THE BEST OF COLIN URQUHART

The Best of Colin Urquhart Omnibus edition first published 1998 by Hodder and Stoughton, a division of Hodder Headline plc

Listen and Live
Copyright © Colin Urquhart 1987. First published in Great Britain in a single volume 1987 by Hodder and Stoughton.

"My Dear Child . . ."
Copyright © Colin Urquhart 1990. First published in Great Britain in a single volume 1990 by Hodder and Stoughton.

The Truth That Sets You Free
Copyright © Colin Urquhart 1993. First published in Great Britain in a single volume 1993 by Hodder and Stoughton.

The right of Colin Urquhart to be identified as the author of each of the above works has been asserted by him in accordance with the Copyright, Designs and Patents Act 1988.

10 9 8 7 6 5 4 3 2 1

British Library Cataloguing in Publication Data
A record for this book is available from the British Library

ISBN 0 340 71396 8

Printed and bound in Great Britain by
Clays Ltd, St Ives plc

Hodder and Stoughton
A Division of Hodder Headline PLC
338 Euston Road
London NW1 3BH

LISTEN
AND
LIVE

LISTEN AND LIVE

Using the Bible in prayer

COLIN URQUHART

Hodder & Stoughton

LONDON SYDNEY AUCKLAND

CONTENTS

· PART FIVE ·

YOUR LIFE IN THE SPIRIT

· PART SIX ·

YOUR LIFE IN THE KINGDOM

ACKNOWLEDGMENTS

At last! A promise fulfilled! Several years ago I wrote a footnote in my book, *Anything You Ask*, to say that the principles of prayer referred to there would soon be published under the title, *Listen and Live*. Ever since then my office has had continual requests for the book. It has been an embarrassment for me whenever people have asked for the book when speaking with them after public engagements.

So it is with joy and relief that the task has now been accomplished. There have been many causes for delay. My good friend, Alan Woodland, and I co-operated in producing the original series of meditations in duplicated form back in the 1960s. This was reproduced several times, but before publishing them in printed form, I wanted to revise them completely.

The revision has become a complete rewrite, so that this book bears little resemblance to the original meditations, although the general form of prayer is the same.

Both Alan and I would acknowledge our gratitude to the late Jim Wilson and to Robert Coulson for principles learned through their teaching on prayer. I should also like to thank all those prayer groups with whom I have shared this way of praying – at Cheshunt, Letchworth, Luton and more recently in the Bethany Fellowship.

In producing this book I am deeply grateful to the Lord for the love and devotion to the task by my assistant, Angela, and my secretary, Janie. My thanks also to Merion and all the members of my household for their help and encouragement.

Above all, my thanks to our heavenly Father who in love draws us close to Him in prayer and who has given me such a lovely wife, Caroline, to be with me in the service of His kingdom. And, needless to say, my children, Claire, Clive and

Andrea, have exercised their usual patience when Dad has been busy writing, even though he spends so little time at home with them.

To God be all the glory!

The Scriptures quoted are from the New International Version and are used with permission.

LISTEN AND LIVE

Many Christians want to know the answer to two basic questions:

1. How can I pray more effectively?
2. How can I receive from God the blessings He promises?

This book contains the answers to such questions – a way of praying that has proved to be both powerful and effective over many years. This method is powerful because it shows you how to use the words of Jesus and other Scriptures in prayer. It is effective because God will always honour His own words.

Some people despise methods because they believe prayer should always be spontaneous. Others like a fixed form because they fear spontaneity. This book will be useful to both. An outline is provided in which there is plenty of room for spontaneous expression. You will find the method readily adaptable to your own needs.

At the same time this method of prayer provides a discipline, but not a legalistic form. This is a way in which you can meet with God in prayer, hear His voice and receive powerfully from Him both for yourself and others.

I have used this method of prayer with many groups of church people, besides finding it a great strength in my own spiritual life. The principal benefits I have received through it are these:

1. It has helped me to appreciate that God's words contain Spirit and life.
2. I have learned how to receive that life through His words.
3. Through such prayer it is possible to receive, at any time the love, joy, peace, power, healing, forgiveness, etc., of which Jesus speaks, at any time.
4. God's power and healing can be conveyed to others, by

taking hold of the healing in God's Word and passing this on to others.

5. This prayer has made it much easier for me to hear God's voice.

6. Many Scriptures have become part of me in such a deep way that my thinking and attitudes have been changed by them. In other words, receiving His words in this way can help you to think as God thinks, and to have His attitudes towards your daily circumstances.

When pastoring a local church in Luton, there were as many as eighteen groups using this method of prayer weekly, including three groups among the staff of the general hospital in the parish. These were called prayer and healing groups and numerous people received miraculous healing from God through the prayer ministry of these groups.

In addition one group met to pray weekly for unconverted members of church families and friends with startling results.

Most of us spend only a limited time in prayer, and do not have the capacity to concentrate for longer periods. You will find this method can be as brief or as long as you want it to be, but that it will aid your ability to concentrate.

Some words of advice: It is better not to maintain any other methods while using this one, simply because you will only burden yourself by doing that. Let this become a framework within which you hear from God, pray to Him and praise His name. It is most important that you meet with God in your prayer time – not say a whole series of prayers because this has been your habit.

And give yourself opportunity to become used to this way of praying. It is very simple and will fast cease to become a 'method'. However, at first it may seem clumsy because you are having to remember what comes next. This is why the outline of the method is given on page 17. You will find it helpful to refer to this for a few days until the order becomes familiar.

THE METHOD

This book is divided into a number of short sections for daily use. Each section can be done in about ten minutes, but you can extend this as much as you want. The theme for each section is given in the title.

You may want to use a different section each day, but you will find great benefit from using the same section every day for a week. Not only are you able to absorb the teaching more fully, but the words of Scripture become part of you, when you use them over a period of time. Even though you use the same material each day, the experience will be entirely different on each occasion.

This method can be used individually or by groups. A new section can be used when the group meets, and then used individually by each member of the group until the next meeting a week later, when the next section can be used.

A group meeting does not have to take a whole afternoon or evening. The business of the whole group can be completed within about half an hour.

POSTURE

Different postures are appropriate for different types of prayer. As the main purpose of this method is to receive from God, sitting is the best posture to use. It is easier to receive when you are relaxed; but if you are too relaxed you are likely to fall asleep! So it is best to use a chair with an upright back, but which is comfortable. Discomfort distracts from concentration.

1. *Opening sentence:* This sets the theme for the section and should be read slowly and thoughtfully.

2. *Brief prayer:* Asking the Lord to fill the time of prayer with His presence. Of course, these short prayers may be expanded if you so desire.

3. *Scripture reading:* This is printed in full for your convenience. The New International Version of the Bible has been used. Read this and the teaching given after the passage. To aid concentration you can do this aloud if you wish, even when using the meditation on your own.

4. *Relax:* Sit with your back upright and both feet on the floor. Let all the tension flow from your body by relaxing your muscles. Start with your facial muscles and work down the

body relaxing shoulders, arms, fingers, feet and toes. Remember it is easier to receive when relaxed, and you will concentrate better if you are not distracted by discomfort.

5. *'Come to me . . .'* Jesus said: 'Come to me, all you who are weary and burdened, and I will give you rest' (Matt. 11:28). Pass your burdens over to the Lord. Ask Him to forgive the sins of which you are conscious; give Him the burden of any anxieties or worries you may have. Do all this within about a minute, so that you do not dwell on these issues. Prayer is not sitting down to think about your problems; it is meeting with God.

It does not take long to ask God to forgive you. But be specific. Vague prayers receive vague answers. Specific prayers receive specific answers. You need to know God's forgiveness for your specific sins. Be assured that if you confess your sins to Him, He forgives you; this is His promise.

You are told to cast all your burdens on the Lord. You do not need to go into long explanations. Simply say: 'Lord Jesus, I give you my anxiety about so and so. I ask you to take the burden of this problem. I hand over my concern about that other need.'

Remember, if Jesus bears the burden, you do not have to carry it as well. It is simply a matter of deciding who is going to carry it.

6. *Forgive others:* Jesus emphasised how important it is to forgive others whenever you pray. In this way, no resentment or anger is stored up within you. 'Forgive us our sins as we forgive those who sin against us.'

Forgiveness is not a feeling; it is an act of the will. You choose to forgive. Be sure to forgive all who have hurt or offended you in any way.

Now you are at peace with God and with others. You are ready to receive from Him.

7. *Meditation sentence:* Prayer is an activity of the spirit more than of the mind. You are going to receive the Word of God into your spirit.

Simply repeat the Scripture sentence slowly again and again. Do not try to work out what it means with your mind. God is speaking His Words to your heart. Receive them. They are words spoken from Him to you. You will find it helpful to add your Christian name to the sentence. This helps to make it more personal; God is speaking His Word personally to you: e.g. 'My peace I give you . . . Colin.'

At times it will seem that nothing is happening; at other times you will sense the Lord's presence, you will be excited by the revelation taking place within your heart. You may even be aware of His power pouring into you.

Generally speaking you will have a deep sense of His peace. But do not judge what is happening by feelings. Even when it seems nothing is happening, God can be working very deeply within you.

As you receive His Words in this way, you are receiving the Spirit and life they contain. Jesus is the Word of God and His life can be received through the words of Scripture.

Continue to receive for about two minutes by repeating the meditation sentence. In time the two minutes can be extended to four or five. But do not try to concentrate for too long too quickly. Better a few minutes of concentration than several minutes of wandering thoughts.

Sometimes you can be engaged in conversation and your attention strays from what the other person is saying. In such circumstances you begin to listen again as soon as you are aware your attention has strayed. If your thoughts do wander, do not be either surprised or dismayed. Simply come back to the meditation sentence, knowing God is speaking His Words to you.

As you are receiving the Word in this way, you will find sometimes that the Holy Spirit will bring to mind other Scriptures, or even speak to you prophetically. Do not be surprised by this; receiving His Words sharpens your ability to hear the Lord speaking to you. As you listen to Him through His Word, so you are able to listen to the voice of His Spirit and make use of His gifts.

Two further Scriptures are given which can be used to supplement the meditation sentence. Their use is entirely optional, but you can use one or both of them between repetition of the main sentence, especially when you are praying for longer periods of time. Do not feel you have to use these additional Scriptures, especially at first when you are becoming used to this way of praying.

Jesus warned against vain repetition – the mechanical repetition of prayers which do not come from the heart. To repeat Scriptures in this way is certainly not vain, for you are allowing God to speak His Words to your heart, and you are receiving the truth, life, Spirit and healing that are in those words.

8. *Prayer for others:* Having received the Words yourself, you can now direct them, and the life they contain, towards others. Into the stillness of God's presence bring the person for whom you wish to pray. Continue to use the meditation sentence adding his or her Christian name to the sentence: e.g. 'My peace I give to you . . . John.' You may like to imagine the person is there before you and that you are laying your hands on his head in the name of Jesus, as you communicate the healing and life of His Word to him.

At times the Holy Spirit may prompt you to add a further word of Scripture for a particular individual because this is relevant for the person's situation.

After about half a minute, thank the Lord for what He has done in that person. You may like to use Jesus's words: 'Father, I thank you that you have heard me. I knew that you always hear me' (John 11:41–2). Then pray for the next person.

Try not to have a list of more than about six or eight people. Better to pray effectively for a few than ineffectively for many.

9. *Praise:* Thank the Lord for His love and presence with you and spend a few moments praising Him. You are given a sentence from Scripture to help you do this. Add to this your own words of thanksgiving and praise.

10. *Closing prayer:* This is a prayer of consecration to the Lord, that you may serve Him faithfully and lovingly, taking His presence into your daily life and relationships. You can use the suggested prayer or one of your own.

I have tried to keep the explanation of this method as brief and simple as possible. I have prepared an audio cassette which gives a fuller explanation and which includes an actual time of meditation as a demonstration. You can obtain this by sending £3.00 to:

> Listen and Live,
> Roffey Place Christian Training Centre,
> Faygate, Horsham.
> West Sussex RH12 4SA

May the Lord Jesus bless you richly in your times of prayer. May you meet with Him in His Word and by the power of His Spirit.

C.U.

PRAYER OUTLINE

1. Opening sentence.
2. Brief prayer.
3. Scripture reading.
4. Relax.
5. 'Come to me, all you who are weary and burdened, and I will give you rest.'
   (a) Confess your sins to the Lord.
   (b) Pass your burdens on to Him.
6. Forgive others.
7. Meditation sentence – repeated several times.
8. Prayer for others – using meditation sentence.
9. Praise.
10. Prayer of consecration: 'Lord I offer myself to you, all that I am, all that I have and all that I do. Work through me by the power of your Holy Spirit that I might please you in all things, and come to the glorious fulfilment of your purposes for me. Amen.'

PART ONE

YOUR
FELLOWSHIP
WITH GOD

1. The God of Love

'We love because he first loved us' (1 JOHN 4:19).

Holy Spirit, please show me the love of Jesus.

READING: 1 JOHN 4:16–18

God is love. Whoever lives in love lives in God, and God in him. Love is made complete among us so that we will have confidence on the day of judgment, because in this world we are like him. There is no fear in love. But perfect love drives out fear, because fear has to do with punishment. The man who fears is not made perfect in love.

'God is love'; this is a truth that needs to become personal revelation for you. Then you will know He loves you personally.

God's love is of a very particular kind; it is given, shared, communicated to others. 'For God so loved the world that he *gave* his one and only Son, that whoever believes in him shall not perish but have eternal life' (John 3:16).

In love He gave His Son for you. In love He wants to give Himself to you now. He loves you so much He wants to live in you in the person of the Holy Spirit. In love He wants to answer your prayers. He wants you to live with a continual awareness of His love, knowing His presence with you always. Instead of dealing with you as you deserve, He is ready to forgive you and to treat you with mercy and graciousness.

The Lord does not look upon you with judgment, criticism or condemnation. He does not accuse you or crush you. It is not His purpose to bruise or hurt you.

In love he wants to encourage you, fill you, provide for you. His love is very practical. He does not sit on His throne, saying, 'I love you', while keeping Himself detached from your needs and circumstances. He wants to be involved in every area of your life.

His love is not born of emotion and does not depend on feelings; it is born of the Spirit. But it touches the emotions and you need not be afraid of this fact. The Holy Spirit living within you desires to influence each area of your soul, including the emotions. If you love the Lord, you will feel love for Him; but loving Him is not based on feelings. If you love Him you will obey His commandments, regardless of feelings. You will express your love in positive, practical obedience.

Loving the Lord, however, is more than a slavish obedience to His will. It involves a *relationship* of love. When you worship Him it is right to feel love for Him, to feel the joy in praise and the beauty of adoration.

Some try to freeze their feelings out of their Christian lives and that can be dangerous. If you are afraid to feel love for God, you will frequently doubt His love for you. There is no fear in love. The existence of the fear is the very proof of an inadequate grasp of His love.

Allow the love of Jesus to fill your spirit and soul as you receive His Word. Because He loves you, He wants you to receive His love. Know that He is speaking His Words of love to you now; that these are not words about love, but Words of love. They contain His love and communicate His love to you.

Meditation:
'I HAVE LOVED YOU,' SAYS THE LORD
(MAL. 1:2).

Fear not, for I have redeemed you; I have called you by name; you are mine (ISA. 43:1).

You are precious and honoured in my sight, and . . . I love you (ISA. 43:4).

Praise:
I love you, O Lord, my strength (PS. 18:1).

23

2. *Father*

'No-one knows the Son except the Father, and no-one knows the Father except the Son and those to whom the Son chooses to reveal him' (MATT. 11:27).

Lord Jesus, please reveal your Father to me.

READING: JOHN 5:17–23

Jesus said to them, 'My Father is always at his work to this very day, and I, too, am working.' For this reason the Jews tried all the harder to kill him; not only was he breaking the Sabbath, but he was even calling God his own Father, making himself equal with God.

Jesus gave them this answer: 'I tell you the truth, the Son can do nothing by himself; he can do only what He sees his Father doing, because whatever the Father does the Son also does. For the Father loves the Son and shows him all he does. Yes, to your amazement he will show him even greater things than these. For just as the Father raises the dead and gives them life, even so the Son gives life to whom he is pleased to give it. Moreover, the Father judges no-one, but has entrusted all judgment to the Son, that all may honour the Son just as they honour the Father. He who does not honour the Son does not honour the Father, who sent him.'

God is Holy, Almighty, Righteous, Truth; but, because you believe in Jesus, He is also your Father. Here is the heart of true relationship with God, that you can call Him 'Father' because you know His love for you, that He has accepted you and made you His own.

'The Father loves the Son and has placed everything in his hands' (John 3:35). 'For the Father loves the Son and shows him all he does' (John 5:20). The Father and the Son maintained a perfect unity throughout His humanity because of the love which bound them together. In love, Jesus remained submissive to His Father at all times, even being prepared to go to the cross. Because He loves you as His child He wants to show you all that He does.

Jesus taught the disciples. 'When you pray, say: "Father . . ."' (Luke 11:2). That one word speaks of the relationship we have with the Lord and in which we pray. Like Jesus He wants you to know your unity and fellowship with Him personally.

The Father's love is always reliable. He is the everlasting Father – His love will last for ever. He never stops loving you; He never withdraws His words of promise.

Jesus said, 'My Father is always at his work' (John 5:17). Understand that He is always wanting to work for you, doing for you what you cannot do for yourself, speaking words of faith and strength to your heart, assuring you of His best purposes for you. He wants to draw you closer to Himself, giving you a greater revelation of His love for you.

He does not want you to settle for anything less than His best. In Christian things the good is the enemy of the best. Reach out for God's best. Every human father wants the best for his children; how much more is this true of the perfect love the heavenly Father has for you.

You will find there are times when you need only one word in prayer: 'Father'. Sometimes you will say it in supplication; you cannot find any other words to pray in such a situation. At other times it will be a simple word of adoration: 'Father', the cry of the child to the one who loves him or her.

As you pray now use this one word. You are calling to your heavenly Father; you are embracing Him in love. You are safe and secure in Him. Let Him be your Father; it was His idea long before you had the desire to know Him. And when you pray for others simply hold them in the Father's love.

Meditation:
'FATHER' (LUKE 11:2).

Father, hallowed be your name (LUKE 11:2).

You are my Son; today I have become your Father
(PS. 2:7).

Praise:
He will call out to me, 'You are my Father, my God,
the Rock my Saviour' (PS. 89:26).

3. Sons of God

'How great is the love the Father has lavished on us, that we
should be called children of God! And that is what we are! The
reason the world does not know us is that it did not know him'
(1 JOHN 3:1).

Father, thank you for making me your child.

READING: LUKE 15:25-32
Meanwhile, the older son was in the field. When he
came near the house, he heard music and dancing. So
he called one of the servants and asked him what was
going on. 'Your brother has come,' he replied, 'and
your father has killed the fattened calf because he has
him back safe and sound.'

The older brother became angry and refused to go
in. So his father went out and pleaded with him. But he
answered his father, 'Look! All these years I've been
slaving for you and never disobeyed your orders. Yet
you never gave me even a young goat so I could
celebrate with my friends. But when this son of yours
who has squandered your property with prostitutes
comes home, you kill the fattened calf for him!'

'My son,' the father said, 'you are always with me,
and everything I have is yours. But we had to celebrate
and be glad, because this brother of yours was dead
and is alive again; he was lost and is found.'

God is love; it is His nature to love; it is His nature to give. Because He loves you He wants to give to you.

It is your responsibility to come to Him and ask, believing it is His purpose to give to you. As you move towards God in prayer so He moves towards you in blessing.

Seek **Him** for Himself not simply for His blessings. Desire to draw near to Him because He is your Father and you are His child. You will discover, like the younger son in this parable, that the Father comes to meet you; and even though you feel unworthy in yourself, nevertheless He wants to give to you the very best.

When you receive from Him you can overflow in giving to others. The prodigal son in the parable squandered his inheritance on himself and realised his mistake. The older brother was equally wasteful because he never claimed his inheritance. Like him, it is possible to be full of self-righteousness and pride in the way you serve the Lord and work diligently for Him, without realising you are a son with a rich inheritance.

God does not want you standing outside looking at the feast. As a forgiven sinner, you belong at the table eating the fattened calf, wearing the robe of righteousness Jesus has given you, with a ring on your finger and shoes on your feet! If you are one who has sought to love and serve Him diligently, His word to you is: 'My son you are always with me, and everything I have is yours' (Luke 15:31).

Whether male or female you are a son of God by faith in Christ Jesus because sons have the first right of inheritance, and every born-again child of God has the same inheritance in Christ. God loves you; He has accepted you; He owns you as His child and He wants to give to you.

Receive the truth of His words now. Hear the Father speaking to your heart . . .

———————

Meditation:
MY SON YOU ARE ALWAYS WITH ME,
AND EVERYTHING I HAVE IS YOURS
(LUKE 15:31).

27

You are all sons of God through faith in Christ Jesus (GAL. 3:26).

Surely they are my people, sons who will not be false to me (ISA. 63:8).

Praise:
My lips will shout for joy when I sing praise to you – I, whom you have redeemed (PS. 71:23).

4. Forgiven

'For God so loved the world that he gave his one and only Son, that whoever believes in him shall not perish but have eternal life' (JOHN 3:16).

Thank you, Jesus, that you died for me.

READING: ISAIAH 53:5–6
But he was pierced for our transgressions, he was crushed for our iniquities; the punishment that brought us peace was upon him, and by his wounds we are healed. We all, like sheep, have gone astray, each of us has turned to his own way; and the Lord has laid on him the iniquity of us all.

The nature of God's love for us is seen supremely in the cross. Because He is both holy and just, God could not shrug His shoulders at our sin and say, 'It doesn't matter'. All have sinned and fallen short of God's glory. Sin is unholiness; whatever offends the Lord. The Holy One cannot be united with the unholy. It was necessary for God to do something to cleanse us of unholiness so that we might have fellowship with

Him. There was only one alternative: we would die eternally and miss His glory.

Because of our sin we deserve eternal separation from God; we deserve hell, not heaven. We could never earn the right to have fellowship with God. This is a gift of His grace – God giving to those who deserve nothing. So He sent His Son into the world, not that men should be condemned, but saved – from sin and eternal death.

Those who believe in Jesus will not be condemned, but are given the gift of eternal life now. Because He is the Son of God and your Saviour, you need to confess your sins to Him and ask for His forgiveness.

On the cross he offered to the Father His sinless life on your behalf as a sinner; He gave His perfect life for your imperfections, His holy life for your unholiness. God's love is so great for you, He deliberately sent His Son to make such an offering on your behalf: 'For the transgression of my people he was stricken' (Isa. 53:8).

Jesus died the death of a criminal because He was experiencing the punishment you deserve, 'the punishment that brought us peace was upon him' (Isa. 53:5). You do not need to suffer punishment from God for your sins. He will not punish twice for the same offence. If Jesus has borne your punishment, you can be freely forgiven. And when God forgives, He forgets.

Jesus could cry out in triumph on the cross, 'It is finished', or 'It is accomplished'. Everything for our forgiveness and salvation was accomplished. Jesus had made the supreme sacrifice of love that we might be set free.

John tells us plainly: 'If we claim to be without sin, we deceive ourselves and the truth is not in us. If we confess our sins, he is faithful and just and will forgive us our sins and purify us from all unrighteousness. If we claim we have not sinned, we make him out to be a liar and his word has no place in our lives' (1 John 1:8–10).

When God forgives you, He makes you righteous in His sight; you are put right with Him. Rejoice in what Jesus has done for you and know that every time you pray, you can pass all the burdens of your sins on to the Lord. He is willing to take them. He wants to forgive you and He died to make this possible. He wants to see you freed from sin and guilt, rejoicing in His peace. He wants to see you enjoying your relationship with Him as your loving heavenly Father.

Meditation:
BUT HE WAS PIERCED FOR OUR TRANS-GRESSIONS, HE WAS CRUSHED FOR OUR INIQUITIES (ISA. 53:5).

For I will forgive their wickedness and will remember their sins no more (JER. 31:34).

In him we have redemption through his blood, the forgiveness of sins (EPH. 1:7).

Praise:
'It is finished' (JOHN 19:30).

5. *Fellowship with God*

'God, who has called you into fellowship with his Son Jesus Christ our Lord, is faithful' (1 COR. 1:9).

Holy Spirit, please speak the Word to my heart.

READING: 1 JOHN 1:2–4
The life appeared; we have seen it and testify to it, and we proclaim to you the eternal life, which was with the Father and has appeared to us. We proclaim to you what we have seen and heard, so that you also may have fellowship with us. And our fellowship is with the Father and with his Son, Jesus Christ. We write this to make our joy complete.

God has made you to live in close fellowship with Him. Fellowship means 'the sharing of life'. Jesus shed His blood on the cross so that you might share in His life and live in harmony with Him.

Many people think that living close to God is something reserved for great men of faith. This is not the case. You can live in constant fellowship with the Father. He wants you to share His life with Him.

Do you really experience this?

It is difficult to be in harmony with God if you disagree with Him! It is possible to argue with Him without intending to do so. If He says one thing and you say the opposite, someone has to be wrong! Every time you complain about the circumstances of your life you are expressing dissatisfaction with God, with His love and care for you. Paul says, 'Do everything without complaining or arguing' (Phil. 2:14).

Every time you think of yourself with self-pity you deny what God says in His Word: You have received everything you need for life and godliness (2 Pet. 1:3); your God will meet every need of yours according to His glorious riches which are yours in Christ Jesus (Phil. 4:19); you have come to fullness of life in Him (Col. 2:9).

If I am living in fellowship with God and not disagreeing with Him, then I know that God will meet every need of mine, not according to my worthiness, but according to His riches in Christ Jesus. So instead of grumbling, the Christian is to recognise the Lord as his provider. Recognise the truth of what Jesus says: 'But seek first his kingdom and his righteousness, and all these things will be given to you as well' (Matt. 6:33).

Instead of disagreeing with God begin to agree with what He says. Receive His Word; hear Him speaking to your heart. Know that the more you agree with Him, the closer will be your fellowship with Him.

As you pray, He is speaking His Word personally to you because He loves you. He wants you to pay close attention to what He is saying.

Meditation:
MY SON, PAY ATTENTION TO WHAT I
SAY; LISTEN CLOSELY TO MY WORDS
(PROV. 4:20).

I love those who love me, and those who seek me find
me (PROV. 8:17).

Lay hold of my words with all your heart; keep my
commands and you will live (PROV. 4:4).

Praise:
I will sing to the Lord all my life; I will sing praise to
my God as long as I live (PS. 104:33).

PART TWO

YOUR LORD AND YOUR GOD

6. I am your Creator

'Is he not your Father, your Creator, who made you and formed you?' (DEUT. 32:6).

Thank you, Lord, that you have a purpose for me.

READING: ROMANS 8:26–30
In the same way, the Spirit helps us in our weakness. We do not know what we ought to pray, but the Spirit himself intercedes for us with groans that words cannot express. And he who searches our hearts knows the mind of the Spirit, because the Spirit intercedes for the saints in accordance with God's will.

And we know that in all things God works for the good of those who love him, who have been called according to his purpose. For those God foreknew he also predestined to be conformed to the likeness of his Son, that he might be the firstborn among many brothers. And those he predestined, he also called; those he called, he also justified; those he justified, he also glorified.

Some doubt the existence of God and imagine the world and all life on it has come into being through a series of accidents. This takes no account of the order and pattern in creation, nor does it answer the problem as to how matter came into being in the first place.

Others, even some who would call themselves Christians, believe there is a Creator God, but having brought the world, and ultimately man, into being He then left creation to its own devices. Man has to run the world as best he can, without expecting any supernatural interventions from God.

All this conflicts completely with the Biblical view of God. He created deliberately, not by some chance. He sustains His creation by His Word and everything is moving towards the fulfilment of the purpose He has for His creation. Because He made us with free-will, each individual man or woman can choose to co-operate with the Lord in His purposes, or can refuse to do so.

Within His whole creation, He has a plan and purpose for you. In common with all His beloved children who know Him and love Him, He assures you His purposes are good. '"For I know the plans I have for you," declares the Lord, "plans to prosper you and not to harm you, plans to give you hope and a future"' (Jer. 29:11).

Those who do not know the Lord often accuse Him of being responsible for the devil's activities. The Lord does not desire evil for those He loves. That would be a complete contradiction of His Fatherhood. In His love He plans for your welfare. He has set this hope before you, that He will keep you faithful to the end, that He will raise you up at the last day, that when you see Him face to face you will be like Him. He will not cast you off or leave you to be condemned. In love He has saved you and made you His own.

You are an heir of God and a fellow-heir with Christ. You share in the rich inheritance of God's heavenly kingdom.

Some have placed predestination and free-will in opposition to each other and have said it is impossible to believe in both. The Bible teaches both and holds them together. The Lord has a particular purpose for you, but He works with your co-operation. He wants you to use your free-will to co-operate with Him. He will not force His way into your life, or make you walk in His ways. You can choose to walk in your ways in which there will be no blessing, or in His ways: 'See, I set before you today life and prosperity, death and destruction. For I command you today to love the Lord your God, to walk in his ways, and to keep his commands, decrees and laws; then you will live and increase, and the Lord your God will bless you in the land you are entering to possess' (Deut. 30:15–16).

God has predestined in His love that you should belong to Him, that you should be adopted as His child through Jesus Christ (Eph. 1:5). And yet He waited for your free response to His call. 'In him we were also chosen, having been predestined according to the plan of him who works out everything in conformity with the purpose of his will, in order that we, who were the first to hope in Christ, might be for the praise of his glory' (Eph. 1:11–12). It is His purpose to keep you in His way and He is determined to see His purpose for you fulfilled.

Hear the Lord speaking to you now, giving you assurance that your life is in His hands. He knows you, loves you, cares for you and has a purpose for you. What is more, He will lead you to the fulfilment of His plans for you.

Meditation:
SURELY, AS I HAVE PLANNED, SO IT WILL BE, AND AS I HAVE PURPOSED, SO IT WILL STAND (ISA. 14:24).

I am the Lord, and there is no other; apart from me there is no God (ISA. 45:5).

For I know the plans I have for you . . . to prosper you and not to harm you, plans to give you hope and a future (JER. 29:11).

Praise:
Let them praise the name of the Lord, for he commanded and they were created (PS. 148:5).

7. *I am with you*

'I have told you these things, so that in me you may have peace. In this world you will have trouble. But take heart! I have overcome the world' (JOHN 16:33).

Lord, please deliver me from all my fears.

READING: ISAIAH 43:1–3, 4–7

'Fear not, for I have redeemed you; I have called you by name; you are mine.

'When you pass through the waters, I will be with you; and when you pass through the rivers, they will not sweep over you.

'When you walk through the fire, you will not be burned; the flames will not set you ablaze.

'For I am the Lord, your God, the Holy One of Israel, your Saviour.

'Since you are precious and honoured in my sight, and because I love you, I will give men in exchange for you, and people in exchange for your life.

'Do not be afraid, for I am with you; I will bring your children from the east and gather you from the west.

'I will say to the north, "Give them up!" and to the south, "Do not hold them back."

'Bring my sons from afar and my daughters from the ends of the earth – everyone who is called by my name, whom I created for my glory, whom I formed and made.'

Fear is the enemy of faith, and there is no fear in love. Fear is sin because it exists only when we fail to trust in the Lord. There is a good acrostic for fear: False Expectations Appearing Real. The enemy likes to try and plant suggestions in our minds that he knows will encourage fear and which usually prove to be false; the expectation is worse than the deed.

Time and time again the Lord gives His antidote to fear – *Fear not*. That sounds simplistic, but He gives good reasons for our not being afraid.

There is nothing to fear because you belong to Him; He has redeemed you by paying the price for you with His own blood. He has called you by name and He is able to keep all who are His. He promises He will never leave you or forsake you.

The one who has purchased you is the Holy One, your Saviour. He is the Lord whose authority and power far outstrip all who oppose Him. So it does not matter how difficult the circumstances, He promises to preserve those who are His. 'When you pass through the waters, I will be with you; and when you pass through the rivers, they will not sweep over you. When you walk through the fire, you will not be burned; the flames will not set you ablaze' (Isa. 43:2).

When you fear it is because you do not fully appreciate the nature of God's love. The more you believe the reality of His love for you, the less you will fear. You are precious and honoured in His sight and He loves you.

I used to be a very fearful person myself. The more I have grown to appreciate the Lord's love for me, the greater the freedom from fear I have experienced. Even if my first natural reaction to some situations is to be afraid, the Spirit reminds me: 'Do not be afraid, for I am with you' (Isa. 43:5). We are made for the glory of God, not to be creatures bound by fear. Paul reminds Timothy of the nature of the Holy Spirit who lives in us: 'For God did not give us a spirit of timidity, but a spirit of power, of love and of self-discipline' (2 Tim. 1:7).

Is God's love and care for His children not much greater than the love of the best human father towards his children? He sent Jesus to die for us because He wants to gather around Himself the children He loves, those who are precious to Him and honoured in His sight.

How blessed you are to belong to the Lord, to have God as your Father, Jesus as your Saviour, the Holy Spirit living in you. 'But blessed is the man who trusts in the Lord, whose confidence is in him. He will be like a tree planted by the water that sends out its roots by the stream. It does not fear when heat comes; its leaves are always green. It has no worries in a year of drought and never fails to bear fruit' (Jer. 17:7–8).

When the Lord called Gideon, He found him hiding in fear in a wine-press. Yet He addressed him as a 'mighty warrior' (Jdg. 6:12). God could see him as the man he would become. See yourself as God sees you, living in Christ in whom there is no fear, with the Spirit of power, love and a sound mind living within you.

The Lord speaks to you now. He tells you not to fear; He has redeemed you. He has bought you with His blood and you belong to Him. He has called you by name and chosen you to be His.

———————

Meditation:
FEAR NOT, FOR I HAVE REDEEMED YOU; I HAVE CALLED YOU BY NAME; YOU ARE MINE (ISA. 43:1).

Do not be afraid, for I am with you (ISA. 43:5).

So do not fear, for I am with you; do not be dismayed, for I am your God (ISA. 41:10).

Praise:
In God I trust, I will not be afraid (PS. 56:4).

8. I am your Salvation

'Great is the Lord and most worthy of praise; his greatness no-one can fathom' (PS. 145:3).

Lord Jesus, please give me complete assurance of my salvation through your love.

READING: PSALM 103:1–5

Praise the Lord, O my soul; all my inmost being, praise his holy name. Praise the Lord, O my soul, and forget not all his benefits. He forgives all my sins and heals all my diseases; he redeems my life from the pit and crowns me with love and compassion. He satisfies my desires with good things so that my youth is renewed like the eagle's.

When we consider all that God has done for us in Jesus, we are filled with praise and thanksgiving. We want to bless the Lord, to worship Him and proclaim His greatness.

When you first came into a personal relationship with Jesus Christ, you recognised Him as your Saviour. He wants you to continue to relate to Him as Saviour in your daily experience.

When you focus on the problems you encounter, or the difficult situations which confront you, or the negative feelings within you, the last thing you want to do is to praise the Lord. Sometimes it requires a real act of the will to begin to praise Him. Praising the Lord focuses on Him and away from yourself. Then you begin to see everything in a different light, you gain something of God's perspective on the things that concern you. As a result, faith begins to rise within you and you hear the Holy Spirit witnessing to your heart the relevant promises from God's Word.

The Lord is gracious and compassionate, slow to anger and rich in love. The Lord is good to all; he has compassion on all he has made. All you have made will praise you, O Lord; your saints will extol you. They will tell of the glory of your kingdom and speak of your might, so that all men may know of your mighty acts and the glorious splendour of your kingdom (Ps. 145:8–12).

What a contrast this is to the negative complaints sometimes heard from Christians. As a saint you are the one who is to tell of the glory of God's kingdom and speak of His might. When you complain, you inadvertently suggest that God's salvation and provision for you is somehow incomplete or inadequate.

David knew what it was to suffer opposition, and felt hemmed in by his enemies. He could feel oppressed and discouraged. But he learned the effectiveness of praise. In Psalm 103 he speaks to his own soul as if to say to himself, 'Take your eyes off your problems, David, and remember all that God has done for you: the salvation, the healing and deliverance that is yours through His love and mercy.'

He gives himself five good reasons for praising the Lord:

> He forgives all my sins;
> He heals all my diseases;
> He redeems my life from the pit;
> He crowns me with love and compassion;
> He satisfies my desires with good things.

See how many aspects of salvation are included in those few verses. And this was centuries before the coming of Jesus! Through Him God has blessed you with every spiritual blessing in heavenly places. Praising God for your salvation is the antidote to fear! 'In the time of my favour I heard you, and in the day of salvation I helped you. I tell you, now is the time of God's favour, now is the day of salvation' (2 Cor. 6:2).

Jesus says to you personally that He is your salvation. The Church is not your salvation; your spiritual life is not your salvation; your good works are not your salvation. *He* is your salvation. Trust in Him.

Meditation:
I AM YOUR SALVATION (PS. 35:3).

But salvation will last for ever, my righteousness will never fail (ISA. 51:6).

I will not forget you! See, I have engraved you on the palms of my hands (ISA. 49:15–16).

Praise:
He alone is my rock and my salvation (PS. 62:6).

9. I am the Lord

'Now to him who is able to do immeasurably more than all we ask or imagine, according to his power that is at work within us, to him be glory in the church and in Christ Jesus throughout all generations, for ever and ever! Amen' (EPH. 3:20–1).

Jesus, you are my Lord.

READING: JEREMIAH 32:38–41
They will be my people, and I will be their God. I will give them singleness of heart and action, so that they will always fear me for their own good and the good of their children after them. I will make an everlasting covenant with them: I will never stop doing good to them, and I will inspire them to fear me, so that they will never turn away from me. I will rejoice in doing them good and will assuredly plant them in this land with all my heart and soul.

Every day of your life you need to know there is one greater than you, who loves you and who wants to give to you. This God is almighty, for Him nothing is impossible. He is the Lord, the one who is above all He has made, the one with ultimate authority and power.

So great and so personal is His love for you, that He knows your need even before you ask. He is able to do immeasurably more than you could ask, or even imagine Him doing for you. He tells you to:

Ask and it will be given to you; seek and you will find; knock and the door will be opened to you. For everyone who asks receives; he who seeks finds; and to him who knocks, the door will be opened. Which of you, if his son asks for bread, will give him a stone? Or if he asks for a fish, will give him a snake? If you, then, though you are evil, know how to give good gifts to your children, how much more will your Father in heaven give good gifts to those who ask him! (Matt. 7:7–11).

If God is all-knowing and all-powerful, why should He want us to ask? If His love for us is so perfect, why doesn't He do what we need without asking?

This is the way God has chosen to work, because in asking we are declaring our faith in His love. We are saying He is the almighty God for whom nothing is impossible, and who wants to give to us. Day by day He is the Lord of miracles, whether small or large. This means we expect Him to intervene supernaturally in our affairs in response to our prayers.

Obviously, what you believe is central to your effectiveness in prayer. It is not a question of simply calling Jesus 'Lord', or saying He is almighty, of praying formal prayers ending with the phrase, 'in the name of Jesus'. It is the prayer of the heart that God promises to answer. He will always honour the faith in your heart; He answers what you truly believe. He has committed Himself to do this.

The faith with which you pray depends largely on your understanding of who the Lord is, and therefore of what He is able to do. This is why it is so important to receive revelation of God's Words in your heart. Consider the faith-building truths in the brief passage above:

You are one of God's chosen people;
He is your personal God;
He promises to give you 'singleness of heart and action';
Then you will fear the Lord, you will be in awe of His holiness and power;
This will be for your good and for the good of your children;
The Lord has made an everlasting covenant, or binding agreement, with you;
Under that covenant He has pledged that He will never stop doing good to you;
He will teach you to fear Him so that you will not turn away from Him;
He rejoices to do you good;
With all His heart He wants to lead you into your rich inheritance.

What a Lord! What a Lord!

You will find it helpful to analyse passages of Scripture like this, and to write down what God says to you about yourself and the wonderful love He has for you.

He wants you to know He is Lord, not only in your head but in your heart. He wants you to believe He is almighty in the circumstances of your life, that nothing is impossible for Him. This is much more than believing in some academic sense that He is the almighty God. Rather it is trusting in His might and power in the daily circumstances of your life. 'Amen! Praise and glory and wisdom and thanks and honour and power and strength be to our God for ever and ever. Amen!' (Rev. 7:12).

Jesus wants to speak to your heart now, assuring you there is nothing too hard for Him to accomplish in your life. Listen to Him.

Meditation:
I AM THE LORD, THE GOD OF ALL MAN-KIND: IS ANYTHING TOO HARD FOR ME? (JER. 32:27).

I am who I am (EXOD. 3:14).

I am the Lord your God (DEUT. 5:6).

Praise:
The Lord is near to all who call on him, to all who call
on him in truth. He fulfils the desires of those who fear
him; he hears their cry and saves them (PS. 145:18–19).

10. *I am the Light of the World*

'The Lord is my light and my salvation – whom shall I fear?'
(PS. 27:1).

Lord, I want your light to shine through my life.

READING: JOHN 12:35–6
Then Jesus told them: 'You are going to have the light
just a little while longer. Walk while you have the
light, before darkness overtakes you. The man who
walks in the dark does not know where he is going.
Put your trust in the light while you have it, so that
you may become sons of light.' When he had finished
speaking, Jesus left and hid himself from them.

Jesus came as light into the spiritual darkness of the world.
'The true light that gives light to every man was coming into
the world' (John 1:9). However, not everybody was prepared
to receive the light.

This is the verdict: Light has come into the world, but men
loved darkness instead of light because their deeds were evil.

Everyone who does evil hates the light, and will not come into the light for fear that his deeds will be exposed. But whoever lives by the truth comes into the light, so that it may be seen plainly that what he has done has been done through God (John 3:19–21).

John affirms what he heard Jesus teach: 'This is the message we have heard from him and declare to you: God is light; in him there is no darkness at all' (1 John 1:5). We are to walk in the light as the children of light. We are not to be ashamed of our actions or words so that we need to hide them under the cover of darkness.

Sin is often worked in darkness and secretiveness. The Christian can be open about what he does because he wants the light of Jesus to shine through every part of his life.

The Holy Spirit does an ever-deepening work in the believer. On the surface all may appear to be well, but there are areas of darkness, of sin, fear and need, lurking beneath the surface. The value of this kind of prayer in which we receive the life in His Word, is that His truth can penetrate beneath the conscious level of the mind. The Holy Spirit takes the words and speaks them to your spirit, the deepest part of your being. His truth, His life, His light, can then radiate throughout your thinking and can influence your actions for good.

Not only the thinking part of you needs to be converted and brought under the Lordship of Jesus, but every area of your life. The Word and the Spirit flush out the areas of unbelief, of resentment and bitterness, the wrong motives and desires, bringing God's light and wholeness into your life. 'The entrance of your words gives light; it gives understanding to the simple' (Ps. 119:130). This is a continual process.

'Whoever loves his brother lives in the light, and there is nothi   n him to make him stumble' (1 John 2:10). The Lord desire to cleanse you of everything that is not of love so that you can be full of light and walk as Jesus did.

It is good to have someone who loves you and whom you can trust, with whom you can 'walk in the light', sharing your heart, your problems and needs. This needs to be someone who will not reject you or judge you no matter what you reveal about yourself; but someone who will accept and encourage you, pray for you and stand with you in a unity of faith.

Do not fear to bring what is hidden in the darkness into the light of Christ. You will not find judgment and condemnation awaiting you, but love, grace and mercy, 'for the Lord will be your everlasting light, and your God will be your glory' (Isa. 60:19).

Hear Jesus assuring you that He is the light of life in your life. He will never lead you into darkness. To follow Him is to follow this light and to walk in light. He will lighten the way with His love, joy and peace.

Meditation:
I AM THE LIGHT OF THE WORLD, WHO-
EVER FOLLOWS ME . . . WILL HAVE THE
LIGHT OF LIFE (JOHN 8:12).

For the Lord will be your everlasting light, and your God will be your glory (ISA. 60:19).

God is light; in him there is no darkness at all (1 JOHN 1:5).

Praise:
You are resplendent with light (PS. 76:4).

11. I am the Way, the Truth and the Life

'For as the Father has life in himself, so he has granted the Son to have life in himself' (JOHN 5:26).

Jesus, you are my life.

READING: JOHN 14:6–10

Jesus answered, 'I am the way and the truth and the life. No-one comes to the Father except through me. If you really knew me, you would know my Father as well. From now on, you do know him and have seen him.'

Philip said, 'Lord, show us the Father and that will be enough for us.'

Jesus answered: 'Don't you know me, Philip, even after I have been among you such a long time? Anyone who has seen me has seen the Father. How can you say, "Show us the Father"? Don't you believe that I am in the Father, and that the Father is in me? The words I say to you are not just my own. Rather, it is the Father, living in me, who is doing his work.'

Some say there are many different ways to God; others that everyone will go to heaven. Both beliefs contradict what Jesus says – and He should know, because He was the man sent from heaven. Nobody, except Jesus, has been born into this world that has come from heaven and knows what it is like there! People only make such statements because they do not understand that God is holy and righteous, and man is sinful by nature. Nobody can be made acceptable to the Father without a Saviour; and Jesus is the only Saviour. He is the only one who has made a holy, righteous, sinless sacrifice of His life to the

Father for our sakes. It is only through Him and His sacrifice on the cross that you or anyone else can come to the Father.

Jesus, then, is the only way to the Father, not simply beyond death, but now.

Many others claim to have truth; but only Jesus makes such a relationship with God possible – and *now*. Only through Jesus is it possible to receive eternal life *now*. Only through Jesus does the Father give the gift of His kingdom *now*. Only through Jesus are people healed and needs met *now*. Heaven and earth will pass away, but the words of Jesus will remain for ever, for they are the words of truth – and the truth is always the truth. It never changes.

Some modern thinkers want to change the words of Jesus to fit their own ideas. They consider the Bible out of date. But their opinions do not lead others to receive new life, the gift of God's kingdom, the power of the Holy Spirit of healing: 'I, the Lord, speak the truth; I declare what is right' (Isa. 45:19). Instead of setting our minds against the truth, we need to bow our hearts and minds before the revelation of God's truth. Then we are able to receive all that Jesus came to give.

The new life within you is the life of Jesus. He gave His life for you that you may receive His life, and only through Him can God's purpose for you be fulfilled.

You have come to the Father through Jesus. He has given you salvation. You can walk in His way, holding fast to His truth, and enjoying the life He alone could give.

Meditation:
I AM THE WAY AND THE TRUTH AND THE LIFE. NO—ONE COMES TO THE FATHER EXCEPT THROUGH ME (JOHN 14:6).

I give them eternal life, and they shall never perish; no–one can snatch them out of my hand (JOHN 10:28).

I, the Lord, speak the truth; I declare what is right (ISA. 45:19).

Praise:
For with you is the fountain of life (PS. 36:9).

12. I am the Bread of Life

'Do not work for food that spoils, but for food that endures to eternal life, which the Son of Man will give you. On him God the Father has placed his seal of approval' (JOHN 6:27).

Lord Jesus, please feed me with your words of life.

READING: JOHN 6:35–40
Then Jesus declared, 'I am the bread of life. He who comes to me will never go hungry, and he who believes in me will never be thirsty. But as I told you, you have seen me and still you do not believe. All that the Father gives me will come to me, and whoever comes to me I will never drive away. For I have come down from heaven not to do my will but to do the will of him who sent me. And this is the will of him who sent me, that I shall lose none of all that he has given me, but raise them up at the last day. For my Father's will is that everyone who looks to the Son and believes in him shall have eternal life, and I will raise him up at the last day.'

Jesus is the bread of life. To feed on His words is to feed on Him. As you receive His words of eternal life, you receive Him. He alone can give you the food that endures for ever.

Jesus will never reject those who respond to His Father's call. When we put our faith in Him, the Father takes us and places us in His Son. He then feeds us with true spiritual food.

He feeds us with the words of life, power and healing. To feed on His words is to feed on Jesus Himself.

Whenever we celebrate Holy Communion, repeating the actions of Jesus at the Last Supper, we proclaim all that His death means and conveys to us. We can enter afresh into the fullness of the life He has made possible, renewing the gift of our lives to Him and allowing Him to renew the gift of Himself to us. Jesus said:

I tell you the truth, unless you eat the flesh of the Son of Man and drink his blood, you have no life in you. Whoever eats my flesh and drinks my blood has eternal life, and I will raise him up at the last day. For my flesh is real food and my blood is real drink. Whoever eats my flesh and drinks my blood remains in me, and I in him. Just as the living Father sent me and I live because of the Father, so the one who feeds on me will live because of me. This is the bread that came down from heaven. Your forefathers ate manna and died, but he who feeds on this bread will live for ever (John 6:53–8).

The Lord wants to feed you with His words of truth, and the Spirit and life contained in those words. He wants you to live in the power of the cross, knowing that in the giving of His body, Jesus made every provision for your physical and material well-being; and in the giving of His blood He has met every spiritual need, cleansing you from sin and breaking every power of the enemy.

Jesus is the bread of your life. Feed on Him whenever you receive Holy Communion. Feed on Him now as you hear Him speaking His Word to you. You will never go hungry or thirsty because of His loving care for you. He will meet every need, whether spiritual or material.

Meditation:
I AM THE BREAD OF LIFE. HE WHO COMES TO ME WILL NEVER GO HUNGRY, AND HE WHO BELIEVES IN ME WILL NEVER BE THIRSTY (JOHN 6:35).

I am the living bread that came down from heaven (JOHN 6:51).

If anyone hears my voice and opens the door, I will come in and eat with him, and he with me (REV. 3:20).

Praise:
The eyes of all look to you, and you give them their food at the proper time. You open your hand and satisfy the desires of every living thing (PS. 145:15–16).

13. *I am the Good Shepherd*

'The sheep listen to his voice. He calls his own sheep by name and leads them out' (JOHN 10:3).

Lord Jesus, you are my shepherd; I want to know your voice and follow you.

READING: JOHN 10:14–18

I am the good shepherd; I know my sheep and my sheep know me – just as the Father knows me and I know the Father – and I lay down my life for the sheep. I have other sheep that are not of this sheep pen. I must bring them also. They too will listen to my voice, and there shall be one flock and one shepherd. The reason my Father loves me is that I lay down my life – only to take it up again. No-one takes it from me, but I lay it down of my own accord. I have authority to lay it down and authority to take it up again. This command I received from my Father.

The job of the shepherd is to care for the sheep. In countries like Israel, the shepherd would do this by leading them several miles a day to find sufficient pasture. David said: 'The Lord is my shepherd, I shall lack nothing' (Ps. 23:1). 'He leads me beside quiet waters' (v.2). 'He guides me in paths of righteousness for his name's sake' (v.3).

A good shepherd provides for the needs of his flock by exercising the proper leadership. However, the Lord complained that Israel's shepherds had failed in their calling: 'Should not shepherds take care of the flock? . . . You have not strengthened the weak or healed the sick or bound up the injured. You have not brought back the strays or searched for the lost' (Ezek. 34:2–4).

So the Lord promises that He Himself will shepherd the people: 'I myself will search for my sheep and look after them. I myself will tend my sheep and make them lie down, declares the Sovereign Lord. I will search for the lost and bring back the strays. I will bind up the injured and strengthen the weak' (Ezek. 34:11, 15–16).

Jesus fulfils this prophecy when He comes as the Good Shepherd, who is prepared to lay down His life for the sheep. This is the measure of His love for them. If they are to be led to the rich pasture He desires for them, it is important that they recognise His voice. Sheep, as opposed to goats, are prepared to listen to Him and follow Him.

Those who do not belong to Him do not recognise His voice, nor listen to His words. They are not concerned to follow Him, and so they miss the rich inheritance which belongs to those who love the Lord.

Jesus lays down His life for all – those who follow Him and those who do not. But those who turn to Him in faith are able to benefit from His great love. They know they are loved personally and that the shepherd calls them by name. They belong to Him and are prepared to follow Him. 'My sheep listen to my voice; I know them, and they follow me. I give them eternal life, and they shall never perish; no-one can snatch them out of my Father's hand' (John 10:27–8).

You have the security of knowing that Jesus has called you personally by name. You are His. What was true for David is true for you; so you can say, 'The Lord is my shepherd, I shall lack nothing' (Ps. 23:1).

Hear His words to you; receive them in your heart. Rejoice that Jesus knows you and you know Him, that He has laid His life down for you that you might receive the fullness of His life.

Meditation:
I AM THE GOOD SHEPHERD; I KNOW MY SHEEP AND MY SHEEP KNOW ME (JOHN 10:14).

My sheep listen to my voice; I know them, and they follow me (JOHN 10:27).

The Lord is my shepherd, I shall lack nothing (PS. 23:1).

Praise:
It is God who arms me with strength and makes my way perfect (PS. 18:32).

14. *I am the Resurrection and the Life*

'For as the Father has life in himself, so he has granted the Son to have life in himself' (JOHN 5:26).

Thank you, Father, for your gift of eternal life to me.

READING: 1 PETER 1:3–9

Praise be to the God and Father of our Lord Jesus Christ! In His great mercy he has given us new birth into a living hope through the resurrection of Jesus Christ from the dead, and into an inheritance that can never perish, spoil or fade – kept in heaven for you, who through faith are shielded by God's power until the coming of the salvation that is ready to be revealed in the last time. In this you greatly rejoice, though now for a little while you may have had to suffer grief in all kinds of trials. These have come so that your faith – of greater worth than gold, which perishes even though refined by fire – may be proved genuine and may result in praise, glory and honour when Jesus Christ is revealed. Though you have not seen him, you love him; and even though you do not see him now, you believe in him and are filled with an inexpressible and glorious joy, for you are receiving the goal of your faith, the salvation of your souls.

When God raised Jesus from the dead, He raised all those who believe in Him. In Christ you are raised to a new victorious life in Jesus. God already sees you sitting in heavenly places in Him. 'And God raised us up with Christ and seated us with him in the heavenly realms in Christ Jesus' (Eph. 2:6).

This is not to say that your physical resurrection has already taken place, but that the Lord wants you to have assurance of your salvation, to know that He sees as already accomplished in eternity, what you do not yet see in time.

The Christian, then, does not need to fear death. He does not know what dying will be like, neither can he experience what lies beyond death until he dies physically. But he does know that death is not the end of his existence, only the threshold to the greater revelation of God and His glory. What he has begun to appropriate now by faith, he will then know fully. The life of the kingdom partially experienced already, will then be fully revealed.

So, like Paul, we can say it is better to go to be with the Lord, but not before God's appointed time. We do not need to fear death or judgment: 'I tell you the truth, whoever hears my word and believes him who sent me has eternal life and will not be condemned; he has crossed over from death to life' (John 5:24).

However, we shall all have to give an account of our stewardship, of how we have used the spiritual and material resources God has made available to us. He does not want us to waste His gifts, but to see our potential realised.

This is accomplished by living in the victory of His cross and resurrection. You are to live in the power you possess as a believer, what Paul describes as, his incomparably great power for us who believe (Eph. 1:19). Fear does not need to dominate your life, because you are a child of God, called to live by faith. 'The life I live in the body, I live by faith in the Son of God, who loved me and gave himself for me' (Gal. 2:20).

Your inheritance can never perish, spoil or fade. It is kept for you in heaven. Your faith is more precious than gold, and the outcome of that faith will be everlasting glory. You can know the victory of faith in your life now, and be assured of the ultimate victory, even over death. You are receiving the goal of your faith, the salvation of your soul.

One of the saddest sights is to see people become elderly without Jesus; to watch people face death with great uncertainty as to what lies beyond. You can be thankful that you will never need to live without Him either in this life or beyond death. You can rejoice that Jesus is your resurrection and life. And you can use the opportunities you have to point others to Him as Saviour and Lord.

Hear Him speak His words of truth to your heart now.

Meditation:
I AM THE RESURRECTION AND THE LIFE (JOHN 11:25).

Whoever hears my word and believes him who sent me has eternal life (JOHN 5:24).

Whoever eats my flesh and drinks my blood has eternal life, and I will raise him up at the last day (JOHN 6:54).

Praise:
To him belongs eternal praise (PS. 111:10).

PART THREE

YOUR LIFE IN CHRIST

15. See yourself in Christ

'It is because of him that you are in Christ Jesus, who has become for us wisdom from God – that is, our righteousness, holiness and redemption' (1 COR. 1:30).

Holy Spirit, please give me the revelation that I am in Christ.

> **READING:** 1 JOHN 4:13–15
> We know that we live in him and he in us, because he has given us of his Spirit. And we have seen and testify that the Father has sent his Son to be the Saviour of the world. If anyone acknowledges that Jesus is the Son of God, God lives in him and he in God.

God has chosen to take hold of your life and place you in Christ Jesus, that you might live in Him. You could never deserve such a privilege, neither could you work your way into such a position. Your heavenly Father has chosen to make you His child and place you in His Son – it is because of Him that you are in Christ Jesus.

You do not have to strive to be placed in Jesus. You are already in Him by God's gracious act. You do not have to attain to some advanced level of spirituality before you can be 'in Christ'. This is where the Father puts you at the beginning of your Christian experience.

He sees you 'in Christ' and He wants you to see yourself 'in Christ'.

How can you know you are in Him? John answers the question: If you believe Jesus is the Son of God, who died on the cross to save you from your sins, this is evidence that God lives in you and you in God. You believe Jesus was not merely a good man, or a great prophet or teacher; He was God in human flesh who gave His life for you – to be your Saviour.

When you submit your life to Him as your Lord, you are born again and God's Spirit comes to live in you. To have received the gift of God's Holy Spirit is the very evidence that He loves you, forgives you, accepts you and that He has made it possible for you to live in Him and for Him to live in you. 'We know that we live in him and he in us, because he has given us of his Spirit' (1 John 4:13).

Every day you are to think of yourself as living in Christ with all His heavenly riches available to you.

When you know you are in Christ you accept Him as your wisdom from God. You cannot have a righteousness of your own before the righteous God; Jesus is your righteousness. God sees you in His beloved Son, clothed with His righteousness, made acceptable and worthy through Him.

He is your holiness and has made you one with the Holy Father. He is your redemption; He has paid the price for you with His own blood that you might belong to His Father eternally.

Because you are in Christ, everything He is and has becomes yours. Hear Him speaking His words to you now.

Meditation:
IT IS BECAUSE OF HIM THAT YOU ARE IN CHRIST JESUS (1 COR. 1:30).

For in him we live and move and have our being (ACTS 17:28).

For in him you have been enriched in every way (1 COR. 1:5).

Praise:
Praise the Lord, O my soul, and forget not all his benefits. He forgives all my sins and heals all my diseases; he redeems my life from the pit and crowns me with love and compassion (PS. 103:2–4).

16. Your Inheritance in Christ

'Now if we are children, then we are heirs – heirs of God and co-heirs with Christ' (ROM. 8:17).

Father, may I live in the knowledge of the rich inheritance you have given me in Christ.

READING: EPHESIANS 1:3–6

Praise be to the God and Father of our Lord Jesus Christ, who has blessed us in the heavenly realms with every spiritual blessing in Christ. For he chose us in him before the creation of the world to be holy and blameless in his sight. In love he predestined us to be adopted as his sons through Jesus Christ, in accordance with his pleasure and will – to the praise of his glorious grace, which he has freely given us in the One he loves.

Because you are in Christ Jesus, nothing can separate you from God's love. Jesus says the Father and the Son have come to make their home with you (John 14:23). You live in Him and He lives in you. You have all the resources of heaven available to you: everything that God has given Christ He has given you, because you too are His child and Jesus is your brother.

You received salvation by putting your faith in what Jesus did for you on the cross. You believed in God's grace, that He was willing to bless you although you deserved nothing from Him.

In the same way you learn to appropriate your inheritance in Christ by faith. It is possible to live in Christ without availing yourself of the rich inheritance which is yours through Him. God intends your life in Christ to be a constant reaching up to heaven to take to yourself whatever you need from His riches.

Because you are in Christ He has already given you every blessing heaven has to offer! That does not mean that you have received or appropriated every blessing, but that He has already given them. He has given you in Christ full salvation of body, soul and spirit. So Paul can positively affirm, 'And my God will meet all your needs according to his glorious riches in Christ Jesus' (Phil. 4:19).

You can be confident that all your needs *will* be met because all your needs *have* been met in Jesus. You live in Him who is your sufficiency at all times and in all situations. 'And God is able to make all grace abound to you, so that in all things at all times, having all that you need, you will abound in every good work' (2 Cor. 9:8). Did you know that this is God's purpose for you?

Let the words be personal for *you*. The Father of your Lord Jesus Christ has blessed *you* with every spiritual blessing in Christ. He wants *you* to hear that truth again and again in your heart. Keep saying to yourself: God has blessed me with every spiritual blessing in Christ.

Meditation:
GOD ... HAS BLESSED US IN THE HEAVENLY REALMS WITH EVERY SPIRI- TUAL BLESSING IN CHRIST (EPH. 1:3).

And my God will meet all your needs according to his glorious riches in Christ Jesus (PHIL. 4:19).

You have been given fulness in Christ (COL. 2:10).

Praise:
Now to him who is able to do immeasurably more than all we ask or imagine, according to his power that is at work within us, to him be glory in the church and in Christ Jesus throughout all generations, for ever and ever! Amen (EPH. 3:20–1).

17. Appropriate your Inheritance with Confidence

'This is the assurance we have in approaching God: that if we ask anything according to his will, he hears us' (1 JOHN 5:14).

Thank you, Lord, that I can draw near to you with confidence.

READING: HEBREWS 10:19–23
Therefore, brothers, since we have confidence to enter the Most Holy Place by the blood of Jesus, by a new and living way opened for us through the curtain, that is, his body, and since we have a great priest over the house of God, let us draw near to God with a sincere heart in full assurance of faith, having our hearts sprinkled to cleanse us from a guilty conscience and having our bodies washed with pure water. Let us hold unswervingly to the hope we profess, for he who promised is faithful.

Suppose someone left you a million pounds in his will, and you knew nothing about this inheritance. Obviously you would not be able to use the money. However, as soon as you were informed about this great inheritance you could begin to draw upon it, to use it in the right way.

God does not give you a million pounds, but a million blessings: every blessing in Christ. Now you can begin to draw on this rich inheritance. If you knew nothing about it before, you certainly do now. As far as God is concerned these blessings have your name on them and He is longing to release them into your life.

Because he knew the Lord, David could say: 'The Lord is my shepherd, I shall lack nothing' (Ps. 23:1).

The Lord is *your* shepherd. He will never lead you into want. He desires to provide for you and meet all your needs, to lead you beside quiet waters, to restore your soul, to guide you in righteous ways. He has spread a table before you in the face of all your problems and difficulties. He wants your cup to overflow because of His anointing on your life. He invites you to take from Him, for He loves to give to you.

Some approach Him tentatively, questioning His love, wondering if He truly wants to give to them. They doubt His love and grace.

You are told to come with confidence into His presence, to come with 'a sincere heart in full assurance of faith'. If you come to Him with confidence you expect to receive from Him what you ask. You do not imagine that you will be turned away empty handed. 'This is the assurance we have in approaching God: that if we ask anything according to his will, he hears us' (1 John 5:14).

Some have been ignorant of their heavenly blessings. Others, through unbelief, have left them deposited in heaven without availing themselves of these riches. The Lord wants you to transfer these blessings into the current account of your experience. His Word will show you what His will is. So when you pray according to His Word you pray according to His will.

Now you can see how important it is to pray His Word; to hear Him, believe Him and confidently ask Him to meet all your needs. 'From the fullness of his grace we have all received one blessing after another' (John 1:16).

Jesus is speaking to you now. He is inviting you to draw near to Him because He loves you and wants to make His holy presence known to you. Hear Him calling you and know you can take His presence into the world around you.

Meditation:
DRAW NEAR TO GOD WITH A SINCERE HEART IN FULL ASSURANCE OF FAITH (HEB. 10:22).

From the fullness of his grace we have all received one blessing after another (JOHN 1:16).

Let us then approach the throne of grace with confidence, so that we may receive mercy and find grace to help us in our time of need (HEB. 4:16).

Praise:
Blessed are those who have learned to acclaim you, who walk in the light of your presence, O Lord (PS. 89:15).

18. Hear and Believe

'I tell you the truth, whoever hears my word and believes him who sent me has eternal life and will not be condemned; he has crossed over from death to life' (JOHN 5:24).

Holy Spirit, I need to understand that I have died and that my life is now hidden with Christ in God. Please speak this truth to my heart.

READING: JOHN 5:19–24
Jesus gave them this answer: 'I tell you the truth, the Son can do nothing by himself; he can only do what he sees his Father doing, because whatever the Father does the Son also does. For the Father loves the Son and shows him all he does. Yes, to your amazement he will show him even greater things than these. For just

as the Father raises the dead and gives them life, even so the Son gives life to whom he is pleased to give it. Moreover, the Father judges no-one, but has entrusted all judgment to the Son, that all may honour the Son just as they honour the Father. He who does not honour the Son does not honour the Father, who sent him. 'I tell you the truth, whoever hears my word and believes him who sent me has eternal life and will not be condemned; he has crossed over from death to life.'

Have you received the gift of eternal life? If you have been born again, you have! God has taken you out of the kingdom of darkness where Satan rules and He has brought you into the kingdom of the Son He loves. He has put you into Christ and given you the gift of eternal life.

Paul is clear about when this transference took place: 'And you also were included in Christ when you heard the word of truth, the gospel of your salvation. Having believed, you were marked in him with a seal, the promised Holy Spirit, who is a deposit guaranteeing our inheritance' (Eph. 1:13–14).

This echoes what Jesus Himself taught. Those who hear His words and believe they are spoken from God the Father by His Son, have eternal life. They do not have to fear being condemned, separated from God and cast off from Him. They have passed from darkness to light, from death to life.

The words you believe are the words you live by. You have passed from death to life. You have died to your old life separated from God: 'your life is now hidden with Christ in God' (Col. 3:3). You no longer belong to the darkness; you are a child of light. Satan no longer has any hold or authority over you because Jesus is your Lord. You do not need to fear being condemned; you are a child of God's grace.

Hear these words of truth in your heart, for faith comes from hearing in this way. This is the truth about you, the truth that needs to undergird every part of your life.

Because you are in fellowship with God as your Father, you do not have to act independently of Him, striving in self-effort. Jesus said that the Son can do nothing by Himself, and

He reminded the disciples that they could do nothing apart from Him. The Son gives life to whom He is pleased to give it. He has been pleased to give it to you. He wants you to live in the power of this life and truth, not in independence. 'Let the word of Christ dwell in you richly' (Col. 3:16).

You may find it difficult to understand with your mind, but receive the truth in your spirit. You have died to a life separated from God. Now your life is hidden with Christ in God.

Meditation:
FOR YOU DIED, AND YOUR LIFE IS NOW HIDDEN WITH CHRIST IN GOD (COL. 3:3).

Apart from me you can do nothing (JOHN 15:5).

Now if we died with Christ, we believe that we will also live with him (ROM. 6:8).

Praise:
Like your name, O God, your praise reaches to the ends of the earth; your right hand is filled with righteousness (PS. 48:10).

19. The Truth about Yourself

'Therefore, if anyone is in Christ, he is a new creation; the old has gone, the new has come!' (2 COR. 5:17).

Lord, please help me to know that I am set free from my past and can now live a new life.

READING: REVELATION 21:3–5
And I heard a loud voice from the throne saying, 'Now the dwelling of God is with men, and he will live with them. They will be his people, and God himself will be with them and be their God. He will wipe every tear from their eyes. There will be no more death or mourning or crying or pain, for the old order of things has passed away.'
He who was seated on the throne said, 'I am making everything new!'

God's Word is truth; that is why it is so important to read His Word, to feed on it and to receive the Spirit, life and truth that are in His Word. Remember, agree with God: agree with what He says about you and about all who are in Christ, even if you do not fully understand what the Scriptures mean. Affirm the truths for yourself.

Therefore, there is now no condemnation for those who are in Christ Jesus (Rom. 8:1). I deserved to be condemned, but God by His loving grace has saved me. I do not have to allow the enemy to put me under any feelings of condemnation. God has put me into Christ – and there can be no condemnation in Him! I am not rejected by God; I am accepted by Him!

Christ is in me so my spirit is alive because of righteousness. I need no longer consider myself unrighteous because God has made me righteous in His sight. I have Christ as my righteousness because God has put me in Him.

I can walk not according to the flesh but according to the Spirit. To walk according to the flesh is death. To set my mind on pleasing myself, to dwell on my feelings, doubts and fears is spiritual death. Harmony and fellowship with the Lord are not possible if what I believe and say is hostile to God's Word. To set my mind on the Spirit, who declares God's Word to me – that is life and peace.

I can live in the Spirit, not in the flesh, because the Spirit of God dwells in me. What belongs to my old nature no longer need control my life. Because the old is dead I do not have to fight it. I reckon it as dead. God wants me to believe and declare that I am a new creature in Christ. I am a new creation.

I am led by the Spirit of God because I am a son of God. Since His Spirit is leading me, I can walk in the confidence and assurance that He will lead me in the path that He wants. If I start diverging from His way I shall soon lose my peace because my fellowship with Him is marred.

I did not receive the spirit of slavery to fall back into fear, but I have received the spirit of sonship. Every time I say 'Abba' 'Father' it is the Spirit Himself bearing witness with my spirit that I am a child of God. If I am His child then I am an heir of God and a fellow-heir with Christ (See Rom. 8:15). I am a child of God. He is my Father. The Holy Spirit within me bears witness to this truth. As a child of God I am a fellow-heir with Christ.

Notice the way in which the truths of Scripture are personally appropriated. I see myself as God sees me and speak to myself as He speaks of me in His Word. These same truths are true for you. As you learn to be still and to receive from God you will find His Words will become part of your thinking and believing.

Hear the Spirit taking the truth of God's Word and declaring it to you now. You are a new creation. The old has gone in your life and the new *has* come. Hear Him and believe Him.

Meditation:
THEREFORE, IF ANYONE IS IN CHRIST, HE IS A NEW CREATION; THE OLD HAS GONE, THE NEW HAS COME! (2 COR. 5:17).

I am making everything new (REV. 21:5).

Put on the new self, created to be like God in true righteousness and holiness (EPH. 4:24).

Praise:
For you make me glad by your deeds, O Lord; I sing for joy at the works of your hands (PS. 92:4).

20. *Confession of Faith*

'Put away perversity from your mouth; keep corrupt talk far from your lips' (PROV. 4:24).

Holy Spirit, give me the grace to speak the truths of your word about myself.

READING: PROVERBS 4:20–7
My son, pay attention to what I say; listen closely to my words. Do not let them out of your sight, keep them within your heart; for they are life to those who find them and health to a man's whole body. Above all else, guard your heart, for it is the wellspring of life. Put away perversity from your mouth; keep corrupt talk far from your lips. Let your eyes look straight ahead, fix your gaze directly before you. Make level paths for your feet and take only ways that are firm. Do not swerve to the right or the left; keep your foot from evil.

In order to fight the good fight of faith, we need to 'confess' – to speak out – our faith. We are not only to 'confess' sins, but to 'confess' faith. For example, when we speak as if we were

71

still living in the old life, rather than in the new life given us in Christ, we deny the very Spirit of God within us. Many Christians wage war against the old life and experience defeat because they are fighting a battle already won.

They need to realise they have died to the old life and need live in it no longer. Now they can live the new life, because they are not in bondage to the past. Believing the revelation of Scripture means they can see the power of God expressed in their lives far more freely. They can experience for themselves the victory He has already won.

Such a confession would say:

Father I have failed you. I'm sorry and I ask you to forgive me. I thank you that you have forgiven me because your Word says: 'If we confess our sins he is faithful and just and will forgive us our sins and purify us from all unrighteousness' (1 John 1:9). I believe you have forgiven me, Father, that I am righteous in your sight because you have cleansed me from all unrighteousness by the blood of Jesus. I confess that you are my Father and I am your child; and that you have given me your Spirit. I confess that you live in me by the power of your Spirit. I confess that you have made me an heir with Christ of all you have to give. I confess, Father, that every spiritual blessing in the heavenly realms is already mine. I confess, Father, that according to your Word I am more than a conqueror. I confess that according to your Word you always lead me in triumph. I confess that according to your Word you have not given me a spirit of fear, but of power and love and a sound mind. I confess that I am already justified, sanctified and glorified, not by what I have done but by what you have done for me in Christ; I am accepted, made holy and seated in heavenly places in Christ. I confess that although of myself I was unworthy, you have made me worthy by the blood of Jesus.

When you make such a confession as this, you agree with God concerning what He says about you. Holding fast to the truth will enable you to overcome temptation, fear and a sense of total inadequacy. When you think of yourself as God thinks, this has practical consequences for you. Of course He is wanting you to live up to your high calling in Christ. Even when you fail to do so, He is ready to restore you as soon as you turn to Him in repentance. What love!

In love He has called and chosen you to be His child. In love He has incorporated you into Christ. In love He has given you a rich inheritance. When you live in Him you live in the one who is love.

Listen to Him speak His words of love to you now. Jesus is telling you that He loves you in the same way the Father loved Him. What a glorious truth! He tells you to live in that truth, to remain in His love.

Meditation:
I HAVE PUT MY WORDS IN YOUR MOUTH (JER. 1:9).

I open my lips to speak what is right (PROV. 8:6).

My mouth speaks what is true (PROV. 8:7).

Praise:
May the words of my mouth and the meditation of my heart be pleasing in your sight, O Lord, my Rock and my Redeemer (PS. 19:14).

21. Feelings or Truth

'Heaven and earth will pass away, but my words will never pass away' (MATT. 24:35).

Lord, I do not want to live by my feelings, but by your truth.

> **READING:** JOHN 8:31–2, 36
> To the Jews who had believed him, Jesus said, 'If you hold to my teaching, you are really my disciples. Then you will know the truth, and the truth will set you free . . . So if the Son sets you free, you will be free indeed.'

When your feelings contradict what God says in His Word, both cannot be right!

Feelings are totally unreliable because they change so rapidly as you react to what goes on around you. You can feel great one moment, only to feel completely deflated the next because someone has said something unloving or critical to you, or because you have received bad news.

Many live in bondage to their feelings. They do what they feel like doing, and refuse to do what they do not want to do. Satan feeds negative things in people's minds in an attempt to make them feel oppressed or depressed. Even good feelings can do great harm leading to much of the permissive thinking so prevalent today: 'If it feels good, do it!'

God wants to teach you how to live in fellowship with Him, to agree with Him – and not allow your feelings to control you. If you speak only as you feel, you will often contradict what God says about you. In which case you cannot then be speaking the truth. God is truth; His words are truth. Therefore, whatever disagrees with Him cannot be truth. Anyone denying the Word of God cannot be speaking the truth.

Some say, 'I can't deny my feelings, it would be unreal to do so.' God is asking you to control your feelings and not to let them control you. Let the Word of God determine the course of your life, not your feelings which fluctuate so easily. You can be in bondage to your feelings, or be set free by the truth.

Heaven and earth will pass away, but my words will never pass away (Matt. 24:35).
. . . the word of our God stands for ever (Isa. 40:8).
(My words) are life to those who find them and health to a man's whole body (Prov. 4:22).
The words I have spoken to you are spirit and they are life (John 6:63).

Believe the power and authority of God's Word to be the ultimate truth, not your feelings, nor your circumstances, nor the lies of Satan, nor the opinions of men, nor your own understanding of events. None of these is to be trusted. But God's Word is trustworthy and the Holy Spirit wants to speak those words to your heart.

This is where the role of the Spirit and the Word come together. Jesus Christ said that the Holy Spirit will guide you into all truth (John 16:13). 'The Spirit will take from what is mine and make it known to you' (John 16:15). Your feelings will often lead you into trouble; the truth will set you free. Then you will have a greater control over your feelings; they will come under the ruling of the Holy Spirit.

Every time you pray in this way, you are able to receive the Spirit and life that are in God's Word. Know He is renewing His gifts to you now; He is breathing His Spirit and life into you as you pray.

Meditation:
THE WORDS I HAVE SPOKEN TO YOU ARE SPIRIT AND THEY ARE LIFE (JOHN 6:63).

The Spirit will take from what is mine and make it known to you (JOHN 16:15).

Praise:
Praise the Lord, O my soul; all my inmost being,
praise his holy name (PS. 103:1).

22. Freedom in Christ

'It is for freedom that Christ has set us free' (GAL. 5:1).

Father, I want to live in the freedom you have given me
through Jesus.

READING: GALATIANS 5:1, 13
It is for freedom that Christ has set us free. Stand firm,
then, and do not let yourselves be burdened again by a
yoke of slavery . . . You, my brothers, were called to
be free. But do not use your freedom to indulge the
sinful nature; rather, serve one another in love.

Paul speaks of 'the glorious freedom of the children of God'
(Rom. 8:21). God wants you to be free. Jesus died to set you
free. What He has done, He has done. It is finished, accomplished. *He has set you free*. And Jesus Himself said: 'So if the
Son sets you free, you will be free indeed' (John 8:36).

Speak this truth to yourself about yourself: Christ has set *me*
free. Christ *has* set me free. Christ has set me *free*. He has done
it. The Spirit of God bears witness to the truth of God's Word.
I am set free through Jesus Christ. I have the glorious freedom
of the children of God. Hallelujah!

Some believe this and live in freedom; others doubt it and
live in bondage. This freedom needs to be expressed in every
area of your life. Some feel there are certain things that restrict
or inhibit them. Often they point to events in the past, or the
way they were brought up. They claim they cannot be free
now because they are victims of their past.

But Christ has done everything to set you free. Because you

are born again the old has passed away and the new has come. The only hurts from the past that continue to have influence in your life are those you have not forgiven. If someone hurts you and you forgive him or her, that is the end of the matter. But if you do not forgive, the bitterness, resentment and anger seethe deep within you making the wound worse. Resentment is like a spiritual cancer eating away inside a person. You can become a hurt or wounded person who expects to be rejected and hurt further by others, if you do not forgive.

Do not allow any such hurt to rob you of your freedom in Christ. Forgive any who have hurt you; pray for them; and invite the Holy Spirit to come into the wounded areas of your life. Know that Jesus frees you in those areas; He was wounded to free you from all your wounds. The truth of what Jesus has done for you sets you free.

Live in His words of truth and rejoice in the freedom He has given you. Hear Him speaking His Words to you now.

Meditation:
IF THE SON SETS YOU FREE, YOU WILL BE FREE INDEED (JOHN 8:36).

It is for freedom that Christ has set us free (GAL. 5:1).

In my anguish I cried to the Lord, and he answered by setting me free (PS. 118:5).

Praise:
You are my God, and I will give thanks; you are my God, and I will exalt you (PS. 118:28).

23. No Condemnation

'Therefore, there is now no condemnation for those who are in Christ Jesus' (ROM. 8:1).

Thank you, Father, that there is no condemnation for me.

READING: JOHN 3:16–18
For God so loved the world that he gave his one and only Son, that whoever believes in him shall not perish but have eternal life. For God did not send his Son into the world to condemn the world, but to save the world through him. Whoever believes in him is not condemned, but whoever does not believe stands condemned already because he has not believed in the name of God's one and only Son.

You are in Christ Jesus. You are part of God's kingdom. You live in Him and He lives in you. One of the most important consequences which arises from these truths is that there is no condemnation for you.

Before you came to faith in Jesus you were under condemnation: 'Whoever believes in him is not condemned, but whoever does not believe stands condemned already because he has not believed in the name of God's one and only Son' (John 3:18). When you became a believer, God took hold of your life and placed you 'in Christ Jesus'. He rescued you from the dominion of darkness and brought you into the kingdom of the Son He loves.

In Christ there can be no condemnation, no sentence of death, no alienation from God. Outside of Him all are condemned because of their unbelief; they remain in darkness, subject to the prince of darkness.

Jesus has rescued you from condemnation and there is nothing Satan can do about that. He cannot undo what God has done in your life, but he can try to prevent you from living in the good of it. And one of his chief weapons is to create a false sense of condemnation.

Jesus died on the cross to free you from the shame and guilt of sin and from all condemnation. He suffered the punishment you deserve so you may be spared from punishment.

But Satan wants you to believe you are not truly forgiven, not really accepted by God. He feeds negative thoughts to you suggesting you are too unworthy to receive anything from the Lord. He questions whether God truly loves you; if so, why does He allow difficulties in your life? He suggests you are a spiritual failure and delights to point out all your blemishes to you, trying to make you feel you could not expect to receive blessing from the Lord.

He persists with his slanderous accusations trying to drive us into feelings of failure, frustration, defeat and even despair.

But God's Word here proclaims a great truth to our hearts. There is no condemnation for those in Christ. You are not condemned; you are forgiven and accepted. You do not have to listen to the enemy's lies. Even when you sin, God does not condemn you. He does not throw you out of His kingdom or withdraw your inheritance from you. He convicts you of your sin through the Holy Spirit working in you, drawing you to repentance and back into unity with Him and His purposes.

Conviction, the Holy Spirit pointing out your sin to draw you to repentance and forgiveness, leads to freedom; condemnation is like a prison. God has freed you from the prison of unbelief and condemnation. Resist the lies of the enemy and he will have to flee from you. As you live out your life in Christ Jesus there never will be any condemnation in this life or beyond. Alleluia!

Hear the words in your heart now. There is no condemnation for you because you are in Christ.

Meditation:
THEREFORE, THERE IS NOW NO CON-
DEMNATION FOR THOSE WHO ARE IN
CHRIST JESUS (ROM. 8:1).

Whoever believes in him [Jesus] is not condemned (JOHN 3:18).

The prince of this world [Satan] now stands condemned (JOHN 16:11).

Praise:
The Lord is compassionate and gracious, slow to anger, abounding in love (PS. 103:8).

24. *The Truth in Love*

'You, therefore, have no excuse, you who pass judgment on someone else, for at whatever point you judge the other, you are condemning yourself, because you who pass judgment do the same things' (ROM. 2:1).

Please, Father, help me by your Holy Spirit not to judge and condemn others.

READING: COLOSSIANS 3:12–14
Therefore, as God's chosen people, holy and dearly loved, clothe yourselves with compassion, kindness, humility, gentleness and patience. Bear with each other and forgive whatever grievances you may have against one another. Forgive as the Lord forgave you. And over all these virtues put on love, which binds them all together in perfect unity.

Condemnation does not only come directly from the enemy. Believing the negative things others say to you can bring a sense of condemnation. People gossip, criticise and condemn. Jesus said, 'Do not judge, or you too will be judged. For in the same way you judge others, you will be judged, and with the measure you use, it will be measured to you' (Matt. 7:1–2).

Judging others is completely the opposite to the forgiving, accepting and loving way in which God deals with us. He could judge us but chooses not to.

Satan is the accuser of the brethren, but he can use the mouths of others to do his accusing work for him. Many of the things others say are a denial of the truth about who you are in Christ. It is so easy to listen to, and believe, these negative things, especially if you have a low opinion of yourself already. The negative suggestions and criticisms of others will only confirm what you already believe about yourself, adding to your sense of personal failure.

When the woman caught in the act of adultery was brought before Jesus, He said: 'If any one of you is without sin, let him be the first to throw a stone at her' (John 8:7). One by one the crowd left until Jesus was alone with the woman. 'Has no-one condemned you?' He asked her. When she answered, 'No-one sir,' 'Then neither do I condemn you,' Jesus declared. 'Go now and leave your life of sin' (vv.10–11).

Many people criticise and condemn others because they are so insecure themselves. If they can make others seem worse, this will build their own self-confidence and pride, they imagine. In fact, it only adds to their insecurity for the reasons Jesus gives. You receive back from others what you give to others.

This does not mean that we should close our ears to helpful and objective criticism. Listen to those who are productive in the Lord. Often you will find that those who condemn, produce little themselves. Always assess what people say against the revelation of Scripture, and do not listen to the wild accusations of a single voice. If criticism is valid there will be at least two or three witnesses of the same mind.

To speak the truth in love to someone means that you will point them to the positive truth of what God has done for them in Christ; you are seeking to encourage them, not to be negative and destructive. Speak always in love, and only correct others when you know you do so in genuine love.

The truth brings conviction of sin, but never condemnation. There is *no* condemnation for those who are in Christ – no condemnation either from Satan or others.

Don't allow others to condemn you, and avoid feeding condemning thoughts to others. Know the Lord is merciful and gracious and wants to express those qualities through you to others.

Hear the Lord speaking to you now, knowing the Holy Spirit will help you to fulfil His words.

———

Meditation:
DO NOT JUDGE, AND YOU WILL NOT BE JUDGED. DO NOT CONDEMN, AND YOU WILL NOT BE CONDEMNED. FORGIVE, AND YOU WILL BE FORGIVEN (LUKE 6:37).

Then neither do I condemn you (JOHN 8:11).

Therefore, let us stop passing judgment on one another (ROM. 14:13).

Praise:
In God, whose word I praise, in the Lord, whose word I praise – in God I trust; I will not be afraid. What can man do to me? (PS. 56:10–11).

25. A False Cage

'Ask and it will be given to you' (LUKE 11:9).

Holy Spirit, help me to be faithful by being positive in my attitudes.

READING: PHILIPPIANS 4:4–7
Rejoice in the Lord always. I will say it again: Rejoice! Let your gentleness be evident to all. The Lord is near. Do not be anxious about anything, but in everything, by prayer and petition, with thanksgiving, present your requests to God. And the peace of God, which transcends all understanding, will guard your hearts and your minds in Christ Jesus.

We can create cages for ourselves by our words, making ourselves feel condemned. Unbelief is like a prison and is often evident by the things we say. Although there is no condemnation for those who are in Christ, we can feel condemned when guilty of negative unbelief, saying such things as:

'I don't believe it is God's will to heal me'; or
'God wouldn't be concerned about this matter'; or
'I don't want to bother God with my need'; or
'There are many far worse off than I am'.

By words such as these we both limit God and argue with Him, for His Word says He is almighty and for Him nothing is impossible. Never question His love and concern, nor doubt His graciousness. You will not see God do anything about your situation while you do not believe that He will. Jesus tells you to ask and promises you will receive, for He is always ready to be merciful to you.

Paul reinforces Jesus's words. He tells you not to be anxious about *anything*. You can entrust every situation to the Lord, no matter how large or seemingly insignificant. In *everything* you are to present your requests to God. Everything means everything!

Some say they do not want to ask anything for themselves. This is not humility; it is rank disobedience to God's Word and is also evidence of unbelief. Only a fool would fail to ask God to meet his need if he believed the answer was only a prayer away.

When you pray and present your petitions to God, you can do so with thanksgiving, confident that He hears and answers you. This is the kind of faith the Lord wants to produce in you.

It is a natural reaction to become anxious about difficult circumstances, but you are told to cast all your anxiety on the Lord for He cares for you. This is why at the beginning of your time of meditation it is so important to spend a few moments passing your burdens on to Him – not spending time dwelling upon them, but recognising that He is willing to take the weight of them from you.

'Come to me, all you who are weary and burdened, and I will give you rest' (Matt. 11:28). Anxiety never helps and is a contradiction to faith in Jesus. He is the Lord who loves you and wants to carry the weight of any problem and give you rest. To know He is willing to undertake for you enables the peace of Jesus to fill your heart and mind.

To pray with thanksgiving is evidence that you believe God has heard you and answered, even before there is anything to show for such faith. Such thanksgiving demonstrates a confidence in the gracious love and faithfulness of the Lord. To pray with thanksgiving and to speak with positive faith demonstrates that you refuse to be imprisoned in a false cage of unbelief. You will not condemn yourself with negative thinking.

Meditation:
ASK AND YOU WILL RECEIVE, AND YOUR JOY WILL BE COMPLETE (JOHN 16:24).

in everything, by prayer and petition, with thanksgiving, present your requests to God (PHIL. 4:6).

And the peace of God, which transcends all understanding, will guard your hearts and your minds in Christ Jesus (PHIL. 4:7).

Praise:
I sought the Lord, and he answered me; he delivered me from all my fears. Those who look to him are radiant; their faces are never covered with shame (PS. 34:4–5).

26. Encourage Others

'Whoever loves his brother lives in the light, and there is nothing in him to make him stumble' (1 JOHN 2:10).

Holy Spirit, help me to encourage others.

READING: COLOSSIANS 3:15–17
Let the peace of Christ rule in your hearts, since as members of one body you were called to peace. And be thankful. Let the word of Christ dwell in you richly as you teach and admonish one another with all wisdom, and as you sing psalms, hymns and spiritual songs with gratitude in your hearts to God. And whatever you do, whether in word or deed, do it all in the name of the Lord Jesus, giving thanks to God the Father through him.

We have a great responsibility to build up one another in love, to encourage one another in truth. When Christians criticise and judge each other they only glorify the accuser of the brethren. We need to eradicate destructive criticism and begin to encourage faith in the Word.

This needs to be done sensitively – the Word spoken in the power of the Spirit encourages faith. Jesus intends you to have a ministry of encouragement to your brothers and sisters. The Word spoken without love can leave people feeling devastated even if what is said is true. It is not only what you say that matters but how you say it! You need to speak the truth in love, and be open to receive encouragement from others without feeling resentful or pressed.

Every truth you have appropriated for yourself about your new life in Christ is equally true for other Christians. Your responsibility is to point them to those truths:

They are not alone.
He is with them.
He is the strength of their life.
There is no condemnation for those in Christ Jesus.
God will meet their needs according to His riches in Christ
  Jesus.

You can point them to the truth of God's Word so they can believe and speak victoriously instead of confessing misery, failure, doubt and defeat. You can speak to them in the name of Jesus, saying what He wants to say to encourage them.

Jesus says, 'if two of you on earth agree about anything you ask for, it will be done for you by my Father in heaven' (Matt. 18:19). By this Jesus means that the two people should agree in their hearts about what they believe; they are in complete harmony about the matter. They do not merely agree to a formula of words, one praying a prayer, the other saying, 'Amen'! What they pray comes from their heart–conviction as to what God will do about the matter.

It is good to talk together with others and allow the Holy Spirit to bring you to a common mind as to what you are to believe. Whatever you agree together in *faith* will be done by your Father in heaven. When you arrive at a common mind, you can pray with confidence, knowing that 'it will be done for you'.

Honesty is vital here, both with God and with yourself, especially if faith is lacking at first. An honest admission of unbelief gives another person opportunity to speak faith to you and show you what the Lord promises in His Word. As you hear the truth together through one another your confidence is strengthened. You can encourage faith in others and they can encourage faith in you. When one wavers the other can remain strong. We need each other in our faith walk with the Lord.

Hear now the words of Jesus. Allow His truth to fill your heart. His prayer promises are for *you*.

Meditation:
IF TWO OF YOU ON EARTH AGREE ABOUT ANYTHING YOU ASK FOR, IT WILL BE DONE FOR YOU BY MY FATHER IN HEAVEN (MATT. 18:19).

Therefore encourage one another and build each other up (1 THESS. 5:11).

And whatever you do, whether in word or deed, do it all in the name of the Lord Jesus (COL. 3:17).

Praise:
May the peoples praise you, O God; may all the peoples praise you (PS. 67:3).

PART FOUR

YOUR LIFE OF FAITH

27. Faith in God

'Have faith in God' (MARK 11:22).

Holy Spirit, help me to have faith in God at all times.

READING: MARK 11:22–5

'Have faith in God,' Jesus answered. 'I tell you the truth, if anyone says to this mountain, "Go, throw yourself into the sea," and does not doubt in his heart but believes that what he says will happen, it will be done for him. Therefore I tell you, whatever you ask for in prayer, believe that you have received it, and it will be yours. And when you stand praying, if you hold anything against anyone, forgive him, so that your Father in heaven may forgive you your sins.'

Jesus teaches His disciples to pray with faith. First, He says, it is important to have faith in God. That might seem self-evident, but it is only too easy to concentrate on the need or problem, on your feelings or fears. If you do this, faith rapidly drains away.

To have faith in God is to have faith in His Word. Your faith in Jesus demonstrates you are able to believe without seeing. Doubting Thomas refused to believe Jesus had risen until he saw Him for Himself. When he saw he worshipped, saying, '"My Lord and my God!" Then Jesus told him, "Because you have seen me, you have believed; blessed are those who have not seen and yet have believed"' (John 20:28–9).

So you are a blessed one. You believe without seeing. When you pray with faith, God wants you to believe in the result of your prayer before there is anything to see. The world says: See and then believe. Jesus says: Believe and then see!

As you receive the Word, see with the eyes of faith the answer to your need. You can end every prayer with thanksgiving because you believe the Father answers you, whether you are praying for yourself or for someone else. 'Do not be anxious about anything, but in everything, by prayer and petition, with thanksgiving, present your requests to God' (Phil. 4:6).

This is how Jesus Himself prayed. He stood before the tomb of Lazarus and said: 'Father, I thank you that you have heard me. I knew that you always hear me' (John 11:41–2). He said this *before* Lazarus was raised. This is the confidence that comes from knowing the faithfulness of your Father in heaven.

You have this relationship because you are a child of God. You can be so confident of your Father's desire to give to you that you can be still at any moment and in any place, and receive from Him through His Word and by His Spirit. You have faith in God. He hears you and meets with you every time you wait on Him.

Hear Jesus encouraging you now, urging you to exercise your faith in God, for He knows His Father will never fail you.

Meditation:
HAVE FAITH IN GOD (MARK 11:22).

According to your faith will it be done to you (MATT. 9:29).

Trust in God; trust also in me (JOHN 14:1).

Praise:
Then they believed his promises and sang his praise (PS. 106:12).

28. Speak to the Mountains

'Jesus replied, "I tell you truth, if you have faith and do not doubt, not only can you do what was done to the fig tree, but also you can say to this mountain, 'Go, throw yourself into the sea,' and it will be done"' (MATT. 21:21).

Lord, I want to learn to speak to mountains and see them moved.

> **READING:** MARK 11:22-5
> 'Have faith in God,' Jesus answered. 'I tell you the truth, if anyone says to this mountain, "Go, throw yourself into the sea," and does not doubt in his heart but believes that what he says will happen, it will be done for him. Therefore I tell you, whatever you ask for in prayer, believe that you have received it, and it will be yours. And when you stand praying, if you hold anything against anyone, forgive him, so that your Father in heaven may forgive you your sins.'

Do you speak to your problems? Jesus tells you to do so. He says you are to speak to the mountains and command them to move. Obviously these are not physical mountains of rock, but mountains of need, the problems that have to be removed from your life.

Faith gives you confidence to speak to the mountains in your life. God has not put them there, and He wants them removed. Wrong thinking leads to unbelief. If you imagine your problems come from God, you will not have faith to ask Him to take them away, nor will you have confidence to speak to the needs.

It is the enemy who wants to put hindrances in your way. Jesus wants you to exercise your authority over all the power of the devil. If you resist him, he will flee from you. If you come against the mountains he puts in your way, you can command them to be thrown into the sea.

Sometimes Christians accept their problems instead of coming against them in faith. The devil loves such passive attitudes. Even as you pray, receiving the Spirit and life in God's Word know that you are coming against these mountains with all His resources behind you. The mountains must give way. God's power is greater than any need.

There is a kind of godly indignation at the spoiling tactics of the enemy. Instead of passively accepting problems, Christians should rise up in indignation against the negative things which cause upset, pain and chaos in people's lives. Jesus expressed such indignation against the Pharisees, against the money-lenders in the temple, against demonic forces and sickness, and against the devil himself.

You can speak to the mountains in your experience with all the authority of one who lives in Christ. You are given the privilege of speaking in His name, on His behalf, in the way He would speak to the problems you encounter. See them as He would see them, and deal with them as He would.

Listen to these words of Jesus. He is saying *you* can speak to the particular mountain before you and it will be moved. Don't believe in the mountain: trust Him.

Meditation:
YOU CAN SAY TO THIS MOUNTAIN, 'GO, THROW YOURSELF INTO THE SEA,' AND IT WILL BE DONE (MATT. 21:21).

Nothing will be impossible for you (MATT. 17:21).

Everything is possible for him who believes (MARK 9:23).

Praise:
Every day I will praise you and extol your name for ever and ever (PS. 145:2).

29. Believe you have Received

'If you believe, you will receive whatever you ask for in prayer' (MATT. 21:22).

Father, I want to pray always with faith.

READING: MARK 11:22–5

'Have faith in God,' Jesus answered. 'I tell you the truth, if anyone says to this mountain, "Go, throw yourself into the sea," and does not doubt in his heart but believes that what he says will happen, it will be done for him. Therefore I tell you, whatever you ask for in prayer, believe that you have received it, and it will be yours. And when you stand praying, if you hold anything against anyone, forgive him, so that your Father in heaven may forgive you your sins.'

The enemy will try to persuade you that you do not have enough faith to be able to receive from God. Don't listen to him! You do have faith. You believe God wants to give to you and every time you pray in this way you are able to receive from Him.

To pray with faith is not to say that God will do something at some time in the future. That is hope, not faith. When you pray with faith, you believe you have received it.

This type of prayer helps you greatly in this respect. You believe God is giving to you as you receive His Word in prayer. Although the total answer to your need may not be manifested immediately, nevertheless you believe the outcome is already settled. You have received your answer by faith and every time you pray like this you are appropriating your answer.

It is great when God meets with us in miraculous ways, when needs, even of a critical or substantial nature, are met spontaneously. But this is not the only way God answers prayer, neither is it the only way of receiving from Him.

I receive some answers immediately, but others come gradually. This is true of healing, for example. I see God heal many people spontaneously, but I hear of many others who receive their healing over a period of time. This is true of medically incurable diseases, or of more minor matters.

Faith does not question the final outcome. You believe you have received the total answer, even though this may be manifested gradually. Every occasion of receiving through prayer is a further step towards the ultimate victory.

Come against the need in your life. Speak to the mountain and command that it be moved. The Lord does not want you living with that problem; He wants it thrown into the sea and sunk without trace. With the eyes of faith, see this as accomplished, and know that every time you pray you receive the answer to your need.

Your Father hears you when you pray. He wants you to be so sure of His love and faithfulness, to have such faith in the power of His Word, that every time you pray you believe you receive from Him.

Meditation:
IF YOU BELIEVE, YOU WILL RECEIVE WHATEVER YOU ASK FOR IN PRAYER (MATT. 21:22).

And I will do whatever you ask in my name, so that the Son may bring glory to the Father (JOHN 14:13).

You may ask me for anything in my name, and I will do it (JOHN 14:14).

Praise:
Trust in the Lord for ever, for the Lord, the Lord, is the Rock eternal (ISA. 26:4).

30. Receiving

'And when you stand praying, if you hold anything against anyone, forgive him, so that your Father in heaven may forgive you your sins' (MARK 11:25).

Holy Spirit, help me always to have a forgiving attitude.

READING: MATTHEW 18:21–35

Then Peter came to Jesus and asked, 'Lord, how many times shall I forgive my brother when he sins against me? Up to seven times?' Jesus answered, 'I tell you, not seven times, but seventy-seven times.

'Therefore, the kingdom of heaven is like a king who wanted to settle accounts with his servants. As he began the settlement, a man who owed him ten thousand talents was brought to him. Since he was not able to pay, the master ordered that he and his wife and his children and all that he had be sold to repay the debt.

'The servant fell on his knees before him. "Be patient with me," he begged, "and I will pay back everything." The servant's master took pity on him, cancelled the debt and let him go.

'But when that servant went out, he found one of his fellow servants who owed him a hundred denarii. He grabbed him and began to choke him. "Pay back what you owe me!" he demanded.

'His fellow servant fell to his knees and begged him, "Be patient with me, and I will pay you back."

'But he refused. Instead, he went off and had the man thrown into prison until he could pay the debt. When the other servants saw what had happened, they were greatly distressed and went and told their master everything that had happened.

'Then the master called the servant in. "You wicked

servant," he said, "I cancelled all that debt of yours because you begged me to. Shouldn't you have had mercy on your fellow servant just as I had on you?" In anger his master turned him over to the jailers until he should pay back all he owed.

'This is how my heavenly Father will treat each of you unless you forgive your brother from your heart.'

Jesus made it very clear how important it is to forgive: 'For if you forgive men when they sin against you, your heavenly Father will also forgive you. But if you do not forgive men their sins, your Father will not forgive your sins' (Matt. 6:14–15).

If you do not forgive, you are not yourself forgiven, and if you are not forgiven it is extremely difficult to receive from God, no matter how much faith you have. Forgiveness is an expression of love and mercy from God to you. And He expects you to extend similar love and mercy towards others. Paul warns, 'if I have a faith that can move mountains, but have not love, I am nothing' (1 Cor. 13:2).

Jesus told the parable of the unmerciful servant to warn us of the consequences of refusing to forgive others.

In your preparation to receive, ask God to forgive you *and extend your forgiveness towards others*. You are to maintain an attitude of mercy no matter how many times you have to forgive. Forgiveness needs to become a natural reaction when others wrong you. Instead of burning with anger or resentment, forgive. Instead of waiting until the other apologises before forgiving, have a forgiving attitude immediately you are aware of the wrong, so that the sore has no opportunity to fester.

Whenever you pray you are to forgive, that is what Jesus says. Not sometimes, but *whenever*: and whenever means every time you pray.

I have known many to receive healing of physical or emotional needs as a result of forgiving others. No doubt the Lord wanted to release their healing to them before, but the lack of forgiveness prevented this. For example, a woman in the advanced stages of multiple sclerosis came to a meeting in her wheel-chair. Through the preaching the Lord convicted her of her need to forgive someone who had caused a deep hurt in her life. From that moment she began to be healed of her disease. She was soon out of her wheel-chair and walking around normally.

No one prayed with her; Jesus ministered His Word to her heart. When she responded she was set free. 'Forgive us our debts, as we also have forgiven our debtors' (Matt. 6:12).

Let the words of this meditation become part of you, so that on every occasion your instinctive reaction is to forgive. You are to forgive – as the Lord forgave you. He never wants to withhold that forgiveness from you if you do not withhold your forgiveness from others.

Meditation:
FORGIVE AS THE LORD FORGAVE YOU
(COL. 3:13).

If you hold anything against anyone, forgive him (MARK 11:25).

For if you forgive men when they sin against you, your heavenly Father will also forgive you (MATT. 6:14).

Praise:
As far as the east is from the west, so far has he removed our transgressions from us (PS. 103:12).

31. Acting out your Faith

'Then Jesus said, "Did I not tell you that if you believed, you would see the glory of God?"' (JOHN 11:40).

Father, may I know your faithfulness in always answering my prayer.

READING: JOHN 11:40–2
Then Jesus said, 'Did I not tell you that if you believed, you would see the glory of God?'
   So they took away the stone. Then Jesus looked up and said, 'Father, I thank you that you have heard me. I knew that you always hear me, but I said this for the benefit of the people standing here, that they may believe that you sent me.'

Faith is not a feeling; it is an activity. Faith is expressed in what you say and do. Jesus says that from the overflow of the heart the mouth speaks. If there is faith in your heart, your mouth will proclaim that faith, and your actions will declare it.

When Jesus heard that His great friend Lazarus was sick, His immediate reaction was one of faith: 'This sickness will not end in death' (John 11:4). This is His faith reaction to the news. The enemy might want to steal the life of His beloved friend through sickness, but he will not be allowed to prevail. This is a statement of faith, and of godly indignation!

Because there is faith in His heart, Jesus does not hurry to the scene. With His eyes of faith He sees Lazarus being raised long before the event. It is four days before He arrives at the tomb. Each of His actions demonstrates the reality of His faith. '"Take away the stone," he said' (John 11:38). What would be the point of saying this unless He expected a miracle?

He is concerned to see God glorified: 'This sickness will not end in death. No, it is for God's glory so that God's Son may be glorified through it' (John 11:4). 'Did I not tell you that if you believed, you would see the glory of God?' (John 11:40).

He wants to see His Father glorified in the situation – Satan's seeming triumph will be turned to defeat. His Father's glory will be reflected in the Son as He proceeds with faith.

He stands before the tomb and prays: 'Father, I thank you that you have heard me. I knew that you always hear me, but I said this for the benefit of the people standing here, that they may believe that you sent me' (John 11:41–2).

This is prayer with faith. Jesus knows His Father always hears Him. He believes He has received His answer before there is anything to show for such confidence. The way in which He prays is an example to all those around.

Then He speaks to the 'mountain' with a word of authority: 'Lazarus, come out!' (John 11:43). And he does!

Remember what Jesus teaches, 'believe that you have received it, and it will be yours' (Mark 11:24). Do you see how this principle operates in practice? Jesus has faith; He is confident of the outcome from the very beginning. He knows in His heart what will happen.

You may not have to raise the dead very often, but every day you need to pray with faith. Remember, it is not only what you say at the time of prayer that matters. Like Jesus, you need to have faith attitudes in your heart. All your words and actions are to spring from these heart attitudes. Faith that is an external veneer is not real faith! It is the prayer and desire of the heart that God promises to answer.

You are about to pray to the Father with the words of Jesus. Because you live in Him, these words are as true for you as for Him. Your heavenly Father always hears you, and He promises to answer the cry of your heart.

Meditation:
FATHER, I THANK YOU THAT YOU HAVE HEARD ME. I KNOW THAT YOU ALWAYS HEAR ME (JOHN 11:41–2).

How much more will your Father in heaven give good gifts to those who ask him! (MATT. 7:11).

To your name be the glory, because of your love and faithfulness (PS. 115:1).

Praise:
This is the assurance we have in approaching God: that if we ask anything according to his will, he hears us. And if we know that he hears us – whatever we ask – we know that we have what we asked of Him (1 JOHN 5:14–15).

32. *Faithful Speech*

'Make a tree good and its fruit will be good, or make a tree bad and its fruit will be bad, for a tree is recognised by its fruit' (MATT. 12:33).

Holy Spirit, help me to speak positive words of faith.

READING: MATTHEW 12:35–7
The good man brings good things out of the good stored up in him, and the evil man brings evil things out of the evil stored up in him. But I tell you that men will have to give account on the day of judgment for every careless word they have spoken. For by your words you will be acquitted, and by your words you will be condemned.

These are some of the most awesome words Jesus spoke, and they point to the importance of the way in which we use our mouths. James warns us: 'With the tongue we praise our Lord and Father, and with it we curse men, who have been made in God's likeness. Out of the same mouth come praise and cursing. My brothers, this should not be. Can both fresh water and salt water flow from the same spring?' (Jas. 3:9–11).

The way you speak indicates what you believe. If you are full of positive faith, your mouth will speak positive words. If you are full of fear and unbelief you will speak negatively. If you are double-minded you will speak in confusion, vacillating from faith to doubt and back to faith again, not sure what you really believe.

A good tree can only produce good fruit. A positive heart can only produce positive words of faith and encouragement. A praising heart will rejoice in the Lord, regardless of the circumstances. What is happening around the person will not change his heart attitudes.

There is an important lesson to learn here, for many speak as if their problems cause their negative responses. This is not the case; the problem has simply revealed the negative heart attitude already there. It has not created the negative reaction, only revealed it. What has been hidden in the dark has been drawn out into the light.

For this reason two people can react in entirely different ways to identical circumstances. One will immediately be dejected and frustrated, fearful and angry even. Another will look to Jesus, entrusting the matter into His hands, confident He will not fail. It all depends on what is already in the heart.

This is why it is so important to store the truth of God's Word in your heart, so that it may be a wellspring of life within you. If the truth is already in your heart, your mouth will proclaim it. Your words will be like the sounding of a true note in harmony with God's Word, rather than one which is out of tune, at discord with His will.

The answer to fear and doubt is not to ask the Lord to remove them; rather begin to make a positive confession. There is no condemnation in being attacked by negative doubts; this is Satan's work and he loves to try and undermine the faith of God's children. The way to overcome him is to resist him in the way Jesus did: 'It is written . . .' (Luke 4:4, 8, 10).

You will find that to speak the positive truth of God's Word will help that Word live in you. As you declare it, believe it. This is what God says about the matter. You will experience positive results as you steadfastly maintain that confession in the face of all the difficulties. This is much more powerful than expressing the negatives of the world, the flesh and the devil.

Store the good things within you – and good things will flow out of you. God has given you a mouth. You have the ability to speak the negative words of unbelief, fear and sickness; or, like Jesus, you can speak the positive words of faith.

Meditation:
LET THE WORD OF CHRIST DWELL IN YOU RICHLY (COL. 3:16).

Above all else, guard your heart, for it is the wellspring of life (PROV. 4:23).

Keep my commands in your heart, for they will prolong your life many years and bring you prosperity (PROV. 3:1–2).

Praise:
I will sing of the Lord's great love for ever; with my mouth I will make your faithfulness known through all generations (PS. 89:1).

33. Hold Fast

'[My words] are life to those who find them and health to a man's whole body' (PROV. 4:22).

Father, I believe you will watch over your Word to perform it in my life.

READING: LUKE 8:11–15
This is the meaning of the parable: The seed is the word of God. Those along the path are the ones who hear, and then the devil comes and takes away the word from their hearts, so that they cannot believe and be saved. Those on the rock are the ones who receive the word with joy when they hear it, but they have no root. They believe for a while, but in the time of testing they fall away. The seed that fell among thorns stands for those who hear, but as they go on their way they are choked by life's worries, riches and pleasures, and they do not mature. But the seed on good soil stands for those with a noble and good heart, who hear the word, retain it, and by persevering produce a crop.

God will never deny His Word, but will perform what He has promised. Often your experience does not measure up to these promises, but God wants to raise your experience to the level of His Word, not reduce His Word to the level of your experience. There is no room for question-marks as to God's will when He clearly expresses His purpose in His Word. God's will never contradict His Word. If God was ever to deny His Word, He would deny His Son. That He will never do for He is not divided against Himself. He will honour the covenant, the binding agreement, He has made with His children and which is sealed, or ratified, with the precious blood of Jesus.

God wants you to take Him at His Word. If you believe what He says, you will hold fast to His Words with all your heart, even in the face of adverse circumstances.

Abraham inherited God's promises by faith with patience. Jesus never promised instantaneous answers to all our prayers. Often patient endurance is needed until the promise is fulfilled, and that can be the real test of faith. During the waiting period you need to continue to receive His Words, and hold fast *with an honest and good heart*.

Every time you waver in your faith, you have to come back to God and confess your doubt. He will forgive you and you can return to the positive affirmation of His truth, praising Him for His faithfulness.

Nobody can prevent God from doing what He says He is going to do. This is why it is so important to hear Him speaking His words of promise to your heart. He watches over His Word to perform it. Those who bear a hundredfold fruit in Jesus's parable are those 'who hear the word, retain it, and by persevering produce a crop' (Luke 8:15).

Meditation:
I THE LORD HAVE SPOKEN, AND I WILL DO IT (EZEK. 36:36).

The Lord is faithful to all his promises (PS. 145:13).

God, who has called you into fellowship with his Son Jesus Christ our Lord, is faithful (1 COR. 1:9).

Praise:
My son, do not forget my teaching, but keep my commands in your heart, for they will prolong your life many years and bring you prosperity (PROV. 3:1–2).

34. The Lord your Healer

'I am the Lord who heals you' (EXOD. 15:26).

Father, I want to know you as my healer.

READING: LUKE 4:14–21

Jesus returned to Galilee in the power of the Spirit, and news about him spread through the whole country-side. He taught in their synagogues, and everyone praised him.

He went to Nazareth, where he had been brought up, and on the Sabbath day he went into the syna-gogue, as was his custom. And he stood up to read. The scroll of the prophet Isaiah was handed to him. Unrolling it, he found the place where it is written:

'The Spirit of the Lord is on me, because he has anointed me to preach good news to the poor. He has sent me to proclaim freedom for the prisoners and recovery of sight for the blind, to release the oppressed, to proclaim the year of the Lord's favour.'

Then he rolled up the scroll, gave it back to the attendant and sat down. The eyes of everyone in the synagogue were fastened on him, and he began by saying to them, 'Today this scripture is fulfilled in your hearing.'

It is God's nature to heal. He revealed himself to Israel as the Lord who heals. Jesus came to do the will of His Father; He did only the things He saw His Father doing – and He spent much of His public ministry healing the sick. When He went to the cross He made provision for our total healing, spirit, soul and body.

Jesus expressed the Father's desire to heal. In one sense all God does in our lives is part of His healing purpose, saving us from sin, sickness, poverty and death. His Words are words of healing, 'they are life to those who find them and health to a man's whole body' (Prov. 4:22).

You can receive healing every time you sit down quietly and 'receive' His Words into your spirit. Hear the Lord speak to your heart saying, 'I am the Lord who heals you.' Know that these are not words *about* healing; they are words *of* healing. Yes, God's healing power can come to you through His Word.

Understand that the Lord is speaking to you personally: 'I am the Lord who heals *you*.' And He is conveying His healing life and power to you as you receive His Words.

In times of particular need, you can spend a few minutes several times a day receiving healing from the Lord as you receive His Words of healing in this way. Remember, faith comes from hearing the Word of Christ proclaimed to your heart. It may seem little is happening at first. But there will come the point at which the Spirit will declare those words of truth to your heart. At that moment they become personal to you; they are the voice of God to you.

As you pray, believe that the Holy Spirit comes upon you to bring God's healing into your life and body. Both the Word and the Spirit are agencies of God's healing grace to you. What a combination when you bring the two together!

What is more, the Holy Spirit will work through you to bring healing to others, to members of your family, to friends and fellow Christians. Teach them to be still, to hear the Lord speak words of healing to their hearts. You may feel it right to help them by laying hands on them, praying for the Holy Spirit to come upon them to heal. Whether you do this or not, know there is healing life and power in God's Words and He is going to speak healing into your life now.

Meditation:
I AM THE LORD WHO HEALS YOU (EXOD. 15:26).

He drove out the spirits with a word and healed all the sick (MATT. 8:16).

But just say the word, and my servant will be healed (MATT. 8:8).

Praise:
I trust in the Lord. I will be glad and rejoice in your love, for you saw my affliction and knew the anguish of my soul (PS. 31:6–7).

35. *Health*

'By his wounds you have been healed' (1 PET. 2:24).

Jesus, I need the revelation in my heart that I am healed by your wounds.

READING: ISAIAH 53:4–10
Surely he took up our infirmities and carried our sorrows, yet we considered him stricken by God, smitten by him, and afflicted. But he was pierced for our transgressions, he was crushed for our iniquities; the punishment that brought us peace was upon him, and by his wounds we are healed. We all, like sheep, have gone astray, each of us has turned to his own way; and the Lord has laid on him the iniquity of us all.

He was oppressed and afflicted, yet he did not open his mouth; he was led like a lamb to the slaughter, and as a sheep before her shearers is silent, so he did not open his mouth. By oppression and judgment, he was taken away. And who can speak of his descendants? For he was cut off from the land of the living; for the transgression of my people he was stricken. He was assigned a grave with the wicked, and with the rich in his death, though he had done no violence, nor was any deceit in his mouth.

Yet it was the Lord's will to crush him and cause him

to suffer, and though the Lord makes his life a guilt
offering, he will see his offspring and prolong his days,
and the will of the Lord will prosper in his hand.

When a need for healing arises in your life it is easy to speak
negatively about the dreadful pain, the discomfort and the
weakness. The more you concentrate on the problem, the
more you place yourself in the grip of that problem. You
believe in your heart what your mouth speaks. How much
healthier to speak words of healing because the truth is stored
in your heart.

There are several ways of receiving healing through Jesus.
The key is to understand that He dealt with your need on the
cross. 'Surely he took up our infirmities and carried our
sorrows.' He dealt with every emotional and physical need as
well as all our spiritual needs.

Jesus took up your infirmities and sorrows. He was rejected
and oppressed so that you may be set free from rejection and
oppression. He suffered for you in order to free you. By His
wounds you are healed in every way, in spirit, soul and body.
Affirm for yourself:

By His stripes I am healed.

You do not need to see yourself as 'Poor me'. Neither are you
to feel condemned for being sick. Here is an opportunity to see
the manifestation of the victory of the healing of Jesus, won for
you on the cross. You need to make the positive confession of
faith in God's power and will to heal you. Without that
confession which stems from faith, you may well deprive
yourself of your healing, no matter how often you ask others
to pray for you. God hears the prayer of your heart and He
knows what you really believe. Faith does not say, 'God will
heal me.' Faith says: 'By His wounds I have been healed'; He
has done it.

This truth needs to be revelation in your heart. Know that
every time you sit down and receive the words of healing,

God's healing is actually taking place in you. Affirm the truth: *Jesus has carried my infirmities and my sorrows.*

You do not need to question whether it is God's desire to heal you. Instead you can affirm: 'In Christ, He has met my need.' Through His mercy and by the power of the Holy Spirit you are able to receive His healing. As you repeat this Scripture know that the Lord is conveying healing to you personally.

Remember, He often heals from the inside outwards. You may experience considerable healing within you before you see all the physical needs met. Whatever way He works in your situation, you can be thankful that by the wounds of Jesus you have been healed.

Do not be discouraged if your healing does not take place instantaneously or in a miraculous fashion. Some healings take place like that, others take a period of time. Nobody manifests the perfect healing of spirit, soul and body during this life; but as you feed on God's Word His healing purposes are being furthered in your experience.

Meditation:
BY HIS WOUNDS YOU HAVE BEEN HEALED
(1 PET. 2:24).

Surely he took up our infirmities and carried our sorrows (ISA. 53:4).

Go! It will be done just as you believed it would (MATT. 8:13).

Praise:
One generation will commend your works to another; they will tell of your mighty acts (PS. 145:4).

N B. For a further treatment of the whole subject of healing see the author's book, *Receive Your Healing.*

36. The Holy Spirit Helps

'When the Counsellor comes, whom I will send to you from the Father, the Spirit of truth who goes out from the Father, he will testify about me' (JOHN 15:26).

Holy Spirit, please fill me with your healing life and power.

READING: JOHN 16:12–15
I have much more to say to you, more than you can now bear. But when he, the Spirit of truth, comes, he will guide you into all truth. He will not speak on his own; he will speak only what he hears, and he will tell you what is yet to come. He will bring glory to me by taking from what is mine and making it known to you. All that belongs to the Father is mine. That is why I said the Spirit will take from what is mine and make it known to you.

The Holy Spirit will help you to confess the positive truth of God's Word. This is part of His job, of His ministry to you. 'But the Counsellor, the Holy Spirit, whom the Father will send in my name, will teach you all things and will remind you of everything I have said to you' (John 14:26).

Do not feel condemned when attacked by the negative. The Holy Spirit will bring to your mind the positive truths that will counteract the negative.

If you feel afraid, speak out the positive words of faith, such as, 'I am with you always'. When you live faith and learn to confess the Word in faith, you will find yourself beginning to live in a new dimension, no longer believing experiences and waiting passively for the next problem. You appreciate that you live in Christ and He in you, and you have available from God all the resources needed to meet every situation.

If you speak need, you have need. If you speak as one provided for, you will see the Lord's provision.

If you speak sickness, you will remain sick. If you speak healing, you will experience healing.

If you speak despair, you will feel everything is hopeless. If you speak encouragement, you will be encouraged yourself and will appreciate that God is able to meet with you in every situation.

These are not formulae of speech to be repeated mechanically, for the words you speak need to flow from the heart. This is why it is so important to receive the positive truth of God's Word into your heart.

Pray for the Holy Spirit to help you in this. You are not expected to struggle on in your own strength, but to flow in His power. He will help you. It is His job, His desire to do so. Call on the Holy Spirit any moment of the day or night – and He will help you. He will declare God's Word to you, bringing to the conscious level of your mind the truth you need to be reminded of at that particular time.

Hear Jesus speak to you now the words He spoke to His disciples. Let Him breathe His Spirit into you afresh. Believe He is doing that as you pray.

Meditation:
RECEIVE THE HOLY SPIRIT (JOHN 20:22).

The Holy Spirit . . . will remind you of everything I have said to you (JOHN 14:26).

The Spirit will take from what is mine and make it known to you (JOHN 16:15).

Praise:
The Lord has done great things for us, and we are filled with joy (PS. 126:3).

37. Authority over Satan

'The one who is in you is greater than the one who is in the world' (1 JOHN 4:4).

Lord Jesus, I want to exercise the authority you give me over the evil one.

READING: 1 JOHN 4:2–5
This is how you can recognise the Spirit of God: Every spirit that acknowledges that Jesus Christ has come in the flesh is from God, but every spirit that does not acknowledge Jesus is not from God. This is the spirit of the antichrist, which you have heard is coming and even now is already in the world.

You, dear children, are from God and have overcome them, because the one who is in you is greater than the one who is in the world. They are from the world and therefore speak from the viewpoint of the world, and the world listens to them.

When Jesus was led by the Spirit of God into the wilderness and Satan came to tempt Him, Jesus dismissed him with the Word of God. Learn to do this. You have the authority to dismiss him as your defeated enemy. With the spiritual armour God gives you, He fills both your hands. In one hand you hold the shield of faith 'with which you can extinguish all the flaming arrows of the evil one' (Eph. 6:16). With that shield in position you say to the enemy, 'I'm not going to listen to any of your accusations or lies.' In the other hand you have the sword of the Spirit which is the Word of God. These are the words of truth which are powerful and to which Satan has no answer. He knows the truth of those words.

But Satan is glorified when your speech disagrees with God's Word. Because he is the father of all lies, he delights to hear Christians making negative statements. In his role as deceiver and accuser he tries to persuade you to doubt the promises of God and concentrate on your unworthiness before God. He wants to deceive you into contradicting the truths of Scripture.

The Spirit is the one who is always declaring God to you in the here and now. He is wanting you to look up and to look forward, not to look back or look in on yourself. Satan, however, feeds all the negative things that are there within you. He could score a victory now if you allow him to make you feel condemned by all the negative confessions you have made. But you know the truth: 'Therefore, there is now no condemnation for those who are in Christ Jesus' (Rom. 8:1).

God has forgiven all your past failures and wants you now to live in the power of His Word. No longer are you going to live as the victim of your feelings and fears. You are not merely on the defensive expecting one attack after another; you are moving on to the offensive against the enemy. 'The weapons we fight with are not the weapons of the world. On the contrary, they have divine power to demolish strongholds. We demolish arguments and every pretension that sets itself up against the knowledge of God, and we take captive every thought to make it obedient to Christ' (2 Cor. 10:4-5).

You believe the Spirit of God, not the lies of the enemy. As you pray the Spirit will witness to your heart the truths you repeat to yourself again and again. It is by the Holy Spirit's activity that these become part of you and He will bring them to your consciousness whenever you have need, the right Word for the right occasion.

The Spirit of God within you is greater than the power of the enemy. As a believer you have been given authority over all the works of the devil. Don't let him kick you around. Show him who is boss! Exercise the authority you have been given.

Meditation:
I HAVE GIVEN YOU AUTHORITY . . . TO OVERCOME ALL THE POWER OF THE ENEMY; NOTHING WILL HARM YOU (LUKE 10:19).

Resist the devil, and he will flee from you (JAS. 4:7).

He . . . gave them authority to drive out evil spirits and to heal every disease and sickness (MATT. 10:1).

Praise:
From the lips of children and infants you have ordained praise because of your enemies, to silence the foe and the avenger (PS. 8:2).

38. *Watered with Praise*

'Serve the Lord with gladness; come before him with joyful songs. Know that the Lord is God. It is he who made us, and we are his; we are his people, the sheep of his pasture' (PS. 100:2–3).

Holy Spirit, may there be a continual song of praise in my heart.

READING: PSALM 34:1–3
I will extol the Lord at all times; his praise will always be on my lips. My soul will boast in the Lord; let the afflicted hear and rejoice. Glorify the Lord with me: let us exalt his name together.

Your prayer to God is like a seed of faith that you plant and which needs to be watered with praise. Praise concentrates on the Lord Himself, rather than His gifts and blessings to us. The more your attention is fixed on Him, the more you are able to understand that He is far bigger than your situation or need. You can rejoice in Him and in His victory and provision made possible through Jesus. The more you know the Lord, the more you will want to praise Him; and the more you praise

Him, the more you will know Him. Those who express a dislike for praise betray their lack of relationship with Jesus.

Praise is a way of life. It is far more than singing hymns and spiritual songs to the Lord; it is an activity of the whole being and is to be expressed in every area of your life.

David was a man who could experience the depths of despair and desolation; yet when surrounded by his enemies, with the situation looking disastrous, he could say: 'Why are you downcast, O my soul? Why so disturbed within me? Put your hope in God, for I will yet praise him, my Saviour and my God' (Ps. 42:11).

God's love for you is steadfast, certain and sure: He is always worthy of your praise. The essence of worship is to express to God what He is worth. Whether you feel like praising or worshipping Him or not, He is worthy of your praise. There will be times when you are conscious of God's light and times when all *appears* dark and difficult. God, though, is light all the time; in Him there is never any darkness. Even when He is revealing some area of darkness in you in order to deal with it, His light remains undiminished. Praise directs your attention away from yourself, your negative feelings and any darkness you may experience.

The darker the situation, the more in need you are of God's light; the greater therefore you need to praise Him. And yet this is the very opposite to what many people do. The greater the difficulty, the less they feel inclined to praise. Instead they concentrate on the problem and their own feelings.

Praise needs to be continuous in your Christian life because it is so easy to look in on yourself, and analyse yourself instead of allowing the Spirit to direct your focus to the light and glory of God in the wonder of praise.

Do not listen to the lies of the enemy. He suggests that it would not be real to praise God unless you felt like it. He will even suggest it will be hypocritical to do so. How the deceiver can deceive! He will do anything to try and prevent you from praising the Lord and focusing your attention on Him.

It is good to read one or two psalms of praise whenever you begin to pray, particularly when you feel prayer is difficult. This method of meditation centres your heart and mind on the

Lord Himself, and that helps to put your own situation in proper perspective. No matter what your circumstances He loves you, cares for you and wants the best for you.

Meditation:
PRAISE THE LORD, O MY SOUL; ALL MY INMOST BEING, PRAISE HIS HOLY NAME (PS. 103:1).

Rejoice in the Lord always. I will say it again: Rejoice! (PHIL. 4:4).

Be joyful always; pray continually; give thanks in all circumstances, for this is God's will for you in Christ Jesus (1 THESS. 5:16–18).

Praise:
Let everything that has breath praise the Lord (PS. 150:6).

39. *Victory*

'But thanks be to God! He gives us the victory through our Lord Jesus Christ' (1 COR. 15:57).

Lord Jesus, I want to live as one who is more than a conqueror because of your victory.

READING: ROMANS 8:31–9
What, then, shall we say in response to this? If God is for us, who can be against us? He who did not spare His own Son, but gave him up for us all – how will he not also, along with him, graciously give us all things?

Who will bring any charge against those whom God has chosen? It is God who justifies. Who is he that condemns? Christ Jesus, who died – more than that, who was raised to life – is at the right hand of God and is also interceding for us. Who shall separate us from the love of Christ? Shall trouble or hardship or persecution or famine or nakedness or danger or sword? As it is written: 'For your sake we face death all day long; we are considered as sheep to be slaughtered.' No, in all these things we are more than conquerors through him who loved us. For I am convinced that neither death nor life, neither angels nor demons, neither the present nor the future, nor any powers, neither height nor depth, nor anything else in all creation, will be able to separate us from the love of God that is in Christ Jesus our Lord.

Confess the truth of God's Word to yourself: *I am more than a conqueror through Him who loves me!* What makes you more than a conqueror? You live in the victory Jesus has already achieved.

Nothing can separate you from the love of Christ. You can conquer 'trouble or hardship or persecution or famine or danger or sword' through Him. You have the victory over death and anything that comes against you in this life. Nothing in the present or the future can separate you from His love.

Jesus does not promise His followers an easy life. 'In this world you will have trouble,' He says; but continues by pointing them to the victory: 'But take heart! I have overcome the world' (John 16:33). When your faith is in Him, you overcome the world too. 'This is the victory that has overcome the world, even our faith. Who is it that overcomes the world? Only he who believes that Jesus is the Son of God' (1 John 5:4–5). You can exercise your faith and say confidently: *Through my faith in Jesus as God's Son I have overcome the world*.

No wonder Paul says God 'always leads us in triumphal procession in Christ' (2 Cor. 2:14). You cannot imagine Jesus leading us into failure or despair, pain or sickness, temptation or disaster. He leads God's children in the ways of peace and prosperity, of health and wholeness, of power and provision. Jesus did not come to support you in your need, but to supply your need. So you can affirm positively: *God always leads me in triumph*. If you know the truth, you can be confident, no matter how adverse the circumstances are. You can say to the God who never lies, 'Lord you are going to lead me in triumph. I am going to see your victory in this situation. Alleluia!' He promises, 'I will never leave you nor forsake you.' (Jos 1:5). So you can go forward with confidence; nothing can separate you from His love.

Look at the trials in your life as opportunities to see the victory of Jesus manifested again. God allows the trials to refine us, but he never wants us to be overcome by any situation. He has put the victory within our grasp.

The world sees the Church not as a body full of faith and power, but as a weak institution consisting of people with as many fears and anxieties as others. If we are born again into a new life in the Spirit, this is not the picture the world should have. People should see evidence of victory in our lives, as distinct from the despair and defeat of those outside Christ Jesus. Even in death a Christian is victorious because he is at one with the risen Christ. We only experience and manifest failure when we are not asserting our life in Christ and His life in us.

Hear the Word of God spoken to you personally by His Spirit. You are more than a conqueror through Jesus because of His love for you. You have a victorious faith that overcomes the world, the flesh and the devil!

Meditation:
NO, IN ALL THESE THINGS WE ARE MORE THAN CONQUERORS THROUGH HIM WHO LOVED US (ROM. 8:37).

But take heart! I have overcome the world (JOHN 16:33).

This is the victory that has overcome the world, even our faith (1 JOHN 5:4).

Praise:
You give me your shield of victory, and your right hand sustains me (PS. 18:35).

PART FIVE

YOUR LIFE IN
THE SPIRIT

40. A New Heart

'I will give you a new heart and put a new spirit in you; I will remove from you your heart of stone and give you a heart of flesh' (EZEK. 36:26).

Thank you, Father, for giving me a new heart.

READING: ROMANS 8:2–4
Through Christ Jesus the law of the Spirit of life set me free from the law of sin and death. For what the law was powerless to do in that it was weakened by the sinful nature, God did by sending his own Son in the likeness of sinful man to be a sin offering. And so he condemned sin in sinful man, in order that the righteous requirements of the law might be fully met in us, who do not live according to the sinful nature but according to the Spirit.

Under the Old Covenant, God revealed His purposes to His people through the commandments He gave them. But the law gave them no motivation or power to enable them to obey the Lord. Instead they chose to please themselves; to please God required such great effort and determination of will. Their hearts often became hardened against Him, because they wanted to satisfy their own desires instead.

Under the New Covenant, God promised to replace their stony hearts with new hearts. His law would no longer be written on tablets of stone, but on their new hearts. Then they will want to please Him.

The Lord has given you a brand new heart! You do not need to strive to please God in your own way; by the power of His Spirit you have His love and ability working within you. You have the heart to please Him and the ability to do so. You now have a heart that *desires* to praise, love and obey Him. 'I desire to do your will, O my God' (Ps. 40:8).

Paul says, 'the old has gone, the new has come!' (2 Cor. 5:17). God has taken away your old heart and given you a new one. Your old life without Jesus has ended; your new life in Him has begun. The deepest desire of the Spirit within you is to please the Lord – not out of a begrudging obedience, but out of a genuine longing to please Him. The Spirit of Jesus lives in your new heart, inspires your love for God and enables you to do what He desires. This spiritual heart wants to influence your soul (your mind, your will and your feelings), which have not yet become fully submitted to God. On occasions you still choose to please self instead of the Lord. This is walking in the flesh rather than the Spirit. What God puts into the heart has to radiate through the whole of your life.

The problem lies in the fact that you experience a mixture within yourself which leads to conflict. On the one hand you want to please self because of the self-love that persists in your life. On the other hand Jesus wants to bring you to the end of that self-love, for the more fully you submit yourself to Him, the more contented and peaceful you will become. Do not be surprised or alarmed at the conflict you experience within yourself. This is evidence that the Holy Spirit is doing His work within you, pointing you to the Word and the way of Jesus. Whenever you obey His prompting you bless Him; when you yield to the flesh, your natural instincts, you grieve Him. Even then you can turn back to Him seeking His forgiveness and submitting yourself afresh to His will.

Let the Lord renew His gift to you now. Hear His words of promise and know He is pouring the life of the Spirit into you as you pray.

———————————

Meditation:
I WILL GIVE YOU A NEW HEART AND PUT A NEW SPIRIT IN YOU (EZEK. 36:26).

Love the Lord your God with all your heart (MARK 12:30).

I am gentle and humble in heart (MATT. 11:29).

Praise:
Rejoice in the Lord, you who are righteous, and praise his holy name (PS. 97:12).

41. The Role of the Holy Spirit

'But when he, the Spirit of truth, comes, he will guide you into all truth' (JOHN 16:13).

Thank you, Holy Spirit, for living in me.

READING: PSALM 51:10–13
Create in me a pure heart, O God, and renew a steadfast spirit within me. Do not cast me from your presence or take your Holy Spirit from me. Restore to me the joy of your salvation and grant me a willing spirit, to sustain me. Then I will teach transgressors your ways, and sinners will turn back to you.

Jesus tells us, 'the Spirit will take from what is mine and make it known to you' (John 16:15). Jesus also said the Holy Spirit 'will guide you into all truth' (John 16:13).

The Spirit will teach you everything – therefore you are to set your mind on the things of the Spirit. Paul tells the Romans: 'You, however, are controlled not by the sinful nature but by the Spirit, if the Spirit of God lives in you' (Rom. 8:9).

You do not have to allow your mind to be dominated by fleshly desires when you have the Spirit of God in your heart, wanting to guide your thoughts and speech to be consistent with His thoughts and words. In the old life you lived to please yourself; now you live to please Him. But if, even now, you set your mind on the sinful desires of the flesh you will grieve the Lord, denying the work of the Holy Spirit within you.

Your new heart can become tainted by wrong desires, when you set your mind on fleshly things. When you are willing to turn back to the Lord, to embrace His best purposes for you, like David you will want to pray, 'Create in me a pure heart, O God, and renew a steadfast spirit within me' (Ps. 51:10).

When you turn to Him with renewed repentance, He releases afresh within you the power of His Holy Spirit. Once again you feel clean before Him and your desire to walk in His ways is restored.

'But we have the mind of Christ' (1 Cor. 2:16). The Holy Spirit wants to inform your mind of God's mind, so that you think according to His ways rather than your own natural ways. Because your mind has been conditioned to think naturally and even negatively, opposing the Word of God, it takes time for your thinking to be renewed. And what you think determines what you do. This is why Paul says 'those who live in accordance with the Spirit have their minds set on what the Spirit desires' (Rom. 8:5).

We have the warning of Scripture not to lean on our own understanding. We need to realise that God's thoughts might differ totally from our thoughts, but that His thoughts are higher than ours. His thoughts are truth.

Our bodies try to distract us from God's purpose by making us aware of their desire for gratification. We know conflict between the spirit and the flesh, but we have God's promise that He will never allow us to be tempted beyond what we can endure. The Lord is in the centre of such conflict with you because His Spirit is within you. It is His life within you that is to fight against the world, the flesh and the devil. '. . . the one who is in you is greater than the one who is in the world' (1 John 4:4).

When Jesus spoke of the Holy Spirit, He also said that rivers of living water would flow out from your innermost being, from out of your heart. 'By this he meant the Spirit, whom those who believed in him were later to receive. Up to that time the Spirit had not been given, since Jesus had not yet been glorified' (John 7:39).

Now that Jesus has been glorified, and His Spirit has been poured out, many rivers can flow from your heart. The rivers are not rivers of negative thinking and critical speech, but of praise to God, of faith in what He has done, and of love towards others.

The positive life of God's Spirit within you is greater than all the negatives around you. God is far greater than Satan. The Spirit is more powerful than the flesh. Jesus has overcome the world. So hear the Lord speaking His words into your heart to encourage your faith.

Meditation:
THE ONE WHO IS IN YOU IS GREATER THAN THE ONE WHO IS IN THE WORLD
(1 JOHN 4:4).

The mind controlled by the Spirit is life and peace (ROM. 8:6).

Live by the Spirit, and you will not gratify the desires of the sinful nature (GAL. 5:16).

Praise:
Surely the righteous will praise your name and the upright will live before you (PS. 140:13).

42. *The Spirit within Me*

'For God did not give us a spirit of timidity but a spirit of power, of love and of self-discipline' (2 TIM. 1:7).

Lord, give me boldness by your Holy Spirit, please.

READING: 2 TIMOTHY. 1:6–9

I remind you to fan into flame the gift of God, which is in you through the laying on of my hands. For God did not give us a spirit of timidity, but a spirit of power, of love and of self-discipline.

So do not be ashamed to testify about our Lord, or ashamed of me his prisoner. But join with me in suffering for the gospel, by the power of God, who has saved us and called us to a holy life – not because of anything we have done but because of his own purpose and grace.

If you are to speak the truth about yourself as someone with a new heart and in whom God has put His Spirit, you need to say:

I have a spirit of power;
I have a spirit of love;
I have a spirit of self-discipline.

You can never say truthfully that you lack the resources to share God's love and power with others.

Jesus promised: 'But you will receive power when the Holy Spirit comes on you; and you will be my witnesses in Jerusalem, and in all Judea and Samaria, and to the ends of the earth' (Acts 1:8). Because you have received the Holy Spirit the power of God is within you. You do not have to be afraid because his presence is within you and His power is available to you. That power is greater than any worldly or demonic power. It is God's power, which will enable you to do anything He asks of you.

You have a spirit of power – God's power. Jesus prayed that 'the love you have for me may be in them and that I myself may be in them' (John 17:26). This prayer was fulfilled in you when you received the Holy Spirit. You have the love of the Father and the Son within you. This demonstrates the immensity of His love for you and His desire for this love to be expressed through you. *You have a spirit of love* – not of fear or hate or lust, which are all opposites of love.

Self-discipline is part of the fruit of the Holy Spirit (Gal. 5:23), one of the qualities He produces in the believer. The Amplified Bible translates this as having a 'well balanced mind and discipline and self-control'. You are able to be in control of your thinking and do not have to receive the fearful, negative, accusing, condemning thoughts that the enemy wants to plant in your mind. If you think correctly, you will act in accordance with God's will. *You have a spirit of self-discipline*, a sound mind.

Your mind is not to be a plaything of the enemy. This is his first line of attack. Yes, he knows that if he can encourage you to think incorrectly then you will also speak and act incorrectly. By contrast, the Holy Spirit informs your mind of God's thoughts, reminding you of His Words. In every situation He wants you to be attentive to His voice. It is so important, therefore, to receive His Words and to store them within your heart.

You can live in freedom from fear; Jesus is with you always. He lives in you and you live in Him. In Him there is no fear. He loves you and His perfect love casts out all fear (1 John 4:18). Praise Him that He has given you a spirit of power, love and self-discipline. Your life does not need to be dominated by negative thoughts or feelings. Your trust is in Him who loves you perfectly.

Meditation:
FOR GOD DID NOT GIVE US A SPIRIT OF
TIMIDITY, BUT A SPIRIT OF POWER, OF
LOVE AND OF SELF-DISCIPLINE (2 TIM.
1:7).

But you will receive power when the Holy Spirit
comes on you (ACTS 1:8).

Do not be afraid . . . You are my witnesses (ISA. 44:8).

Praise:
God is our refuge and strength, an ever present help in
trouble. Therefore we will not fear, though the earth
give way and the mountains fall into the heart of the
sea (PS. 46:1–2).

43. Heart, Mind and Body

'You, however, are controlled not by the sinful nature but by
the Spirit, if the Spirit of God lives in you' (ROM. 8:9).

Holy Spirit, I want to walk in your ways, not those of the
flesh.

READING: ROMANS 12:1–2
Therefore, I urge you, brothers, in view of God's
mercy, to offer your bodies as living sacrifices, holy
and pleasing to God – which is your spiritual worship.
Do not conform any longer to the pattern of this
world, but be transformed by the renewing of your
mind. Then you will be able to test and approve what
God's will is – his good, pleasing and perfect will.

The Lord wants to produce in your life all the ninefold fruit of the Spirit. As you allow the Holy Spirit freedom in your life, He will produce in you the fruit of love, joy, peace, patience, kindness, goodness, faithfulness, gentleness and self-control. He will release His power and healing in your life. From you will flow rivers of love towards others as you seek to serve them in the name of Jesus.

Your body is to express the new life He has put within you. It is not enough to possess the Holy Spirit; God wants to see His life expressed in your life. He has made you holy in His sight, so you are to offer your body to Him as a living sacrifice. This is the worship He desires: a body offered to Him to express His holy life. He is renewing your thinking so that you know what His perfect will is, and He is empowering you with His Spirit to enable you to do it.

The ways of the world are often at odds with the ways of God. Every day you will have to make decisions as to whether you will act in ways the world admires, pleasing the flesh and honouring the devil, or whether you will choose to deny self and follow Jesus.

There is nothing wrong with the new heart God has given you. As you use your mind and mouth correctly, you can begin to express the abundance that God has put in your heart in positive action. You can stop using your mouth in ways which deny the truth of God's Spirit within you. God will transform your thinking and speaking.

To be always submitted in these ways involves the daily offering of yourselves to Him. 'Finally, brothers, whatever is true, whatever is noble, whatever is right, whatever is pure, whatever is lovely, whatever is admirable – if anything is excellent or praiseworthy – think about such things. Whatever you have learned or received or heard from me, or seen in me – put it into practice. And the God of peace will be with you' (Phil. 4:8–9).

As you use your mind in the right way, so you will then act in the right way. Your bodily appetites will not rule you. Your new heart will rule the mind, and the mind the body. In this way the reign of Jesus, who is your Lord, will be expressed in your life. You will do what He wants you to do.

Receiving the Word of God is vital to this whole process. The Holy Spirit working in your heart witnesses to the truth of the Word. Your mind absorbs the Word and your will translates it into action.

The secret is not to concentrate on the flesh and try to fight it, but to concentrate on the Lord Jesus and pray that the Holy Spirit will keep you in His ways. When you are pleasing the Lord, the flesh has no room to express itself.

Jesus wants to speak personally to you, encouraging you not only to receive the Holy Spirit, but to live by the Spirit. God wants every part of you, spirit, soul and body, to express His life which is within you.

Meditation:
LIVE BY THE SPIRIT, AND YOU WILL NOT GRATIFY THE DESIRES OF THE SINFUL NATURE (GAL. 5:16).

Pursue righteousness, faith, love and peace, along with those who call on the Lord out of a pure heart (2 TIM. 2:22).

The grace of our Lord was poured out on me abundantly, along with the faith and love that are in Christ Jesus (1 TIM. 1:14).

Praise:
Your ways, O God, are holy. What god is so great as our God? (PS. 77:13).

44. Loving Obedience

'If you love me, you will obey what I command' (JOHN 14:15).

Lord Jesus, I want to show my love for you by obeying you.

READING: LUKE 6:46–9

Why do you call me, 'Lord, Lord,' and do not do what I say? I will show you what he is like who comes to me and hears my words and puts them into practice. He is like a man building a house, who dug down deep and laid the foundation on rock. When the flood came, the torrent struck that house but could not shake it, because it was well built. But the one who hears my words and does not put them into practice is like a man who built a house on the ground without a foundation. The moment the torrent struck that house, it collapsed and its destruction was complete.

It is easy to imagine these two houses in the midst of a violent storm. One withstands the might of the wind and rain; the other is swept away, its collapse and destruction complete. The first is built on rock, the other on sand, without a foundation.

Those who build on the rock are those who hear the words of Jesus *and put them into practice*. It is not enough to hear the Word; we are to live the Word. It is worth digging deeply to ensure your life is based on the solid rock of God's Word.

The man who builds on sand also hears the words of Jesus, but does not put them into practice. Because he is not practising the Word he cannot withstand the storms of life.

Through this method of prayer, and in other ways, God speaks His words to our hearts. Faith comes from hearing those words *and is expressed in acting upon them*. We are to be not only doers, but doers of the Word.

Jesus points us to the absolute security to be found in obeying what He says. Obedience is an outworking of our love for the Lord. 'Whoever has my commands and obeys them, he is the one who loves me. He who loves me will be loved by my Father, and I too will love him and show myself to him' (John 14:21).

The rewards for obedience are amazing: 'Jesus replied, "If anyone loves me, he will obey my teaching. My Father will love him, and we will come to him and make our home with him"' (John 14:23). The message is clear. Jesus does not ask us simply to agree with His teaching, but to live it as an outworking of our love for Him.

Our love for Jesus, and our obedience to Him, is a response to His amazing love for us. It is impossible to express adequately in words the nature of that love. We can only experience it continually and increasingly, and be grateful for it. The knowledge of that love is like rock beneath our feet.

As Christians it is our desire to express God's love to others every day of our lives. We do this in our relationships, our acceptance and forgiveness of others; we do this in the ways we serve and encourage people. All this is like living on rock, for it is living His Word. To love one another, as He has loved us is building on rock; to hear that but to live a life of hatred, lust, greed and selfishness is building on sand.

To live by faith is to build on rock. To speak and live as one who is in Christ is to build on rock. To put the resources of God's kingdom to work in your life is to build on rock. To appropriate His promises is to build on rock. To resist the devil and all his works is to build on rock. For these are all ways of putting the Word into practice.

When you depend on yourself instead of the Lord, it is like stepping on to sand. You may know and believe the Word, but are not practising it at that point. The same is true when you speak negatively, think of yourself outside of Christ, look to men and natural resources instead of the Lord and His heavenly resources. It is also like walking on sand when you disbelieve the promises God gives you, and allow the devil to trample all over you.

Make sure your house is built on rock so that you live on the

rock, and don't step out of His provision on to shifting sand.
Know that the Father and Son have come to make their home
with you.

Meditation:
IF YOU LOVE ME, YOU WILL OBEY
WHAT I COMMAND (JOHN 14:15).

Whoever has my commands and obeys them, he is the
one who loves me (JOHN 14:21).

He who loves me will be loved by my Father, and I too
will love him and show myself to him (JOHN 14:21).

Praise:
He set my feet on a rock and gave me a firm place to
stand (PS. 40:2).

45. The Fruit of the Spirit is
... Joy

'But the angel said to them, "Do not be afraid. I bring you
good news of great joy that will be for all the people"' (LUKE
2:10).

Holy Spirit, please fill me with joy.

READING: JOHN 16:20–4
I tell you the truth, you will weep and mourn while the
world rejoices. You will grieve, but your grief will
turn to joy. A woman giving birth to a child has pain
because her time has come; but when her baby is born

she forgets the anguish because of her joy that a child is born into the world. So with you: Now is your time of grief, but I will see you again and you will rejoice, and no-one will take away your joy. In that day you will no longer ask me anything. I tell you the truth, my Father will give you whatever you ask in my name. Until now you have not asked for anything in my name. Ask and you will receive, and your joy will be complete.

Because God is love, the first-fruit of the Holy Spirit is love. He is the Spirit of love living within you and wanting to guide you in loving obedience. However, the Spirit will produce other fruit in you as well.

Jesus was a man of joy. When God describes His own Son, He says: 'You have loved righteousness and hated wickedness; therefore God, your God, has set you above your companions by anointing you with the oil of joy' (Heb. 1:9). The righteous life is a joyful life.

Sometimes Christians appear very dour and sombre, without conveying the joy which comes from knowing Jesus. God intends your joy to be full. 'Ask and you will receive, and your joy will be complete' (John 16:24).

Jesus tells us to live in His love so we can be full of joy. 'I have told you this so that my joy may be in you and that your joy may be complete' (John 15:11). No one can take from you the joy of knowing the risen Christ; 'no-one will take away your joy' (John 16:22).

Because joy is part of the fruit of the Holy Spirit God has put in you, He wants to see this joy expressed in your life. Just as God's love is not based on emotion, although it is bound to touch your emotions, so with His joy. We are speaking of the joy of the Spirit, who is constantly within you no matter what your feelings and circumstances. It is this joy that no man, no situation, no demonic force can take from you. You have this joy whether you feel joyful or not.

God calls you to a life of faith, and joy is the barometer of your faith. A person cannot be in a position of faith without being joyful. Your situation may appear to be completely hopeless, but the joy of the Lord is your strength! You know He is present with you; you know He will never leave you or forsake you. You know He hears your cry for help and answers you – even though there may not be any immediate evidence of that.

Even repentance can be joyful, not that we enjoy confessing our sins, but because turning away from sin and back to Him leads to a fresh revelation of His love.

Jesus was 'full of joy through the Holy Spirit' (Luke 10:21), and that is God's purpose for you. Express that joy in praise and worship, in loving and serving others, in giving to God and others with a joyful heart.

Meditation:
I HAVE TOLD YOU THIS SO THAT MY JOY MAY BE IN YOU AND THAT YOUR JOY MAY BE COMPLETE (JOHN 15:11).

No–one will take away your joy (JOHN 16:22).

Those on the rock are the ones who receive the word with joy when they hear it (LUKE 8:13).

Praise:
You have made known to me the path of life; you will fill me with joy in your presence (PS. 16:11).

46. The Fruit of the Spirit is . . . Peace

'And the peace of God, which transcends all understanding, will guard your hearts and your minds in Christ Jesus' (PHIL. 4:7).

Jesus, you are my peace.

> **READING:** JOHN 14:26–7
> But the Counsellor, the Holy Spirit, whom the Father will send in my name, will teach you all things and will remind you of everything I have said to you. Peace I leave with you; my peace I give you. I do not give to you as the world gives. Do not let your hearts be troubled and do not be afraid.

Jesus stood among the disciples in His risen body and gave them His peace. 'Peace be with you,' He said (John 20:19). This fulfilled the promise He had given them earlier. These words are not simply a greeting, they convey His peace to His disciples, who at the time were in a fearful state.

God's peace is different from the world's idea of peace. People think of peace being the absence of war, or the lack of noise when the children have gone to bed. But God's peace is part of the fruit of the Spirit because 'he himself is our peace' (Eph. 2:14). It is a positive gift from God to His children.

Paul describes this peace as being beyond our understanding. 'And the peace of God, which transcends all understanding, will guard your hearts and your minds in Christ Jesus' (Phil. 4:7). You receive this peace in three dimensions.

First, you are at peace with God, which means there is a sense of well-being between the Lord and yourself. There is no conviction of sin because you know you are cleansed and forgiven. You can experience this peace because Jesus has made 'peace through his blood, shed on the cross' (Col. 1:20).

Second, you can be at peace with others: 'Let the peace of Christ rule in your hearts, since as members of one body you were called to peace. And be thankful' (Col. 3:15). Your peace with God is expressed in your unity and peace with others. 'Live in peace with each other' (1 Thess. 5:13).

Third, because you are at peace with God and others you have peace within yourself. 'Now may the Lord of peace himself give you peace at all times and in every way' (2 Thess. 3:16).

The Lord gives this peace through the activity of His Spirit within you. 'May God himself, the God of peace, sanctify you through and through. May your whole spirit, soul and body be kept blameless at the coming of our Lord Jesus Christ' (1 Thess. 5:23).

You will know His peace as you follow the leading of His Spirit. When you walk in the flesh, you lose your peace with God; you are not at peace with yourself and it is not long before your relationships with others begin to be affected. When you are at peace with the Lord you have the sense of well-being, even in the middle of what appears to be turmoil and confusion, for that peace comes from your heavenly circumstances not your earthly ones.

Whenever you feel anxious and are distracted by your situation use this sentence in meditation. Sit down quietly and receive the peace of God, for Jesus is with you, speaking His words of peace. Remember, these are not words about peace, but words which convey His peace to you.

Meditation:
PEACE I LEAVE WITH YOU; MY PEACE I GIVE YOU (JOHN 14:27).

Peace be with you! (JOHN 20:19).

Now may the Lord of peace himself give you peace at all times and in every way (2 THESS. 3:16).

47. *The Fruit of the Spirit is . . . Patience*

'Love is patient' (1 COR. 13:4).

Holy Spirit, produce the fruit of patience in me, please.

READING: COLOSSIANS 1:10–14

And we pray this in order that you may live a life worthy of the Lord and may please him in every way: bearing fruit in every good work, growing in the knowledge of God, being strengthened with all power according to his glorious might so that you may have great endurance and patience, and joyfully giving thanks to the Father, who has qualified you to share in the inheritance of the saints in the kingdom of light. For he has rescued us from the dominion of darkness and brought us into the kingdom of the Son he loves, in whom we have redemption, the forgiveness of sins.

The Lord is infinitely patient with us. It is an aspect of His character and therefore part of the personality of the Holy Spirit. So He wants to produce the fruit of patience in you.

Many recognise their need for more patience. In public they usually manage to control themselves and their tempers. In private they relax their guard and take out their frustrations and disappointments on those they love most, on husband or wife and children. This causes them distress because they do not want to hurt those who are most precious to them.

'Love is patient,' says Paul. In love a husband or wife learns to put up with the failings of his or her partner and the constant demands of the children. It is an expression of their love. But we all recognise the limitations of our human love and therefore our human patience. We recognise the need to avail ourselves of the Lord's resources, of the patience which comes by the Spirit.

'Lord, give me patience – but hurry' is a common joke, but expresses something which is often true in our attitudes.

Fruit takes time to grow. The more conscious you are of God's love at work in you, the more the fruit of patience will be evident in your life. It is not a matter of simply asking God for patience. Because this comes as part of the fruit of the Spirit working within you, it will grow alongside other aspects of the Spirit's activity within you.

Abraham inherited the promises of God by faith with patience. It is that patience which is so often lacking with us. We would like instantaneous answers to every prayer. The Holy Spirit helps us to maintain our faith position until we see the promises fulfilled.

We are to be patient in the face of adversity, patient with those who scoff at us because we believe, with those who cannot understand the gospel because they are bound by unbelief.

We are to be patient as we await the return of Jesus in glory and triumph.

And we are to be patient with one another, expressing the love of Jesus to one another in forgiveness and encouragement. 'But for that very reason I was shown mercy so that in me, the worst of sinners, Christ Jesus might display his unlimited patience as an example for those who would believe on him and receive eternal life' (1 Tim. 1:16).

Hear the Lord encouraging you now. The Spirit desires to create in you the humility, gentleness and patience of which these words speak.

Meditation:
BE COMPLETELY HUMBLE AND GEN-
TLE; BE PATIENT, BEARING WITH ONE
ANOTHER IN LOVE (EPH. 4:2).

Love is patient (1 COR. 13:4).

He is patient with you (2 PET. 3:9).

Be patient with everyone (1 THESS. 5:14).

Praise:
I waited patiently for the Lord; he turned to me and heard my cry (PS. 40:1).

48. *The Fruit of the Spirit is . . . Kindness*

'Love is kind' (1 COR. 13:4).

Jesus, I want to express your kindness through the Holy Spirit working in me.

READING: EPHESIANS 2:4–10
But because of His great love for us, God, who is rich in mercy, made us alive with Christ even when we were dead in transgressions – it is by grace you have been saved. And God raised us up with Christ and seated us with him in the heavenly realms in Christ Jesus, in order that in the coming ages he might show the incomparable riches of his grace, expressed in his kindness to us in Christ Jesus. For it is by grace you have been saved, through faith – and this not from yourselves, it is the gift of God – not by works, so that no-one can boast. For we are God's workmanship, created in Christ Jesus to do good works, which God prepared in advance for us to do.

All the fruits of the Spirit abound in Jesus's life. His kindness is shown in the loving way He dealt with those in need, in His willingness to forgive the disciples regularly for their unbelief, in His patience with them in all their failures.

And so the Holy Spirit wants to reproduce His kindness in us. We are told to 'Be kind and compassionate to one another, forgiving each other, just as in Christ God forgave you' (Eph. 4:32). Paul also says, '. . . always try to be kind to each other and to everyone else' (1 Thess. 5:15). 'And the Lord's servant . . . must be kind to everyone' he says (2 Tim. 2:24). We are to clothe ourselves with kindness (Col. 3:12).

Of course it is easier to be kind to those you find easy to love. But your call is to love all your Christian brethren, and your neighbour as yourself. God's intention is that you express kindness to all, which is easier said than done!

The quality of Christian witness suffers seriously when kindness is lacking in relationships. None of us is perfect in our expression of Jesus's love, but Christians too often deal with one another in thoughtless and unloving ways, thinking little of the consequences of their words and actions and their effects upon others. This results in hurt and sometimes deep bitterness, and is the consequence of fleshly decisions and actions rather than those filled with Holy Spirit activity.

Jesus needed to be stern at times, even with the disciples. But He was never unkind. He reflected the fact that God's anger is tempered by mercy and grace. He confronted the Pharisees and others with their hypocrisy; yet loving kindness awaited those who turned to Him.

Love is often expressed in acts of positive kindness – in not dealing with people as they deserve, but with graciousness, love and mercy. It helps to remember the ways in which God has expressed His kindness to you. This will help motivate you to be kind to others, depending not on yourself, but on the resources of God's Spirit within you.

The kingdom principle applies once again: The measure you give is the measure you get back. 'A kind man benefits himself, but a cruel man brings himself harm' (Prov. 11:17). Never forget, kindness is the fruit of God's Spirit working within you to express the life of Jesus through you. The more the Spirit abounds in your life, the more that kindness will be manifested.

As you receive God's Word, believe the Spirit is working within you to enable you to clothe yourself with kindness in your dealings with others.

Meditation:
CLOTHE YOURSELVES WITH . . . KINDNESS (COL. 3:12).

Love is kind (1 COR. 13:4).

Be kind and compassionate to one another, forgiving each other, just as in Christ God forgave you (EPH. 4:32).

Praise:
He shows unfailing kindness to his anointed (PS. 18:50).

49. *The Fruit of the Spirit is . . . Goodness*

'"Why do you call me good?" Jesus answered. "No-one is good – except God alone"' (MARK 10:18).

Holy Spirit, help me at all times to do what is good.

READING: LUKE 6:43–5
No good tree bears bad fruit, nor does a bad tree bear good fruit. Each tree is recognised by its own fruit. People do not pick figs from thorn-bushes, or grapes from briers. The good man brings good things out of the good stored up in his heart, and the evil man brings evil things out of the evil stored up in his heart. For out of the overflow of his heart his mouth speaks.

Paul gives a clear description of man in his natural state: 'There is no-one righteous, not even one; there is no-one who understands, no-one who seeks God. All have turned away, they have together become worthless' (Rom. 3:10–12). No one is good in himself, no matter how many 'good works' he accomplishes. Everyone is born with a rebellious spirit and desires naturally to walk in his own ways. God alone is good, says Jesus (Mark 10:18).

This conflicts with modern rational thinking, in which man is thought to be good in himself. So many people think of themselves as living 'good' lives, by which they mean that they are law-abiding citizens who do not harm others and may even seek to help them.

This fails to take into account the fact of sin. Even those who try to lead 'good' lives sin regularly against the Lord. Without a Saviour their sin renders them unacceptable to God. Even if it seems many of their actions would please Him, they themselves can only please the Holy God when washed of their sins and made holy in His sight.

The blood of Jesus cleanses us from the things which are not good in God's eyes and the Holy Spirit creates in us what is good. Jesus reflected perfectly His Father's goodness. He, in turn, wants you to reflect His goodness. But this is not some inherent goodness you have within yourself, but the goodness which comes from the Holy Spirit's activity within you.

Before conversion, your spiritual heart was diseased; when you were born again the Lord gave you a new heart. It does not matter how bad the tree was beforehand, God makes you a new creation, a new tree, a good tree, able to bear good fruit.

John the Baptist told people to prove their repentance by the fruit they produced in their lives. Jesus says something similar; a good tree cannot bear bad fruit; a bad tree cannot bear good fruit.

This does not mean you are to strive in your own strength to be good. The tree produces fruit as a result of the life-producing sap flowing through its branches. The goodness God wants to see in your life flows from the sap of the Holy Spirit producing the positive works of goodness and love within you. He prompts you to do what is good and right in each situation, but also supplies the ability to do it.

You want to do what is best for those you love. This will require correction and discipline at times; but mainly it is a question of giving to them, because their good is your concern. Such goodness is to flow out of you as a river of living water towards all around you; seeking the good and welfare of others, expressing God's goodness to them. You will have the right motivation to obey the leading of the Spirit to do this if you remain aware of His constant goodness towards you.

Goodness is expressed in the moral choices you make, as well as in your willingness to serve others. Because you are a child of His kingdom, He wants the life of this kingdom to be evidenced in the choices you make, because you live by the principles of the kingdom, which are always good. You cannot reflect the life of the king or His kingdom through making wrong choices.

Goodness is to be shown to all, even to those who hate you, because you are Jesus's witness wherever you are, regardless of what is happening to you. As you receive His words today, remember that the Lord supplies all the grace you need to accomplish what He asks of you.

Meditation:
TRUST IN THE LORD AND DO GOOD
(PS. 37:3).

The Lord is good to all (PS. 145:9).

He satisfies my desires with good things (PS. 103:5).

Praise:
I will extol the Lord at all times; his praise will always
be on my lips (PS. 34:1).

145

50. The Fruit of the Spirit is . . . Faithfulness

'I will betroth you in faithfulness, and you will acknowledge the Lord' (HOS. 2:20).

Holy Spirit, please keep me faithful.

READING: PSALM 89:1–8

I will sing of the Lord's great love for ever; with my mouth I will make your faithfulness known through all generations. I will declare that your love stands firm for ever, that you established your faithfulness in heaven itself.

You said, 'I have made a covenant with my chosen one, I have sworn to David my servant, I will establish your line forever and make your throne firm through all generations.'

The heavens praise your wonders, O Lord, your faithfulness too, in the assembly of the holy ones. For who in the skies above can compare with the Lord? Who is like the Lord among the heavenly beings? In the council of the holy ones God is greatly feared; he is more awesome than all who surround him. O Lord God Almighty, who is like you? You are mighty, O Lord, and your faithfulness surrounds you.

God is always faithful. He will never fail His children. He will never deny Himself by acting unfaithfully. He will always honour His Word; He watches over it to see it fulfilled. He is always ready to honour His covenant promises to those who belong to Him.

Because faithfulness is an essential part of His being, He wants the Holy Spirit to reproduce that faithfulness in you.

The word faithful can mean two things. First, it involves being full of faith, full of trust and confidence in God's Word, in His love and faithfulness. God is so faithful to His Word, His Spirit will constantly direct you to that Word.

Second, faithful means to remain true to the Lord, reflecting His own faithfulness. The Bible is full of statements concerning God's faithfulness. 'You are mighty, O Lord, and your faithfulness surrounds you' (Ps. 89:8). Later in the same Psalm we read, 'but I will not take my love from him, nor will I ever betray my faithfulness' (v.33).

Paul makes it clear that our lack of faith cannot 'nullify God's faithfulness' (Rom. 3:3). He will always remain faithful, even if His children are not always faithful. But He rewards those who do remain faithful to Him. 'Be faithful, even to the point of death, and I will give you the crown of life' (Rev. 2:10).

The enemy tries to encourage God's children to fear they would not be faithful if their faith was to be subjected to some serious trial. However, God always gives grace as and when it is needed. Faithfulness is a work of the Holy Spirit within your life. He will not leave you to your own devices, and is always ready to help whenever you turn to Him and trust in Him. It is His purpose to keep you faithful to the end, and He will do it. 'May God himself, the God of peace, sanctify you through and through. May your whole spirit, soul and body be kept blameless at the coming of our Lord Jesus Christ. The one who calls you is faithful and he will do it' (1 Thess. 5:23–4).

When you appreciate this truth, you will be liberated from the constant temptation to strive. You will never prove faithful by your own efforts; only by the precious work of the Holy Spirit within you. You can be faithful only because He is faithful, and is ready to produce the fruit of faithfulness within you. 'The Lord is faithful to all his promises and loving towards all he has made' (Ps. 145:13).

The Spirit is ready to lead and guide you in the way God wants you to go. He prompts you to co-operate with Him by making the decisions pleasing to Him. Even when you fail to hear and obey Him, He remains faithful to you because of His commitment to you as your Father. When you confess your sins He is faithful to the atoning work of Jesus and forgives your sins, cleansing you from all unrighteousness.

Whichever way you turn, the Lord is there in His faithful love, wanting to give to you and encourage you. Even when you go through the greatest times of testing, He will never fail in His love for you. Neither does He want you to fail in your faithfulness to Him. Your faithfulness is a response to His faithfulness.

Hear Jesus speaking these words to your heart. Once they become part of you, they will be a constant source of encouragement to you.

Meditation:
I WILL NEVER LEAVE YOU NOR FOR-
SAKE YOU (JOSH. 1:5).

Be faithful . . . and I will give you the crown of life
(REV. 2:10).

The faithfulness of the Lord endures for ever (PS.
117:2).

Praise:
His compassions never fail. They are new every morning; great is your faithfulness (LAM. 3:22–3).

51. The Fruit of the Spirit is . . . Gentleness

'Let your gentleness be evident to all. The Lord is near' (PHIL. 4:5).

Lord Jesus, I can only be gentle through your grace.

READING: MATTHEW 11:28–30
Come to me, all you who are weary and burdened, and I will give you rest. Take my yoke upon you and learn from me, for I am gentle and humble in heart, and you will find rest for your souls. For my yoke is easy and my burden is light.

Perhaps gentleness is the most misunderstood part of the Holy Spirit's fruit. People often associate gentleness with weakness. Yet Jesus Himself said that He was gentle, and you could not accuse Him of weakness.

We are to be completely humble and gentle (Eph. 4:2); and let our gentleness be evident to all (Phil. 4:5). So this is a quality the Lord wants to see in all His children. Indeed, it is His desire to see every part of the fruit of the Spirit reproduced in the lives of all who belong to Him.

Notice the way gentleness and being humble are linked together by both Jesus and Paul. Jesus described Himself as gentle and humble in heart. When He rode in triumph into Jerusalem He was 'gentle and riding on a donkey' (Matt. 21:5). Paul says, 'Be completely humble and gentle' (Eph. 4:2).

Pride causes a strident harshness in people's lives, and therefore in their dealings with others. There is great strength in humility. Jesus came as the servant of all, but He was the man of authority and power. It is not weak to be humble and gentle.

Gentleness is another aspect of love. Love 'does not boast, it is not proud' (1 Cor. 13:4). There is a gentleness about love, a desire to protect those loved from harm.

The Lord disciplines us in His love, but He does not do so harshly. He does not lord it over us in a worldly way. Because of His great love for us He is exceedingly gentle, pointing us in the right direction, prompting us to obey His will, giving time for repentance, but never forcing us into a begrudging obedience. That is an expression of His gentle and humble heart.

And so He desires that we treat others similarly. Instead of being resentful we are to forgive. When a brother sins we are to try and restore him. We are to encourage one another, not judge and condemn.

These things are not possible when there is no love. The Spirit produces gentleness as an expression of God's love in our lives. When you express His love, you will be gentle with others. As with other aspects of His life, you will find it easier to show gentleness towards others by being consistently thankful of God's gentleness with you. 'In everything, do to others what you would have them do to you' says Jesus (Matt. 7:12). This becomes possible when you know you can do for others what God has already done for you!

Meditation:
I AM GENTLE AND HUMBLE IN HEART
(MATT. 11:29).

Be completely humble and gentle (EPH. 4:2).

Let your gentleness be evident to all. The Lord is near (PHIL. 4:5).

Praise:
For the Lord takes delight in his people; he crowns the humble with salvation (PS. 149:4).

52. The Fruit of the Spirit is . . . Self-control

'Therefore, prepare your minds for action; be self-controlled; set your hope fully on the grace to be given you when Jesus Christ is revealed' (1 PET. 1:13).

Holy Spirit, help me to be self-controlled at all times.

READING: 1 THESSALONIANS 5:5–11

You are all sons of the light and sons of the day. We do not belong to the night or to the darkness. So then, let us not be like others, who are asleep, but let us be alert and self-controlled. For those who sleep, sleep at night, and those who get drunk, get drunk at night. But since we belong to the day, let us be self-controlled, putting on faith and love as a breastplate, and the hope of salvation as a helmet. For God did not appoint us to suffer wrath but to receive salvation through our Lord Jesus Christ. He died for us so that, whether we are awake or asleep, we may live together with him. Therefore encourage one another and build each other up, just as in fact you are doing.

Selfishness and self-seeking lead to a lack of self-control. Expressing the 'self' life, the life of the flesh, opposes the work of the Spirit within us. The Holy Spirit wants to keep that self life under control. Love 'is not self-seeking' (1 Cor. 13:5). So the Spirit sounds warning bells within us when we are in danger of grieving the Lord.

God lives within you to express His life through you. If the things that self desires oppose the purposes of God, those selfish impulses have to be denied. Then the life of His Spirit can flow readily through your life.

Peter warns: 'Be self-controlled and alert. Your enemy the devil prowls around like a roaring lion looking for someone to devour. Resist him, standing firm in the faith' (1 Pet. 5:8–9). The enemy wants to stir up all the wrong desires, motives and intentions. He wants you to act in ways that are unloving and which oppose the Spirit. The Lord, on the other hand, wants to produce the qualities of Jesus in you by the power of the Holy Spirit, bringing your spirit, soul and body willingly and lovingly under His control.

The devil inspires hatred, selfishness and greed; the Spirit produces love. The enemy wants you to be joyless, complaining, morose, defeated and dejected: the Holy Spirit gives you joy. Satan wants to create tension, anxiety and disunity; the Spirit produces peace in you. The enemy wants you to judge and criticise; the Spirit wants you to be kind.

The devil tempts you to selfishness and self-gratification; the Holy Spirit gives you the ability to be self-controlled, to deny the attempts of the world, the flesh and the devil to lead you away from the purposes of God.

As you receive God's Word, He encourages you to put on faith and love as a breastplate. God is working within you by His Spirit to keep the self life under control and enable that love and faith to be a defence for you.

Meditation:
LET US BE SELF-CONTROLLED, PUTTING ON FAITH AND LOVE AS A BREASTPLATE (1 THESS. 5:8).

Love . . . is not self-seeking (1 COR. 13:4–5).

You, however, are controlled . . . by the Spirit, if the Spirit of God lives in you (ROM. 8:9).

Praise:
The Lord reigns, let the earth be glad (PS. 97:1).

PART SIX

YOUR LIFE IN THE KINGDOM

53. The Kingdom of God

'Do not be afraid, little flock, for your Father has been pleased to give you the kingdom' (LUKE 12:32).

Lord, I need to have the revelation that the kingdom is within me.

READING: LUKE 17:20–1
Once, having been asked by the Pharisees when the kingdom of God would come, Jesus replied, 'The kingdom of God does not come visibly, nor will people say, "Here it is," or "There it is," because the kingdom of God is within you.'

When Jesus began to teach and preach, He had a simple proclamation: 'Repent, for the kingdom of heaven is near' (Matt. 4:17). The king of heaven had come to dwell among men and brought His kingdom within their reach. When they submitted their lives to Him, they came under His rule and reign. At the same time all the riches and resources of this kingdom became their inheritance, an inheritance which they can begin to appropriate immediately.

When Jesus reigns in your life you are not only part of His kingdom, you possess the kingdom of God or the kingdom of heaven. This is not a visible kingdom. You cannot say it is over here or over there: it is within you.

When you put your faith in Jesus, God gave you the gift of His kingdom. In His many parables Jesus teaches about the nature of this kingdom. It is like a tiny mustard seed which, when fully grown, becomes a tree that birds can nest in. Contained within that seed is all that will potentially grow from it, just as everything the oak tree becomes is contained potentially in the acorn. All the seed needs is the right soil and water, in order to grow to fruitfulness.

The Lord has planted the seed of His kingdom in your heart and life. All the life and resources of that kingdom are yours potentially. Your life is to be good soil that will produce thirtyfold, sixtyfold, or a hundred times what was sown. He has watered that seed with the power of the Holy Spirit – God living within you to enable you to live as a child of the kingdom.

So the kingdom is not something you are given when you die if you prove worthy enough to receive it. God has already given you this gift because of the worthiness of Jesus. You have the life of the kingdom within you. The Holy Spirit enables you to live as a child of God's kingdom, enjoying the privileges, but also facing the responsibilities of such a position.

When you die and go to be with the Lord, you will know the fullness of the kingdom. Until then, He wants to see you appropriating His riches, and expressing the life of His kingdom in your life. He teaches you to pray, 'your kingdom come, your will be done on earth as it is in heaven' (Matt. 6:10). He tells you to seek first the kingdom and His righteousness and you will not need to be anxious about anything. For the king of heaven is the king of love and He cares perfectly for those who are His subjects.

Because His kingdom is within you, He wants you to be subject to Him in all things so that nothing can hinder the flow of His kingdom life through you. Receive this revelation in your heart, for it is the revelation Jesus came to give you.

Meditation:
THE KINGDOM OF GOD IS WITHIN YOU (LUKE 17:21).

But seek first his kingdom and his righteousness, and all these things will be given to you as well (MATT. 6:33).

Your kingdom come, your will be done on earth as it is in heaven (MATT. 6:10).

Praise:
They will tell of the glory of your kingdom and speak of your might, so that all men may know of your mighty acts (PS. 145:11–12).

54. *The Privileges of the Kingdom*

'Therefore, since we are receiving a kingdom that cannot be shaken, let us be thankful, and so worship God acceptably with reverence and awe' (HEB. 12:28).

Father, thank you for giving me your kingdom.

READING: MARK 4:26–9
He also said, 'This is what the kingdom of God is like. A man scatters seed on the ground. Night and day, whether he sleeps or gets up, the seed sprouts and grows, though he does not know how. All by itself the soil produces corn – first the stalk, then the ear, then the full kernel in the ear. As soon as the grain is ripe, he puts the sickle to it, because the harvest has come.'

The kingdom of God, or the kingdom of heaven, has come with Jesus. It is coming still as His reign is established in the lives of more people. It will come in its fullness when Jesus returns in glory.

The kingdom of heaven is within you as a believer and among men because we believe. The seed of the kingdom will continue to grow in you: first the blade then the ear, then the full corn in the ear.

God wants to see you enjoying the privileges of His kingdom. The kingdom reflects the nature of the king. God is love, so His is a kingdom of love. He is almighty; His is a kingdom of power. He is supernatural; so His kingdom is supernatural. He is righteous; His is a kingdom of righteousness – and so on. The kingdom reflects the nature of the king who rules over it.

There are two spiritual kingdoms, not one. The dominion of darkness reflects the nature of the one who rules over it. Satan does not act according to principles such as those which govern God's kingdom. No, he is unprincipled, a thief who steals, kills and destroys; the deceiver and father of lies, the accuser of the brethren.

But he is no match for God. His dominion is obviously present in the world around us. Many, whether they realise it or not, have submitted their lives to His rule, rather than to the reign of God. Yet when light meets darkness the light prevails. So when we have turned to Christ, Paul explains that God 'has rescued us from the dominion of darkness and brought us into the kingdom of the Son he loves' (Col. 1:13).

You do not belong to the darkness, but to the light. 'For the kingdom of God is not a matter of talk but of power' (1 Cor. 4:20). You have the power of God's positive kingdom which is far greater than the power of Satan's negative kingdom. You have the power to love rather than hate; to forgive rather than be resentful; to give rather than steal; to encourage rather than be jealous – and so on.

Desire that these positive attitudes of the king and His kingdom are demonstrated more and more fully in your life. You can frequently ask yourself; 'Is what I am saying or doing positive or negative? Does it express the life of Jesus and His kingdom?'

You will learn to reign over your circumstances, instead of allowing your circumstances to rule over you. '. . . those who receive God's abundant provision of grace and the gift of righteousness reign in life through the one man, Jesus Christ' (Rom. 5:17). You are to reign in life because you live in the king. You can express His life, His power and His authority. Your life is no longer ruled by the unprincipled prince of darkness, but by the principles of God's kingdom of light. His kingdom is unshakeable.

As you hear and receive the words of Jesus, know that to be

given the kingdom is to have all the riches and resources of this kingdom. It is a kingdom of power, the power that will enable you to reign in life.

Meditation:
YOUR FATHER HAS BEEN PLEASED TO GIVE YOU THE KINGDOM (LUKE 12:32).

For the kingdom of God is not a matter of talk but of power (1 COR. 4:20).

For the kingdom of God is . . . righteousness, peace and joy in the Holy Spirit (ROM. 14:17).

Praise:
Say to God, 'How awesome are your deeds! So great is your power that your enemies cringe before you' (PS. 66:3).

55. *The Power of the Kingdom*

'I tell you the truth, whatever you bind on earth will be bound in heaven, and whatever you loose on earth will be loosed in heaven' (MATT. 18:18).

Holy Spirit, please enable me to live in the power of the kingdom.

READING: MATTHEW 10:7–8
As you go, preach this message: 'The kingdom of heaven is near.' Heal the sick, raise the dead, cleanse those who have leprosy, drive out demons. Freely you have received, freely give.

The privileges of being part of God's kingdom are yours; He has blessed you in Christ with every spiritual blessing in heavenly places. You are a co-heir with Christ of all the Father has to give.

Jesus sent the disciples out with the message of the kingdom, but also to express its power. In His own ministry His words were verified by His works. The same was to be true of His followers. Freely they had received the gift of the kingdom: now they were to give freely of its life and power.

When He sent out the larger number of disciples His instructions were similar: 'When you enter a town and are welcomed, eat what is set before you. Heal the sick who are there and tell them, "The kingdom of God is near you"' (Luke 10:8–9). When they returned they were overjoyed that even the demons had submitted to the authority they had in Jesus's name. Jesus used the opportunity to teach them an important lesson: 'I saw Satan fall like lightning from heaven. I have given you authority to trample on snakes and scorpions and to overcome all the power of the enemy; nothing will harm you. However, do not rejoice that the spirits submit to you, but rejoice that your names are written in heaven' (Luke 10:18–20).

Their names were written in heaven; they belonged to God's kingdom. Satan had been thrown out of heaven when he rebelled against the Lord. So, of course, they had victory over the powers of darkness, and sickness and death. It was not the victory that should be the cause of their joy, but why they had the victory. They belonged to the kingdom of heaven; they possessed the power and authority of God's kingdom.

This is true of you also. Jesus wants to see you exercise the authority you possess as a child of His kingdom. 'I tell you the truth, whatever you bind on earth will be bound in heaven, and whatever you loose on earth will be loosed in heaven' (Matt. 18:18).

You have the authority to act in the name of Jesus, heal in His name, pray in His name. You do not have a gospel of words only, but of power. As you follow the leading of the Holy Spirit, He enables you to exercise this power and authority.

God does not want to see His Church weak, infiltrated by unbelief and the powers of darkness. His children are to be light, a city set on a hill that cannot be hidden. The world is to see and understand that we have the power and authority to bring the victory of Jesus into our personal circumstances and in the situations around us; to reign, not be overcome by events.

The ability to reign begins within you, in the heart attitudes you adopt to your circumstances. You are not the worthless, powerless, weak, spiritual failure you would be without Christ. You live in Him and He in you. Begin to reign over your own circumstances, speaking positively of yourself and of what God will do through you. See each situation as Jesus Himself would view it. Adopt the attitude He would have because you live in Him. The Holy Spirit will help you to do this.

> What would Jesus think?
> What would His attitude be?
> What would He say?
> What would He pray?
> What would He do?

You are in Him. You have the privilege of acting in His name, speaking in His name, praying in His name. As you ask yourself such questions you will be surprised how often the answers will be clear. If this is how Jesus would think, pray, believe and act, then this is what you are to do in this situation. You have the power to do so, but sometimes you may realise you lack the faith to step out in obedience. If this is the case, confess your unbelief to the Lord and He will forgive you. And then spend time 'receiving' His Word, which will inspire faith within you.

Meditation:
FOR THE KINGDOM OF GOD IS NOT A MATTER OF TALK BUT OF POWER (1 COR. 4:20).

Rejoice that your names are written in heaven (LUKE 10:20).

As you go, preach this message: 'The kingdom of heaven is near' (MATT. 10:7).

Praise:
O my Strength, I sing praise to you; you, O God, are my fortress, my loving God (PS. 59:17).

56. Give and Receive

'But just as you excel in everything – in faith, in speech, in knowledge, in complete earnestness and in your love for us – see that you also excel in this grace of giving' (2 COR. 8:7).

Father, I want to be generous to others; just as you are so generous to me.

READING: 2 CORINTHIANS 9:6–9
Remember this: whoever sows sparingly will also reap sparingly, and whoever sows generously will also reap generously. Each man should give what he has decided in his heart to give, not reluctantly or under compulsion, for God loves a cheerful giver. And God is able to make all grace abound to you, so that in all things at all times, having all that you need, you will abound in every good work. As it is written: 'He has scattered abroad his gifts to the poor; his righteousness endures forever.'

Any gardener knows that, no matter how well the soil is prepared, there will be no harvest unless he first plants the seed. If he puts a small amount of seed into the soil he can expect only a small harvest. If he sows generously he will reap generously.

It is a matter of quality as well as of quantity; the wise farmer sows plenty of the finest seed so that he gets a bountiful harvest of the richest quality.

God has chosen to work by the principle of giving in order to receive. He wanted a rich harvest of souls for His kingdom so He sowed the very best seed: He sent His only Son, the Word made flesh. 'I tell you the truth, unless an ear of wheat falls to the ground and dies, it remains only a single seed. But if it dies, it produces many seeds' (John 12:24). If this is the kingdom principle by which God works, we must learn to work along with Him, instead of insisting on receiving first.

It is by the measure you give that you are able to receive the abundance of life He has for you. When you first came to the cross and gave yourself to Jesus, you experienced His life being given to you. He waited until you were prepared to give yourself to Him before He gave Himself to you. This is the principle of God's kingdom at work: 'Give, and it will be given to you. A good measure, pressed down, shaken together and running over, will be poured into your lap. For with the measure you use, it will be measured to you' (Luke 6:38).

Some do not receive answers to prayer because of their lack of giving to God and to others. They are not in a fit spiritual state to be able to do so if they are not 'givers'. Paul gives His teaching on sowing and reaping when speaking of money. There is no doubt that God expects us to be faithful in our financial giving. If we are, we shall receive His abundant measure in return. The world says, 'If you give you will have less.' Jesus says the opposite: 'If you give you will have more.'

This principle relates not only to money, but also to the giving of their lives in every way. To love is to give. John tells us that if we imagine we love God but are not giving to our brothers in need, we are deceiving ourselves. God desires us to be using every opportunity to be giving to Him by giving to one another.

In particular He wants us to be giving into the work of the

kingdom that His purposes may be fulfilled, that His kingdom will come and His will be done on earth as in heaven.

When you plant seed expect a harvest, expect God's abundant measure back to meet your need. When you plant your seed of prayer with faith, water it with praise and continue to thank God until you see the harvest. Jesus taught His disciples to *believe* the harvest as they prayed, rather than waiting for the evidence before they believed.

We know that our God has so much to give; by His grace we have as much to receive. I have hardly begun to receive all that God has to give. What is already mine is still waiting to be appropriated by faith. As I live, not to receive but to give to God, He pours into my life a rich abundance. You will find this is true for you because it is the Word of God. The measure you give will be the measure you get back, but with God it is 'good measure, pressed down, shaken together and running over' (Luke 6:38).

Seek to live by the principles of God's kingdom. These are the principles Jesus lived by and they work!

Meditation:
GIVE, AND IT WILL BE GIVEN TO YOU (LUKE 6:38).

Whoever sows generously will also reap generously (2 COR. 9:6).

See that you also excel in this grace of giving (2 COR. 8:7).

Praise:
Praise be to God, who has not rejected my prayer or withheld his love from me! (PS. 66:20).

163

57. The Measure you Give

'Blessed are the merciful, for they will be shown mercy' (MATT. 5:7).

Father, I want to give to you and to others in the ways that will please you.

READING: LUKE 6:37–8
Do not judge, and you will not be judged. Do not condemn, and you will not be condemned. Forgive, and you will be forgiven. Give, and it will be given to you. A good measure, pressed down, shaken together and running over, will be poured into your lap. For with the measure you use, it will be measured to you.

Because the principle of giving and receiving is a basic principle of God's kingdom, it applies to many areas of Jesus's teaching. 'For with the measure you use, it will be measured to you.' In other words you receive according to the way you give.

This is true of attitudes towards others: 'Do not judge, and you will not be judged.' The inference is clear that if you do judge others you will yourself be judged in the same way. The same is true of condemnation. 'Do not condemn, and you will not be condemned.'

It makes no sense for Jesus to die on the cross to save us from judgment and condemnation, only for us to place ourselves back under judgment and condemnation because of the way in which we treat others!

'Forgive, and you will be forgiven.' The principle works with the positive as well as the negative. But Jesus warns: 'But if you do not forgive me their sins, your Father will not forgive your sins' (Matt. 6:15).

The Lord wants us to express love to others. To receive

love, you need to give love. Some people wait to receive love from others, and are often bitter and accusing that they receive so little. They need to understand the truth that it is in giving they receive. 'Give, and it will be given to you. A good measure, pressed down, shaken together and running over, will be poured into your lap . . .' (Luke 6:38). This is true of love as of everything else.

You gave your life to Him, He gave His life for you. That is a pretty good deal! But you needed to give first. The same is true about receiving the Holy Spirit, healing or any particular anointing or need from God. We give first, surrendering ourselves to Him and then He gives to us.

If you are ever short on receiving from God, consider what you are giving to Him. Let the words of Jesus sink deep into your heart. Give love, forgiveness, mercy; give generously of yourself to Him and to others and expect the good measure in return. 'Blessed are the merciful, for they will be shown mercy' (Matt. 5:7).

If you need to receive from others, stop and consider what you are giving to others. 'It is more blessed to give than to receive' (Acts 20:35). That means you will actually be blessed more in the giving than seeking only to receive!

Meditation:
FOR WITH THE MEASURE YOU USE, IT WILL BE MEASURED TO YOU (LUKE 6:38).

It is more blessed to give than to receive (ACTS 20:35).

For where your treasure is, there your heart will be also (MATT. 6:21).

Praise:
Righteousness and justice are the foundation of your throne; love and faithfulness go before you (PS. 89:14).

58. The Command to Love

'How great is the love the Father has lavished on us, that we should be called children of God!' (1 JOHN 3:1).

Holy Spirit, fill me with your love.

READING: JOHN 15:9–14

As the Father has loved me, so have I loved you. Now remain in my love. If you obey my commands, you will remain in my love, just as I have obeyed my Father's commands and remain in his love. I have told you this so that my joy may be in you and that your joy may be complete. My command is this: Love each other as I have loved you. Greater love has no-one than this, that he lay down his life for his friends. You are my friends if you do what I command.

God has expressed His love for us in Jesus – supremely in the cross, but also throughout His ministry.

The Father's love for Jesus was perfect. Whenever Jesus spoke, the Father spoke and acted through Him. He was so concerned to maintain the unity in relationship that if He could not find time to pray in the day because of the pressing demands upon Him from the crowd, then He drew aside quietly at night to be with His Father.

'The Father and I are one,' says everything about their unity, a relationship based on love. The Father was faithful to His Son, leading and guiding Him throughout His earthly ministry, taking Him to the cross, where in love He could pour out His life for us. In love and triumph the Father raised Jesus from the dead.

And Jesus makes this incredible statement. 'As the Father has loved me, so have I loved you.' The Father's love for the Son was perfect and was expressed in practical power throughout His life and ministry. This means that Jesus's love for you is perfect and He desires to express that in practical ways. He will be faithful to you; He will lead you and guide you by His Spirit; He will carry you through traumas and difficulties bringing you to victory.

Jesus says; 'Now remain in my love.' The tense in Greek is continuous: 'Go on continually living in my love, remaining and resting in my love.'

You need never ask Jesus to love you; He already does. You need never question His love for He will not withdraw His love from you. His love is a fact, the greatest fact upon which to build your life.

The way to remain in the knowledge and power of Jesus's love is to obey His words. Love is not sentiment, but is expressed in a true desire to do God's will in your life.

Because He is love, His command to us is to love. 'And this is His command: to believe in the name of his Son, Jesus Christ, and to love one another as he commanded us' (1 John 3:23). He loves us as the Father has loved Him; and so Jesus tells us to love one another in the same way He loves us. This means laying down our lives for one another, even as He laid His life down for us, being faithful to one another, reliable and dependable; encouraging one another; forgiving, merciful and gracious; ready to serve humbly.

The more you know of God's love for you, the more love you will share with others. John points out; 'Dear friends, since God so loved us, we also ought to love one another. No-one has ever seen God; but if we love each other, God lives in us and his love is made complete in us' (1 John 4:11–12).

Hear Jesus speaking to you now, assuring you that He loves you in the same way that the Father loved Him. His love for you is both perfect and practical. All His divine power is behind this love, the love in which He tells you to abide.

Meditation:
AS THE FATHER HAS LOVED ME, SO HAVE I LOVED YOU. NOW REMAIN IN MY LOVE (JOHN 15:9).

If you obey my commands, you will remain in my love (JOHN 15:10).

Love each other as I have loved you (JOHN 15:12).

Praise:
Give thanks to the Lord of lords: his love endures for ever (PS. 136:3).

59. Love one Another

'Whoever loves his brother lives in the light, and there is nothing in him to make him stumble' (1 JOHN 2:10).

Lord Jesus, please help me to love others as you have loved me.

READING: 1 JOHN 4:7–12
Dear friends, let us love one another, for love comes from God. Everyone who loves has been born of God and knows God. Whoever does not love does not know God, because God is love. This is how God showed his love among us: He sent his one and only Son into the world that we might live through him. This is love: not that we loved God, but that he loved us and sent his Son as an atoning sacrifice for our sins.
Dear friends, since God so loved us, we also ought to love one another.

When Jesus gave this command to love one another as He has loved us, He explained this would mean laying down our lives for our friends. What does this involve? Living not for your own ends, but to love and serve others. By doing this, you love and serve the Lord.

The message of John's first epistle is challenging and un-compromising; you can assess your true relationship with God by the way in which you relate to fellow Christians. The one is a reflection of the other. You cannot truly love God, unless you love your brother also. Listen to what the Holy Spirit says through John: 'This is the message you heard from the beginning: We should love one another' (1 John 3:11). 'This is how we know what love is: Jesus Christ laid down his life for us. And we ought to lay down our lives for our brothers' (1 John 3:16).

He explains what this involves in practice:

If anyone has material possessions and sees his brother in need but has no pity on him, how can the love of God be in him? Dear children, let us not love with words or tongue but with actions and in truth (1 John 3:17–18).

Dear friends, let us love one another, for love comes from God. Everyone who loves has been born of God and knows God (1 John 4:7).

No-one has ever seen God: but if we love each other, God lives in us and his love is made complete in us (1 John 4:12).

We love because he first loved us. If anyone says, 'I love God,' yet hates his brother, he is a liar . . . (1 John 4:19–20).

And he has given us this command: Whoever loves God must also love his brother (1 John 4:21).

This is how we know that we love the children of God: by loving God and carrying out his commands (1 John 5:2).

These verses speak for themselves. There is no such thing as a costless Christianity. It cost Jesus His life to love us, and it costs us our lives to express His love to others. Wherever you go as a Christian you are a witness of His love and you have practical opportunities to express that love. How much you will do so depends on the extent to which you have died to yourself in order that you might live for Jesus.

He never expects you to love without making the resources of His love available to you. And so John also reminds his readers, 'But you have an anointing from the Holy One' (1 John 2:20). '. . . the anointing you received from him remains in you' (1 John 2:27). 'And so we know and rely on the love God has for us' (1 John 4:16).

Receive His love afresh as you receive His words. And rejoice that you are one through whom He has chosen to express His love to others.

Understand that your life can be a great blessing to the Lord and to others as you express His love He has put within by the Holy Spirit.

Meditation:
AS I HAVE LOVED YOU, SO YOU MUST LOVE ONE ANOTHER (JOHN 13:34).

Dear friends, let us love one another, for love comes from God (1 JOHN 4:7).

If we love each other, God lives in us and his love is made complete in us (1 JOHN 4:12).

Praise:
How priceless is your unfailing love! (PS. 36:7).

60. The Spirit's Love

'Dear children, let us not love with words or tongue but with actions and in truth' (1 JOHN 3:18).

Father, I want to express your love in my life.

READING: 1 CORINTHIANS 13:4–8
Love is patient, love is kind. It does not envy, it does not boast, it is not proud. It is not rude, it is not self-seeking, it is not easily angered, it keeps no record of wrongs. Love does not delight in evil but rejoices with the truth. It always protects, always trusts, always hopes, always perseveres.
Love never fails.

Paul speaks here of the qualities of God's love, the love the Holy Spirit puts within our hearts. Naturally we can be very impatient, unkind, envious, boasting, proud, rude, self-seeking, angry and unforgiving. These are the expressions of the flesh opposed to the Spirit. To each individual some of these will be greater problems than others. But all of us would have to acknowledge our guilt in the wrong attitudes and reactions we have towards some people at certain times.

However, the Holy Spirit creates within us the attitudes and reactions of Jesus. You cannot imagine any of these fleshly expressions in His life. The amazing thing about the Spirit's activity within us is that He changes us so that we can express more of Jesus in our relationships.

Unfortunately, the Holy Spirit does not produce instant perfection in our lives. If you examine your relationships, even briefly, you will see that you express many of the positive aspects of love mentioned by Paul – towards certain people! However, there may be others of whom you are less tolerant and to whom it seems very difficult to express God's love.

These are the relationships with which He wants to help if you will allow Him. As you confess the unloving things, so then you can ask the Spirit to produce in you the positive aspects of Jesus's love.

He wants to teach us to love others for their sake, and not out of selfish motives. Jesus reminds us that even unbelievers love those who will love them in return. The Christian is called to love, even if his love is taken for granted, or even rejected.

Often our unwillingness to love others comes out of our own insecurity. For some reason we are afraid to love or allow others to love us. Ultimately this is an indication of a person's lack of assurance in God's love for him. You can love if you are confident in God's love for you, even if that love is rebuffed. Perhaps you rejected love shown you by other Christians before you came to know Him, because you felt challenged in some way or convicted about your need of God. Similarly your love is likely to be rejected on occasions. Do not allow this to deter you from loving others. Try to understand what is going on in the other person and make allowances for any insecurities they may be experiencing.

A lack of love can be the result of a lack of brokenness in the believer. He has not truly submitted himself to the Lord. He wants to remain in the driving seat in his life and is ruled in many ways by pride and selfishness. He is likely to love only when it suits him, when it is not too demanding or inconvenient to do so.

We can rejoice in the provision God has made for us by filling us with His Spirit of love. The one who is filled has to use that love, expressing it to others. His willingness to do this will depend on His willingness to co-operate with God in His purposes.

Fresh resources of His love are always available for He never comes to the end of His giving to us. As you feed on God's Word know that He is speaking love and communicating that love to you.

Meditation:
THE SPIRIT WILL TAKE FROM WHAT IS
MINE AND MAKE IT KNOWN TO YOU
(JOHN 16:15).

The anointing you received from him remains in you
(1 JOHN 2:27).

We love because he first loved us (1 JOHN 4:19).

Praise:
Give thanks to the Lord, for he is good. His love
endures for ever (PS. 136:1).

61. *His Witnesses*

'Listen, my dear brothers: Has not God chosen those who are
poor in the eyes of the world to be rich in faith and to inherit
the kingdom he promised those who love him?' (JAS. 2:5).

Father, I want to bear much fruit for your glory.

READING: JAMES 2:14–22
What good is it, my brothers, if a man claims to have
faith but has no deeds? Can such faith save him?
Suppose a brother or sister is without clothes and
daily food. If one of you says to him, 'Go, I wish you
well; keep warm and well fed,' but does nothing about
his physical needs, what good is it? In the same way,
faith by itself, if it is not accompanied by action, is
dead.

But someone will say, 'You have faith; I have
deeds.'

Show me your faith without deeds, and I will show
you my faith by what I do. You believe that there is

one God. Good! Even the demons believe that – and shudder.

You foolish man, do you want evidence that faith without deeds is useless? Was not our ancestor Abraham considered righteous for what he did when he offered his son Isaac on the altar? You see that his faith and his actions were working together, and his faith was made complete by what he did.

Faith will result in positive action. Faith comes through hearing God's Word, believing what He says *and acting upon it*.

Love is not true love unless it results in positive action, laying down our lives for our friends – living for them rather than for ourselves, rejoicing in the opportunities we have to give and to serve.

The enemy wants you to be passive. He does not mind very much if people indulge in super-spiritual talk so long as they do not produce any fruit. Jesus said, 'This is to my Father's glory, that you bear much fruit, showing yourselves to be my disciples' (John 15:8).

God wants you to be active, not passive. This does not mean that you are to go around in a blaze of self-effort; rather you are to follow the leading of the Spirit who will lead you into what the Father wants you to be doing actively, at the same time empowering you to do it.

To James, faith without works is dead. In other words, it is not true faith unless it results in positive action. Some try to put an unreal division between what James and Paul say about faith. The faith that justifies, which makes us acceptable to God and leads to new birth, will result in fruitfulness. When God speaks He expects obedience, which always leads to fruitfulness. He leads His children into activity, not passivity.

James says something else of great importance here. Believing there is a God is not sufficient to please Him, or to bring salvation into a person's life. Even demons believe there is only one God, but that does not make them Christian! They are utterly opposed to all things Christian.

Your faith is not a series of verbal statements outlining what you believe about God, but the putting of your trust in Him in everyday practical situations, believing He will manifest His love and power through you; His supernatural life shining through your natural life. So, James says, faith and action go together.

The fields are ripe for the harvest. God is able to use you to bring the gospel of His kingdom to others in practical ways; through the way you love others by serving them; through your faith bringing God's supernatural power into daily events; through your witness in word and deed.

What does God want you to do specifically? He will show you if you want to know. But you can begin where you are by loving and serving those around you, by expecting His supernatural power to change circumstances, by telling others the good news that God wants to give them a kingdom.

Hear Jesus encouraging you to fruitfulness. He wants to see His Father glorified in your life by what the Holy Spirit does through you. Remember, Paul says that the only thing that counts is faith being expressed in love.

Meditation:
THIS IS TO MY FATHER'S GLORY, THAT YOU BEAR MUCH FRUIT, SHOWING YOURSELVES TO BE MY DISCIPLES (JOHN 15:8).

If a man remains in me and I in him, he will bear much fruit; apart from me you can do nothing (JOHN 15:5).

The only thing that counts is faith expressing itself through love (GAL. 5:6).

Praise:
I am still confident of this: I will see the goodness of the Lord in the land of the living (PS. 27:13).

175

62. Unity

'If I give all I possess to the poor and surrender my body to the flames, but have not love, I gain nothing' (1 COR. 13:3).

Holy Spirit, help me to know my unity with all who are in Christ.

READING: EPHESIANS 4:1–6

I urge you to live a life worthy of the calling you have received. Be completely humble and gentle; be patient, bearing with one another in love. Make every effort to keep the unity of the Spirit through the bond of peace. There is one body and one Spirit – just as you were called to one hope when you were called – one Lord, one faith, one baptism; one God and Father of all, who is over all and through all and in all.

The Holy Spirit is able to produce a unity of love that transcends any differences between Christians. To the world there appears to be many churches, but in fact there is only one Church, the Church of the Lord Jesus Christ. All who are born again of the Spirit are part of that one Church, regardless of their denominational affiliation. Jesus Christ Himself is the head of that one Church.

He desires to see unity in His body, which is the way Paul describes the Church. Jesus prayed for this unity before going to the cross. 'May they be brought to complete unity to let the world know that you sent me and have loved them even as you have loved me' (John 17:23). This unity is to be a witness of God's love to the world. Jesus is speaking about unity in the relationship between Christians, even among those who are part of the same expression of local fellowship.

Jesus reveals Himself to Christians 'in order that the love you have for me may be in them and that I myself may be in them' (John 17:26). This is an amazing prayer, that the

Father's own love for the Son might be in us; and that Jesus Himself might live in us.

When we love, we allow the presence of Jesus to shine through our lives as light in the midst of darkness. How important, then, not to allow differences to divide us, to have a proper respect for other born-again believers, whether you agree on all points of doctrine or not. The Spirit of truth will guide us into all the truth, says Jesus. That is not the starting-point but where the Spirit will lead us.

How important to honour one another, encourage each other and speak well of one another. We are not involved in competition with other believers, but are seeking to express the love and faith of Jesus to an unbelieving world. So Paul says: 'Be devoted to one another in brotherly love. Honour one another above yourselves' (Rom. 12:10).

We can further the disunity of the Church by the negative attitudes we have and the negative things we say, even about others in our own fellowship. Or we can increase the unity among Christians by concentrating on the love and faith which unite us, using every opportunity to work with others to see God's kingdom on earth.

Unfortunately, Christians often concentrate on what divides them instead of finding their true unity in the love of Christ. Openness to the influence of God's Spirit will draw believers into a new sense of unity not necessarily of ecclesiastical order, but of love and faith.

Confess the unity you have with others and express that in the love the Spirit gives you. Use opportunities that arise to understand and listen to what other Christians can teach you of your common life in Christ. Stand against any unbelief or compromise of God's Word – but always with love. You are to love your brother in Christ, even if you don't agree with everything he says!

Meditation:
BE PATIENT, BEARING WITH ONE ANOTHER IN LOVE (EPH. 4:2).

I pray . . . that all of them may be one, Father, just as you are in me and I am in you (JOHN 17:20–1).

Make every effort to keep the unity of the Spirit through the bond of peace (EPH. 4:3).

Praise:
How good and pleasant it is when brothers live together in unity! . . . For there the Lord bestows his blessing (PS. 133:1, 3).

63. Spread the Kingdom

'The creation waits in eager expectation for the sons of God to be revealed' (ROM. 8:19).

Father, please use me to show others the way into your kingdom.

READING: PHILIPPIANS 2:14–16
Do everything without complaining or arguing, so that you may become blameless and pure, children of God without fault in a crooked and depraved generation, in which you shine like stars in the universe as you hold out the word of life – in order that I may boast on the day of Christ that I did not run or labour for nothing.

The world is full of people in great need physically, socially and economically. Yet their greatest need is to be made alive spiritually, and this can only happen through a personal relationship with Jesus. The Christian is not to try to make himself acceptable to others by adopting the standards and ideals of the world. He wants to bring his thoughts, speech and actions into line with God's will, to live as a child of God's kingdom, demonstrating to others the benefits of belonging to His kingdom.

'The creation waits in eager expectation for the sons of God to be revealed' (Rom. 8:19). You are one of these sons. The world needs to hear the Word of God, not the ideas and opinions of men. They will pass away with them, but God's words are eternal truth. When God's children speak His Word under the authority of the Holy Spirit the truth can penetrate to the heart and evoke a definite response. But that Word needs to live in the one who speaks it; then he will be able to speak heart to heart, rather than mind to mind.

The initial response can sometimes appear negative because the truth can seem uncomfortable. It is better for someone to feel uncomfortable if this will lead him or her to repentance and new life! Paul said: 'You know that I have not hesitated to preach anything that would be helpful to you' (Acts 20:20). Paul appreciated that there was bound to be friction where the kingdom of light confronts the kingdom of darkness, the kingdom of this world.

God's Word will work for anyone who believes because it is truth. A fundamental truth such as 'God loves you' needs to be supplemented with an understanding of the nature of His grace, mercy and forgiveness. People need to know He is the God of promise, who is faithful to His Word, and they need to be shown how they can receive the gift of His kingdom from Him. He wants to meet with them in their daily situations in His supernatural power, to exercise His reign over them that they also may 'reign in life'.

You can help these things to live for others if they are real for you. The rich inheritance you have in Christ will become more real as you share your faith with others. 'I pray that you may be active in sharing your faith, so that you will have full understanding of every good thing we have in Christ' (Philem. v.6). Take this truth to heart!

Do not allow fear and self-consciousness to prevent you from speaking out what needs to be said. And don't allow your conversation to be reduced to the negative level of the world around you, where others complain and argue without faith, where there is much bitterness, resentment, jealousy and anger. Speak as a child of God's kingdom, the kingdom of righteousness, joy and peace in the Holy Spirit. Spread these qualities by the things you say and do.

If the Word is spoken in the power of the Spirit, things will happen to people because 'the word of God is living and active. Sharper than any double-edged sword, it penetrates even to dividing soul and spirit' (Heb. 4:12). It cuts straight to the heart of the listener. Sinners are brought under conviction, saints are encouraged and God confirms His Word with demonstrations of power.

This was how Jesus and the early Church communicated the gospel. This is the method needed in this generation. We need to speak the truth to the world in the power of the Holy Spirit and see that Word confirmed with signs and wonders.

Meditation:
FREELY YOU HAVE RECEIVED, FREELY GIVE (MATT. 10:8).

Whoever acknowledges me before men, I will also acknowledge him before my Father in heaven (MATT. 10:32).

What I tell you in the dark, speak in the daylight (MATT. 10:27).

Praise:
Declare his glory among the nations, his marvellous deeds among all peoples (PS. 96:3).

PART SEVEN

YOUR LIFE OF DISCIPLESHIP

64. Following Christ

Anyone who does not take his cross and follow me is not worthy of me (MATT. 10:38).

I want to follow you, Jesus.

> **READING:** LUKE 9:23-6
> Then he said to them all: 'If anyone would come after me, he must deny himself and take up his cross daily and follow me. For whoever wants to save his life will lose it, but whoever loses his life for me will save it. What good is it for a man to gain the whole world, and yet lose or forfeit his very self? If anyone is ashamed of me and my words, the Son of Man will be ashamed of him when he comes in his glory and in the glory of the Father and of the holy angels.'

As soon as Jesus began to speak about His rejection and crucifixion, He also spoke about a cross the disciples would have to carry. This cross was not only for the original twelve, but for anyone who wanted to follow Jesus.

The cross all disciples have to carry is different from that which Jesus Himself suffered. The crucifixion of God's Son was a unique event, never to be repeated. He carried the sin of all humanity, our pain and sickness, grief and sorrow. On the cross He overcame the devil and all his works.

There is nothing that has to be, or could ever be, added to the victory of the cross. God's intention is that we learn to live in the power of this victory He has gained for us.

We must be careful, therefore, that we do not carry the wrong cross. Sometimes Christians talk about being punished for their sins and suggest that is the cross they must carry. This is not right. Jesus bore our punishment on the cross so that we might know God's gracious mercy and forgiveness, and be spared the punishment we rightly deserve.

Sometimes it is suggested that sickness is the cross we have to carry. But Jesus bore our infirmities and sicknesses on the cross and by His stripes we have been healed. The cross was the answer to sickness. If someone imagines that being sick is suffering for the kingdom, they had better examine the Scriptures more carefully.

Jesus makes clear the nature of our cross as Christians or as His disciples. It is the cross of self-denial: 'If anyone would come after me, *he must deny himself* and take up his cross daily and follow me' (Luke 9:23). This involves surrendering ourselves to the Lordship of Jesus. It is not what we want that matters, but what He wants.

He makes it clear that those who follow Him will experience persecution, rejection and ridicule. There will be plenty of cost. But this cross is something we willingly take up every day. We are prepared to face the cost of being faithful witnesses in a world full of negative unbelief and darkness.

We do not enjoy the cost but it is inevitable, if we are to be faithful to the Lord. Jesus experienced such cost throughout His ministry, but with the right attitude; 'who for the joy set before him endured the cross, scorning its shame' (Heb. 12:2). For us the cost can take a variety of forms: making sacrifices of time or money in order to serve others; the cost of a disciplined spiritual life in prayer and meditation; the submission of our wills to God's will, agreeing to do what we do not want to do; the cost of loving others, of bringing the gospel to those who do not know Jesus; persecution and ridicule for professing faith in Him; standing by the principles of the Word, even if this includes financial loss.

And so James tells us: 'Consider it pure joy, my brothers, whenever you face trials of many kinds, because you know that the testing of your faith develops perseverance' (Jas. 1:2–3). Whatever the cost, the rewards are always much greater. And no cost we face could possibly compare with what Jesus suffered for us.

Hear the promise of Jesus's words. Don't concentrate on the cost but on the joy of knowing you are serving Him. Remember that you cannot give to Him without receiving a much greater reward.

Meditation:
WHOEVER LOSES HIS LIFE FOR ME WILL
FIND IT (MATT. 16:25).

Come, follow me (MATT. 4:19).

Anyone who does not take his cross and follow me is
not worthy of me (MATT. 10:38).

Praise:
How beautiful on the mountains are the feet of those
who bring good news, who proclaim peace, who
bring good tidings, who proclaim salvation, who say
to Zion, 'Your God reigns!' (ISA. 52:7).

65. *Crucified with Christ*

'I have been crucified with Christ and I no longer live, but
Christ lives in me. The life I live in the body, I live by faith in
the Son of God, who loved me and gave himself for me' (GAL.
2:20).

Father, I recognise my life belongs totally to you.

READING: 1 CORINTHIANS 6:19–20
Do you not know that your body is a temple of the
Holy Spirit, who is in you, whom you have received
from God? You are not your own; you were bought at
a price. Therefore honour God with your body.

Jesus took you, not only your sin to the cross. Through His
blood you can receive forgiveness for your sins. Through the
cross the power of sin can be broken in your life. This is why
Paul said: 'I have been crucified with Christ and I no longer

live, but Christ lives in me. The life I live in the body, I live by faith in the Son of God, who loved me and gave himself for me' (Gal. 2:20). Jesus not only took Saul's sin to the cross: He took Saul of Tarsus so that his old life might be put to death and he be given a new life, a new nature.

This not only shows you the great power of the cross but faces you with another truth. Your life does not belong to you. Everything you are and all that you have belongs to the Lord.

When Jesus went to the cross, God the Father paid the price for you with the blood of His Son, in order that you would belong completely to Him. You have no life, no identity, nothing apart from Him. The Father wanted *you* for His child and *you* in the kingdom, not your sins. He cleansed you to make you a sacred temple of His presence in the world.

The Lord desires more than mental assent to the truth that everything you are and have belongs to Him. The test comes when he wants to take possession of some part of your life, but comes into conflict with your will. We do not always want to be obedient. Even when we know what is right, we do not necessarily want to do it. To live as a child of His kingdom is to recognise the rights God has over us and the claims He can rightly make upon us.

God does not seek to take away from you as you commit your life to Him; He already owns every part of you. This is a revelation that brings great freedom into your life. Whatever you yield to the Lord is His already; to hold something back from Him denies His ownership of your life. His desire is to work in and through you. Paul speaks of 'the glorious riches of this mystery, which is Christ in you, the hope of glory' (Col. 1:27).

Because the old Saul no longer lived, Christ could live in the new man, Paul. The apostle could now live by faith in God's Son and all the riches He had made available.

Consider this: Christ lives in you to express His life and love through you by the power of the Holy Spirit. The person you once were is dead and buried with Christ, as signified in your water baptism. He wants to flow out of your innermost being like rivers of living water. You belong to Him. By co-operating with Him and His purposes for your life, He will have His way and make you a blessing to Him and to others. It is no longer you who lives but Christ in you.

You are set free from the bondage of self. You do not have to strive to accomplish things for God; He will work through you as you recognise who holds the true ownership of your life and submit to His purposes. His commands need not be burdensome; you will delight to do His will.

The Holy God is able to express His holy life through you by His Holy Spirit. All He needs is your co-operation. Consider the privileges of being called and chosen by God. Why you? This is a question you will never answer satisfactorily. You can only be thankful for all His love and grace in choosing you to be His own possession, one in whom He lives.

Meditation:

YOU ARE NOT YOUR OWN; YOU WERE BOUGHT AT A PRICE. THEREFORE HONOUR GOD WITH YOUR BODY (1 COR. 6:19–20).

Your body is a temple of the Holy Spirit, who is in you (1 COR. 6:19).

The life I live in the body, I live by faith in the Son of God, who loved me and gave himself for me (GAL. 2:20).

Praise:

For with you is the fountain of life; in your light we see light (PS. 36:9).

66. Agreeing with God

'Blessed rather are those who hear the word of God and obey it' (LUKE 11:28).

Lord Jesus, may I never argue with your words.

READING: MATTHEW 16:13–23

When Jesus came to the region of Caesarea Philippi, he asked his disciples, 'Who do people say the Son of Man is?' They replied, 'Some say John the Baptist; others say Elijah; and still others, Jeremiah or one of the prophets.'

'But what about you?' he asked. 'Who do you say I am?'

Simon Peter answered. 'You are the Christ, the Son of the living God.'

Jesus replied, 'Blessed are you, Simon son of Jonah, for this was not revealed to you by man, but by my Father in heaven. And I tell you that you are Peter, and on this rock I will build my church, and the gates of Hades will not overcome it. I will give you the keys of the kingdom of heaven; whatever you bind on earth will be bound in heaven, and whatever you loose on earth will be loosed in heaven.' Then he warned his disciples not to tell anyone that he was the Christ.

From that time on Jesus began to explain to his disciples that he must go to Jerusalem and suffer many things at the hands of the elders, chief priests and teachers of the law, and that he must be killed and on the third day be raised to life.

Peter took him aside and began to rebuke him. 'Never, Lord!' he said. 'This shall never happen to you!'

Jesus turned and said to Peter, 'Out of my sight,

Satan! You are a stumbling block to me; you do not
have in mind the things of God, but the things of men.'

This is the moment of truth, the time for the disciples to
understand who Jesus is. It is Peter who comes out with the
heaven-inspired declaration: 'You are the Christ, the Son of
the living God.' Jesus commends him and uses this opportunity to tell the disciples they share His authority to bind and
loose. But He also prophesies His forthcoming passion,
crucifixion and resurrection.

This is too much for Peter. He wants to argue. How can
such a thing be true for the Messiah, the Christ, God's Son?
'Never Lord! This shall never happen to you!' (Matt. 16:22) he
says.

Peter has made a serious mistake. One minute he is recognising the divinity of Jesus, acknowledging Him as God's Son:
the next he is daring to argue with Him. Satan is the one who
argues with God's Word. From being the mouthpiece of a
revelation from the Father, Peter has become a spokesman for
the enemy!

What a warning for us all. When we speak against God's
Word, when we want to argue with what He says, we are
siding with His enemy. This is not a clever thing to do! We
argue sometimes because what God says is beyond our understanding; and other times because we do not like what He is
saying.

Peter could not, at this stage, understand why Jesus should
need to go to the cross. Neither did he like what he had heard.
He listened to his emotions rather than to the Lord. He had
grown to love Jesus and could not bear the thought of His
'suffering many things' and being killed.

The lesson we need to learn from this is to submit intellectual understanding, our emotions and wills to God's Word,
every part of our souls being brought into line with what He
says.

This does not mean the Lord wants us to be non-intellectual.
Far from it. Peter's mind needed to be expanded and his

understanding of Old Testament prophecies extended, before he could appreciate the need for the cross. The Spirit of God challenges us to think expansively. The natural mind diminishes God and His abilities.

There are always those who want to raise their reason above the inspiration of Scripture. In effect, their thinking is too small to encompass God's thoughts and understanding. Because of their pride they imagine the Lord must be confined to their own understanding of Him, which is often minute.

Allow the Scriptures to speak to you, enlarging your understanding as well as speaking life and healing to you. Every word is food for you as a disciple of Jesus. When He speaks to you don't argue with Him. Whatever He asks of you, do it. Learn from what He says and believe His promises.

Meditation:
MAN DOES NOT LIVE ON BREAD ALONE, BUT ON EVERY WORD THAT COMES FROM THE MOUTH OF GOD (MATT. 4:4).

My food . . . is to do the will of him who sent me and to finish his work (JOHN 4:34).

Do whatever he tells you (JOHN 2:5).

Praise:
How sweet are your promises to my taste, sweeter than honey to my mouth! (PS. 119:103).

189

67. Serving in His Name

'I have made you known to them, and will continue to make you known in order that the love you have for me may be in them and that I myself may be in them' (JOHN 17:26).

Lord Jesus, help me to serve humbly.

READING: MATTHEW 25:34–6
Then the King will say to those on his right, 'Come, you who are blessed by my Father; take your inheritance, the kingdom prepared for you since the creation of the world. For I was hungry and you gave me something to eat, I was thirsty and you gave me something to drink, I was a stranger and you invited me in, I needed clothes and you clothed me, I was sick and you looked after me, I was in prison and you came to visit me.'

The greatest in the kingdom shall be the least of all, the one who is willing to serve. This is another kingdom principle. Because Jesus lived the kingdom life perfectly while on earth, He came as the humble servant of all. 'Instead, the greatest among you should be like the youngest, and the one who rules like the one who serves' (Luke 22:26).

What a privilege to be used by the king! What a privilege that He should live in you and work through you. Even when you have done everything He wants, you are still an unworthy servant, says Jesus (Luke 17:10). And yet He gives back to you immeasurably more than you give to others, promising to reward you for all that you do.

It is as we reach out with the life, the love and the power of the king that we fulfil our mission now as children of the kingdom. The love of God is very practical and if this is to be expressed in our lives this will involve being prepared to serve others in whatsoever ways He asks us. We shall not be fruitful by closing our eyes to the needs around us. Love is practical and is expressed in giving and serving others. What you are prepared to give to God is shown by what you give to serve others, the ways in which you use your time, abilities or money.

You can look at yourself and say, 'I don't have enough love', or you can recognise the truth that God has given you the Father's love for the Son. This means you can give, love and act instead of only talking about what needs to be done. 'For the kingdom of God is not a matter of talk but of power' (1 Cor. 4:20). It is not enough to express concern if you have the resources to meet the need. God has given you the power to love, to serve, to work miracles in His name.

Before you aspire to great things in God, remember that Jesus says you are to prove faithful in small things. Many want to achieve spectacular results which will appear impressive, but they don't want to get their hands dirty. They want recognition, but not humbly to serve others.

You do not have to go searching for a ministry. God puts in front of your eyes and under your nose what He wants you to do, and the people He wants you to love. And He never asks you to do anything without making available to you the resources to do it. You do not have to rely upon your natural resources and abilities. When these are submitted to Him and His use, you find His supernatural resources and ability are readily available.

In the above passage, those who had served the Lord faithfully were astonished at the way He commended them. What they had done seemed so natural to them, expressing the love and compassion He had placed in their hearts. By comparison, those who were filled with self-concern were oblivious to the needs around them.

Often you may feel incapable and inadequate to love, serve and meet the needs of others. Be encouraged; the secret is Christ in you. The Holy Spirit will help and enable you. Even now you can receive afresh the resources of God's love; they are always available to you.

Meditation:
I AM AMONG YOU AS ONE WHO SERVES
(LUKE 22:27).

Serve wholeheartedly, as if you were serving the Lord
(EPH. 6:7).

Not everyone who says to me, 'Lord, Lord,' will enter
the kingdom of heaven, but only he who does the will
of my Father who is in heaven (MATT. 7:21).

Praise:
Your love, O Lord, reaches to the heavens, your
faithfulness to the skies (PS. 36:5).

68. *Using Your Authority*

'Or again, how can anyone enter a strong man's house and
carry off his possessions unless he first ties up the strong man?
Then he can rob his house' (MATT. 12:29).

Lord Jesus, I want to exercise the authority you give me.

READING: 2 CORINTHIANS 10:3–5
For though we live in the world, we do not wage war
as the world does. The weapons we fight with are not
the weapons of the world. On the contrary, they have
divine power to demolish strongholds. We demolish
arguments and every pretension that sets itself up
against the knowledge of God, and we take captive
every thought to make it obedient to Christ.

Some come to initial faith in Jesus proclaiming, 'You are the Christ', without moving on in obedience to the Lord. God calls us not only to initial faith, but to a lifetime of faith in Him. For faith brings the victory of Jesus into the present circumstances.

Many Christians are ignorant of the spiritual warfare in which they need to be engaged. They do not appreciate the truth of what Paul teaches: 'For our struggle is not against flesh and blood, but against the rulers, against the authorities, against the powers of this dark world and against the spiritual forces of evil in the heavenly realms' (Eph. 6:12).

Christians need to take authority over spiritual forces which seek to rule over nations, places and individuals; to bind the oppressive powers of Satan which want to hinder them in their walk of faith and obedience. They need to pray for people, but also against the powers of darkness which oppose them.

Some do not recognise the powers behind the difficulties they experience. They pray about a situation without binding these powers and commanding them to release the situation. Some do not receive the victory in their sickness because they fail to exercise their authority as children of the kingdom, praying against the powers of darkness which perpetrate sickness. There were several occasions when Jesus commanded healing by releasing people from bondage to evil powers.

Satan wants to capitalise on any area of weakness in your life and to try and put you into oppressive bondage. When this happens you need repentance for the sin, but you also need to exercise authority over the enemy, standing firm against him and commanding him to go. In this way you will be loosed from the oppression and you can then ask the Holy Spirit to strengthen you. You will be amazed at the victory which comes into your life when you do this.

You do not gain the victory by raking around in the past, or looking in upon yourself, but by proclaiming the power of the blood of Jesus which frees you from the past and from every form of oppressive evil. Do not be afraid to dismiss the powers of darkness with the authority you have as God's child. Command them to depart, to stop oppressing you. When confronting the powers of darkness it is worth remembering that if you expect a battle you will have a battle; if you anticipate victory you will have victory. 'I proclaim the victory of Jesus over Satan and all his works. Depart from me all you powers of darkness, you have no claim upon my life.' When you deal with the enemy be firm as you would be with a naughty child. You are telling him what to do.

There may be times when you will sense you are engaged in a spiritual battle as you pray in the Holy Spirit. Continue to 'pray through' until you are assured you have the victory. This is the phrase many of the great men of prayer have used. Persevere; do not give up, even if you experience on occasions that you have not established the victory completely in one session. Remember, the spiritual forces of heaven are infinitely greater than those of the evil one.

First you need to hear the Lord giving personal revelation of your authority as a child of His kingdom.

Meditation:
SUBMIT YOURSELVES, THEN, TO GOD. RESIST THE DEVIL, AND HE WILL FLEE FROM YOU (JAS. 4:7).

He drove out the spirits with a word and healed all the sick (MATT. 8:16).

Encourage and rebuke with all authority (TITUS 2:15).

Praise:
The Lord reigns for ever; he has established his throne for judgment (PS. 9:7).

69. The Name of Jesus

'And everyone who calls on the name of the Lord will be saved' (ACTS 2:21).

Father, I want to use the name of Jesus with power and authority.

READING: ACTS 3:1–10, 16

One day Peter and John were going up to the temple at the time of prayer – at three in the afternoon. Now a man crippled from birth was being carried to the temple gate called Beautiful, where he was put every day to beg from those going into the temple courts. When he saw Peter and John about to enter, he asked them for money. Peter looked straight at him, as did John. Then Peter said, 'Look at us!' So the man gave them his attention, expecting to get something from them.

Then Peter said, 'Silver or gold I do not have, but what I have I give you. In the name of Jesus Christ of Nazareth, walk.' Taking him by the right hand, he helped him up, and instantly the man's feet and ankles became strong. He jumped to his feet and began to walk. Then he went with them into the temple courts, walking and jumping, and praising God. When all the people saw him walking and praising God, they recognised him as the same man who used to sit begging at the temple gate called Beautiful, and they were filled with wonder and amazement at what had happened to him . . . By faith in the name of Jesus, this man whom you see and know was made strong. It is Jesus' name and the faith that comes through him that has given this complete healing to him, as you can all see.

The name of Jesus is above every other name and means 'Saviour' or 'the Lord saves'. Jesus saves from sin and death, from condemnation and darkness, from the devil and the powers of hell, from sickness and grief. He saves us for Himself, choosing a people who will live for Him, extending His kingdom on earth; a people who will be holy and blameless in His sight.

Because His name is above every other name, at the name of Jesus every knee shall bow 'in heaven and on earth and under the earth, and every tongue confess that Jesus Christ is Lord, to the glory of God the Father' (PHIL. 2:10–11). All will ultimately have to acknowledge the authority of Jesus and the power of His name. 'Salvation is found in no–one else, for there is no other name under heaven given to men by which we must be saved' (Acts 4:12).

Salvation means healing. The name of Jesus stands for the total salvation of spirit, soul and body made possible through the life, death and resurrection of God's Son. When He gives His commission to the Church, Jesus says that believers will drive out demons in His name and 'they will place their hands on sick people, and they will get well' (Mark 16:18).

We see these words being fulfilled by Peter and John as they heal the crippled beggar. When they had to explain to the people why the man had been healed, they made it clear: 'It is Jesus' name and the faith that comes through him that has given this complete healing to him, as you can all see' (Acts 3:16).

Later when hauled before the Jewish Council they repeated this assertion: 'It is by the name of Jesus Christ of Nazareth . . . that this man stands before you completely healed' (Acts 4:10).

The name of Jesus has lost none of its significance, meaning, power or authority since Bible times. His name is still the name above every other name. His name is still the only name by which men can be saved. By faith in this name, the sick man can still be healed for the glory of God.

The name of Jesus can be powerful and effective in your life. You are 'surnamed' in Christ Jesus. You are told to pray in His name and that everything you do and say is to be in His name. 'And whatever you do, whether in word or deed, do it all in the name of the Lord Jesus, giving thanks to God the Father through him' (Col. 3:17).

Understand, therefore, the enormous privilege God gives you when inviting you to pray in His name. Imagine what could happen in your experience as you begin to speak and act in His name. See what you could accomplish as you obey God's command to heal the sick, because by faith in the name of Jesus people are healed today.

Hear His words of promise to you. Let these words sink into your heart. Jesus speaks them to you!

Meditation:
I WILL DO WHATEVER YOU ASK IN MY NAME (JOHN 14:13).

And everyone who calls on the name of the Lord will be saved (ACTS 2:21).

In the name of Jesus Christ of Nazareth, walk (ACTS 3:6).

Praise:
Ascribe to the Lord the glory due to his name (PS. 29:2).

70. I Strengthen You

'The Lord gives strength to his people; the Lord blesses His people with peace' (PS. 29:11).

Thank you, Lord, that you promise to strengthen me.

READING: ISAIAH 41:9–13

I took you from the ends of the earth, from its farthest corners I called you. I said, 'You are my servant'; I have chosen you and not rejected you. So do not fear for I am with you; do not be dismayed, for I am your God. I will strengthen you and help you; I will uphold you with my righteous right hand. 'All who rage against you will surely be ashamed and disgraced; those who oppose you will be as nothing and perish. Though you search for your enemies, you will not find them. Those who wage war against you will be as nothing at all. For I am the Lord, your God, who takes hold of your right hand and says to you, Do not fear; I will help you.'

The Lord is the strength of your life. There will be many occasions when you will feel weak and useless, totally inadequate, a failure even. It will seem that the Lord will reach deep within you to expose your insecurities. Then He will show you His love. Yes, His love is for the real you, not some projection of yourself that you want others to believe in.

It is *you* He has called and chosen, *you* He has made acceptable, *you* in whom He lives by the power of His Holy Spirit. It is you to whom He has given a new life.

You do not have to be bound by your past, by your sins, failure and inadequacy. Yet the Lord can work through your weakness in His strength. This was the lesson Paul learned well. 'My grace is sufficient for you, for my power is made perfect in weakness' (2 Cor. 12:9). This does not mean that

God's power is ever imperfect, but that the complete scope of His power can be manifested through your weakness. He has chosen 'the weak things of the world to shame the strong' (1 Cor. 1:27).

Again and again the Lord tells us not to fear, because He knows that often this will be our natural reaction; 'I have chosen you and have not rejected you. So do not fear for I am with you; do not be dismayed, for I am your God. I will strengthen you and help you; I will uphold you with my righteous right hand' (Isa. 41:9–10).

So you can learn to stand firm in the knowledge of what you mean to Him and what He has done for you. You can give yourself to Him knowing He will use you and work through you despite all your inadequacies. 'Therefore, my dear brothers, stand firm. Let nothing move you. Always give yourselves fully to the work of the Lord, because you know that your labour in the Lord is not in vain' (1 Cor. 15:58).

Again Paul urges: 'Be on your guard; stand firm in the faith; be men of courage; be strong. Do everything in love' (1 Cor. 16:13–14). Stand firm in the faith of who you are in Christ. Be bold in your faith, for you know the Lord will not fail you when you put your trust in Him. You may feel very weak, but He will not allow you to fall or be overcome by events as you look to Him. Be strong, not only by your own efforts, but by resting in His strength.

When you feel a failure in your inability to love, know that the Holy Spirit has given you all the resources of His love. When you sense you have such little power, know His almighty power can flow through your weakness.

'It is for freedom that Christ has set us free. Stand firm, then, and do not let yourselves be burdened again by a yoke of slavery' (Gal. 5:1). Stand firm against all the devices of the enemy who wants you to believe that you are a useless failure.

You are God's child, loved and appreciated by Him. He watches over you and strengthens you in your weakness. He speaks into your areas of insecurity to free you from them and to teach you that He is more than adequate for your every need. He has accepted *you* and loves *you*.

Meditation:
I AM WITH YOU . . . I WILL STRENGTHEN
YOU AND HELP YOU (ISA. 41:10).

My grace is sufficient for you, for my power is made
perfect in weakness (2 COR. 12:9).

God chose the weak things of the world to shame the
strong (1 COR. 1:27).

Praise:
The Lord is my strength and my song (PS. 118:14).

71. *Always Giving Thanks*

'Be joyful always; pray continually; give thanks in all circumstances, for this is God's will for you in Christ Jesus'
(1 THESS. 5:16–18).

Father, I want to be thankful in every situation and so fulfil
your purpose for me.

READING: PSALM 30:11–12
You turned my wailing into dancing; you removed
my sackcloth and clothed me with joy, that my heart
may sing to you and not be silent. O Lord my God, I
will give you thanks for ever.

One of the most destructive things in the Christian life is
self-pity. When our difficulties are compared to those of Paul,
for example, we have hardly any right to call them problems!
Yet, he rejoiced no matter what his circumstances. He wrote
to the Philippians from prison telling them to rejoice in the
Lord always. When thrown into prison Peter sang hymns! As

he praised God the doors were flung open! Praise releases the supernatural power of God into the situation.

Turning the direction of our hearts and minds to the Lord with joy and thanksgiving is no flippant gesture. It is not a matter of saying, 'Praise the Lord, anyway!' We learn to be grateful that in every situation the Lord is present with us, ready to help and encourage, to forgive and to heal, to enable and guide us.

When wanting to encourage others it's not a question of slapping them on the back and saying; 'Well, you have a lot for which to be thankful!' True as that is, we have to learn to, 'Rejoice with those who rejoice; mourn with those who mourn' (Rom. 12:15). Sensitively you can try to identify with the person you want to help and understand his position. Then you can direct his attention to the Lord, to His love and provision showing him why he can be thankful:

Thankful that He is with them;
Thankful that He never fails;
Thankful that He is faithful;
Thankful that He reigns in victory;
Thankful that He understands us because He has shared
  our humanity;
Thankful that His love and power is more than sufficient
  for every situation.

But remember, much harm can be done by giving the right answer in the wrong way. There are times when you cannot know another's grief, even if you may have experienced something similar yourself. What matters is that you are there, able to express God's love to the person, to show His mercy and compassion. In that way the person in grief can identify with you and when that identification has taken place, you can begin to turn that person's eyes in the right direction. You can start lovingly to thank the Lord, even in that situation. There have been many times when I have been amazed at the effect of thanksgiving on someone in deep distress. When praying with them I have simply begun to thank the Lord and before long the needy one is beginning to view his or her circumstances with an entirely new perspective.

The whole world can so easily seem distorted by what is going on within us. This is why we need to help one another to focus on the Lord. My moods, feelings and situations may change, but He is the great unchanging one. He is the solid rock on which my life is built. If my trust is in Him, the Lord will see me through. He even promises: 'I have made you and I will carry you; I will sustain you and I will rescue you' (Isa. 46:4).

When you are unable to walk through a situation, He will even carry you! He knows when you need to be carried and when you are to walk on your own two feet, without adopting a self-reliant attitude that says, 'I'll get there by myself!'

At times when it is difficult to pray, let alone praise God, the gift of speaking in tongues can be an immense help. 'He who speaks in a tongue edifies himself' (1 Cor. 14:4). The Spirit within you can always pray, and He knows exactly what to say! The Spirit ministers to you as you pray in tongues. Gradually your spirit is lifted and you are aware that God has replaced the heaviness with praise and thanksgiving for Him. He is the Lord who turns your wailing into dancing, who clothes you with joy.

Again and again the Spirit will want to encourage you to rejoice in the Lord and to give Him thanks. Hear Him now and set your heart and mind on putting this word into operation in your life every day.

Meditation:
GIVE THANKS IN ALL CIRCUMSTANCES
(1 THESS. 5:18).

I have made you and I will carry you (ISA. 46:4).

Rejoice in the Lord always . . . Rejoice! (PHIL. 4:4).

Praise:
In God we make our boast all day long, and we will praise your name for ever (PS. 44:8).

PART EIGHT

YOUR LIFE IN HOLINESS AND GLORY

72. I am Holy

'For he chose us in him before the creation of the world to be holy and blameless in his sight' (EPH. 1:4).

You alone can make me holy, O Lord.

READING: REVELATION 4:8–11

Each of the four living creatures had six wings and was covered with eyes all around, even under his wings. Day and night they never stop saying: 'Holy, holy, holy is the Lord God Almighty, who was, and is, and is to come.' Whenever the living creatures give glory, honour and thanks to him who sits on the throne and who lives for ever and ever, the twenty-four elders fall down before him who sits on the throne, and worship him who lives for ever and ever. They lay their crowns before the throne and say: 'You are worthy, our Lord and God, to receive glory and honour and power, for you created all things, and by your will they were created and have their being.'

God's essential nature is to be holy. It is impossible to describe adequately what this means, for the Lord in the essential nature of His being, is beyond description. We can say He is whole, complete and perfect in Himself; but this is a very inadequate definition of His holiness. He is above and beyond all He has made, and above anything we can conceive. 'I am the Lord, your Holy One' (Isa. 43:15).

What does a holy God want with us who are obviously so unholy in ourselves? To make us holy and fit to reign with Him in His holy heaven.

The heavenly host is holy, but even the creatures, elders and angels who surround God's throne bow before Him as they sing day and night the hymn which proclaims His holiness.

The holiness of God is somehow so much greater than the holiness of any He has made, in heaven or on earth.

Jesus came to make you holy, fit to come before His holy throne in worship and prayer. You can 'have confidence to enter the Most Holy Place by the blood of Jesus' (Heb. 10:19).

Paul says: 'It is God's will that you should be holy' (1 Thess. 4:3). But the very word 'holiness' sends a shiver down the spine of many Christians. They immediately think of legalistic holiness movements in which there is little joy or power. Or they imagine holiness is something beyond them, for great spiritual 'saints'. Yet, according to the New Testament, every Christian is a saint, one who is set apart for God and called to be holy.

You are not a Christian unless you are a saint! And here is the secret of living in holiness. This is not a goal that you will inevitably fail to attain. It is the essential nature of God's own Spirit who lives within you. He is the *Holy* Spirit. To live a holy life is to follow the leading of the Holy Spirit and obey the Lord. He will never lead you into unholiness or what God considers unrighteous.

The Holy Spirit does more than show you what to do; He enables you to do it! He is the Spirit of holiness within you wanting to be expressed in your life.

Jesus lived the holy life here on earth. To be holy in practical ways is to be like Him. You need to have a positive view of holiness and to see that it is possible for you to live in holiness because you have the presence, the life and the power of the Holy One within you. To be holy is to be full of love, full of joy, full of peace and power and forgiveness, full of the fruit of the Holy Spirit.

The words of this meditation are not only a command; they are a promise. There may be many ways in which you fail to be like Jesus; but He is at work in you changing you into His likeness from one degree of glory to another. Do not be discouraged. Know that the Lord will complete the work He has begun in you. 'May God himself, the God of peace, sanctify you through and through. May your whole spirit, soul and body be kept blameless at the coming of our Lord

Jesus Christ. The one who calls you is faithful and he will do it'
(1 Thess. 5:23–4).

Above all remember the revelation of God's Word; you are
already made holy in Christ, sanctified in Him (1 Cor. 1:30).
The Lord sees this as an accomplished fact. Your holiness is
not what you accomplish, but the holiness you have in Christ.
His holiness has become your holiness. No wonder you are
accepted by the Father. You live in the Holy One, and the
Holy One lives in you!

Meditation:

BE HOLY BECAUSE I, THE LORD YOUR
GOD, AM HOLY (LEV. 19:2).

It is God's will that you should be holy (1 THESS. 4:3).

[You are] sanctified in Christ Jesus and called to be
holy (1 COR. 1:2).

Praise:

Your ways, O God, are holy. What god is so great as
our God? (PS. 77:13).

73. I have Wisdom

'I guide you in the way of wisdom and lead you along straight paths' (PROV. 4:11).

Father, I ask for wisdom and believe you give this to me by your Holy Spirit.

READING: 1 CORINTHIANS 1:25–31
For the foolishness of God is wiser than man's wisdom, and the weakness of God is stronger than man's strength.

Brothers, think of what you were when you were called. Not many of you were wise by human standards; not many were influential; not many were of noble birth. But God chose the foolish things of the world to shame the wise; God chose the weak things of the world to shame the strong. He chose the lowly things of this world and the despised things – and the things that are not – to nullify the things that are, so that no-one may boast before him. It is because of him that you are in Christ Jesus, who has become for us wisdom from God – that is, our righteousness, holiness and redemption. Therefore, as it is written: 'Let him who boasts boast in the Lord.'

The Lord is wise. Even man's greatest wisdom is only foolishness in God's sight. '"For my thoughts are not your thoughts, neither are your ways my ways," declares the Lord. "As the heavens are higher than the earth, so are my ways higher than your ways and my thoughts than your thoughts"' (Isa. 55:8–9).

Intellectual pride is one of the greatest sins in modern society, keeping many from faith and the salvation God desires to give. Those who judge God make themselves out to be greater and wiser than He. Those who humble themselves before Him not only come to know Him, but also find their thinking enlarged by God's supernatural thinking.

If you accept the Lord's words and store up His commands within you,

> turning your ear to wisdom and applying your heart to understanding, and if you call out for insight and cry aloud for understanding, and if you look for it as for silver and search for it as for hidden treasure, then you will understand the fear of the Lord and find the knowledge of God. For the Lord gives wisdom, and from his mouth come knowledge and understanding (Prov. 2:2–6).

To be wise with God's wisdom is to be wise indeed. To be wise in the world's eyes is mere foolishness before God. And He is always willing to give you His wisdom when you acknowledge your need of it. James says that, 'If any of you lacks wisdom, he should ask God, who gives generously to all without finding fault, and it will be given to him' (Jas. 1:5). However, the one who asks must believe and not doubt when he asks. James later describes the nature of this wisdom. 'But the wisdom that comes from heaven is first of all pure; then peace-loving, considerate, submissive, full of mercy and good fruit, impartial and sincere' (Jas. 3:17).

The Holy Spirit is the Spirit of wisdom and the means by which God imparts His wisdom to us. Those who set their minds in opposition to God's truth display their foolishness. Who is wiser than God? Who has more knowledge than His Son?

Often God chooses those who seem of little consequence in worldly terms, in order that He might work through them in His sovereign power. Then it is clearly seen that what is accomplished is not man's work, but God working through man.

Jesus is wisdom personified, our wisdom from God. The wisdom of God is seen in His life and ministry and the Holy Spirit wants to produce those same qualities in us. James describes these as purity, peace, love, consideration, submission, mercy, faithfulness, impartiality and sincerity. It is wise to live in purity; impurity leads to a sense of guilt and shame and makes it impossible to have confidence before the Holy God. It is wise to be at peace; not to be anxious and fretful, not to be at odds with others. It is wise to love; for only then can you reflect the Lord's love and receive all He wants to give you. It is wise to be considerate towards others. It is wise to be submissive, for God does not walk with the proud: He dwells with the humble of heart. It is wise to be merciful, for then you shall obtain mercy, the mercies of God that are new for you every morning.

It is wise to be faithful for then you can inherit the promises of God, knowing His faithfulness towards you. It is wise to be impartial and to seek to live in peace with all men. It is wise to be sincere, for God hates hypocrisy and insincerity, for He is truth.

These are the practical outworkings of God's holiness and righteousness in your life. Because Jesus is wisdom from God for us, He is our righteousness, holiness and redemption, Paul says. We realise we can produce nothing of lasting value in ourselves; our total dependence is therefore on the Lord to work in us and through us.

'I am the Lord your God, who teaches you what is best for you, who directs you in the way you should go. If only you had paid attention to my commands, your peace would have been like a river, your righteousness like the waves of the sea' (Isa. 48:17–18).

The wisdom of God brings true counsel and insight as well as understanding and power into your daily life. When perplexed, the Holy Spirit is willing to speak a word of wisdom to you. When you ask for wisdom, God is ready to give it to you. He wants you to understand things from His perspective so that you come to the right decisions that are pleasing to Him.

Sometimes we opt for the foolishness of sin. But the Lord with His constant patience brings us back to a realisation that it is always wiser to walk in His ways, and receive the riches that are the benefit of His wisdom.

Meditation:
COUNSEL AND SOUND JUDGMENT ARE
MINE; I HAVE UNDERSTANDING AND
POWER (PROV. 8:14).

I am the Lord your God, who teaches you what is best
for you (ISA. 48:17).

For the Lord gives wisdom, and from his mouth come
knowledge and understanding (PROV. 2:6).

Praise:
I will praise the Lord, who counsels me (PS. 16:7).

74. *Walking as Jesus Did*

'Whoever claims to live in him must walk as Jesus did' (1 JOHN
2:6).

Holy Spirit, please help me to walk as Jesus did.

READING: 1 PETER 1:13–23
Therefore, prepare your minds for action; be self-
controlled; set your hope fully on the grace to be given
you when Jesus Christ is revealed. As obedient children, do not conform to the evil desires you had when
you lived in ignorance. But just as he who called you is
holy, so be holy in all you do; for it is written: 'Be holy,
because I am holy.'
    Since you call on a Father who judges each man's
work impartially, live your lives as strangers here in
reverent fear. For you know that it was not with
perishable things such as silver or gold that you were
redeemed from the empty way of life handed down to

you from your forefathers, but with the precious blood of Christ, a lamb without blemish or defect. He was chosen before the creation of the world, but was revealed in these last times for your sake. Through him you believe in God, who raised him from the dead and glorified him, and so your faith and hope are in God.

Now that you have purified yourselves by obeying the truth so that you have sincere love for your brothers, love one another deeply, from the heart. For you have been born again, not of perishable seed, but of imperishable, through the living and enduring word of God.

Jesus was tempted in every way as we are, yet never sinned. Paul tells us: 'No temptation has seized you except what is common to man. And God is faithful; he will not let you be tempted beyond what you can bear. But when you are tempted, he will also provide a way out so that you can stand up under it' (1 Cor. 10:13).

The Holy Spirit working within us, encourages us to refuse temptation. There is no sin in being tempted, only in yielding to the temptation. John says we are to walk as Jesus did. At first this seems like an impossible ideal because we know of His sinless character. At the same time we also recognise our own proneness to yield to temptation and so fail to walk as Jesus did.

The Holy Spirit helps you do what Jesus would do in your position. There is no need to fear holiness. This is God expressing His life through your imperfect life. Be thankful for the ways in which this already happens. If you recognise there are things in your life that are opposed to His purposes, ask the Lord to forgive you, and call upon the Holy Spirit to help you.

There is a right kind of fear of God, when we are in awe of Him and do not desire in any way to displease Him. Peter says that you purify yourself by obeying the truth. We have peace with God when we know our hearts are pure before Him and that we desire only what He wants. 'Who may ascend the hill of the Lord? Who may stand in his holy place? He who has clean hands and a pure heart' (Ps. 24:3–4).

Such purity of heart is expressed in true, selfless love for the brethren; love that is deep and comes from the heart. Every one of Jesus's actions was motivated by such love, first for His Father and then for those to whom He ministered.

God continues the process of refining your heart, showing you the hidden faults. Do not be discouraged when He does this; it is part of the way in which He expresses His love for you. Peter later says; 'Dear friends, I urge you, as aliens and strangers in the world, to abstain from sinful desires, which war against your soul. Live such good lives among the pagans that, though they accuse you of doing wrong, they may see your good deeds and glorify God on the day he visits us' (1 Pet. 2:11–12).

When you agree to do what Jesus would do you know you bring glory to the Father. If you decide to do anything He would not do, this will cause grief both to Him and yourself. There is peace in walking as Jesus did; only confusion and upset if you choose your own path instead. 'He himself bore our sins in his body on the tree, so that we might die to sins and live for righteousness' (1 Pet. 2:24).

God always has your best interests at heart. He knows how you will benefit by walking in righteousness and truth, conquering temptation and expressing His love. 'Finally, all of you, live in harmony with one another; be sympathetic, love as brothers, be compassionate and humble. Do not repay evil with evil or insult with insult, but with blessing, because to this you were called so that you may inherit a blessing' (1 Pet. 3:8–9).

Meditation:
WHOEVER CLAIMS TO LIVE IN HIM MUST WALK AS JESUS DID (1 JOHN 2:6).

For he chose us in him . . . to be holy and blameless in his sight (EPH. 1:4).

God disciplines us for our good, that we may share in his holiness (HEB. 12:10).

Praise:
Show me your ways, O Lord, teach me your paths (PS. 25:4).

75. *The Open Door*

'See, I have placed before you an open door that no-one can shut' (REV. 3:8).

Lord, draw me into your holy presence, please.

READING: REVELATION 4:1–2
After this I looked, and there before me was a door standing open in heaven. And the voice I had first heard speaking to me like a trumpet said, 'Come up here, and I will show you what must take place after this.' At once I was in the Spirit, and there before me was a throne in heaven with someone sitting on it.

God is holy. Heaven is the dwelling-place of His holy presence. The hymn the heavenly host sings day and night is: 'Holy, holy, holy is the Lord God Almighty, who was, and is, and is to come' (Rev. 4:8).

And yet it is into this holy place that the Lord welcomes you. Jesus has gone to prepare a place for you; today and every day He calls you into the holy of holies to enjoy fellowship with you.

It seems inexplicable that the holy God should delight in fellowship with us. It is the overwhelming evidence of His love that He should send His Son to endure suffering and death to make this possible.

How it must grieve the Lord, therefore, when we pray from a distance without drawing near. He has set an open door before you. Because He has opened it, no one can shut it. This is the door into His glory and He encourages you to walk through it.

It is not surprising that you hesitate at first. It seems inconceivable that we could be worthy enough to go through this doorway into the holy presence of the Lord and enjoy His glory. Of yourself you could never be worthy of such a privilege. However, Jesus has made you worthy. When you are cleansed from your sins you are made righteous in His sight. And you live in Christ Jesus. Because you are in Him you belong to the glory: 'And God raised us up with Christ and seated us with him in the heavenly realms in Christ Jesus' (Eph. 2:6).

The secret to going through that open door is knowing you are able to do so. Many Christians worship the Lord faithfully without ever realising they have such a privilege.

Imagine you are in a large room. Along one wall is a doorway with the door thrown open. Through the opening, shafts of light stream into the room. You are in the room next to the glory. Hear the Lord say to you, as He said to John: 'Come up here, and I will show you what must take place after this' (Rev. 4:1).

Perhaps you have often asked the Lord to come to you. Now He is asking you to come to Him. Such an invitation can hardly be refused. Why do you hesitate? Is it because you realise that certain things in your life are not holy and do not belong in the glory? Would you be ashamed to come before God's very throne in such a state?

Very well, then, leave behind in the room next to the glory these things which do not belong to the glory. Spend time throwing off 'everything that hinders and the sin that so easily entangles' (Heb. 12:1). Ask Jesus to forgive the sins, all the things of which you are ashamed, those things about you that are not like Him and cannot reflect His glory.

Take off the burdens, those things that cause anxiety and

fear. Be sure you forgive any who have hurt you in any way. Hold nothing back from Him who sees all. Be humble and honest with Him.

Know that Jesus is saying to you, 'your sins are forgiven' (Mark 2:5). This means He has freed you from everything that could deter you from passing through the open doorway.

Use your imagination to picture the scene. See yourself approaching the doorway. The streams of God's glory fall upon you and you hear His voice, 'Come up here.' He is waiting for you; He is ready to welcome you.

You pass through the doorway. There before you is a throne, immense in size; and on it Someone is sitting, the King of Glory. He is surrounded by His heavenly hosts bowing before Him in worship. Join them; worship the King from your heart.

See His hands extended to you in love. Then see the marks of the cross, the cost of bringing you into this holy place. Hear His words of assurance; He loves you, accepts you, wants you to reign with Him eternally.

Perhaps you will see Him lift you into His arms. Perhaps you will hear a word spoken to your heart, a word of encouragement or correction as He reveals His purpose to you. Perhaps you will understand He is asking what you want Him to do for you. Answer Him, with the boldness of faith that comes with knowing you have access to the throne. He may give you a commission, something He is sending you to do in His name.

Every time I pass through this doorway, the experience is different. However, you are not seeking experiences, but to draw near to the holy Lord, who is your God and Father.

Meditation:
COME UP HERE, AND I WILL SHOW YOU
WHAT MUST TAKE PLACE AFTER THIS
(REV. 4:1).

See, I have placed before you an open door that no–one can shut (REV. 3:8).

Holy, holy, holy is the Lord God Almighty, who was, and is, and is to come (REV. 4:8).

Praise:
Holy, holy, holy is the Lord God Almighty; the whole earth is full of His glory (ISA. 6:3).

76. Confidence before God

'I tell you the truth, whoever hears my word and believes him who sent me has eternal life and will not be condemned; he has crossed over from death to life' (JOHN 5:24).

Lord Jesus, may I always have the confidence to know you hear me and answer me when I pray.

READING: 1 JOHN 3:21–4
Dear friends, if our hearts do not condemn us, we have confidence before God and receive from him anything we ask, because we obey his commands and do what pleases him. And this is his command: to believe in the name of his Son, Jesus Christ, and to love one another as he commanded us. Those who obey his commands live in him, and he in them. And this is how we know that he lives in us: We know it by the Spirit he gave us.

Without condemnation we can have confidence before God, 'we have confidence to enter the Most Holy Place by the blood of Jesus, by a new and living way opened for us through the curtain, that is, his body' (Heb. 10:19–20).

The blood of Jesus has freed you from all condemnation and has opened the way for you into the Lord's Holy Presence. You can stand before His throne, clothed in the righteousness of Jesus, knowing the Father loves you and accepts you and wants to meet you in your need.

John heard Jesus give His wonderful prayer promises. About fifty years later he wrote his first Epistle. Those were fifty years of Spirit-filled ministry in which he had ample opportunity to test those promises in practice. He discovered they were true within the context in which Jesus gave them: 'If you remain in me and my words remain in you, ask whatever you wish, and it will be given you' (John 15:7).

If you continue in Jesus and allow His words to live in you, your heart will not be condemned and you will have confidence before God that He will answer your prayer. This does not mean you have to attain a certain degree of sanctity before God will listen to you. He hears the cry from the heart of every one of His children. It does mean He wants you to walk in faithful obedience to the Word He sets before you.

John discovered that we receive whatever we ask because:

1. *Our hearts do not condemn us;*
2. *We obey the Lord;*
3. *We do what pleases Him – offering our hearts and lives to Him that He may have His way with us.*

To pray in the name of Jesus, is to pray as He would pray, seeing the situation from His perspective and believing God will deal with the matter. We cannot imagine Jesus praying without such faith. 'Now faith is being sure of what we hope for and certain of what we do not see' (Heb. 11:1).

If we are seeking to please the Lord, living by faith in Him, our hearts will not condemn us. We shall not always get everything right, but when we sin or fail we turn to the Lord in His mercy and graciousness and receive forgiveness – not allowing ourselves to feel condemned by the enemy, by others, or by our own sense of failure. We have confidence because we are sure of who God is, the Faithful One who is perfect love, for whom nothing is impossible; the One in whom we live, and move and have our being. It is so important to ensure you are right with God and others, that nothing may destroy your confidence in Him.

Draw right into His Holy Presence, whenever you pray. See yourself before His throne. This is where you belong. This is the place He has prepared for you. You do not have to stand far off. Because you are in Christ you can draw near with a sincere heart in full assurance of faith (Heb. 10:22). 'This is the assurance we have in approaching God: that if we ask anything according to his will, he hears us. And if we know that he hears us – whatever we ask – we know that we have what we asked of him' (1 John 5:14–15).

Meditation:
WE HAVE CONFIDENCE BEFORE GOD AND RECEIVE FROM HIM ANYTHING WE ASK (1 JOHN 3:21).

If we ask anything according to his will, he hears us (1 JOHN 5:14).

Such confidence as this is ours through Christ before God (2 COR. 3:4).

Praise:
Lift up your hands in the sanctuary and praise the Lord (PS. 134:2).

77. The Glory of the Lord

'To them God has chosen to make known among the Gentiles the glorious riches of this mystery, which is Christ in you, the hope of glory' (COL. 1:27).

Lord, please continue to change me from one degree of glory to another.

READING: REVELATION 22:1–5
Then the angel showed me the river of the water of life, as clear as crystal, flowing from the throne of God and of the Lamb down the middle of the great street of the city. On each side of the river stood the tree of life, bearing twelve crops of fruit, yielding its fruit every month. And the leaves of the tree are for the healing of the nations. No longer will there be any curse. The throne of God and of the Lamb will be in the city, and his servants will serve him. They will see his face, and his name will be on their foreheads. There will be no more night. They will not need the light of a lamp or the light of the sun, for the Lord God will give them light. And they will reign for ever and ever.

What is God's purpose for you? To know His glory. All have sinned and as a consequence have fallen short, or misused the glory God intended for them. That is the devastating consequence of sin; it deprives men and women of the glory for which they were created.

Praise be to God! He has provided us with a saviour – we can be cleansed of our sins and receive the revelation of God's glory. 'And we, who with unveiled faces all reflect the Lord's glory, are being transformed into his likeness with ever-increasing glory, which comes from the Lord, who is the Spirit' (2 Cor. 3:18). Jesus has removed the veil that separated man from God and now you can know His glory. Even more amazing is that God says in His Word that you 'reflect the Lord's glory'. How can such a thing be true?

Jesus prayed that the Father would glorify Him as He went obediently to the cross. The glory for us is on the other side of the cross. Once we have known the cleansing of His blood we can receive the revelation of His glory. Jesus prayed: 'I have given them the glory that you gave me, that they may be one as we are one' (John 17:22).

Jesus displayed God's glory in the things He did. 'I have brought you glory on earth by completing the work you gave me to do. And now, Father, glorify me in your presence with the glory I had with you before the world began' (John 17:4–5). As God's children we too are to show His glory in the works He performs through us. God is glorified every time a sinner turns to Him in repentance and receives salvation, every time someone is baptised in the Holy Spirit or healed. He loves to give to His children and it blesses Him to see His life expressed in their lives.

We glorify the Lord in our lives as we live by faith putting our trust in His words of promise. We glorify Him by a life of faithful obedience, being prepared to deny ourselves in order that we might follow Him. We glorify Him when we allow His love to flow through us to others. '. . . live lives worthy of God, who calls you into his kingdom and glory' (1 Thess. 2:12).

As you pray He wants to reveal His heavenly glory to you, giving you a foretaste of the awesome joys that are to come. Such times are a great blessing; you sense a release in your heart and want to express your wonder, love and praise to Him.

The Holy Spirit is leading you to a greater revelation of God's glory, to the fulfilment of His purpose. When you see Him face to face, you will be like Him, radiant in His glory. 'He called you to this through our gospel, that you might share in the glory of our Lord Jesus Christ' (2 Thess. 2:14).

You are a fellow-heir with Christ. That means you are to share the inheritance He has received. You share now in the cost of living as a child of His kingdom in the world, of being a faithful witness in the face of misunderstanding and opposition, so that you will share in the glory to come.

The Lord sees this as accomplished: 'And those he predestined, he also called; those he called, he also justified; those he justified, he also glorified' (Rom. 8:30). He sees the whole process from beginning to end. What He has begun in you He will surely bring to completion for He sees it as already completed. The work is done totally in Jesus. 'Then Jesus said, "Did I not tell you that if you believed, you would see the glory of God?"' (John 11:40).

This was Jesus's prayer for you and all who believe in Him: 'Father, I want those you have given me to be with me where I am, and to see my glory, the glory you have given me because you loved me before the creation of the world' (John 17:24).

Meditation:
I HAVE GIVEN THEM THE GLORY THAT YOU GAVE ME, THAT THEY MAY BE ONE AS WE ARE ONE (JOHN 17:22).

I am going . . . to prepare a place for you (JOHN 14:2).

I will come back and take you to be with me that you also may be where I am (JOHN 14:3).

Praise:
Ascribe to the Lord the glory due to his name (PS. 29:2).

78. Press On

'Therefore, since we are surrounded by such a great cloud of witnesses, let us throw off everything that hinders and the sin that so easily entangles, and let us run with perseverance the race marked out for us. Let us fix our eyes on Jesus, the author and perfecter of our faith' (HEB. 12:1-2).

Dear Father, please give me the grace to remain faithful to the end.

READING: PHILIPPIANS 3:7-14

But whatever was to my profit I now consider loss for the sake of Christ. What is more, I consider everything a loss compared to the surpassing greatness of knowing Christ Jesus my Lord, for whose sake I have lost all things. I consider them rubbish, that I may gain Christ and be found in him, not having a righteousness of my own that comes from the law, but that which is through faith in Christ – the righteousness that comes from God and is by faith. I want to know Christ and the power of his resurrection and the fellowship of sharing in his sufferings, becoming like him in his death, and so, somehow, to attain to the resurrection from the dead.

Not that I have already obtained all this, or have already been made perfect, but I press on to take hold of that for which Christ Jesus took hold of me. Brothers, I do not consider myself yet to have taken hold of it. But one thing I do: Forgetting what is behind and straining towards what is ahead, I press on towards the goal to win the prize for which God has called me heavenwards in Christ Jesus.

Life is a matter of priorities. Every day is full of decisions. Paul counted everything else as rubbish in comparison with knowing the Lord Jesus. He never wanted to be a Christian originally, let alone an apostle; but God took hold of his life because He loved him and wanted to make him holy, like Jesus. His ministry was to be that of an apostle extending His kingdom, not persecuting the Church.

Paul knew God had taken hold of his life for a purpose and he wanted to 'press on to take hold of that for which Christ Jesus took hold of me' (Phil. 3:12). So he learned to look forward to what lay ahead. He was reaching out for the next thing that God wanted to do in his life or the next way in which He wanted to use him.

We should all do well to follow Paul's advice. Ahead of you lies a greater revelation of God's love for you than you have so far received. Ahead of you there will be more challenges to your faith, which will result in a strengthening of your trust in Jesus. Ahead of you the Father will do more pruning in your life, but you will be more fruitful as a result, and you will reflect more of His holiness and glory.

Yes, there will be difficulties and disappointments and even failure when you trust in yourself, but there will also be rich blessing and victory. The Lord in His goodness will lead you through each situation. And all the time, like Paul, you will be drawing nearer towards the goal. 'I press on towards the goal to win the prize for which God has called me heavenwards in Christ Jesus' (v.14).

Remember, 'we know that in all things God works for the good of those who love him, who have been called according to his purpose. For those God foreknew he also predestined to be conformed to the likeness of his Son, that he might be the firstborn among many brothers' (Rom. 8:28–9). How comforting to know you are in God's purpose and that He will ensure the plan for your life is fulfilled. Day by day you can co-operate with Him in this, rejoicing that He has made you His own.

Your love for Him creates in you the desire to make Him known to others, to pray for those who do not know Him: the lost, the desperate, the lonely, the depressed. You will know

the need to pray for revival in the Church, that the life, love
and power of Jesus might be revealed to the world through His
people; to look forward to the time when there will be a great
spiritual awakening in the nation and many are brought into
God's kingdom.

We live, not for ourselves, but for His kingdom, to see His
reign extended on earth, His will done here as in heaven. We
live to make Him known, that men and women may be saved
from death and brought to a saving knowledge of Jesus, being
brought into His kingdom and receiving the gift of eternal life.
We live to glorify the King, giving Him the praise and honour
He alone deserves.

And we long for the time when the King will return in glory
to claim all who belong to Him!

Meditation:
HALLELUJAH! FOR OUR LORD GOD
ALMIGHTY REIGNS (REV. 19:6).

Whoever is thirsty let him come; and whoever wishes,
let him take the free gift of the water of life (REV. 22:17).

Amen. Come, Lord Jesus (REV. 22:20).

Praise:
The Lord Almighty is with us; the God of Jacob is our
fortress (PS. 46:7).

"MY DEAR CHILD . . ."

"My Dear Child . . ."

Colin Urquhart

Hodder & Stoughton

LONDON SYDNEY AUCKLAND

To Anthea
and all those who,
through this book,
will hear the Lord say:
'My dear child . . .'

Contents

Acknowledgments

It is no exaggeration to say that the experience of writing this book has changed my life. I have received so much from the Lord and cannot adequately express my thanks to him.

Anthea, my secretary, has done far more to assist than type and retype the text. She has helped considerably with the editing process and I am grateful for her sensitivity to the Lord and her devotion to the task. She has been on the receiving end of the revelation God has given, and her life has been changed as a result.

My thanks also to Laura who has collated the scripture references, and to Katya.

Of course, this book could not have been written without the loving support of my wife Caroline, my family, and all at Kingdom Faith Ministries.

This is a book written from the Heavenly Father's heart to the hearts of his children. Obviously it is not scripture, nor is it in any way intended to stand alongside the Word of God in significance.

Prophecy is one of the gifts of the Holy Spirit: God speaking into the lives of his people. So this book is a form of prophecy, and I believe many will experience God speaking to their hearts concerning issues which are of deep and immediate concern to them.

To write this book the Lord asked me to draw aside for several days to listen to what was in his heart. The experience of doing this has changed me as a person in many respects. I have a clearer understanding of who God is and of the nature of his love for each of his children. This is reflected in the text of this book, and I believe you will receive a greater revelation of God's love for you as you read it.

The Lord wanted to open his heart to me about himself, revealing several aspects of his nature – not only his love, grace and mercy, but also his wrath, justice and judgment.

The Lord asked me to write this book at a time when I had not made provision for writing in my full schedule. But the impact of what he has said has made this task a joy and not a burden. I count it a great privilege to have been called aside by the Lord to spend this time with him and to be his 'mouthpiece' in writing this book. He has greatly encouraged me in faith and love by what he has said.

The form of the book is simple: God is speaking to 'My dear child'. This child is a believer in the Lord Jesus Christ and is in a personal relationship with him, and therefore with the Father. My prayer is that you will hear his voice in these pages and will meet personally with your Heavenly Father as a result.

This book is ideally suited to use during your daily time with the Lord. It could also be used in a prayer group. In either case, you will find it helpful to read the text aloud. The language has deliberately been kept conversational in style.

I have spent time listening to him every day for over twenty-five years. Paul warns us that our prophecy is imperfect, and I have done my best to keep the human element to a minimum. Of course it is impossible to eliminate this completely, because in prophecy God is speaking through an imperfect channel. But nothing would be gained by trying to put my own ideas or opinions into his mouth!

An appendix of scripture references relevant to each section is included for your study. This is only a small selection of the scriptures that could be quoted. I have also made an audio cassette tape of readings from *My Dear Child* . . . and this is available from:

Kingdom Faith Ministries,
Roffey Place,
Crawley Road,
Faygate,
Horsham,
West Sussex RH12 4SA

Please accept this book as a contribution to your spiritual life from a Christian brother who has sought to hear the Father honestly and convey what is on his heart. May you rejoice eternally in his love.

May your roots go down deep into the soil of God's marvellous love; and may you be able to feel and understand, as all God's children should, how long, how wide, how deep and how high his love really is; and to experience this love for yourselves, though it is so great that you will never see the end of it or fully know or understand it. (Eph 3:17–19, Living Bible)

Colin Urquhart

1

I Have Personality

———— o ————

My dear child, I created heaven and earth. Many have wondered how creation came into being. For me it was simple. I spoke. This is all I had to do. Whatever I speak comes into being; it happens. Can you imagine the creative power and energy of my words?

Yet I am not a man; I am Spirit. People think of spiritual forces as powers which have no personality, like the wind. I am an almighty, powerful Spirit who has personality.

My power is only used in relation to my character. I am love and I have the power to create. Put the two together, and you can see that I create in love. You must understand that there are no other creative forces. **I am the only Creator.** This is another way of saying I am the only God. Men have always tried to imagine what I am like and have had all sorts of wrong ideas. They have created gods according to their own understanding. Clearly this is false and shows how important it is to know me, the only true God.

Throughout the centuries I have spoken to men and women to show them what I am really like, and this is why I am speaking to you now.

This earth is but a minute part of what I have made. But I love this planet and all I have made to live on it,

— 19 —

including you. At first there was no life on the earth, so I set about bringing form and order. If you look at creation, you will see how orderly it is, how carefully I have planned and made things.

I won't dwell on the details of the plants and animals because I want to concentrate on you. Yes, I made you. You are only one of millions, I know. Yet because I have made everything in love, I have made you in love. You may not understand what this means, but you will.

The word that comes out of my mouth has personality. This word can express everything I am. It expresses my love, my life, my joy, my power, my will – everything about me. There is nothing about me that cannot be expressed through my word.

Why should this be so important for you to understand? Because a day came when the personality of my word took human form. This word, my creative word, became a man and lived among other men.

Do you know what this means? It signifies that, although I created the entire universe, I decided to become a man for a short period of time. I had very good reasons for doing this, as you will see.

During this time, I didn't cease being God. No, there could never be a time when I didn't exist. I continued in the full personality of my spiritual life and power; but the word through which I created became a man so that everyone could hear my voice clearly. Yes, I wanted to speak to everyone, to show men and women what I was really like. I wanted them to understand why I had created them, what in their lives pleased me and what grieved me.

Those who please me are truly happy. But those who disregard me can never experience real fulfilment in their lives. They become frustrated and fearful.

2

In My Image

—— o ——

My dear child, I have made you in my image. This does not mean you are exactly like me, but you are to reflect my character and personality. Whatever I am, I want to see reflected in you. **I see you as the real master-work of my creative ability.**

I have made mountains, rivers, seas and trees, animals, birds and fish. But I have not made anything else like you. You see, all the other aspects of my creation can give me glory by being what they are. However, I can be glorified by you in a very particular way.

Animals can't have a loving, spontaneous, joy-filled relationship with me like you can.

3

No Accident

———— o ————

I created you in love, for love. Isn't that good? My real
expectation is that you will know my love, be filled
with my love, express my love, return my love, give my
love to others and enjoy my love. My whole purpose for
you is centred around love. Always remember this.

When I created, there was no order on the earth. I
enjoyed bringing order out of chaos and seeing everything come together as I had envisaged in my mind.
When you look at the creation around you, you can see
how ingenious I have been. I have created order in
everything from a snowflake to a leaf, from the limbs of
an animal to your brain, heart and every other part of
your body. No man could have devised or thought up
such a scheme of creation, let alone produce it.

I laugh at those who say it is an accident. Accidents
end in chaos, confusion and disaster. No accident ends
in such finely planned and thought-out order. Deliberate
action on my part was at the inception of everything.

So, my child, you were no accident. **You are part of my
overall plan.** Sometimes you think that if it had not been
for a man and a woman making love, you would not
exist. But who made that man and woman? Who made
them able to have a sexual relationship? Who had oversight of your birth?

When you were a young baby you were not able to think, understand and believe as you can now. But I have watched over you and am bringing to fulfilment my plan for your life.

I am a most extraordinary inventor, aren't I? Even when things appear to go wrong, I am able to work in the situation. I can turn everything to good for my purposes.

4

Created In Love

—— ○ ——

My dear child, I am your Almighty God, and I am your Father. I love you.

I know your understanding of words such as 'Father' and 'love' are coloured by your experience. But my heart is not like that of any human father. My love transcends any other. You can't judge my love by human standards, no matter how good your experience of love.

You see, my child, before the world was created, I knew you. I appreciate this is impossible for you to understand fully. But I don't dwell within the limitations of time; I am eternal. I am able to see the beginning and the ending of all things at any given moment.

So, **even before you were born, I knew you.** From the moment of your conception I have watched over you. I have seen your conflicts, turmoil, trauma even. I know your fears, your sins, inadequacy and insecurity. You have often wondered why I made you in such a way if I truly loved you. But I didn't make you like that. **I made you to be like me.**

I knew I would draw you to this moment when I could speak to you heart to heart. I want to explain my love to you in such a way that you can experience that love and be set free from all the things that have made it difficult, impossible even, to reflect my love in your life.

When you lose sight of my love for you, real problems arise. Sadly, some of my children do lose sight of the centrality of my love, and become hard-hearted. I want you to enjoy your relationship with me, child. Then you will always respect me as your Creator, the Holy One who is Almighty.

Because I created you in love, I had to give you free will. This means you are able to hate as well as love, to be selfish and proud if you wish. Everybody has been created with the ability to choose what to do and how to behave.

You are no exception. Because you have free will, you have the ability to respond to my love. Many choose not to do so, but that doesn't stop me loving them and longing for them to be set free from the things that deny my love. I would like everyone to know and enjoy my love and express this in their relationships.

My child, this is what I want for you.

5

My Plan for You

——— o ———

Before creation began, I decided to have a number of people like you who would be my children, and respond to my love. Out of the chaos and confusion of their lives I decided to bring my divine order to prepare and equip them for heaven.

This is no small task. At first everybody rebels. They sin and are cut off from my love. **I sent my Son to restore them to relationship with me.** As soon as they give their lives to Jesus, my divine order for their lives is established. My Holy Spirit works in each of my children to bring my plan to fulfilment.

So, my dear child, this is what is happening in your life. **You will be transformed into my likeness, changed from one degree of glory to another.** You will one day see me face to face. Then you will be like me, and you will reign eternally with me in glory. I am looking forward to that so much. I want you to look forward to that time, my child. Please co-operate with me in all I need to do in preparing you for this.

You will share my sadness for all those who are unconcerned about my reason for creating them. They want to make their own way through life. Sadly, if they decide to do without me now, they will do without me eternally. If they look to their own works for salvation, their own works will have to save them. This is impossible, isn't it? Nobody can know the glory of my heaven through their own works.

6

My Way of Salvation

— ○ —

I was not taken by surprise when man sinned. I had already planned what I would do when this happened.

Some people talk as if I was taken by surprise and had to alter my strategy to bring men back on course. How mistaken they are. They don't understand that I live in eternity and can see the end from the beginning. I knew very well what would happen.

Like everyone else, you fell short of my glory and what I wanted for you. You were proud and selfish, wanting your own way.

So, my dear child, **I planned for Jesus to take all your sin, failure, fear and inadequacy to the cross. I sent him to take your punishment so that I would have no cause to be angry with you. His blood and your faith have saved you from my wrath. He died for you so that you could have a new life, and become a new creation. I** needed to liberate you from spiritual darkness and make you a child of light. The only way for anyone to know me is through Jesus. This is why you have had to put your faith in him, and all he has done for you.

My dear child, I am so pleased you have done this. Now you and I can have a great life together.

7

I Care for You

———— o ————

I didn't create you to suffer at the hands of others, although I knew this to be inevitable. My Son, Jesus, was subjected to opposition, rejection, abuse and hatred. I allowed this because I love you so much.

You see, my dear child, I wanted to free you from the effects of sin, failure and fear. **I wanted you to be able to receive my life,** a life so real and full that you could allow yourself to love and be loved without fear of hurt or rejection.

Jesus had to be vulnerable in the same way as you to make this possible. As I have watched over you and seen the hurts that have accumulated, I have longed to bring you close to Jesus. For if you are close to him, you are close to me.

So don't think I have been unconcerned about your needs. I have been waiting for you to give me the time and opportunity to set you free from the things that have caused the shame and hurt you have experienced.

I have spoken to you in love many times. Often you've pushed away what I have said. I've spoken to you through others, but you've refused to listen. So I rejoice that now you will sit at my feet and allow me to give you understanding of my love. **I want to speak from my heart to your heart.**

8

You Are Saved

——— o ———

My dear child, I have saved murderers, prostitutes, drug addicts, alcoholics and criminals. Don't you think I am able to save you? I have saved people from communism, hinduism, buddhism and many other 'isms'. Don't you think I can save you?

Why do you always think you are the difficult one? Why do you think it should be more difficult for you to receive from me than anybody else? Why do you give the impression that Christ died for everybody else except you? This doesn't seem to make any sense. You suggest I have one law for everybody else, and a different one for you. I am allowed to bless, heal and save others, but not you.

You keep saying to yourself that there is nothing special about you. Yet you treat yourself as a special case, as if you are the only one I cannot forgive, heal, save or liberate.

I think it's time for you to repent of your pride, don't you? You think such attitudes are the fruit of being humble; but they are not. You are saying you know better than I do! I know more about this salvation business than you!

If you confess your sins, I am faithful and just to forgive you and cleanse you from all unrighteousness.

— 31 —

Believe what I say. I am faithful and just. I have forgiven you and cleansed you from all unrighteousness.

Accept that you are saved because you have asked me to forgive you and you have put your faith in Jesus. You are accepted by me.

Begin to look at yourself as I see you, instead of telling me you are not what you are. You even suggest I couldn't do for you what I have already done. It's very frustrating being your Father if you don't believe my love, and question my goodness and generosity to you!

9

Let Me Love You

———— o ————

I will always speak to you in human terms you can understand. I want to draw you close to me, child. As your Father, I want to hold you in my arms. I won't force myself on you. There have been times when I wanted to enfold you in my love, but you pushed me away. So I've had to be patient, waiting for the time when you would be prepared to open yourself to me, when you would dare to trust me enough to let me love you.

When you receive my love, you know my peace. Then you begin to experience the joy of being loved by me. Instead of feeling vulnerable, you have a new security.

You have feared what people would think if they knew you loved me. Such concerns don't matter. Your need of my love is much more important than other people's reactions, wouldn't you agree?

You have also been slow to believe the reality of my love for you. Many of your fears have been the result of your doubts.

Trust me. I want to teach you how to rest in my love without thinking you have to do something to deserve it. This doesn't seem right to you, does it? But you cannot earn my love, and you don't have to; I already love you.

So enjoy my love. Because I love you, I enjoy you. Why do you find this difficult to believe? **I want you to enjoy me.** I want you to know times when you can rest in my love and enjoy me.

To you this seems like selfish indulgence; yet this is the greatest need in your life. Don't you see that the more you allow yourself to rest in my love, the more able you are to take my love to others? Often the love you have given others has been frantic, not a resting, trusting love.

You don't need to justify my love for you; and you don't have to be afraid to entrust yourself to me. You've really longed to know my love for you, haven't you? My child, as you learn to find time to rest in my love, so you will be able to take that rest into every other area of your life. In the midst of all your difficulties, you will be able to trust in me and know the love I have for you.

10

The Lost Child

—— o ——

A child sat in tears in the middle of the crowd. She was lost, separated from her parents. Some walked past unconcerned. The child didn't belong to them so they ignored the problem.

Then someone went up to the child, took her by the hand and tried to console her. At first the child wouldn't respond because this was not her mother or father. She gave no answer to the questions but continued to sob uncontrollably.

Then from the crowd appeared a distraught mother who enfolded the child in her arms. The sobbing gave way to cries of relief from both mother and child. She lifted her up, hugging her closely, assuring, soothing.

My dear child, do you ever feel lost in the crowd? Others may try to soothe you, but I am the only one who can lift you up and meet your need.

I Love You Because I Love You

———— o ————

My love for you does not depend on your performance or achievements. **I love you because I love
you.** I have called and chosen you. You have been afraid
to come closer to me because of your sense of inadequacy; but **I want you close to me**. I like you.

You have often thought it's my divine job to love you
because I am God. But you have doubted that I really like
you. You see so many things about yourself you don't
like, things you know are not my will for you. If you
don't like yourself because of these things, you have
concluded that I don't like you either! I haven't liked your
sin, which is why you have felt uncomfortable when you
grieved me. But I don't love you only when you are good.
I don't love you only on your obedient days. I love you
because I love you; and I like what I am doing in your life.

I like to bring about changes which free you from the
things you don't like about yourself. I like to see repentance which leads to forgiveness and a release from your
guilt. I like it when you become less religious and more
loving! I like you, my child. I really like you.

I Love You More Than You
Love Yourself

———— o ————

Don't you realise, child, **I love you more than you love yourself**? I like you more than you like yourself. I am more patient with you than you are with yourself.

What do you think I should do with you when you step out of line and disappoint me? What should I do when you deliberately avoid what I am saying, and blind yourself to the truth? Should I punish you? Should I push you away from me because you no longer deserve my love? Do you think my love is only for good, perfect people who always obey me? If this was the case, I wouldn't have anyone left to love!

Imagine a mother holding a young baby in her arms. Does she ask for her child to be perfect, mature and obedient immediately? She knows the child will need training, teaching and discipline. When he learns to walk, he will touch what he shouldn't touch and do what he shouldn't do. He will show little discernment as to what is right or wrong.

But the mother doesn't reject her child, saying she cannot love such a disobedient failure. No, she draws the child closer, saying to herself, 'I will train him and love him and discipline him when necessary. He will grow up to be a fine boy.' And she will defend him against any who criticise him. He is so precious to her.

Hear my father's heart beating as I tell you these things. Don't you see that this is how I regard you? I know you haven't reached perfection and maturity; you are still learning to walk in my ways and do what pleases me.

You are like that small child. You are hurt by doing things you shouldn't, aren't you? This is the way you learn. **It is in your own best interests to do what I say.**

My child, my love for you is not a passing or fleeting infatuation. I have committed myself to you, to love you, to be faithful and true to you through all phases of your growth and training. I have promised to bring you to maturity and to the fulfilment of my purposes. I will bring you to perfection, but I don't treat you as if you are already perfect!

13

Don't Be Afraid of Love

———— ° ————

I don't like all I see in you now, because I am righteous; but I have you in hand.

Sometimes I touch vulnerable areas of your life and you want to wriggle free from my grasp, at least for a while; you feel the pressure is too great. No sooner have you shaken me off, than you long to be in my arms again! You miss the comfort, strength and peace of knowing my presence with you. Slowly you learn to submit to me and my ways. At first you obey me begrudgingly, but later you rejoice in doing what I ask of you.

There are still areas of your life that you consider to be your own. Either you've not submitted these to me, or you've felt that I am not interested in your weakness and need.

I haven't touched those parts you've not wanted me to touch. I have respected your free will and waited for your invitation.

I am able to heal the delicate wounds inflicted by others in the past. My touch is not like their touch. Their touch has hurt you; **my touch will heal you.** Trust me.

Every way in which I touch your life will be for your good. Even when I discipline you, it is always in love. You don't have to shield yourself from me. I don't withdraw from you, but continue to hold you until you relax and are ready to receive from me.

Why be so tense, my child? Why keep from me what is mine? I love you, every part of you. **I don't love an image of what you ought to be, but you; the person you really are, with all your faults and failings.**

I assure you of my love. Nothing is hidden from my sight. I wait until you allow me to touch those vulnerable areas of yourself from which you have excluded me.

14

I Am Gentle With You

———— ° ————

Why do you imagine that my touch will hurt and wound you? I am gentle. I want to touch you with my tenderness. I care about you and deal lovingly with you. I don't work in your life by wounding you, making further healing necessary. **I want to heal you through the revelation of my love.**

I enjoy tender moments with you. I want you to give yourself time to enjoy me. Please don't come rushing in and out of my presence in prayer, without letting me speak lovingly to your heart. I encourage those I love. It's not my purpose to destroy you, but to build you up in faith.

I came as one who served. I came to wash the feet of my disciples. Many of my children find it difficult to let me serve them by washing their feet. They must always serve me rather than me serve them! They fail to realise that unless they receive from me, they cannot give to others. Living in fellowship with me doesn't mean you have to strive to accomplish things all the time.

My dear child, learn to be still and know that I am God.

People imagine I break hard hearts through violent action, judgment and punishment. No, I break hard hearts by melting them with my love. So I keep loving and loving and loving, no matter what response is given me.

Understand then, my child, there is never a moment in time when I don't love you. You are the apple of my eye. **You are one in whom I delight.** I can never love any of my children with anything less than a perfect, unchanging love. I embrace you in love, in whatever way is right for you at that time. **You are never out of my thoughts.**

15

I Am Your Father

——— o ———

My child, don't judge me by your human experience of a father. Your natural father was a man and failed in many ways. You were aware of his weaknesses as well as his strengths.

Some people have suffered rejection at the hands of their human fathers because they were men who could not be trusted. They were unjust or unconcerned about their children. I never abuse my children. **I am near to all who call on me.** I am never distant. I comfort, strengthen and heal them. So I am not to be compared with any other father.

I am not a man. There are no weak, vulnerable areas in my life. There is never inadequacy in me, or inability to meet a need. I love you with my everlasting love that will never fade; it will never be withdrawn from you. As your Father, I watch over your development and I am concerned to protect you from things that are dangerous and harmful to you.

You haven't always heeded my warnings; so at times you've been hurt. But I have always been on hand to heal you and meet your need. Sometimes you've allowed me to do this; at other times you haven't.

I never deal with you as you deserve, but only with compassion and grace. This is difficult for you to understand. I give and give and go on giving to you. I never come to the end of my giving.

You often think to yourself, 'Who am I that I should receive such love, that I should know the personal affection of my God?' You are fearful that my love might suddenly be withdrawn and then you would feel rejected. If you were to open yourself fully to me and then I turned away, you would be devastated. But I would never treat you like that.

I don't withdraw my love. I don't commit myself to you only for a set period of time. My commitment to you is unending, as a commitment of love must always be. Love cannot be real if it is suddenly withdrawn.

I already know you, every part of you – and yet I love you. I see what you try to hide from me. So, hiding is futile. I will not stop loving you because I uncover some unsavoury part of your character. My love for you is real. It doesn't depend on who you are but who I am!

16

You Make It Difficult for Yourself to Receive Love

———— ○ ————

My dear child, when you accuse, judge and condemn yourself, instead of believing what I say, you find it difficult to receive my love, don't you? You concentrate on your inadequacy and problems, wondering if it could be true that I love you.

You've listened to the enemy sometimes, haven't you? He tries to sow seeds of accusation in your mind and encourages your sense of inadequacy, making you feel unworthy of my love. Don't be deceived by any of his tactics. He is a liar. He has no right to accuse you.

I don't regard your inadequacy and failure as the truth about you. The truth is that I love you. You are precious in my sight and I honour you. I see you as one who is slowly but surely responding to me, whose heart is being melted by my love. I see you as my child belonging to my family, made acceptable to me through the blood of Jesus.

You could do nothing to deserve my love; I am so much higher and greater than you. So why not accept the fact that **you can never earn my love, only gratefully receive it?** My dear child, I don't disapprove of those who approve of me! If I did so, who would be left for me to approve? Don't think I regard you in the same way as I regard those who still belong to the kingdom of darkness. The enemy shall not have you. The destroyer shall not touch you, for you are mine.

Sometimes you are concerned because I give you so much, and you give me so little in return. This is *false* guilt. One of the most loving things you can do for me is to allow me to give to you in the way I choose. Then many others will receive my love through you, if you are to love them as I love you.

As a channel of my love you will radiate my love in your character and actions.

always found, my child, that I would place what is behind the masks but this is not true.

come to you again and I say ... that I love and say to you 'Don't be afraid. I love you and long to hear from you.'

17

I Love the Person You Really Are

———— o ————

My child, I am never deceived by appearances. You find that disconcerting. There have been many times when you have put on an appearance for my benefit or for others. You have tried to be what you know you ought to be. But it has never worked, has it? **I see through the barriers and behind the masks you wear.** So why imagine they make you more acceptable to me? I don't accept you because of any of that. None of those masks encourage me to love you any more than I do already. They only make it more difficult for you to receive my love.

I love the person you really are. I sent my Son to die for the real you – not some superficial, false expression of who you are. I don't like masks and barriers. I love people. I don't love what they ought to be; I love them as they are. You have vainly imagined that the masks would be more acceptable to me than the reality of what goes on inside you. I look at the heart. I know the longings of your heart and the conflicts also. You give people the impression you don't need to be loved; but I know differently. You try to persuade others that you are fine as you are. You are able to cope, even though often you feel so lonely within yourself.

I love to come behind the masks and barriers to touch the lonely with my presence, to touch the fearful and inadequate ones with the assurance of my love. You have always feared, my child, that I would reject what lay behind the mask; but this is not true.

I come where nobody else can come. I am Spirit, and I come into your spirit and fill you with my love and say to you, 'Don't be afraid. There is nothing to fear from me.'

18

You Don't Need to Pretend

—— ○ ——

My dear child, why are you so concerned about what others think of you? This occupies so much of your time and gets you into pitiful muddles, doesn't it? Others have the same problem about you. They wonder how you regard them. And I watch all this going on.

Everybody wonders what others think of them. I see them fencing and sparring with one another and they become defensive and fearful. If only they would be open and honest, they would be so much happier. They would discover that they don't have to put on a performance for one another.

Are you listening to me, child? This is very relevant for you, isn't it? **Be yourself and stop trying to be someone else.** Then life will be so much easier for you. You imagine that if anybody knew you for who you are, they would reject you. So the somebody else you try to be is rejected, because everyone knows this is not the real you!

I know who you really are, and I accept you.

19

Your Appearance

———— o ————

My dear child, you spend a lot of time being concerned about your appearance. I like you to look clean and presentable. When Jesus walked about on earth he didn't go around dirty and scruffy. Neither did he wear his best suit all the time.

But, my child, you spend so much time preening the outside, while I am concerned with what is on the inside. It doesn't matter how smart or expensive your appearance, if your heart is poverty stricken! When my love shines through your life, it doesn't matter whether you are wearing your pyjamas, jeans or your best clothes.

Sometimes I look at congregations of smartly dressed people in church and I think to myself, 'Who are they trying to fool?' They say they put on their best clothes for me. The best clothes they could wear for me are a pure heart and a good conscience. These delight me.

Those with pure hearts and clean hands ascend the hill of praise, holiness and true worship. So, present your body as a living sacrifice, holy and acceptable to me. Even your best clothes wear out, but a pure heart doesn't; it is eternal.

My dear child, I wish you would spend as much time being concerned about your heart as your appearance. I

say this gently to you, but it is something you need to hear.

You are often complaining you are the wrong shape. This makes me smile. I see people doing all kinds of things to change their shape. Sometimes it is important that they do, especially if they are guilty of gluttony and are overweight in a way that affects their health. But they would be much healthier if they were more concerned about their spiritual weight and shape!

My Spirit lives within you to encourage the right priorities in your life. So let's work on these things together, shall we? We'll get things in right order. You can look forward to the day when people will be glad to see you because I shine out of your life. Then they won't even notice what you wear, or your shape. What a day that will be, my child!

20

The Real You

———— o ————

My dear child, I think you are beautiful. I really mean that. You are beautiful because you are made in my image, to reflect my glory. I can see my life in you, emerging like a butterfly from a chrysalis. Soon you will be able to spread your wings and fly freely.

Many of the ways in which I touch your life are apparent to others. But nobody else can see those deeply personal times we have together when you shut yourself away in your room to be alone with me.

Do you remember what I promise? I will reward you openly for what I see in secret. At such times you can bare your most intimate thoughts. You can tell me how you really feel. **I never mind, child, what you share with me.** The more open you are, the better I like it. The more real you are, the more I can respond.

This is much more meaningful than formal times of prayer, when you say things you think I want to hear which don't come from your heart. **I want to relate to the real you.**

21

Our Prayer Meetings

———— o ————

Often you need assurance that I am pleased with you. But I am not only pleased with you when you feel the closeness of my presence. Have you ever been in a room with someone you love and yet it is not the appropriate time to hug or kiss them? You can communicate your love in other ways, can't you? It's the same when we are close. Sometimes it is right to enfold you in my love but at other times I want to communicate with you in other ways. I may need to reveal my thoughts to you and give you wisdom.

It would be very boring if every time you drew aside with me the experience was the same. Have you noticed in your relationship with other people, you cannot always predict what they are going to say or do? It is the same with me. I'm not predictable, am I? I don't dance to the tune of any of my children. **There is glorious variety in the ways I meet with you.**

When you don't feel I am close to you, I haven't deserted you, nor have I failed to turn up for the prayer meeting. I certainly haven't taken you off my popularity list. You can always rejoice, whether you feel my presence or not.

Listen child, I am never late for a prayer meeting with you. I am always there before you are, waiting for you to come. You know, sometimes I've been disappointed because you haven't shown up. Does that surprise you?

22

Be Open

———— o ————

My dear child, it is good to talk things through with me, isn't it? Then you let me into the secret places of your heart. You have the spiritual need to open these areas to the influence of my Spirit. When you are open about these hidden things, I can deal with them. Don't say, 'Oh, you know all these things, Lord.' **Take the trouble to tell me about them, and you will experience great release.** Then the enemy cannot take advantage of you in these areas.

While you try to work out things for yourself, he tries to take advantage, doesn't he? I watch what goes on in your mind. You go round and round in circles. The enemy goes round in those circles with you. He tries to increase the confusion.

I never go round in circles. I always come straight to the point and lead you to the answer, child. So when you share your inner turmoil with me, that is the beginning of the end of it; even though it takes time to unravel because you have been in a spiral of confusion.

23

Give and You Will Receive

—— o ——

We are going to have some good times together in the future, aren't we, child? You have been longing to know what is on my heart. Well, you see, **when you share with me what is on your heart, I share with you what is on mine.** You have to share with me first.

The measure you give is the measure you get back. This is a principle of my Kingdom. I am not going to change my principles for you, or for any of my children. Share your heart with me and I will share my heart with you.

24

No Fear in Love

———— o ————

My dear child, there is no fear in my love. My love casts out all fear. You have prayed about your fears and have asked to be set free from them, haven't you? The only way for this to happen is for you to receive my love. Then the fears flee away. In receiving my love, your healing is accomplished, and you are set free from the things that have caused the hurt.

The way you find it most difficult to receive my love is through others. Because my love is born of the Spirit, you want to receive it directly from me as a spiritual experience. This is good; but it's not the only way in which I communicate my love to you.

My Spirit of love lives in others. Just as I want to express this love through you to them, so I express this same love through others to you. But you find it hard to receive in this way because you fear you will be in debt to the one from whom you have received.

What you fail to understand is that **you are also reluctant to receive love from me, because this places you in debt to me.** Better to be independent and self-contained, for then you will not need to be in debt to anyone, even me! But I don't love you to place you in debt or bondage. I love you because I love you. I don't express my love to you through others to place you in debt to them, but because I want to break down your stubborn self-will and independence.

It is humbling, isn't it, to discover your need not only of me but of others also? It is humbling to realise that you cannot fulfil my purposes by being independent and self-contained.

Sometimes you have argued that to receive love from others makes you vulnerable to them and open to hurt. So you have said, 'Better only to receive love from God directly.' Then what will you do with all the love I put within you? Are you going to refuse to give it to others in case they are threatened by your love?

When you experience my love, you want to communicate it and give it to others, don't you, my child? If everyone was like you, afraid to do so, who would receive my love?

There is always a vulnerability in love and the possibility of being rejected or hurt. But because my love is born of the Spirit, that love brings healing. If someone who has communicated my love then hurts you, I will always send someone else to love you and be my instrument of healing to you.

25

You Are Accepted

—— ° ——

S ometimes the enemy attempts to make you feel guilty at having received so much from me. He suggests that it is not your place to receive, only to give. So he encourages you to chase around in a frenzy of constant activity, lest you be rejected by me for doing too little. Even when I encourage you to be still, to receive and rest in me, he suggests that unless you are constantly active you cannot be in my will. Don't listen to such lies.

My child, as you learn to rest in me, your tensions and anxieties ease. You cease to strive. When you believe that I accept you, it becomes evident that you don't have to try and earn my favour. I want you to work because you know you are already in my favour.

You don't have to try to make yourself acceptable to me. You are already accepted because you have put your faith in what Jesus has done for you on the cross. There he dealt with all the unloving things about you – every sin and failure. **Every fear and every need was met.** It is pointless to try to make yourself acceptable when you already are! Believe what I have done for you and live in the good of it.

There is no point in my giving you tender assurance of my love if you don't believe what I say. I have demonstrated my love, not simply by words, but in action. In giving my Son's life on the cross, I showed the full extent of my commitment to you. I was prepared to love you even to the point of death.

26

I Watch Over You

——— o ———

My dear child, I knew you before you were born. You were an object of my desire and my love, even when I planned your life. You wonder how this could be true as you are only one of a multitude of people.

I see the deliberate disobedience of many. **But in every generation I have planned that there will be those who are my own special possession.** They fulfil my heart's desire and radiate my glory in their lives.

You are such a one, child. I watched over the circumstances of your birth, your parents and your family. You wonder at that because things have been far from perfect in your childhood and adolescence. There have been many difficulties and traumas. Did I plan these?

Well, my child, I saw you through them all, didn't I? Those difficulties were important in building your character and in teaching you to look to me and depend on my love. It is quite painful growing up, isn't it? All those tensions you had to go through, and the questions. This is an inevitable process. You had to go through it; but look at you now! You have a heart full of love for me and the rest of your life stretches before you. You can love and serve me for the rest of your life, and you will be with me in glory for evermore. This is comforting to know, isn't it?

Don't fear what is ahead of you. **If I could see you through past problems, I can certainly see you through future experiences.** I have seen new life emerging in you through all these developing processes. Since you put your faith in Jesus, my Spirit has been producing fruit in more and more areas of your life.

I watch this process and it really delights me. You have no idea how it thrills my heart. I love to see myself reflected in my children. This causes them to be really happy and fulfilled.

I love to see my joy breaking through in you. You are learning to rejoice in me, even when things seem really tough. I have been good to you, haven't I?

27

People

———— o ————

Do you know what I like to give you? What you have been most afraid of – people. You see, I love people. I draw my children together in genuine unity. You can be thankful for the friends I have given you. **I want to give you relationships in which you can know my love and unity.** I am present in a very special way among those who love me. I have many more people to give you in the coming years. You can show how much I care for those I bring across your path. You can speak my word into their lives. Others I will bring into your experience as ambassadors of my love to you.

Sometimes others attack and hurt you. I don't want this. But I forgive you when you hurt others, don't I? And I forgive them when they hurt you. I want *you* to forgive them. I won't forgive you if you refuse to forgive others. When you forgive, **I am present to heal the hurts inflicted on you by others.**

Do you remember when it seemed everybody turned against you? You thought the enemy was working through everyone. You hardly knew which way to turn, did you? So you turned to me and I saw you through. I provided for you, precious child. Those past hurts do not seem nearly as significant now, do they? I am still undoing their effects so you can walk in greater liberty.

I like the way you are learning to have real faith about the future, to expect good things. You are not so afraid of the people you meet and the way in which you have to relate to them. This is good, real evidence of my work. You have been able to trust me this far; so trust me for the future.

28

Every Detail

—— o ——

My dear child, I know how many hairs you have on your head. If such a minor detail is known to me, don't you think that more important things about you interest me? You have often thought that I am not concerned about small details because I'm so busy looking after everybody else.

When my Spirit comes to dwell in one of my children, every thought, problem or need is of personal concern to me. This is why you can ask me for anything in the name of Jesus and I will give it to you. It doesn't have to be a big need, but any little thing that worries you.

Some people ridicule those who learn to trust me for little things. They suggest I couldn't be concerned with petty matters. But they are wrong. My love for you is such that I don't regard anything as petty. **If you regard something as important enough to pray about, I regard it as important enough to answer!** Some don't receive because they don't ask. They could receive so much more from me if they only trusted me for small matters.

Don't listen to those who laugh at you because of the way you depend on me. I love you, child. I love to do things for you. I won't allow you to be idle. I won't do for you what you are supposed to do yourself. I am teaching you to be a responsible disciple.

You and I have a love relationship. **Just as you love doing things for me, so I love doing things for you.** It has taken ages for you to appreciate this. You used to be surprised when I did anything for you! Now you are beginning to see the point. You and I can live together in love every day.

29

I Lead You Step by Step

———— o ————

My dear child, sometimes I have asked you to do difficult things. At least, they seemed difficult at first and so you were reluctant to respond. Trust me, do what I say and later you will understand my wisdom.

If I had shown you the whole picture at the beginning, you would have tried to produce the end result in your own way, instead of letting me lead you step by step. On other occasions, if I had shown you where I was leading you, you would have refused through fear. **I work in your heart to prepare you for what lies ahead, changing your mind and desires.** As my will unfolds, you are prepared to accept the next step. Then, when you come to the end of the process, you have a great sense of fulfilment because you know you have done what I asked.

When you look back over this whole process, you marvel at how much I have actually done within you. This sense of fulfilment in knowing you have obeyed me and completed my purpose is my precious gift to you, my child. Sometimes you wonder whether you got everything right. Time and time again I assure you, 'That is good, my child. You have done what I asked.' Even before I send you, I know what you will say and do. I take all that into account.

You get all hot and bothered about things when you listen to the enemy who tries to give you a false sense of failure. Don't allow him to do this. I enjoy what I am doing in you now, despite the fact that sometimes you flounder. **I will enjoy leading you to a further stage of maturity, growth, development, fruitfulness and glory!**

I will enjoy each stage along the path. As far as I am concerned, the whole process is to be an enjoyable one. I don't place false expectations on you. I know what I can expect of you at every stage along the way. What I ask of you now, you are able to fulfil now. A little while ago that would not have been possible, but I have prepared you. My timing is always perfect.

30

Don't Worry About the Future

———— o ————

The future is going to be exciting, child. You don't
have to know the details. Many of my children want
to know everything that is going to happen to them. I can
understand their concern, but I want them to trust me
and be content that my word is a lamp for their feet. I will
take care of their tomorrows. If they obey me step by
step, I will look after them.

**Take no thought for tomorrow. Each day has enough
cares of its own.** The way I programme your life means
that each day will have enough for you to contend with;
but if you take other burdens about the future on yourself, you will carry a load too heavy for you. Then you
will begin to feel unable to cope.

If you can't deal with what is happening now, you
won't have much motivation to allow me to lead you
on. So it is very important for you to obey me by not
worrying about the future.

When I speak to my children to give them direction, I
do so in a variety of ways, once even through a donkey! I
always ensure they hear me.

I know how to speak to every one of my children. Why
should I speak in ways you can't hear?

Sometimes I have to listen to the frustration of those who think I have forgotten them. They have heard nothing more from me because they need to obey what I have already said. When people don't like what I say, they wait for me to say something else. No wonder they get stuck!

But you are not like that, child. **You hear my voice.** You are learning to discern the difference between my will and the spoiling tactics of the enemy. That's good, because I don't want him to distract you.

My sheep know my voice and follow me. You are one of my sheep, child. You know my voice and I rejoice that your heart is mine and that you want to follow me.

31

All of Me

—— o ——

My dear child, how much of me do you possess? **All of me.** You wonder how you could possess all the love of your God, for I have so many others to love as well. But I don't love anybody the way I love you. My love for you is utterly unique.

A human mother and father may have several children, yet love each one with all their hearts. They won't divide their love into portions, giving one part to each child.

I don't divide my love into millions of segments and say to you, 'Here, my child, have one small portion of my love.' No, I give you all of my love. I give you all of myself; I love to live in you by the power of my Spirit. Isn't this wonderful?

I speak many truths into your heart to show you how precious you are to me. Live in the fullness of the glorious inheritance you have through Jesus.

32

All of You

———— o ————

I have another question to ask you. How much of you belongs to me? Everything. **All of you.** You are mine for ever.

I have paid the price for you, haven't I? I didn't purchase part of you with my Son's blood. I purchased the whole of you because I wanted every part of you. So you really are my property, child.

How much of you do I possess in practice? I know every part of you belongs to me, but do you really surrender every part of yourself? Do you still want your own plans and purposes, instead of mine? You know the answers, child. **But just as I am encouraging you to take possession of every part of me, so I am taking possession of every part of you.**

With the blood of my Son I purchased the freehold of your life and I have entered in to take possession of every part of my property. Yes, my child, every part.

I want all of you, not part of you, in heaven. So I am taking possession of what is rightfully mine. Most of the time you enjoy this and co-operate with me, but sometimes, child, you hesitate, don't you? You like the idea of belonging to me completely, but you don't always want to face the practical implications of this, especially when I ask you to do something you don't want to do. I am patient with you at such times. **When you acknowledge that what is mine is mine, then all conflict raging within you will cease!** You will be at peace again. Have you noticed that the more I have possession of you in practice, the happier you are? Do you know why? Every part of you that I take possession of becomes filled with my life, love, joy, peace and power. Why withhold anything from me then, child?

Some try to hold on to their money. They are afraid to let me use it because they think I will take it all from them. They don't believe that whatever is given to me, I measure back abundantly. So if they don't let me have their money, they miss an area of my abundance. Sad, isn't it?

Are you glad I have been patient with you, child? Have you noticed, beloved one, that **the more you let me possess you, the more of me you possess**?

33

I Am Merciful

——— o ———

My dear child, I am merciful: slow to anger and quick to love. You are a branch of the true Vine, Jesus. In my love I prune *every* branch to make each one more fruitful. When I apply my pruning knife to your life, I cut away the superficial.

I have not allowed unrefined parts of your life to interfere with our relationship, or with what you have been able to receive from me. This is an aspect of my mercy for which you need to be thankful.

You wonder how I could have blessed you so much when you have doubted me, questioned my love, disbelieved my word and promises. In my mercy I deal with these things so that the quality of our relationship will be enhanced. **I don't try to deal with everything that needs to be corrected all at once.** I maintain my steadfast love to you despite all these things.

34

True Liberty

———— o ————

Sometimes you experience liberty when you focus on me with praise, only to return to your struggles afterwards. I want you to know liberation which lasts. You are still unaware of many of the things I need to deal with. My mercy will remain new to you every day so that your fellowship with me will not be hindered while I am dealing with you.

Some people give an impression that everything is fine and such a process is not needed in their lives! How foolish and deceived they are.

Most of the pain and fear of the refining process is only in your attitude. When I do the work, it is gentle, isn't it? It is loving, tender and gracious. This is the nature of my heart.

So don't hide your need in praise. Don't pretend everything is fine when it isn't. Trust in my mercy to deal lovingly with you, and encourage others by assuring them I am merciful.

Be very thankful when others express my tenderness and loving forgiveness, when they are compassionate and show the understanding that comes from my heart. You need to pray, my child, that more people will reveal the true nature of my heart, not in harsh judgment, but in tender care.

I am always merciful to those who fear me and to those who are concerned to walk in my ways. Because I am rich in mercy, I have made you alive with Christ. I want you to be rich in mercy, too. **You are merciful by nature, child, because Jesus lives in you.**

35

When I Forgive, I Forget

— ○ —

My dear child, *everybody* needs to be loved. They need to know that I accept and approve of them. You can be an ambassador of this truth to many other people when you believe that I have forgiven and accepted you.

When I forgive, I forget. **Through Jesus' sacrifice your sin is put away from you, and from me, for ever.** So when I look at you today, I don't see you in the light of your past sins and failures. As far as I am concerned, those things no longer exist. It is as if they never were.

Still, you sometimes feel condemned by your past. On one level you accept that I have forgiven you, but on another you don't believe that my forgiveness could be so thorough and so easily obtained. You find it hard to see that I will never hold these things against you. I want to assure you now of the real nature of my forgiveness.

I honour the sacrifice of my Son. **So I forgive you completely.** He suffered the punishment you deserve. You are free from guilt, child, because I have forgiven you. You are free from condemnation because you belong to me.

36

Forgive

—— o ——

As I have forgiven you, so I want you to forgive others.
Forgive those who have wronged you. Forgive
those who have denied you love, or have suffocated you
with it. Forgive those who have brought condemnation
upon you. Forgive as I have forgiven you.

Every time you forgive, fresh resources of my love will
be released in you. **Your heart will be kept tender with
my love.**

The more you understand my heart, the more you will
appreciate how much it grieves me when you don't
forgive. I have shown you such mercy that it offends me
if you are ever unmerciful. But it causes me joy when you
forgive. I love to see myself expressed in you.

37

The Fight

———— o ————

A group of children were playing together. Their game became more and more boisterous. Before long, tempers became frayed and an argument started. Each thought he was right and refused to yield ground to the others. When they returned home, each child looked battered and bruised.

'Just like children – always arguing!' said one mother.

'You wretched child, look at the state of you,' said another.

'I hope you gave as good as you got,' said one father.

'Don't let anyone get the better of you,' said another.

Then one wise father said, 'Child, forgive.'

38

Love is Patient

———— ° ————

My dear child, I have had to be patient with you and **I want you to be patient with others**. You're not always, are you?

Just as I have to make room for your mistakes, so you have to be tolerant towards others without judging or condemning them. I have to be patient with you while you learn; so you have to be patient with them while they learn. You are more patient than you used to be, aren't you? But I think you notice some room for improvement!

You know, **love is not proud.** Pride is often the cause of your impatience. You think others ought to do things as you do them, and see things as you see them.

I give you revelation, child. You must be patient with those who have not received the same revelation. Sometimes they judge you, don't they? But don't judge them in return. Be patient with them.

39

Love Does Not Boast

——— o ———

You can boast about me, child, but not about yourself.
Love does not boast. Everything I give you is a gift of
grace. Everything I do through you is the fruit of my
Spirit. All these things are done for my glory and not for
your self-esteem.

Never envy what I do in others. I do quite enough in
you to keep you well occupied! So don't be jealous of the
way I use others, my call on their lives or the gifts they
have received.

40

Love is Kind

———— o ————

Shall I tell you something that really distresses me? I have a number of children who talk about my love, but they are very rude to others. They take them for granted, make them feel small or even ridicule them. **Love is not rude.**

Don't be rude, child. You know, one small piece of rudeness can ruin your witness in somebody's eyes.

It is better to be kind because **love is kind.** I have never been rude to you, have I? If I had wanted to, I could certainly have said some rude things about you; but it's not my nature. I could have scorned, mocked and criticised you if I had been like some people; but I am not. I am like myself.

Instead of being easily roused to anger, I am merciful, patient, loving and kind. Because my love lives in you, don't be easily angered either, even when people do foolish things.

41

Love Covers Sins Instead of Exposing Them

———— o ————

My love keeps no record of wrongs. I don't keep a record of what I have forgiven. I am not going to produce a catalogue of sins and hold it in front of you, even on the day of judgment. I don't want to remember them. I am only thankful that they are covered by the blood of my Son and no longer exist in my sight. I like to look on righteousness, not sin. On the day Jesus returns, you will stand guiltless before me with others who belong to me.

Another thing that distresses me, child, is seeing people delighting in evil. Some want to join others in their sin. Others delight in uncovering evil. When they do, they make a meal of it. They want to expose their brothers and tell others of their sins. They even claim that they are doing something godly to purify the Body of Christ. I think their actions are despicable. They would not want me to uncover all their sins and parade them in public.

The measure anyone gives is the measure they get back. When people gossip and expose the sins of others, it is only a question of time before their own sins are exposed, unless of course they repent. I hate such actions because really those children of mine are rejoicing in what is evil. They are taking every advantage of it. True love is saddened and grieved at discovering evil.

Love covers a multitude of sins. It does not expose them. I want you and all my children to rejoice in the truth, not in what is evil. I want you to delight in those who do my will and be thankful for every expression of my life you see in others.

Love always protects. So if you love your brother, you will always protect him. You will never expose and criticise him before others, or listen to criticism of him from others. Your love of others will always protect them. My father-love for you always protects you.

I planted my love in you so that you can always protect those whom you love. My love does wrong to no one. Others will value my love in you when they see that protective quality being expressed.

42

My Sin Record

———— ° ————

43

Your Sin Record

—— o ——

(Once you have been forgiven)

44

Love Never Fails

———— o ————

Love always trusts. Yes, always. If you love me you will always trust me. I want you to prove trustworthy to others.

My love always hopes. This means you can look to the future with positive attitudes, knowing that my promises will be fulfilled. I speak of future events with as much certainty as if they had already taken place.

Don't give up. Persevere, holding on to my word with an honest and good heart. Believe the promises I give you and continue in the glorious hope to which you are called.

You are going to see me face to face, child. You are going to have a new resurrection body. You will live in glory with me. This is your hope.

Love never fails. I will bring you to the fulfilment of all these aspects of your hope. I will not fail you, and I don't want you to fail others. Honour your word to them, just as I honour my word to you.

My love will never pass away. Do you realise, my child, my love for you will never end? And neither will your love for me!

45

Trusting Others

—— ○ ——

My dear child, I know you find the whole business of trusting people confusing. Others are only trustworthy when they abide in my love. **I can trust you when you abide in my love.** I know then that you will fulfil my purpose and do what I say.

I am not asking you to be foolish. Be wise as a serpent and innocent as a dove.

You know by the witness of my Spirit within you when people are not trustworthy, just as Jesus did. He didn't put his confidence in man. So my Spirit will give you the witness, child, of when it is safe to trust people and when you need to be wary of them.

Jesus didn't entrust himself to any man. You must love those you doubt are trustworthy, like he did. But don't make yourself vulnerable to them. It is dangerous to be vulnerable to critical, strong-willed, independent people. They are not to be trusted. They will hurt you and cause unnecessary damage in your life.

Put your confidence in me, my child. I will always give you the relationships you need where you can share your heart with others and it will be safe. Those with whom it is safe are those who abide in my love. Trust me. **I will show you how to love each person I put before you.**

46

I Have Chosen You

——— o ———

I call you 'child' because this is what you are: my child. I have called you by name and made you mine by my decision and choice. You have responded to my love, but I took the initiative.

This is still a wonder to you, isn't it? **My love for you is not sentiment. It produces positive results in your life.** You are no longer the person you were. You are a new creation, a child of my grace. I give to you because I have chosen to do so.

Sometimes, my dear child, you feel ashamed because you know you do not measure up to what I want. So you are reluctant to draw near to me in case I reprimand you. And yet **when you do turn to me, you are always met with love, never with harshness.** Have I ever given up on you? Have I ever rejected you, or turned away because you were in disfavour with me? No, my child. I maintain my love to you. It is a steadfast, sure and certain love that will never fail.

Yes, there are times when I have needed to discipline you. There are times when you have not known the closeness of my presence because you have chosen to walk in your ways, and not mine. But I have never withdrawn myself from you. I am with you always, as I promised.

47

I Discipline in Love

———— o ————

My dear child, I discipline in love. But you must understand that my purpose is not always to discipline you. I only do this when necessary. I much prefer to encourage rather than discipline.

I discipline you only when you have been really sinful and rebellious, doing deliberately what I told you not to do. You have stubbornly refused to repent. Then I have had to make you aware that I am the holy God; I am your Lord and you must not treat me or my word lightly.

But when you think back through your life since I became your Lord, there have been very few occasions like that. I very seldom need to punish you and, even when I do, I only take measures that are absolutely necessary to break you of your stubborn self-will and bring you back to obedience to me. **Any loving father punishes his child when necessary.**

Do you realise, my child, that if you are seeking first my Kingdom and righteousness, I certainly will not have any cause to punish you? Instead, my promise is that everything will be added to you, which is totally the opposite. You usually realise when you are at fault and I can easily correct you. When things are not right between us, my Holy Spirit makes you feel uncomfortable. Usually you take notice of what I say, even though it may take a little time. Sometimes the flow of blessing in your life dries up for a while. This is not punishment, but discipline to bring you back to the place where I want you to be.

I only exert pressure on your life when it is for your own good. In all things I am working for your good. I **redeem the testing times and turn them to my advantage and yours.** You don't always appreciate that at the time, do you?

48

I Encourage Your Faith

——— o ———

My dear child, the trying times build and encourage your faith for they teach you how to rely on me. I prove that I will never fail you or leave you, no matter what the situation.

Sometimes there are stubborn problems in your life; it seems that no matter how much you pray about them, they persist. But I am the God of perfect timing. I know precisely when and how to meet with you. Have you noticed how many times you have been in the right place at the right time to hear a particular message, and my Spirit has moved in a way especially relevant for you? These things are not coincidental. They are not accidents. They are evidence of the way in which I plan the details of your life.

I want to lead you and provide for you, but you don't always listen to what I say. I give you a simple command and you question whether you are able to hear my voice so distinctly. Do you think I want to make it hard for you to hear me? Why should I do that? I know how to speak to you, and I am teaching you to recognise my voice.

Faith comes from hearing me. But how many times have I spoken to you and you have not heeded what I said? Later you have thought, 'That must have been the Holy Spirit!' I want you to realise, my child, that **you do hear my voice.**

I don't nag at you like the enemy does. That persistent nagging never comes from me. I gently speak my word to your heart. The enemy shouts at you and tries to drown out my voice. You don't have to listen to his shouts; listen to my still, small voice.

49

You Can Do What I Ask

—— o ——

It is easier for me to hear you than for you to hear me. So why think I don't listen to your prayers? Do you think I am too busy? Or do you imagine you are not sufficiently important for me to take notice of you? Could anyone be more important to me than one of my children, whom I have adopted for myself?

I don't know of anyone more important than you! Does that surprise you? Well, it shouldn't, my child.

You see, I consider each of my children important. One is not more important than another to me, because I love each one equally. So stop thinking you are un-important. I don't like it when you think you are of little significance.

I want to do big things *in* you. I want to do big things *with* you. You find that hard to believe, don't you? You know why? You are afraid of failing me. You fear that you will not hear me correctly, or if you do, you will get it wrong.

Don't you think I know my business, child? If I am the Lord Almighty, would I ask you to do something that would cause you to fail? I am not like that. **I want to see my children succeed.** I wouldn't ask you to do anything too hard for you; I would choose someone else instead.

You see, I am the finest personnel officer; I always appoint the right person for the right job.

Often your first reaction is to think that what I ask of you is impossible, because you know these things could not be accomplished with your natural resources. But whatever I ask of you is possible because I have given you my Spirit. **Everything is possible if you believe.** You believe me, don't you, child?

I know your capabilities. Don't think I only look at you as having potential. The thing I like about you is that you are realised potential. I can see the fruit I have produced in your life. This gives me glory! Yes, child, you give me glory!

50

I Never Despair of You

—— o ——

My dear child, have you noticed how tender my love is for you? So why fear punishment from me? Why fear you will meet with my disapproval if you fail? At times you are disappointed with yourself, child. But I have never despaired of you. I know when you are going to fail.

It is true that I have disapproved of some of the things you have done and said, but **I don't disapprove of you.** You are too precious to me. Sometimes you feel out of sorts spiritually, emotionally or even physically. Almost your first thought is to ask yourself what you have done to cause my disapproval. Oh, my child, this is no way to live.

You can be out of sorts with yourself, but this doesn't mean you are out of sorts with me. In fact, usually when you are like that, I am there with you, waiting for you to turn to me and receive my tender love. When you do, you realise you have been worrying about nothing.

51

My Love Makes You Clean

——— o ———

My dear child, I want to enfold you in my arms of love. I draw you close to me. It is my pleasure. Would I have called and chosen you unless I wanted you? When you held back in fear, I gently persisted. If I hadn't, you would have missed great blessing, wouldn't you? There is no part of your life, my child, that is not a concern to me. I have promised to sanctify you through and through; spirit, soul and body. I will fulfil that purpose.

My love makes you feel clean. I speak my word of forgiveness to you and you feel clean. I touch your life with my Spirit and you feel clean. I heal you and you feel clean. **Whenever you receive from me it has this cleansing effect on you.**

When you fear, you feel unclean. You cower away, fearing that the problem is in you. You think you are so unclean that you cannot receive my love, blessing and healing.

I want you to *be* clean, *feel* clean and *appear* clean because you radiate my holy life. I can't give you anything unclean. The fruit produced in your life by my Spirit is good, pure and wholesome.

52

I Enjoy You

—— o ——

I enjoy you, child. I enjoy knowing you. I enjoy loving you. I enjoy being with you. I enjoy giving to you. I enjoy hearing from you. I enjoy your praises. I am in love with you, child.

53

Enjoy Being You

———— o ————

There are many ways in which I have needed to come deep into your life to liberate you from fear of displeasing me. This is fear of yourself, really. You have been very afraid of yourself, haven't you, child? Can you see the work I am doing in you now, to liberate you from that fear? How can you enjoy being you if you are afraid of yourself?

Precious child, thank you for letting me love you. Thank you for letting me come deep into those secret places. You don't understand all that I am doing in you. That doesn't matter. It's enough to know I understand you, that I heal you and make you whole.

Your days of hiding from me are over, aren't they? You don't need to do that any more, do you? Oh, my dear, dear child. There have been many times when I have longed to give to you, but you have kept yourself out of my reach. How it pleases me that you no longer do that. Not only do you allow me to touch your life with my love but you really want me to. This is a sign of great change in you.

You are beginning to trust my love, aren't you, child? You are beginning to see that there is no need to fear. I always have your best interests at heart, and every touch of my Spirit of love is making you more holy.

I love you, child. There is a sweetness about my peace, isn't there? Have you noticed that you are now able to cope with situations which previously would have caused turmoil within you? This is because you are beginning to see things my way. You have begun to listen to my voice rather than the enemy. In a very gentle way I have moved in your heart so that you yield more fully to me than before. That's good. You can encourage others to open themselves to me, to come deeply into the arms of my love, to receive from me.

54

Receive and Give

— o —

My dear child, do you remember when you felt you had to be continually active for me? It made you satisfied that you were doing something for me; but what was the fruit of it all? You will be more fruitful if you abide in me and I in you.

Don't try to impress me or others with your activity or godliness. You are learning the lesson slowly that **when you receive from me, you become more like me.** It has taken you a long time to appreciate that, but I am glad you know it now.

Would you like to be really useful for me? Would you like to know what would really please me, and how you could glorify me? Let me love you, and then love will pour out of you. Let me give to you, and my gifts will pour through you. It is very simple really, isn't it, my child?

Have you noticed that water keeps falling over a waterfall? It never goes upwards. My love keeps falling on you. It is just like that waterfall. I cannot stop it falling on you. It cannot go upwards and leave you. It can only descend on you. Stand under the waterfall of my love, and receive!

55

I Am Gracious

—— o ——

My dear child, I am the Lord who gives and gives and gives. So you are the child who has to receive and receive and receive. I never come to the end of my giving. Even when you think I could give you no more, I shower further blessings on you.

You judge yourself more harshly than I judge you. According to your assessment, you deserve nothing. This would be true except for my grace.

You know, there are few who really understand my grace. Many preach and talk about it. They concentrate on the fact that people are not worthy to receive from me. But I concentrate on the fact that I am always willing to give. That seems much more helpful!

I know my favour is unmerited, but the emphasis needs to be on my favour. I love to give, child. I am never slow to give when the circumstances are right. Isn't that what I promised through Jesus? He says, **'Everyone who asks receives.'** This is true. Have you noticed that often you have not received because you have been reluctant to ask? When you ask and receive, you wish you had asked for much more and received much earlier. Sweet child, you are learning. That is the important thing.

56

Child of My Grace

——— o ———

You are still surprised when I give to you, my child. You consider that I am bound to give you certain things because I am committed to you. But you only expect the minimum to enable you to do my will.

You don't understand that I want to do beautiful things for you because I love you. You don't think you are very beautiful, do you? I am not talking about physical attraction, but about the person you believe yourself to be. You often wonder why I want to satisfy the desires of your heart.

You are a child of my grace. I fulfil the desire of my heart when I lavish my gifts freely on you. I love it when you pray to me with faith and expect me to answer. I love it when you are not overcome by the need but look to me, knowing I will supply because of my grace. I love that, child.

You wonder whether the desires of your heart are the same as mine. Well, consider this. Where did those desires come from? Selfish desires clearly come from you. But where do those other desires come from? Am I not able to form desires in your heart? Doesn't my Spirit create new desires in you?

57

I Am Generous

——— o ———

I want you to understand my grace more fully, so you can be gracious to others. **I am generous, the God of abundance.** I give far more than the minimum.

I don't want you to give me the minimum, but the maximum. Don't clock in or out for prayer or loving others. You are my child all the time. Those who are generous are always willing to give, no matter the cost, even if nothing can be obtained in return.

My child, sometimes you hold back from giving because you are afraid, thinking others would not want to receive from you. Sometimes you imagine you would spoil what I want to do. You are mistaken. I am able to work through you, expressing my generosity and love.

Your selfishness has annoyed you, hasn't it? My child, it is a matter of the heart, isn't it? **I am ready to make you generous if this is what you want.** I will keep giving to you, as long as you keep giving to others. The measure you give will be the measure you receive: good measure, pressed down, shaken together, running over.

I am the God of grace and I will give and give and give and give and give, even to you!

58

The Old Car

———— o ————

The young man had lost count of the number of times he had had to fix his old car. One thing after another went wrong and needed attention. Yet what was the alternative? A new car was beyond his means. He could see no way in which to buy one. So he would have to make do with the old, patching it up as best he could—unless someone gave him what he could never afford himself!

59

The Way of Love

——— o ———

When you face difficult decisions and are not sure which way to turn, you can always ask yourself what Jesus would do. **He would always choose the way of love.** You will find that when you face such dilemmas, it will be obvious to you which of the alternatives before you is the way of love.

It is tempting to avoid this way because of the cost. Sometimes, people don't want to get involved or take on responsibility. But no one who lets himself be distracted from the work I planned for him is fit for my Kingdom. Whoever loves me will obey my commands. This means they will choose to love others as I have loved them. You have found the cost of that, haven't you, child?

Sometimes I've been disappointed in you because you have chosen the selfish way and then tried to convince yourself that this really was the right decision. You have never been very peaceful about it, have you? And peace is not restored until you admit to me, and to yourself, that really you made the wrong decision. But I don't punish you for such mistakes; you punish yourself by losing that beautiful sense of peace. I don't have to take any further measure against you. I wait until you return to the path of love.

60

Love in My Name

——— o ———

When you read about the life of Jesus, you are impressed by the way he loved people, aren't you? Have you noticed that he didn't talk much about love; he did it. He got on with the business of loving. To love with my love is not sentiment, is it?

When I call you to love in my name, telling people that you love them is not enough. You need to listen, serve and give to them; you have to care and pray for them. The way you care for others is a measure of your greatness.

They may simply need you to be with them to give them assurance. At other times you will need to reach into their lives with my power, bringing them healing.

You need love mingled with faith, don't you? Love without faith is insufficient. **You need love expressed in faith, and faith that works through love.**

When you reach out to others in my name, take my compassion and the faith that believes I will change their circumstances and meet their needs. This is what Jesus did, isn't it, child? **He was not content to love people in their need; he met their need.**

61

A Heart of Love

—— o ——

It took some time for you to appreciate that you were really involved with Jesus on the cross. I know you understood quite readily that Jesus died for you. But Jesus took you to the cross with him. You have been crucified with him. It is no longer you that live but he who lives in you. The old selfish life is dead and buried. Now you have a new life. Don't look back on the past; it's gone.

Look forward to the future. **You are a new creation, created in Christ Jesus to do good works.** These do not produce salvation; they are the fruit of your salvation.

Many people do things for me, believing this pleases me. But unless my love is the motivating force behind their actions, they are futile. Apart from me you can do nothing. You believe that, don't you, child?

I have given you a heart of love. Isn't that good? I don't have to keep persuading you to love. It is becoming your nature. You can see why I am pleased with you. In more and more situations you instinctively love, expressing the life of my Kingdom on earth. You are part of the answer to the prayer, aren't you? In *you* my Kingdom is coming and my will is being done on earth, as in heaven.

62

Go in Love

———— o ————

Love has many healing properties. So I want my love to reach where there is fear, hurt and shame.

I see the poor living in hovels, the starving with swollen bellies. My heart reaches out to them and I commission my children to take my love to them. At the same time I see the greed and selfishness in others; my heart is saddened. I see the corruption of those who take for themselves what is intended for the poor, and I am angry.

You live in a world of need, my child. But this does not mean you should be afraid to know my generosity and abundance yourself. I have impressed on you that **the more you receive from me, the more you can give to others.** I have been working in your heart, filling you with my love so that you have the motivation to pour out your life for others. You are to love them as I have loved you.

You are discovering that I give and give and give yet again. This is how you are to love others.

Give in the way I ask. Some I send to the poor and the destitute; some to the rich, to break through their apathy and indolence. I love to go where there is misery. I go in the hearts of those who love me. I go with the hands of those who reach out in my name. I go in the prayers of those who are deeply concerned.

63

I Go in Love

———— o ————

Miracles happen wherever my children go in my name. I love to go among the addicts where there is misery, violence and abuse. **I go in those who pour out their lives for them without holding back because of the cost of such ministry.**

How I desire that more of my children would make themselves available to reach those who are in the depths of misery and futility.

I love to go among the social outcasts, the unwanted and unloved. I love to show them that someone genuinely cares. But I need bodies through whom to work, serve and show the affection that is so needed. I go in the gifts of those who give freely of their substance because they cannot go in person.

I love to go in my children who will show them the way of salvation. I love to go to all these places with my gospel, not just with natural physical help. What has been accomplished if the body is fed but the spirit is left naked; if physical needs are satisfied but sins remain unforgiven?

So I go in those who show my love and concern for spirit, soul and body. When I go in them, all my resources are available to them through the power of my Holy Spirit.

64

I Go in You

———— o ————

I love to work miracles of healing amongst the destitute who look to me as their only doctor or dentist, those for whom I am the only surgeon available. I love to send people of faith who will look to me for their provision in every situation.

I send a people of love who will not mind the cost of declaring my truth, those who will proclaim my word in the face of abuse. They offer my love although they know it may be rejected. Great will be their reward in heaven.

I love to go in those who risk danger to take my gospel to others. I love to go among the oppressed. I love to go into prisons. Wherever there are captives, I want to set them free by the power of my Spirit. I love to go where people recognise their need of me. They want my love, acceptance and forgiveness. Such hearts are fertile soil to receive the seed of my word.

I love to go in you, my child. Oh, you cannot meet *all* this need. Your heart goes out to such people because you share something of my heart. I have seen the desires within you to reach the poor, the lost, the naked and the blind. I rejoice in your genuine compassion.

I delight when I hear you say, 'Oh Lord, I am ready to go if you will send me.' I love to see my children available to me like that. But I can't send you everywhere, child. I have chosen a particular ministry for you. I direct the footsteps of all who yield their lives to me. **I use you in the most effective way I can** so that many will be touched by my love. My wisdom exceeds yours in this.

65

The Right Time

—— ○ ——

The boy looked up at the mountain. It seemed to tower above him so high, grand and immovable.

'Can I climb this mountain?' he asked his father.

'Why should you want to do that?' came the reply. 'You are too young. You don't understand how dangerous it is.'

The boy was disappointed.

As the years passed, he looked often at this mountain, longing for the time when he would be old enough to make the climb alone. It was a challenge which had to be faced.

One day he set out and began to walk on the lower slopes. It wasn't long before he found the going too hard and had to return home, feeling defeated. His dream was still unfulfilled.

'Why are you looking so discouraged?' asked his father.

'I tried to climb the mountain,' the boy answered. 'But I didn't get very far.'

The father put his arm around his son. 'Didn't I tell you, boy, such high mountains are dangerous and difficult to climb? The task is far too great for someone your age.'

'But I want to climb the mountain,' the boy persisted.

'Then you shall,' said the father, 'but not yet. When the time is right I will guide you, and you will climb the mountain with me. Wait until the time is right, son.'

66

Spread My Love

——— o ———

What matters to me, my child, is that you **spread my love everywhere I lead you.** Give time to those who need time, love to those who need love, money to those who need money, help to those who need help. In all these ways, my child, you will be able to spread my love around you. There is so much need and so few who are willing to face the cost of meeting it.

Do men blame me for the sinfulness of men's hearts, I, who am holy and righteous? Do they blame me for the corruption and abuse of freedom? Do they blame me that men choose to hate instead of love, to be corrupt instead of generous?

I am working in the lives of millions all over the world to right the wrongs that have been brought about by men's selfishness. So my child, I am thankful that your heart is mine and that you are willing to go for me wherever I send you, and do for me whatever I ask of you. Don't be surprised, therefore, if I lavish my love upon you. **For as you give me all you have to give, so I give you all I have to give.**

67

My Kingdom of Love

———— o ————

My dear child, it has been my good pleasure to give you my Kingdom. This is not a place. It is my sovereign reign as King in your life. My Kingdom is within you: I have planted it like a seed in your heart. Contained within that seed is the total life of my Kingdom, all the riches and resources that can develop within you. My Kingdom reflects the nature of the King who rules over it.

My Kingdom is not a matter of talk but of power. This power is not merely a spiritual dynamic that produces miracles; it is revealed in love. Even though you can manifest spiritual gifts, have great faith and demonstrate my power, all these things are worth nothing without love.

My Kingdom is righteousness, peace and joy in the Holy Spirit. When you follow the leading of my Spirit you walk in righteousness, peace and joy. I never lead you to love in wrong ways, by indulging yourself in lust or greed. When people walk in unrighteousness, they lose their peace and joy. **You are an ambassador of my Kingdom of love and power.** I want to express my sovereign reign more fully in your life.

68

You Are Filled With My Power

———— o ————

My dear child, because I am almighty, my Kingdom is a reign of power. Some people wrongly try to separate my love and power; but they belong together.

When Jesus loved people, he reached out with my power. He healed the sick, cleansed the lepers and cast out demons. He even raised the dead on occasions. He performed miracles, turning water into wine, feeding multitudes with a boy's picnic, stilling the raging storm. He even obtained money from a fish.

All these things demonstrate that my love is supernatural. And I express this love through people like you!

My Holy Spirit is supernatural and brings both love and power into your life; he enables you to live the life of my Kingdom. Jesus said, 'You will receive power when the Holy Spirit comes on you.'

So, my child, I want you to realise that you are filled with power. Yes, you really are. You rarely feel full of power, do you? Nevertheless, all the resources of my supernatural power are available to you, and are at work within you.

I have given you power to use in your own life. How can you really move in faith and love unless you learn to use those supernatural resources for yourself? You need to know that I will answer your prayer, that I will heal you when you are sick and provide for you when you are in need.

Those who try to love and serve me without making use of the power I put within them are wasting my resources. They don't listen to my Spirit telling them to use the power and authority I have already given them.

I also give you my supernatural power to enable you to minister to others. Show them how to reach out to me to see their needs met. This is what I want.

I send you into the world in Jesus' name to be like him, and to take his power, love, joy, peace and forgiveness into every situation.

I am glad you see this, child. If you take my love without the power, you can only do half the job.

69

My Power in Love

———— o ————

To take my power without love is no use, either. You may see mighty things happening, but those you help are left with no revelation in their hearts of my love and acceptance.

I have been doing a thorough work in you, my child, teaching you more of who I am and how I work in the lives of my children. I want you to have a balanced ministry. That is a popular saying. Many who talk in this way have unbalanced ministries themselves. They demonstrate little of my power and are weak in supernatural gifts. The only person with a really balanced ministry is Jesus. So I want you to be like him and minister in his love *and* power.

My child, every dimension of my Spirit can flow out of your ministry. **Please don't limit me, but remember to minister my power in love.**

I've taught you much about my gentleness and tenderness. I never want you to lose sight of these qualities. Jesus was gentle and humble in heart, but he still ministered with great power. Some think they will only demonstrate power if they do so loudly and aggressively. But there is great strength in gentleness. Reach out with my supernatural power, knowing my tender touch upon your heart as you do so. You need compassion as well as authority.

70

Not by Might or Power

——— o ———

You know, my child, many of my children say they need more power. But really they need love to release the power I have already given them. The only thing that counts is faith working through love.

Those who want more power to perform spectacular signs and wonders often want to do something really impressive. They think this will give me glory and will be a great example to other people. Of course, it will also enable them to be held in high esteem!

There are times when I do choose to work like that, but often my powerful works are done quietly and unobtrusively. Very few of them are public spectacles. **I will be glorified in every act I perform, and others will not steal the glory from me.**

When people testify to what I've done in their lives, this encourages some to respond to the gospel of my Kingdom. Others don't want to believe, despite the great and powerful signs of which they hear. Many refused to believe Jesus despite the great miracles he performed. The world will not be won by extraordinary signs. In the wilderness, the devil wanted Jesus to do something spectacular to grip people's attention. Jesus refused to be seduced by such an idea.

Don't seek glory for yourself, for I cannot entrust demonstrations of my power to those who will become self-centred and conceited. Their pride gives the impression they are the ones responsible for such miracles. My child, walk in love, faith and power, with the humility and gentleness of Jesus.

71

I Love Working Miracles

———— o ————

Every day I am a miracle-working God. Miracles are not occasional events. I do them daily all over the world.

I like working miracles in you. Ask me for one whenever you have need. If you don't have faith for a miracle, ask me to inspire such faith within you. I am *your* miracle-working God.

72

Let Me Carry the Burden

———— o ————

You have felt defeated when you have tried to take my power to people in great need, those who are crippled and deformed, the blind and those in the depths of depression. You haven't been able to meet their need, have you? You have felt a failure because you know I am almighty and can heal such people. You thought that if you were a better Christian, you would be able to do such things in my name; for if Jesus came into those situations in person, the people would be instantly healed.

But remember this, my child; Jesus didn't heal every sick person when he was on earth. He healed all who *came to him in faith*. This is still the principle by which I work.

Don't take the burden upon yourself. I want to increase your faith and your willingness to see how I can use you. I want you to take my love and power to those desperately needy people. But I don't ask you to take their burdens upon yourself. **I am the one who carries their burdens.** If you go to them in my name, child, then I will always give you the right words to say, the right prayer to pray, and you will see change in their lives. You will not always see dramatic results, however.

It may be that the total need is not met instantly; I don't promise that all the answers to your prayers will be in the form of instantaneous miracles. No, my child, I want to take this false burden of guilt from you.

Go into every situation knowing that you are an instrument of my love and power. You will be fruitful on every occasion if you remember this. Don't set false expectations as your standard. In every situation, **listen to the voice of my Spirit** so that I can make clear to you what I intend to do. You only have to be faithful in doing what I ask you.

Sometimes I use a number of people to minister to one of my children. Each person I send has a distinctive part to play. So take heed to what I say, my child. Then you will not leave with a false sense of condemnation that you are powerless to help. You are not powerless. You can take the resources of my love and power in the way that I teach you.

Of course, my beloved, sometimes you will see mighty things. Give me all the glory for these. But consider this. When you go into a situation and obey the voice of my Spirit, bringing about a small but necessary change in a person, that obedience is as important to me as the times when you stepped out in dynamic faith to see a mighty miracle.

You see, my child, I love obedience. It is the expression of your love for me.

73

Loving Difficult People

———— o ————

My dear child, some people are very difficult to love, aren't they? Especially the demanding ones. They are very insecure, with little assurance of my love and acceptance. Their insecurity produces a pattern of manipulation which usually begins in childhood. They don't expect love from people so they have to manipulate. It's very difficult for them to believe anybody loves them for themselves, even me.

I will send you people to love, but they will never be demanding. In fact, that is how you will distinguish those I send from those the enemy puts in your way to sap your resources of love. Those I send come humbly, sensitive to your needs and aware of the nuisance they might be to you.

Demanding people don't mind how much they drain you or how much time they take. No matter what you give them, they always want more. You give them time and they want more time. You give them love and they want more love. You give them money and they want more money.

Such people will waste much of your time if you let them. They will appear to be better when you have spent time and prayed with them; only to be back on your doorstep a few days later, asking you to go through the whole performance again. Instead of teaching these

— 124 —

people to depend on me, you will find that they become dependent on you. They will drain you of all your energy and abuse your willingness to love them.

The way to love manipulative people is by not yielding to their demands. Don't ignore them but love them with my love, not in the way they demand to be loved. This means you must learn to be strong.

You see, manipulative people are very good at accusing Christians, making them feel condemned. They suggest you don't love them enough: 'You don't really care, you don't really want to love me, do you?' Such accusation makes you feel guilty, as if you have failed the test of love completely. You feel you have to go out of your way to show you genuinely love them.

This is yielding to their demands. Manipulation works by creating a sense of false guilt in others. Manipulative people always seem to get their own way, while everybody else adjusts to them.

Love these people, my child, by being strong. Make it very clear that you will not be manipulated by listening to their accusations. I warn you, my child. Such people will not always take kindly to this; they will get angry. They will say that if you don't love them in the way they demand, they will want nothing more to do with you. You will be accused of rejecting them. Remember, I don't accuse my children.

The enemy accuses through other people and even uses scripture to do so. In relationships such as these, there is a spiritual battle. You are not waging war against flesh and blood but against the spiritual principalities and powers. These people are bound. They have no liberty in the Spirit. I love them and want to use you to help them by refusing to yield to their tactics. Manipulative people resent it when others stand up to them, but find a security in those who are prepared to be strong. In their hearts they know this is what they need.

They must repent of their manipulation and accusations. They need to be brought to a true revelation of my love, acceptance and forgiveness, which cannot be earned or manipulated. I *already* love them with a perfect love.

74

Be Really Fruitful

———— o ————

Insecure people don't enjoy a close relationship with me because I won't yield to their demands. They say they love me but you can see the unreality of this by the way they continue to manipulate.

They don't feel my love because they don't believe my love. Do they want to? I mean, really want to. Will they be prepared to submit themselves to me instead of wanting to run their own lives?

Now listen, my child. **I love these people. I want to see my Kingdom firmly established in their lives.** My Kingdom does not work through manipulation. It is expressed through genuine love, righteousness and power. It is planted in them like a seed but is choked by their own selfish desires and the way in which they allow problems to become more important than my Kingdom.

Some people will not let go of their burdens, even though Jesus carried them to the cross. They hold on to their problems as if they are essential to maintain their identity. They talk about surrendering their lives to me while holding back areas for themselves. They say they give their problems to me, but within hours they take them back again. They even suggest that nobody could really meet their need – not even me! They see themselves as unlovable with impossible problems, even for the Creator of the universe. They will tell you that famous men of God have ministered to them and still they are left in their need.

Have you noticed that one manipulative person like this can cause a lot of distress to many of my children? I regard this as a serious problem within my body. Yielding to these manipulative tactics leaves an area of bondage within my body, exhausting and draining my people and deflecting them from my purposes.

Will you heed what I say to you? Will you be strong and stand up to those people in love? When they accuse you, come back to me and let me reassure you so that you don't feel crushed and bruised by what they say. Don't say to yourself, 'I am too weak to stand up to these people.'

My Kingdom is within you, child. My strong love is in your heart and you are able to do what I tell you. So rejoice, because you are not going to be kicked around any more. Your love is not going to be abused or wasted. I am going to put it to the best possible use. I want you to bear *much* fruit.

I am sending you to those who need love and really want to be helped. I need harvesters in my Kingdom, not gleaners! You have made mistakes in the past, haven't you? I don't condemn you for this. The way you acted was full of good intentions; but you can learn from past mistakes, can't you? In future you can be far more fruitful in your loving of people. My love in you is not to be soft-hearted; it is tender, but strong!

75

Give Yourself Time to Receive

———— o ————

It is good that you have these times to hear me speak to you and receive my love. You become so drained and tired, don't you? So many seem to be taking from you. They look to you for wisdom, prayer, ministry, care, service and love. You seem to be giving and giving, just like I do.

I know you receive as you give, but you also need times like this, my child, when you can draw aside with me and do not have to give; you only have to be still and receive. It is good to receive.

You used to feel very guilty about that. Every time you drew apart with me in prayer, you thought you should be giving to me. So prayer became very tiresome for you. After giving to so many others, you then had to pray and give to me. At times your mind was so preoccupied with other people's problems that you wondered where to start.

My child, you need time to receive from me so that then you can give more effectively, even in prayer.

Sometimes you felt so exhausted that you fell asleep while praying, simply because you were relaxing from all your activity. Then you felt guilty and a failure in prayer, didn't you?

Your times of quiet with me are times when I can speak my word into your heart to encourage, refresh and revive you. Then your heart begins to overflow with worship, thanksgiving and praise. Have you noticed that the flow of praise dries up when you are exhausted?

When you have received from me, you can go back into the world ready to give, not resenting the demands made upon you. I am glad, my child, that you are losing that sense of guilt about receiving. Do you remember when you thought you should only receive a little? So many people had given you completely the wrong idea about prayer.

But I have been re-informing you. Let me put it this way, child. What can you give to me that I don't already have? What can I give to you that you need? Well, it is obvious who should be doing the receiving and who should be doing the giving, isn't it?

Your greatest need is to be loved. I am the only one who can meet that need. So relax, my child. Know my love for you. Receive from me and then go out into the world, sharing that love with others who need to receive it.

76

I Heal

———— o ————

My dear child, I am the Lord who heals. You would think everyone would be happy about this, but they're not; far from it! There are those who claim I don't want to heal, others that I have lost the habit! They believe that although I once healed, now I do so no longer. There are even those who become very angry when I do heal, because this offends their theology!

There are those who say I want to heal some, but not others – as if I view the subject with an arbitrary attitude. Others believe I always want to heal.

Some look for reasons why healing doesn't take place; others speak of my sovereign will, which seems an excuse to believe anything!

It's a very confusing situation, isn't it? Yet to me the matter is simple. So, my dear child, I want you to understand what is in my heart concerning healing. **I heal because I love.** I don't want any of my children to be sick and I certainly don't enjoy seeing them suffer.

Have you noticed, child, that when you are in pain you automatically cry out to me? This is instinctive because you know I love you. When anyone is sick they look to those who love them for support and encouragement.

Of course, it is one thing to cry out to me for help; quite another to believe me to heal. But, nevertheless, those who know me turn to me for some kind of help.

It saddens me if they think my only concern is to support them in their need; it seems such a waste of my healing love and power. But, as you know, I don't like to force myself on people. **If they ask for help, I give them help. If they ask for healing, I am ready to heal.**

77

Causes of Sickness

——— o ———

Consider my heart, child. Listen carefully. Where I see any of my children sick, I want to reach out to them in love. I want to speak the word to them which will set them free. I want to deal with the root cause of every sickness, not simply with the symptoms. The weed needs to be pulled out from the root. The situation often seems confused because the person is concerned with the symptoms and I am concerned with the cause.

Sometimes the cause is sin. Habitual sin has produced a pattern of sickness in the person's life. When sin is the cause, repentance brings amazing results.

Sometimes the cause is hereditary or genetic. I am able to free my children from such sickness. They certainly don't inherit illness from me.

Sometimes the cause is demonic. The enemy is a thief and he will steal physical health if he is able to do so. But I have overcome the power of the evil one. So, when my authority is brought to bear on the situation, the sickness has to depart.

Sometimes the cause is stress. Many of my people worry and grow anxious. This has a distressing effect on their bodies. Remember it is not only the physical disease which concerns, me, but what lies behind it. Repeatedly I tell my children not to fear, for this is a device of the enemy. He wants my children to be afraid because he knows the damaging effects of this on their health. I want my children to know my peace in spirit, soul and body. My Spirit can reach the depths of your being to free you from the negative pressures which have produced tension and disease.

My child, there are several other causes because each situation is unique. I deal with my children as individuals because my love for each is personal.

78

I Don't Want You to Be Sick

——— o ———

My dear child, understand that I never want you or any of my children to be sick. It is not my purpose for you – just as sin is not my purpose for you.

However, I allow you to sin and I can even use it in a positive way. I am able to redeem the situation and turn it to good in your life by drawing you to repentance and fresh obedience.

The fact that I am able to use sin by redeeming it does not make it my will for my children. The fact that sin often precedes a major spiritual breakthrough does not mean I want you to sin. Could the holy and righteous God ever want any of his children to sin? Of course not.

However, because of the weaknesses of those I have chosen, I know that inevitably they will sin. So I take this into account in determining how my purposes are to be worked out in each individual's life. When you sin, I don't disinherit you. It is the same with sickness, my child. **I don't want you to be sick,** but I know you can be. Just as you are prone to sin, so you are also prone to sickness.

I don't plan sin for you; neither do I plan sickness. I have to take account of both, however. I work within you in all circumstances for your good. Just as I do not disinherit you when you sin, so the fact you are sick makes no difference to your promised inheritance. I certainly don't condemn you for being sick. You can be sick as a Christian without incurring my disfavour; isn't that a relief? So don't live in any false fear of my disapproval. Rather, rejoice in my love, my care, my provision and healing.

Just as I can use a sinful situation to produce a major spiritual breakthrough, so I am able to use sickness in a refining, even in a creative way.

It is at this point that many misunderstand. Because **I am able to use sickness positively**, they assume that it must have been my will. They even suggest that I caused it deliberately in order to teach my child a lesson. Such an idea is an offence to my love. **Tell people that I am the Lord who heals.**

79

The Sick Woman

—— ○ ——

The woman lay on her sick-bed. 'I've been here so long,' she thought to herself. 'Doesn't anybody really care?'

She appreciated the friends who brought the flowers and the chocolates, and the cards from those who remembered her.

'But do they really care?' she asked herself. She welcomed those who came and prayed with her; they were so well-meaning and wanted the best for her. 'They seem to care,' she thought.

Then one night she saw her Lord in a dream. 'I care,' he said. When she woke, she left her bed of sickness.

80

Jesus Healed

——— o ———

When I became man in Jesus I clearly demonstrated what I thought of sickness by healing all who came to him with faith, and several others besides. When people came to him, he didn't send them away sick, telling them that I was using the situation to refine them, or that it was for their own good. He didn't tell them I was punishing them for their sins. He didn't say they must learn to live with their sickness.

No, **he healed them**. Yes, everyone who turned to him. He did this because he knew this to be my will. He would never go against my will in anything.

And when he went to the cross he dealt with every expression of evil, including sickness. Do you not perceive, my dear child, that I have created human beings with a desire to be well? They only function fully when they are fit.

81

Sickness is Distressing

——— o ———

I can understand that you often feel perplexed about the amount of suffering and sickness that exists in the world. And I know how distressing it is when someone close to you is ill.

Can you imagine how distressing it is to me? Yes, my child, I am deeply disturbed to see those I love in pain, whether emotional, spiritual or physical. My heart is full of love and compassion for the chronically sick, those who are disabled, deformed or mentally ill. I want to reach them with my love; I want to heal and bring peace to their souls and bodies. **It is my will to make them whole.**

If I want to heal, why do so many remain sick? I often have to settle for something less than my best in the lives of my children. I make the most of every situation. I am ready to give, to heal or deliver. I await the right opportunity.

My dear child, nothing makes you more perplexed than being ill. As soon as there is anything physically wrong with you, even a minor stomach ailment, you instinctively know that this is not my purpose for you and you have a great desire to be well again.

I want you to be strong and healthy. I am glad you are learning to resist sickness. When you feel the first symptoms, stand against them. Rebuke them in the name of Jesus. Don't imagine that you have to yield to the sickness.

Everyone needs healing in some way, for no one is perfect. But there are times when particular sicknesses attack and afflict you, making it difficult for you to do what I want. So, of course, I want to restore you. **I am glorified whenever I heal you.**

Some people think I can be glorified in sickness but this is not strictly true. I can be glorified in any of my *children* who are sick, but I am not glorified in the sickness itself. I regard sickness as something evil. You are not expecting to find sickness in heaven, are you? And Jesus has taught you to pray that my Kingdom shall come and my will shall be done on earth as it is in heaven. So of course I want to see people healed.

82

Receive Your Healing

———— o ————

Sometimes you have been afraid to ask me to heal you in case it doesn't happen. This is a trick of the enemy, isn't it? Fear is his weapon, not mine.

Sometimes you have asked only tentatively, hardly daring to believe I would answer. At other times you have grown stronger much more rapidly than you would have expected. On occasions when you need a miracle, I want to give you the faith to believe me for your healing. Nothing is impossible for me, child. You are beginning to believe this for your own life, aren't you?

There is no such thing as an incurable disease as far as I am concerned. **I am able to heal any sickness**. Human fathers and mothers want to help their children; they don't like watching them suffer pain, sickness or fever. This is even more true about me. I hate to see disease in your body. I am always at hand, child. I am listening to your prayer.

But, remember it is not your words that count but what you believe in your heart.

There have been times when it has not been right for me to heal immediately because there have been other things I have needed to sort out in you, especially when there are some relationships that aren't right. It is my policy to wait until you have forgiven; then I can release my healing power within you.

The secret of receiving healing is to believe that I love you so much that I want to give to you. It is a work of my grace. It helps, doesn't it, when you receive a specific word from me, for this encourages faith.

I heal directly and also through others. It is a wonderful thing when you know that your Creator has touched your life and healed you. It doesn't matter much what method I use, does it? It is the sheer wonder of knowing that you have received from me.

You know I am able to heal, and now you believe I am willing to do so. **When you pray, give me time to answer.** Don't be content with a quick prayer and then go rushing back to your activity. My hand is poised ready to bless but you need time to receive the blessing. I have so much to give, and so few give themselves time to receive. Remember, I don't heal only through instantaneous miracles but also through a continual process which I work out in your life.

83

I Hate Sickness

———— o ————

Tell me child, how do you feel about all those sick people who don't receive healing? Doesn't your heart go out to them? Don't you feel love and compassion for them? Well, this is how I feel too. But my love and compassion for them are far greater than yours. You question why more don't receive healing, especially those who appear to be my devoted followers. I know it perplexes you but I can assure you, child, that I am the only one who sees all the factors involved. Every decision I make is just.

I hate sickness and I would not wish it on any of my children. There are times when I use sickness as judgment on rebellious, stiff-necked, disobedient people. My word is clear about this, but it is certainly not my purpose for those who love me.

Sickness is a work of the devil but my power is so much greater than his. I allow the devil a certain amount of scope, but he never has the victory – not in the lives of any of my children. Death for my children is a release from pain and suffering. It is a release into my glory. I **always have the ultimate victory**. Each of my children is destined to have a new resurrection body which will not waste away.

84

I Was There in the Nightmare

———— o ————

My child, I was there in the middle of the nightmare –
that period of your life when everything seemed to
go wrong. Wherever you turned there were problems.
Despair gripped you, didn't it? You felt as if you were
entirely lost.

I was there when you even contemplated suicide. It
was I who stayed your hand, for I would not want you to
destroy yourself, so great is my love for you.

This was the most difficult time of your life, wasn't it?
But you came through, my child, because I was there
with you in the middle of it all. When you pass through
the waters, I have promised they will not overwhelm
you. When you go through the fire, you will not be
burned.

I know how deeply hurt you felt at the time. You were
experiencing a desolation such as Jesus experienced for
you on the cross when he cried out, 'My God, my God,
why have you forsaken me?' You felt forsaken, didn't
you? Yet I was there all the time. I never left you.

I know the hurts that were inflicted upon you by
others. I know also that those to whom you turned could
not understand your dilemma. You see, they had never
been where you had been. It seemed you were at the
bottom of a great pit and nobody knew how to lift you

out. But I came, didn't I? **I heard you cry. I came and rescued you and lifted you up.** I held you in my loving arms. I saw the joy slowly beginning to come back into your heart. I saw the peace gradually filling your soul; and I rejoiced.

It took some time, didn't it? But did you notice the point at which everything began to change? It was when you forgave. I watched you sink down a spiritual well, and resentment ate at your heart. You felt you had been dealt with so unjustly; one injustice seemed to be heaped on another. People turned against you and insulted you.

You cried out to me for vengeance. That is not what I tell you to do. **Forgive, love your enemies and pray for those who persecute you.** I had to wait until you were obedient to my word. I kept you through those difficult months until you began to rejoice in me and give thanks, even in those dire circumstances. Then everything began to change, didn't it? Have you learned the lesson well, my child?

In future, when others oppose and hurt you, will you let a root of bitterness spring up? Or will you be merciful and forgive? Instead of crying out to me in a rage of self-righteousness, will you praise me, knowing that I am the God of justice and that I vindicate my chosen ones?

I honour the truth and those who hold fast to my word. In my love, I cannot save you from the battles that lie ahead of you; but **I shall always be at your side and my Spirit will work within you for your good**.

85

The Battle Belongs to Me

———— o ————

I am like a mighty warrior who stands at your side with sword unsheathed to protect you from harm. The battle belongs to me. **You are more than a conqueror because of your faith in me**. But you have to live in my word to experience my victory.

I am a wall of protection around you, my child. When you walk in my way you are not vulnerable to the enemy. Even those who assault you, because they allow themselves to be instruments in his hands, will not cause you harm when you stand against them in the truth of my word.

My dear child, I have lifted you out of darkness and deep despair. Never sink back into that again. There is no need for that if you do as I say. Stand against every lie of the evil one. Don't entertain any of his thoughts. Don't believe any of his accusations. Don't accept any condemnation from him. I never want to see you sink into a pit of despair again. And you don't want to either, do you?

So, my child, walk before me in righteousness and in all the good things I have prepared for you. **Rejoice in me and let forgiveness and mercy flow from you as expressions of my love, even towards your enemies.**

86

I Am Light

———— o ————

My dear child, I am light. In me there is no darkness at all. I love to cause my light to shine where there is darkness. Every time this happens, the darkness has to disappear. You have noticed this in your own life, haven't you?

You see, I am engaged in a programme of bringing my light into areas of your life where still there is darkness, or at least shadows. Shadows of fear, unbelief, self-concern and defeat. I shine my light and those shadows disappear.

Sometimes you try to shield yourself from my light. That is never a clever thing to do because it prevents the liberation I want to bring to you. I always have my way in the end, don't I? But you are able to put off the day of your liberation through your hesitation.

I have made you a child of my Kingdom of light. So, walk in the light. Have nothing to do with the sinful deeds of darkness. Be constantly thankful that I have saved you from the corruption of this evil world.

Be one of my instruments in bringing light to those who live in darkness.

87

Powers of Darkness

———— o ————

The world is spiritually dark; evil forces are at work. These powers of darkness grip the lives of multitudes of people without their realising. They experience constant confusion, antagonism, sickness and despair as a result. They are in complete bondage in their social and moral lives, bound by these evil forces.

You see, my child, sin encourages darkness. Those who persist in their sins discover they cannot break free from them. They are enslaved. You can be thankful that I have saved you from such bondage.

I know your heart-concern for those who remain in darkness. All over the world I have raised up evangelists to bring them the light of my gospel. How distressing it is that so many hear the good news but are blinded by the god of this age. So they refuse to repent. They even make jokes about receiving the light! I long to see them turn to me so that **I can dispel their darkness with my light.**

88

I Dispel the Darkness

———— o ————

My dear child, there is a great spiritual battle happening all around you. It saddens me that so many Christians don't understand this. They are aware of the little conflicts within them, but don't believe in demonic powers although my word testifies to their reality. Jesus would not have rebuked demons if they did not exist. He would not have cast them out of people if they were not there in the first place.

People think that such powers belong only to primitive societies or to eastern nations. But I tell you that there are powers of darkness working all around you. They are invoked by those involved in black magic, witchcraft and the occult.

Often the devil appears as an angel of light. Those involved in spiritism imagine they do a great deal of good. But when they use other powers to heal, people are put in bondage to those powers. Calling on spirits of the departed is in direct contravention of my word. So I warn them to avoid every form of evil and be on the watch for deception. I never want to see people in bondage.

When I became man, my light came to live in the midst of the darkness of this world. All the powers of evil were hurled against Jesus but they could not prevail. On the cross, those dark forces were exposed and shattered.

I want you to understand the spiritual authority I have given you. I have made you a person of power and authority. Nothing is able to hinder you from walking in my ways. The powers of darkness cannot touch those who walk in the holy way of my light. They cannot pull them away from the light or drag them back into darkness.

No power of darkness need overcome you. I have given you, my child, authority over Satan and all his works. Whatever you bind on earth is bound in heaven. Whatever you loose on earth is loosed in heaven.

89

The Light of the World

———— o ————

Spiritual forces rule over areas, organisations and nations. They even try to infiltrate churches.

I hold you in my grip and will not allow anything to harm you. You are under the protection of the blood of the Lamb. The Holy Spirit who lives in you is greater than all the spirits of darkness that inhabit the world.

I am not suggesting that you go demon hunting, but you do need to be aware of their existence and the way they influence the society in which you live. They hold captive many whom you meet. Don't be surprised if demons try to attack you with oppression, heaviness or temptation.

You see, my child, I have put you in the front line. Sometimes you don't want to be there; you would much prefer to be among the reserve troops. But there are no reserve troops in my army! Every one of my children must be in the front line. Every believer is bound to be the object of attack from the enemy.

The best method of defence is attack. You are able to attack the enemy in your life and the lives of others. You have authority to set others free. You can command the enemy to depart from their lives as well as your own.

Before you gave your life to me you belonged to the kingdom of darkness. Jesus taught that Satan was your father. The enemy doesn't need to attack those who are already his! Some people even think it is better not to belong to me if they are going to be attacked. But I have delivered you from the dominion of darkness and brought you into my light.

You are no longer under the curse of Satan. My children are the light of the world. So **you are an ambassador of light**, child. This light has to be put on a table – not under it. I want your light to shine before men. Then they will see your good works and give me glory.

Don't be content because you have been delivered from the darkness; take my light where it is needed so that others too may be set free. Whenever you go in my name, I go with you. I watch over you; I care for you. I uphold you with my victorious right hand.

90

Live in Freedom

——— o ———

Often my children concern themselves with petty affairs while a spiritual war is taking place around them. They feel defeated by their circumstances because they are unaware of the true nature of the battle in which they are involved.

I want them to rise up in faith to exercise the authority and power I have given them. I have set my children free from the enemy; but some speak as if they are still bound.

It is for freedom that I have set you free. If I have set you free, you are free indeed. Walk in liberty as a child of God. Live free from the chaos and confusion caused by the evil one. Don't be afraid to come against him when you pray.

Submit yourself to me, resist the devil and he will flee from you. Would I tell you to do this in my word if it was not necessary? It is indeed necessary, my child. When he tries to plant negatives in your mind, resist those thoughts immediately. Don't receive them. If you allow him to affect your thinking, he can undermine your faith. Don't let him do this, my child. Listen to my word, not his lies.

You are not powerless to resist him, neither do you need to be afraid of him. He wants you to believe that if you resist him he will hit back in worse ways.

Your life is not to be lived under a cloud of such fear. I have called you to be a child of faith and to have confidence in me. This is my sovereign will for you.

91

My Sovereign Will

— ○ —

My dear child, people suggest everything that happens is my sovereign will. How they misuse this phrase.

Jesus demonstrated my sovereign will. He showed that I am merciful, that I forgive, heal and deliver my people. Sin, sickness and darkness are not my sovereign will. My will is that you live in me and I in you; that you obey me and live in the wonderful inheritance I have provided for you. **On the cross Jesus was oppressed to free you from all oppression, rejection and sickness.**

By contrast, the enemy wants you to feel ashamed, fearful and of no account. He says you are hopeless, worthless and useless. He discourages you with negative lies. I encourage you with the positive truth.

I am able to use you, and I'm going to do so for my praise and glory. My dear child, don't accept everything that happens as my sovereign will. You will only discover my will from my word. Don't live in fear: live in faith.

92

The Enemy's Tactics

———— o ————

My dear child, I want to explain to you some of the tactics of the enemy. The fruits of his labours are obvious. Wherever there is hatred, fear, destruction, violence, division, abuse, immorality, deception, deceit, corruption or lying, he has been at work. Just as I work through men, so he works through men. Just as I have available to me many angelic forces, so he works through demonic forces.

To look at the state of the world, you would think that Satan had the upper hand, for there is so much that is sinful and destructive. By comparison there seem so few who truly exalt my name. But you know well, my child, that the enemy does not have the upper hand.

Whenever light shines in the darkness, the light always prevails. **Satan is a defeated enemy.** The things you see happening in the world now are his last fling before he is thrown into the abyss for eternity. It is hardly surprising, therefore, that you should encounter opposition from him. He knows that you are on my side. He is like a trapped animal in its death throes, trying to reap as much destruction as possible before his ultimate end. But he shall not have you; you are mine.

He will attack you and seek to seduce you away from my purposes. He will try to deceive you by contradicting my word. He will tempt you to follow your course instead of mine. He will lie to you and accuse you in order to try to destroy your confidence. He will use others to criticise you so that you feel a failure and unworthy to be used in my purposes.

You will need to be alert to all his devices, child.

He seeks to sift you like wheat, but my Son has prayed for you. He intercedes for you in heaven continually. He prays for all who are his. I hear him and I honour his prayer for you.

93

Victory

———o———

I commanded the disciples to heal the sick and drive out demons. What I commanded those first disciples, I command you. Bring my victory into your circumstances and also the lives of others.

Beloved child, **I have defeated the evil one, and so have you.** He is crushed beneath my feet, and yours. Your faith has overcome the world and all the powers of darkness that seek to influence the world. You are no longer subject to them because you are subject to me. I am your Lord; Satan isn't.

I give angels to guard you at all times and my powers of light are infinitely greater than the powers of darkness. Walk in the light as a child of the light, rejoicing that your victory is assured.

All the powers of darkness are under judgment. So are those who invoke them. My judgment shall surely come upon them at the proper time, unless they repent. They will know my divine wrath for they honour the one who seeks to destroy the lives of those I have created.

I have spoken many words of love to you. You wonder whether this could be the same God who speaks of wrath and judgment. Well, it is still I who speak, my child.

You are not a child of wrath. You are a child of God. You are not under judgment and condemnation for my Son has saved you. You are no longer in darkness; now you live in light. You don't belong to the enemy camp. So don't apply to yourself words of judgment reserved for those who follow the enemy.

94

I Am Your Shield

———— o ————

I **am your Deliverer. I am your Stronghold. I am your Defence. I am a mighty Shield about you,** my child. I hold you in my arms of protective love. My gentle hands are also strong hands, able to support you in the midst of the battle.

Be alert and on the watch. The devil prowls around like a lion seeking someone to devour. He will try to attack you, but do not allow him to take advantage of you.

I care for those of my children who do not engage in spiritual warfare. But they don't enjoy my full liberty. They often walk under clouds of heaviness. They become oppressed and take tablets instead of exercising their spiritual authority over those who oppress them.

Fear is one of his chief weapons; but you are not a child of fear. I have not given you a Spirit of fear but of power, love and a sound mind. My Holy Spirit is greater than all the powers of darkness put together. He will lead you in victory, so listen to him.

95

I Hate Darkness

———— o ————

My dear child, there are many who are gripped by foolishness. They don't want to invoke spiritual forces of wickedness. They don't want anything to do with the devil and yet they are involved with works of darkness: the occult, clairvoyance, palmistry, divining and horoscopes. There are organisations which appear to be instruments of light and yet lead people into bondage through secret rites of initiations. They invoke powers of darkness without understanding what they are doing.

Demonic powers work through witchcraft, orgies, drunkenness and satanic rites. But they can also influence people through drugs and consorting with prostitutes. Those involved in such things wonder why their lives are in such turmoil.

Some create and sell children's games which lead young minds into a prison of occult bondage. My righteous judgment is upon those who perpetrate such evil.

I weep over some of my children who smile about such things as if they were not of any significance. They are ignorant and deceived. **What a great task we have, child, to take my truth where there is such deception, to take my heart where there is such darkness. You are a child of my light.** Walk in the light; spread light.

96

Fight the Good Fight

——— o ———

My dear child, I want the devil to be exposed for who he is. He is the deceiver and accuser. He blinds people to spiritual truth. He is the father of lies. The deceit and deception that exist, the corruption that is everywhere in society, are the work of his hands.

He can rightly accuse those who belong to his camp, but not those who belong to my Kingdom. I save them from his accusations.

He is the thief who comes to steal, kill and destroy, even though he may appear as an angel of light. Praise me for giving you victory. I will teach you to fight the good fight of faith, confident that you are able to overcome every device of the evil one. You don't stand in the fight alone. But you are part of a mighty army I am raising up. And I am with you!

People wonder why I allow such powers to influence my world. I have already explained that those who have the ability to love must also have the power to hate. If they are able to walk in the light by choice, they must also be able to walk in darkness. For people to have a genuine choice to love and serve me, they must also be given the choice to serve the enemy.

I don't promise that life in this world will be easy. There will be tribulation, trouble and strife. I cannot save any of my children from being in the front line of the spiritual battle. **It is better to be engaged in the fight than to yield yourself to the powers of darkness.** These are the only alternatives.

Those who try to stand on some middle ground find that it doesn't exist! The enemy is able to rejoice over them and have victories in their lives, again and again.

Stand firm against the enemy. See him flee from you. Refuse to accept the lying, condemning, accusing thoughts, even when he voices these through other people around you. Refuse to compromise your walk in righteousness, holiness and truth. Refuse to have anything to do with the deeds of darkness.

These are important lessons I am teaching you, my dear child. At times you will not succeed. It will seem that the enemy has been allowed to gain the upper hand. Don't despair when this happens. I don't condemn you for your failure.

The evil one is jealous of you. For him there is no forgiveness; he is condemned to ultimate failure. But I forgive you and restore you to my victory. You are a child of light and the powers of darkness have no rightful claim on you.

You see, my child, I have won the victory, and you are able to establish that victory in the circumstances of your life as you exercise the authority I have given you. Persevere in faith until you see my victory.

As you walk in my light, you will rejoice. There will be singing and praises on your lips, for praise is the language of victory. In the middle of the conflict, keep your eyes on Jesus, the conqueror. **You are more than a conqueror through Jesus.**

97

I Am the God of Justice

——— o ———

My dear child, I am the God of justice. **I love justice and hate oppression,** which is a work of the enemy. I hate it when I see men oppressing others, and I love to see my children being liberated from oppression.

When my Son became flesh, he had to suffer oppression to liberate you from the oppressor.

I want you to understand, my child, how I view the nations. Because people see so much injustice, some think I created the world and then left it to its own devices. But no, my child, I oversaw the events of history. I cause nations to be raised up and I pull them down. I can use governments to execute my justice against other nations. Does this seem harsh to you? I never deal with anyone unfairly.

Because I love justice, what am I to do with whole nations who prefer sin and iniquity to righteousness? What am I to do with those who laugh at my name and oppose my purposes? What am I to do with those who exalt their false gods who can give no salvation or eternal life?

Some would like me to smile benignly on everybody. If I did that, I would deny myself. I would say that sin and wickedness didn't matter, that rebellion and blasphemy are not important, and that it doesn't matter which god you serve. All these things are so far from the truth.

I continue to hold out my hand in love, but I cannot force anyone to take it.

98

It Is Finished

——— o ———

My judgment is right, whether it involves nations, peoples or individuals. If I had not provided a sacrifice for sin, all would be consigned to death and eternal separation from me. That is the inevitable consequence of sin. But my justice is tempered with mercy. I don't want to condemn anyone. This is why I have reached out to my people through Jesus.

But what of those who spurn the blood of Jesus? What of those who deny he is my Son? What of those who prefer their own way instead of mine? They will receive the justice their deeds deserve. This saddens me, but I cannot act unjustly. I can't say that sin does not deserve its consequences. I have provided a way of escape from corruption. Can you blame *me* if people refuse my offer?

It saddens me when justice has to be executed in this way. Men reap the consequences of their sins.

Make my salvation known. I don't want to condemn; I want to save. I don't want to judge; I want to be merciful. But my mercy would not be necessary if judgment was not impending.

So many are taken up with their own fears. They are so wrapped up with themselves that they care nothing for the life I am offering them. This grieves me deeply.

Those who need my Son blaspheme him. Those who are in the depths of despair deny him. What more can I do? I can't force anyone to love me, for that would not be true love. I can't send another Saviour for Jesus has already done everything necessary for the salvation of mankind.

If they rejected him, do you really believe they would accept another? No matter at what time or period of history my Son came, he would have been welcomed in exactly the same way. A minority embraced him; the majority rejected him. The world denied him; the religious disowned him.

What has been done has been done. 'It is finished!'

99

My Righteous Judgment

———— o ————

My dear child, I know you are concerned about my righteous judgment on others. You fear for those who have rebelled and turned away from me. You are right to do so. But understand that **I don't enjoy judging anyone.** I don't joyfully test the hearts of those who are unfaithful. But I do rejoice over the faithful ones.

Through my forgiveness I have saved you from the righteous judgment you deserved. But what of those who do not know my forgiveness?

Many unsaved people ask that question. They want a god who will save everyone but make no demands on them. What deception! They don't want to face up to my righteous demands on their lives. So they say they don't believe in me. But who do they cry to when in need?

They don't want to believe in a God of righteousness. If they were to acknowledge me as such, they would have to change their attitudes and actions. They are not prepared to do this. It is easier to believe their own ideas about me instead of the truth. I show my anger from heaven against all sinful, evil men who push away the truth. When they give me up, I give them up to every evil practice they could think of.

Before a person can be forgiven, he must acknowledge his unrighteousness. There is no point in pretending he is right. He has to admit the truth. Those who reject righteousness reject eternal life. This grieves me because, in my love, I want my best for everyone.

100

I Love Everyone

——— o ———

My dear child, people often wonder how I regard those of other religions. They say, 'What about the Muslims, the Buddhists and Hindus, the Mormons and Jehovah's Witnesses? What about those who belong to eastern mystical cults?' Well, first it must be understood that I love them, because I love all men.

Who can think his way to heaven? Who can think his way into my presence? The eastern mystics deceive many by making it appear that this is possible. They suggest that knowing divine reality is an exercise of the mind. This isn't true, is it? It is only through my Spirit that divine truth can be imparted. You receive not only understanding, but life itself.

I know many are sincere, but I am sad that they are also deceived. They imagine they follow the truth when they don't. I am not afraid of competition, you understand! Nobody can compete with me.

But it is so futile, isn't it, that great multitudes of people can be so sincere and not know the forgiveness, mercy and compassion that you have experienced. It is sad, isn't it, that they can't receive the life you have received; life in all its fullness.

It grieves me that they don't receive my Spirit or the salvation I offer through Jesus. It saddens me to see that despite all their religiosity, they are still bound by their sin and guilt.

All I can do is reach out to them through my servants and reveal the truth to them. What am I expected to do if they deny the truth and the offer of life I give? There is nothing so blind as religious prejudice and deception.

People wonder how I will judge them. What is there to judge? They have chosen their gods. They look to them for salvation. How great is their misery if their gods are false. Pray for them, child. I love them.

101

My Covenant People

————— o —————

What of the Jews, my child? I am their God. It was to them that I came with salvation. They had the opportunity to be my instruments of salvation to the world, and for a generation they were just that. For it was through Jewish people that I first took my gospel to the nations. But the obedience of a few in one generation does not save all in other generations.

Rejection of my Son causes me great grief, for these are a covenant people to whom I have bound myself in faithfulness and love. Yes, my child, I truly love my Jewish people. But no one is saved through the law or any righteousness of his own. It is only through faith that a person can find acceptance in my sight and receive my gift of eternal life. This is true for Jew and Gentile alike.

You, my child, are an inheritor of the promises of both the old and new covenant because you have put your faith in Jesus.

Pray for my people the Jews. I have promised that when the Gentile nations have been gathered into my Kingdom then my Spirit will move among them and they shall accept Jesus as their Messiah. I rejoice over everyone who already acknowledges him as such.

I can see the time when there will be a glorious move of repentance and multitudes shall then accept Jesus as the

Christ. My Gospel will be preached to every nation before I come again. There will be a sovereign move of my Spirit among every people and in every land. I can see the end from the beginning, and I can see the harvest of Jewish souls that will be reaped before the end of time. I am he who keeps his word.

102

The Son and I Are One

——— ○ ———

THOSE WHO BELIEVE IN JESUS BELIEVE IN ME.

THOSE WHO DISBELIEVE~~JESUS~~ DISBELIEVE ME.

THOSE WHO LOVE JESUS ~~LOVE~~ ME.

THOSE WHO HATE JESUS HATE ME.

THOSE WHO OBEY JESUS OBEY ME.

THOSE WHO DISOBEY JESUS DISOBEY ME.

I AND JESUS ARE ONE.

103

Judging Others

———— o ————

My dear child, I alone decide those to whom I show mercy. Many are perplexed, wondering why only some are saved.

I don't judge by external appearances, but by the heart. Even when people rebel against me, I can see what will happen to them when they turn to me. I don't reach out only to those who appear to be good people. I reach out to the lost, forsaken, destitute, poor, and those who are bound by sin and walk in spiritual darkness. **I will go anywhere to save those who will be saved.**

Deception is the chief enemy of the truth. People imagine they are right but actually they believe lies. Satan is the father of lies, a liar from the beginning. All who deny the truth of Jesus have the devil as their father. Jesus made that clear. But they are accepted by me when they turn to me, asking for forgiveness and surrendering their lives to me.

No one can be saved in his sins but only from them.

What becomes of those who have never heard of Jesus and don't understand the gospel? I shall give every man justice. I will never deal unfairly with anyone. It is not for you to know what will become of them. You are not the judge of anyone else.

Don't seek to understand things that are too hard for you. I give you knowledge and revelation, but there are some things which are not yours to know. Your eternal destiny is assured, but I **would never give you knowledge which would make you the judge of others.** I would not make you God. Even Jesus in his humanity didn't come to judge. Why then should you be a judge? Isn't it better to leave all judgment to me? Receiving my life does not make you a judge of anyone else, but rather a servant of all. Seek to live in my love and reach out with my truth. This is all I want, dearest one.

104

The Forgiven

——— o ———

'They get what they deserve, those brutes. They don't care about anybody else. They're only interested in themselves. If I had my way, they would all be locked up.'

'Bring back the rod,' his friend replied.

'Why not hang the worst of them?' another said. 'Let's rid the earth of them.'

Another sat quietly in the corner and thought to himself, 'I used to be one of them: violent, selfish, a thief and a liar. But he saved me.'

105

Hell

————— ◦ —————

My dear child, you know me in my love, gentleness and tenderness. You have been spared the harsh reality of my judgments. To keep heaven holy, I had to condemn the devil and his angels to hell. They are held for final judgment.

When I could see righteousness in no one except Noah, I caused the flood as my judgment upon an unbelieving and godless generation. At other times, cities have been wiped out in judgment. Nations have been destroyed and overcome because they chose to follow tyrants instead of me. Make no mistake, my child: **judgment upon the unholy is harsh, even though it is fairly and righteously administered.** The wages of sin are death and eternal separation from me. When I express my wrath in judgment it is never because I have lost my temper. Every judgment I make is a calculated act of justice, having given opportunity for people to respond to my truth.

Hell is a reality. Can you imagine eternal separation from me? Can you envisage what is meant by wailing and grinding of teeth, or being consigned to outer darkness? You cannot imagine these things because you are a child of the light. But I can see the awful reality of what awaits the lost. I don't want my people to be robbed of the eternal destiny I have chosen for them. All have sinned and fall short of my glory but **eternal life is my free gift to all who turn to me.**

106

Men Form Their Own Judgment

———— o ————

Consider the rulers of the nations. Many of them are more concerned with power than the welfare of their people. They are more concerned with their own kingdoms than my heavenly Kingdom. Most care little or nothing for me. What am I to do with them if they avoid the opportunity to bless my people and work for their own welfare instead? What about ordinary people? Are they simply ignorant and blinded? Have they chosen to serve the one who offers worldly riches, position and happiness?

I offer all the riches and resources of my Kingdom. I offer true joy. Some taste my riches but then see the cost of discipleship. They turn back to their own ways and deny me. I grieve for them especially. I long for their return. Many do come back but some are lost for ever. What grief it causes me that men should see the light and yet choose the darkness. This is why I say to you, my child, walk in the light as a child of the light.

My people can choose blessing or curse, life or death. Of course, I want them to choose blessing and life because I love them. But the choice is theirs.

Many misunderstand judgment. They imagine I sit on a throne and make on-the-spot decisions as to what I should do with each person when he dies. I don't have to make any such decisions. People have already made their own, haven't they? They face the inevitable consequences of their decisions.

Each man will receive the just reward for what he has done. Those who have chosen the way of salvation shall surely be saved; but those who have denied Jesus as the only way of salvation shall inevitably be lost.

107

The Narrow Way

—— o ——

Those who judge me don't know my ways, neither do they understand my love. They don't see the heaviness in my heart, or the anger I feel towards the perpetrators of evil who cause death and destruction to my people. Do I not have the right to show fury and power against those who are fit for destruction?

I have my witnesses in every nation. Where there is persecution my people thrive and my Kingdom is extended. Persecution encourages people to be more dependent on me.

Is martyrdom really necessary? Yes! The blood of martyrs is never spilt in vain. Their blood shall be avenged in due course. **Those who oppose my people oppose me.** Don't you know my heaviness of heart concerning all who reject me?

Those who know me are so concerned with the plight of others that they use every opportunity to speak of my salvation. They devote their lives to the cause of my Kingdom.

Religious people are supposed to be enlightened, aren't they, child? Yet still many of them choose to believe what they want to believe, instead of my word. Oh, my child, don't you realise how shameful it is for anyone to confess the name of Jesus and yet side with the perpetrators of evil? They create their own way of following me because they don't like the true way. They confess the name of Jesus, yet choose the broad way that leads to destruction instead of the narrow way that leads to life.

108

Not Under Wrath

—— ∘ ——

I rejoice over you because you remain faithful to me. I am pleased with you and delight in you. You long for me, don't you: to know me better, to be closer to me, to be used effectively by me?

The devil tries to encourage you to believe I am displeased with you, that you are a disappointment to me. But don't you see now, my child, that **my disappointment lies elsewhere. I don't disapprove of you,** but of those who reject my Son. They are the objects of my wrath, not you.

Thank you for accepting me. Thank you for loving me. Thank you for following me. You shall receive your due reward. Thank you, dearest child.

109

I Am the Truth

——— o ———

My dear child, I am the Truth. Yes, truth is a person, not a set of ideals! I am not like the enemy who deceives, or like men who are unreliable. I am light and in me there is no darkness. I don't need to deceive because I am not ashamed of any of my actions.

I have come to the world as the word, Jesus. He came full of grace and truth. He expressed my truth in everything he said and did. He exposed the works of the deceiver. He broke the hold of spiritual darkness over people's lives. He spoke words of truth which set people free – from past bondages, from the grip of evil, from sin and despair, from sickness and need. He set them free to love and serve in ways which are pleasing to me.

Sin is deceptive. When you sin, my child, you feel awkward in my presence, or you want to avoid me altogether. You hope your sin doesn't become exposed. **But when you walk in the truth, you have nothing to hide from me or from anyone else.** You experience the freedom I intend for my children.

Sometimes I have to confront you with the truth of who I am, of my claims on your life, or with what you have done. Don't be surprised or discouraged by this. It is my way of bringing you to freedom.

110

The Truth Works

———— o ————

Can you see that truth works? It grieves me to see some pick and choose when they read my word. They will believe this, but not that. They will accept this, but not that. They will do this, and not that. They sit in judgment on the truth, often on the supernatural dimensions of my word. They forget I am supernatural and try to follow me by trusting their natural reason and ability, and then wonder why they flounder. They don't trust what I say, and then try to excuse themselves for their unbelief.

They suggest my words may not be reliable, that I am incapable of ensuring that only the truth is contained in scripture. In two thousand years of intellectual achievement, have people progressed beyond spiritual truth? During this period, have I lost some of my ability and dynamic power, that I no longer want to love my children by healing them and performing miracles? Have my purposes changed?

I have made clear that **my truth never changes;** heaven and earth will pass away but my words will not pass away.

What am I to do with such an unbelieving and perverse generation? What can I do, except patiently bide my time, and bless all those who hold to the truth of my word with an honest and good heart?

Still, it is good that you believe me, child. To believe I am the truth is to believe what I say. You have learned who is right when your reason and my word conflict!

Over the years I have patiently changed your mind over many issues – not by forcing you but by presenting you with the truth again and again.

You have found some of my promises difficult to accept because you keep looking at your experiences which seem to contradict what I say. If you look at my promises instead, your circumstances will change.

Don't fall into the trap of believing promises without accepting the conditions which go with them. This is a mistake which many make. **Listen carefully to everything I say to you.** Remember who is speaking. I am no mere man; I am your Lord and your God. When I speak it is with all my divine authority. It isn't that some things are more true than others. Truth is truth. Whether I am addressing major situations or giving revelation about details, all I say is the truth.

111

Don't Judge My Word

——— o ———

Who will set himself above me to judge me? Who dares to judge the words of my Son, or to discredit what is written under the inspiration of my Spirit? Could it be that some value their opinions above my word? What pride! What arrogance!

What should I do with such people? They judge themselves by what they believe. If they value their own opinions and ideas, then only their opinions and ideas work for them. **But if they value the truth, the truth will work for them; and I am that truth.**

My dear child, listen to the truths my Spirit of truth impresses upon you. Don't push them away. My truth is the answer to every need. It sets you free!

112

Cling to the Truth

——— o ———

I **am the Truth. Those who cling to me cling to my word.** Instead of believing their feelings, they learn to believe what I say. They put their trust in me rather than in their circumstances. This is what I have been teaching you.

Trust my love, no matter how dark and depressing things may seem. Rejoice in me always, no matter what the circumstances. Maintain your peace even in the midst of turmoil and confusion. Knowing me as the truth will enable you to go through times of conflict and difficulty with triumph.

I have made you a new creation; that is the truth. I have set you free from the law of sin and death; that is the truth. I have come to live in you by the power of my Spirit. I have blessed you with every spiritual blessing in Christ. You are more than a conqueror as you put your trust in me. Constantly I remind you of the truth that nothing is able to separate you from my love. **All this is the truth about you!**

The truth can never be changed. What is true for you is true for each one of my children, whether an international evangelist or the newest believer. Each is precious in my sight. Each has the same inheritance. I don't discriminate between my children. I want all of them to enjoy all of me; and that is the truth! So I have given them everything they need for life and godliness.

You need to be reminded of these things from time to time, don't you, child? Sometimes you flow in the revelation of my truth, rejoicing in all I am and all I have done for you. But sometimes you slip out of gear. You take your eyes off the truth and place them on yourself. Then you begin to struggle.

This is not my purpose for you. **Keep your eyes on me and you will keep your eyes on the truth.** It sounds very simple, I know. But the reality is often more difficult, isn't it?

113

The Man With the Stoop

———— o ————

There was a man who carried a heavy load for many years. He felt weighed down by his problems. They were like a large pack on his back. So great was the weight that the burden caused him to stoop.

One day his burden was removed. He rejoiced that the weight had been lifted from his back. He knew he was set free from it. He knew that only the Lord could have lifted such a burden from him. But still he continued to stoop.

The Lord spoke to him: 'Stand up straight, son.' The man heard these words but in his heart he replied, 'I can't stand up straight. I will have this stoop for the rest of my life because of the burdens I have carried for so long.'

114

Feed on the Truth

—— o ——

The time you spend studying my word is so precious and important, for this is when you build your relationship with the truth. **The truth encourages you,** doesn't it child? I want it to be lodged in your heart.

115

The Walk

———— o ————

There was a man who set out on a very long walk. He knew the general direction in which he had to go but he had no map to guide him. Consequently he took many false turnings which made his journey still longer.

Then one day he came to a village and decided to ask someone which direction he should take. 'Have you no map?' he was asked.

'None,' he replied.

'Here, take this,' said the stranger, thrusting a book into his hand.

'What good is this to me?' said the man. 'When will I have time to read such a long book? I will trust in my own instincts to get me to my destination. Besides, I would only have to carry this book with me.'

And so he threw it aside. Will he ever reach his destination?

116

I Am Faithful

———— o ————

I don't have to explain my actions or justify myself before men. I am righteous, so I always act righteously. I am love, therefore I always act in love. **I am faithful and I always act faithfully.**

My dear child, you must understand that I never deny myself. I will never act contrary to my nature. I reveal myself in what I do.

I have always been faithful to you, even when you have been faithless. I have been utterly reliable and dependable. I have been with you always, loving you through every crisis, watching over you with tender care, even when you have been determined to pursue your own course and not mine. I have seen your impatience when I have not answered prayer in the way you wanted; and then later I have seen your relief that I didn't answer you in that way.

People judge me by the failure of my children. But I am never responsible for their sin. I am responsible for their pardon, forgiveness and restoration.

If I was as fickle as some people imagine, this would be a crazy world. There would be no order, only chaos. But I haven't only created by my word: I sustain creation by my word. If I was to be unfaithful to what I have said, the whole universe would go into confusion and chaos.

The reason why there is so much disorder in the world today is because many listen to the lies and deceit of the enemy, placing themselves under his control. He deceives: I am faithful. So I can truly say that heaven and earth will pass away, but my words will not pass away. I watch over them to ensure they are fulfilled.

117

You Want to Be Faithful

——— o ———

My dear child, I know that one of your deepest fears
is that you will prove unfaithful to me. But if you
keep trusting me, this will not happen. You see, **those
who trust my word obey my word. Faithfulness is
expressed in obedience.** Don't simply believe the promises, but take note of the commands as well. Glorify me in
every aspect of your life.

The enemy tries to persuade you that you want to be
unfaithful. Don't listen to him, even when he persists in
his accusations. Don't feel you have to fulfil these lying
thoughts, or be deceived into thinking this is your
destiny.

These are pernicious lies. They have trapped many
of my children, causing them to be involved in sin
unnecessarily. Don't listen to such accusations. I have
put into your heart a desire to please me in all things.
Your lapses and failures don't amount to persistent sin,
which comes from a rebellious heart. **You want to be
faithful,** don't you? Who put that desire in your heart? I
did. So I will ensure it is fulfilled because you are determined to walk in my ways.

Yes, my child, I need your co-operation. I know I will
have that because you really want to please me. You
build on rock when you build on me. You will be able to
withstand every storm and difficulty. Nothing will cause

your house to fall. **Honour my word at all times.** Those who build their house on the rock are those who hear my word and do it.

I am your Rock. I love to support you, no matter what the situation. I am like a firm foundation that cannot be moved. I'm not a tiny boulder but the bedrock of your life. I am your faithful Father who loves you and cares for you. I am your Provider and your Healer; you shall lack nothing, neither shall you be overcome. I am the Almighty One. Nothing is impossible for me.

118

Do You Believe?

———— ° ————

How many believe I will honour the promises of my word? Some believe them for others, but not for themselves.

They know that I am almighty, all-powerful, and therefore nothing is impossible for me. But do they expect me to do the impossible in their own experience? I tell them they can ask me for anything in the name of Jesus, but do they believe me? Do they think I will be true to such words? Or do they imagine these to be empty promises, a strange spiritual language that bears little or no relation to reality?

Some complain that when they pray with what they imagine to be faith, they still do not see the answers they need. They question my integrity and truthfulness!

It is true that I choose to work in different ways from those they want. Most of my children like instant answers; they don't like to be kept waiting. They snap their prayer fingers and expect me to come running, but are they as responsive when I speak to them? They want me to be faithful without being faithful themselves.

I always answer the prayers of my children with wisdom. I never make mistakes, neither do I fail. Many rush around in a fever of activity, wondering why I don't give them the answers they need. They are neither patient, nor do they persevere in faith. I will answer but in my way, not theirs.

I am always faithful but I come in for much criticism over what they call 'unanswered prayer'. There is no such thing. **I never ignore the prayers of my children.** I don't shut my divine ears to their hearts, or my eyes to their need. I listen intently and always do what they believe I will do, just as I have promised.

Notice that I listen to their hearts. Many pray the right-sounding words but don't believe their own prayers. Am I expected to answer their words or their hearts? **I have promised to answer what they believe in their hearts and I am faithful in doing this.**

119

True Faithfulness

———— o ————

When people accuse me of unfaithfulness, they fail to notice that there may have been other factors which prevented them from receiving what I wanted to give. Some stop praying. So much for their perseverance and faith! Others say they only want me to answer if it is my will. I am certainly not going to give them what is opposed to my will! When people pray like this, they are not sure what they believe or expect.

Jesus teaches you to believe that you have received whatever you ask in prayer. Then it will certainly be yours!

Those with true faith trust me no matter what the circumstances. Even when they don't see an immediate transformation in the situation when they pray, they keep trusting, knowing that **I will fulfil every promise I have made.**

This is the kind of faithfulness that comes from my heart; it is the kind of faith I am producing in you. I like it when you believe my words and act upon them. This will make you really fruitful beyond anything you could have imagined.

Jesus was faithful to me throughout his ministry. You and I can have the same relationship of love and unity, grounded in faithfulness. I am encouraging you not only to believe in my faithfulness but to be faithful yourself.

Be faithful in living out my word. Reflect my faithfulness in your relationships. Don't allow your circumstances to change your love or commitment but maintain your faithfulness, laying down your life for your friends and loving as I have loved you.

Have you noticed that I have maintained my faithfulness to you, no matter what your response to me? Well, in this same way, maintain your faithfulness to others, no matter what their response to you. You will not always find it easy. Nevertheless, this is the only course open to you. Your faithfulness to others truly honours and glorifies me.

120

Trust Me

—— o ——

I am faithful to myself. I am faithful to my word. I am faithful to the blood of my Son. **And I am faithful to you**, my beloved child. The more you put your trust in me, the more you experience my faithfulness. Rejoice in this.

The more you trust my word, the more you will see my word fulfilled in your life. The more you trust in the work of the cross, the more you will live in freedom from guilt, shame, grief, sickness, fear and failure. My Spirit's presence within you is my guarantee that I really will give you all I have promised. The Spirit's seal upon you means I have already purchased you and guarantee to bring you to myself.

The more you trust in my love for you, the more you will enjoy life and know victory in trying circumstances.

I have promised to finish the good work I have begun in you. I will not leave you semi-sanctified! You will be fit for heaven because of all I have done for you and in you. So rejoice!

121

I Am Wisdom

——— o ———

My dear child, I am wisdom. **I always act wisely.** I never do anything foolish. I always speak words of wisdom, whether in scripture or by my Spirit.

I want to eradicate foolishness in you. I often hear you say, 'What a fool I've been'. You look back on things you have said or done and realise how foolish you have appeared to others. This causes you acute embarrassment. It seems worse when others think you are foolish, doesn't it? This confirms all your fears about yourself.

Sin is foolishness. Whatever opposes my will is foolishness. Yielding to temptation is foolishness. I don't condemn you for these things, as you are beginning to realise at last. But my Spirit working within you prompts you to be wise in every situation and on every occasion. So take note of what he says.

My wisdom is pure. So, avoid what is impure in my sight. Sometimes you don't want purity because sin can be fun, at least while it lasts. But when you know you have offended me, you feel dirty and are not clean again until you have repented and received my forgiveness. You don't like feeling dirty, do you? To be clean is to be at peace with me, with nothing to restrict or inhibit your joy.

Jesus made clear that to perform the sin in the mind is as bad as doing the deed itself. Don't misunderstand what he says or you will place yourself in false condemnation. Having the thought or the temptation that the enemy plants is not the sin, but dwelling upon it and making it a focus of desire. If you encourage the thought, it becomes a sinful fantasy.

So in your fight against sin, child, be wise. Dismiss anything impure or opposed to my word. You will be all the better for it. I want to spare you from unnecessary conflict. Remember that Jesus was tempted in every way just as you are, yet he was without sin; he always resisted. I never allow you to be tempted beyond what you are able to endure. I've made that clear to you before, haven't I?

122

Words of Wisdom

———— o ————

My dear child, it is wise to know my word, to be familiar with the truth. They are words of life and healing.

I want my word to be like a reservoir within you. You can draw on this living water in every situation. My Spirit will remind you of my truth. So it is unwise to be ignorant. You don't understand all you read in the Bible, but you understand enough to know what I want in most situations. When you need fresh wisdom or understanding, ask me and I will give it to you.

My Holy Spirit will always lead you in the path of wisdom. This means you will pursue the way of peace, gentleness and kindness – qualities which the world often despises as weakness. Well, they are qualities I possess and I am certainly not weak! I made the universe!

So if you display these same qualities, you will be able to make better use of the power I've given you.

When I reach out to you in the gentleness of my love, something powerful happens in your life, doesn't it? My Spirit works with gentleness, love and affection, and also brings power, deliverance and healing.

Is it your prayer always to act in wisdom? Others will be very quick to pounce on any area of foolishness in your life. **If you walk in wisdom, you will have nothing to fear** from them. You will make mistakes because everybody does. Others may laugh at you as a result, but I don't laugh at you. I encourage and forgive you.

123

This is Wisdom

—— o ——

My dear child, it is wise not only to hear the scriptures but to believe and live them, and do as I say. Believe me when I speak to you, saying that you are lovely in my sight, precious beyond compare. Believe me when I say you are the apple of my eye, that I have redeemed, called and saved you.

I am not a stern Father who remains at a distance, giving wise advice. I am your loving Father who draws near to you, embracing you in love. Walk with me in my ways of wisdom. Be wise as I am wise. Avoid the foolishness of sin and you will rejoice with great joy.

My wisdom leads to peace and is expressed in righteousness, holiness, integrity, truth, love and power. Can you see how all these things are related?

Fear of me is the beginning of wisdom. You are in awe of who I am, so avoid every form of evil and all that is opposed to my word. You are able to have wisdom beyond your years because of the way my Spirit flows through you. Don't despise experience for, although wisdom comes as a gift from me, you learn how to exercise that wisdom by experience. **Wisdom protects you from evil.** It also encourages humility. The foolish are arrogant; Jesus was both wise and humble.

Just as my Spirit of wisdom rested on Jesus, so my Spirit of wisdom rests on you. This is why you feel uneasy if you step outside my purposes. Do you remember that in his humanity, Jesus grew in wisdom? This is what is happening with you. You can only sit at my feet, hear and learn from me because my Spirit of wisdom is operating within you, bringing revelation. This is very different from worldly wisdom which passes away; my wisdom lasts for ever.

Don't think that wisdom is beyond you. You will have sufficient wisdom in every situation. It is time that you really thanked me, child, that I have given you wisdom. **You have my wisdom and can act wisely in every situation.**

124

My Authority

———— o ————

I have total authority over all creation, the whole universe. I have authority in heaven. I have authority over the devil; he only has leave to do what I allow in the testing of men's hearts.

I have complete authority over the nations. I am able to raise up and pull down governments. I can even bring nations into being and cause them to pass away.

I have authority over my Church and **I have authority over you** as one of my children.

My dear child, it is right to respect my Lordship, to be in awe of my majesty and glory, but don't be afraid of me. For although I possess all authority, it is not my purpose to demolish my children. Look how I have encouraged you.

Some people think I don't make a very good job of the exercise of my authority. They point to the conflicts among nations, to the corruption in governments, to the ineffectiveness of my Church and to the failure of some of my children. They judge and condemn me for these things, saying that if I am Lord, I should make a better job of my position!

Some leaders govern well; others oppress through their pride or corruption. Yet in the midst of all this I am at work hearing the heart-cries of my children, establishing righteousness through those who love me. While people are blaming me, I am at work in the situation, changing things!

125

My Critics

—— o ——

My critics want me to act more quickly to eradicate the suffering and need caused by men's corruption. What hypocrisy, for these very critics don't want to acknowledge my authority in their own lives. They don't want me to judge their hearts and actions, but won't repent of their sins. They don't want to bring their lives into conformity to my will or submit to my Lordship.

There is such suffering, injustice and corruption in the world because so many deny my sovereignty.

Some point to the desperate plight of the poor, holding on to their riches while they do so, enjoying their comfortable life-style. Others point to moral depravity while enjoying their own sins. They speak against corruption although their own affairs are not in my order. They complain about the amount of sickness, and yet serve the one who brings sickness, disease and devastation into the lives of people.

They complain about the way they are governed, but don't want to be governed by me. They don't believe my word and neither do they obey me. They criticise me in a futile attempt to justify their disobedience, unbelief and rebellion against my authority.

In my Church many acknowledge my authority only superficially. As a result, the Body of Christ is not the effective instrument in the world it should be. They call me 'Lord' without allowing me to be Lord in their lives.

If everybody who belonged to a church truly submitted their lives to my Lordship, there would be no divisions. Men would not fight with each other for power; they would not squabble, be angry or jealous of one another. Instead they would radiate the life of Jesus more fully and effectively.

126

My Authority in Jesus

———— ° ————

My authority was seen in Jesus. He demonstrated my Lordship in the way he spoke and the actions he performed. He gave the command and the waves obeyed him, demons were driven out of people, the sick were healed. Even the dead were raised.

At the same time he recognised my authority over him. He submitted to my heavenly will, speaking only what I gave him to speak, doing only what he saw me do, obeying me even to the point of death. **He exercised my authority perfectly because he submitted to my authority perfectly.**

This would happen in my Church today if people were prepared to submit to my authority in the same way. But because there is so much disobedience, there is often little truly spiritual authority or evidence of my Lordship.

I cannot be head of rebellion, sin or disobedience. I am obviously not Lord in the life of someone who works in his own ways instead of submitting to mine, no matter how many times he goes to church or prays. Where there is genuine submission to my authority, there my Church appears strong and healthy. My Spirit is able to work powerfully through my people to liberate others.

127

My Authority in Your Life

———— ○ ————

My dear child, when you submit to my Lordship you are an effective witness and a fruitful member of the Body. I can use you to express my life. **You are able to speak and act with my authority.**

So, my child, recognise my authority in your life. This is not a matter of saying, 'Lord, Lord'. Some call me 'Lord' but will not enter my Kingdom because they don't do what I say. To submit to my authority is to submit to my word and my will.

Quietly, lovingly, but with great determination, I have been establishing my authority in your life. You are now in the middle of this process. You acknowledge me as your Lord, but still there are areas where you fail to submit to my authority.

In some ways you don't want to submit to me, do you? You wish I would compromise my demands upon you. You would like me to change my word to conform with your desires.

You know I won't do this, don't you? That would jeopardise the whole purpose I am working out in your life. Instead I change your heart, purify your desires and bring you more in line with my will and authority.

Sometimes I have to speak about a matter several times before you take notice of what I say. My dear child, this is evidence of the fact that you still have some way to go in understanding my authority.

Wouldn't it be wonderful if I only had to speak to you once and immediately you acted upon my word? You delight me on the occasions when this happens. It thrills my heart.

I wait for you to work through many desires and fears before you are ready to accept my will. There are times of conflict when you weigh one thing against another. Will you obey or disobey? Well, my child, I want you to know that I never give up. I continue lovingly, gently, but firmly to impress on you what I desire until you do come to a full acceptance of my will.

Sometimes you think you know better than I do! **But things only work out for the best when you are happy to submit to my authority**. It isn't very comfortable fighting against me, is it?

128

Submit Joyfully

———— o ————

Here's something else you need to understand. I want you to delight to do my will, even when it is not what you want. Doesn't this seem a contradiction? It is. Don't you think it would be much easier to submit at the beginning? This would save you from a load of anguish, anxiety and conflict. Only a suggestion, my dear child! I would love to save you from these inner conflicts in the future.

I know you only too well, and there will be further times of conflict. But I am encouraged by the fact that you are learning through experience. Peace is much better than conflict, isn't it? I want my peace to keep your heart and mind in the knowledge of my love for you.

I always exercise my Lordship in love. Whatever I command, I ask of you in love; I want you to respond in love. You are afraid that I will make demands of you beyond your abilities. You are afraid to draw too close to me because you fear you may lose the freedom to do what you want. But I have impressed on you many times that I will never interfere with your free will, no matter how close you draw to me or how well you know me. I will only work with your co-operation. If the demands seem great to you sometimes, this is only because I know you have reached the point where you are able to meet those demands.

I don't ask things of my children which are beyond them. I take into account that I make my supernatural power available to them. I will never crush my children by putting them in situations where they are trapped, and cannot possibly do what I say.

If you agree to walk in my ways you will not be afraid of my authority. You will be glad to do my will, exercising my authority in your own life and ministry, speaking, praying and acting in my name.

You will be able to speak with my authority to mountains of need and see them moved, to speak to diseases and see them healed. You will speak words of forgiveness to those who have been enslaved by guilt. People will see what you do and hear what you say and they will know that I am your Lord.

129

Authority in My Church

———— o ————

My dear child, I know that sometimes you are perplexed about the way to relate to the authority of men, especially within my Church. It seems to you that it is one thing to recognise and acknowledge my personal authority over you, but it is quite another to have to submit to my authority in others. Yet I ask you to do this.

I want you to listen to me very carefully. **I don't place my children under the spiritual authority of those who are not equipped to exercise such authority.** This is the mistake some of my children make. They feel they have to submit to the authority of men in the places where they are, but these are not the places where I want them.

How can someone exercise spiritual authority in my name if they don't acknowledge my authority in their own lives? How can leaders have spiritual oversight of my people if they are not spiritually alive themselves? This seems so obvious. Why do many imagine they have to submit to unspiritual men in unspiritual churches?

Well, my child, I tell you plainly, that is not my way. I provide appropriate spiritual oversight for my children in order to see them raised in faith and love, and equipped for the ministry to which I call them. Those who submit to unspiritual leadership are not encouraged in their faith, nor in love; neither are they released in ministry. Instead they are suffocated by their circumstances.

My people have often tried to reduce my word to a series of legalistic formulae. Authoritarianism is of the flesh, not of my Spirit. It is men's substitute for the real thing. Spiritual authority comes not from a man's position in any church system, but from his standing with me. **He is only able to exercise authority through the anointing I place on his life.** Does this make things clearer to you?

There is to be great respect among my children for those who lead them. I want spiritual leaders to act in my name and declare my authority in the life of the whole body. How can my children respect the authority of those who are unspiritual? Yet so many of them remain in situations where they cannot respect authority because there is none to respect. This saddens me. I want to see my children growing and prospering in the things of my Spirit.

130

True Authority in Leaders

———— o ————

How it rejoices my heart when leaders exercise authority because they are so submitted to my authority themselves. Such leaders are not men pleasers! They don't simply follow the whims and fancies of any congregation. **They want to please me by leading my people in the way I want them to go.** Such leaders delight me.

Their task is not always easy. Within any fellowship there are those who don't want to submit to my authority. They don't truly want my Lordship over that fellowship. They want to run the church in their own way for their own ends, in order to see their own desires fulfilled. I weep when congregations are manipulated by such people. They cannot be a true expression of my Body.

I want leaders to be people of authority who will declare my purposes without compromise, leading my people unswervingly in the way I want them to go.

Submit to those who are in true authority over you. They will help, encourage and strengthen you in the things of my Spirit. But I don't ask you to submit to those who will hinder, discourage and frustrate you.

However, my child, don't expect perfection in your leaders. They are only human like you. I am working in their lives as I am working in yours – refining, purifying, causing them to increase in love, wisdom and faith.

Don't worry if on occasions they make mistakes. If the leadership consists of those who are truly led by my Spirit, they will soon be convicted of their mistakes and will not continue in pride, trying to maintain they are right on every occasion. They are humble and submit to me. They are humble before the people they lead. Authority is not seen in pride and arrogance but in gentleness, love and sensitivity to the voice of my Spirit.

If you look for perfection in leaders you will never be satisfied, no matter what fellowship you belong to. Learn to respect my authority and submit to one another.

131

I Give My Life

——— o ———

My dear child, no matter how much you have received from me, I still have so much more to give. I am bursting with life, longing to give. Isn't it sad that so many worship me but don't believe I want to give them anything? Yet it blesses me to give: I live to give myself to my children. So I delight when you turn to me to receive, when you are prepared to stop your busy schedule, sit down with me and receive from me. It delights me. This is what I want: to give and give and give to you.

Some people criticise those who want to receive constantly from me. The critics are usually the busy ones rushing around in a fever of activity. But I am wise. I know that the more I give my children of my abundant life, the more that life will flow through them to others. Yes, my child, this is why I want you to receive from me.

Don't be content to receive only occasionally and then try to keep going for a long time in the good of that blessing. **I want to give to you daily, several times a day, in whatever way is needed.**

I am generous by nature. You don't have to persuade me to give.

132

Receive the Holy Spirit

—— o ——

Every time one of my children asks to be filled with the life of my Holy Spirit, I always answer their prayer affirmatively. Some think they haven't received because they haven't trusted me to be faithful in honouring my promise. But I love to give my Holy Spirit to those who ask. Why serve me in your own strength?

I am weary of theological arguments. Some of my children argue about when and how to receive the Holy Spirit, whether a believer can receive only once or often. They argue and argue. Many of them don't come to me to discover the answer. If they did, they would discover I never come to the end of my giving.

If two people love each other, they keep giving to one another. If they ever stop giving, that is a sign that their love has grown cold. They may continue their relationship on a formal or legalistic basis, but they have lost the true spontaneity of love.

I love to give my life to my children at any time, in any place, on any occasion. I love it when they live in the constant flow of my life.

Often this flow is blocked by fear, unbelief, false condemnation and a sense of uselessness. Even though I put my life within them, they feel I couldn't use them to convey that life to others. They listen to the deceiver who says they don't have the necessary qualifications or resources. All the time my life wants to burst free from within them.

You see, my child, when I come to live in someone I don't want to be a prisoner locked up in darkness. I want to break free, to pour out of them as rivers of living water; not a trickle, but rivers.

I love changing lives with my life. It doesn't matter how depraved, hurt or broken a life has been, I am able to heal and deliver. I love to rescue those who have reached the gutters of life. I love to see the transformation that new birth brings to the desperate. I love to see the humble seeking for more of my life. I love to see those who are rich in the eyes of this world recognise their spiritual poverty. My child, I love to give my abundant life!

133

The Garden

—— o ——

The garden was obviously neglected; weeds abounded. The land looked useless, totally unproductive. A certain man looked with interest at this piece of land every time he passed. He saw in his imagination not a wasteland of weeds, but glorious fertile soil bringing birth to a great harvest of crops.

One day the owner stood on the piece of land as the man passed by. 'What a wonderful piece of land,' said the man.

The owner looked at him with satisfaction. 'Then this land is now yours,' he replied.

'Mine?' exclaimed the man.

'Yes,' said the owner. 'I'm giving it to you. Everybody else who has passed has seen only weeds and has complained about this land being neglected. But you have a vision of what you can make of this land; so I am happy to entrust it to you. I know you will pull out the weeds and make it abundantly fruitful.'

134

Praise Me

— ○ —

Listen to this. I don't like the narrow confines that many believe are my limitations. The way I lead is narrow so that you escape the corruption of the world. **But that narrow way is full of life.** I delight in everything good and wholesome. Those who walk close to me along that way walk in the fullness of my life.

Because you know me and have received that life, praise springs up from your heart. The life within you bursts forth with praise and adoration. You can't keep quiet, can you? You even praise me in difficult situations.

Don't feel you have to be so polite and restrained in praising me. If you have a praising, joyful, dancing heart, then be free to express what is in you. Don't worry about what others think. Remember liberty is the work of my Spirit!

Some people fill their lives with petty restrictions and lead others into legalistic bondage. They want me to free others when I am longing to break the bondage in their own lives.

135

Don't Limit Me

———— o ————

I hate it when people try to make me religious. They restrict me within their ecclesiastical systems and tell me that I have to work within the confines of their services. Usually I am only allowed one hour. And then precious few really expect me to do anything! If anyone was to receive fullness of life in the middle of the service he would be dismissed as an emotional freak.

But I see the hearts of those who worship me, even in such situations. **I love them all and I listen to their hearts.** So if one cries to me in repentance, I respond immediately. If one cries out in desperation, I am there to comfort. If I see genuine faith, I am ready to answer.

But I am expected to attend so many boring services. You should hear some of the sermons I have to listen to! If I believed what was said I would cease to exist as the God that I am. But I persevere and don't give up. **I give full measure to all who put their trust in me.**

However, you must know that I am angry with leaders who know of my life but don't enable my people to receive it. Some even prevent and hinder them from receiving. They are accountable to me for their actions.

Every congregation of my people should be abounding with my life, overflowing with love for one another – a company of true joy. Instead I continually see compromise. Even in some churches where the truth is proclaimed, it is not allowed to be expressed. Doesn't it annoy you that people prefer mediocrity, lifelessness and formalism to the fullness of my life? Doesn't it sadden you, my child? What are such people afraid of?

I don't want you to judge others. Take my life to them. Don't be deterred if they shut their religious doors in your face. I know what that feels like myself. I have many of them slammed in my face daily.

136

True Worship

—— o ——

I always go where I am wanted. I always work, even within the limitations put on me by men. How frustrating it is to have so much life, yet be unable to share it with multitudes who are ignorant of what I offer them. I work within ecclesiastical systems despite their problems and restrictions. I work outside these institutions also. Wherever my people gather in my name I am there in their midst. And I rejoice in all who welcome me.

I hate it when my children are jealous of one another, or imagine they are the only ones I know and bless. I hate it when they speak against one another. I don't speak against those who are bound by religious traditionalism or write them off. I love them and want to liberate them by revealing the truth. **I want them to have the fullness of my life.**

Worship must be in spirit and truth. It is not a sweet presentation of music, but the expression of love in the hearts of my people that gives me such pleasure. I want to influence every area of their lives, their minds and decisions, their homes and relationships. I want to be involved in their use of time and money, their work and recreation. I want them to enjoy life to the full, like I do! I want them to enjoy life with me because I am with them. My child, I love life!

137

True Prayer

——— o ———

My dear child, my heart reaches out to you every day. This is why I want you to spend time with me daily. I love it when we can talk together, especially when you open your heart to me. You don't always do that, do you? Sometimes you say the things you think you ought to say, the things you imagine I want to hear. But you don't say what you really mean, what is in your heart. You think I wouldn't approve if you did.

Now listen, I much prefer you to speak the truth from your heart. Tell me how it really is with you. I don't mind. You see, I know already. **I know what is in your heart;** so what point is there in trying to conceal it from me? That seems futile. And it doesn't please me to listen to a whole lot of false pleasantries. That may sound like prayer to you, but it doesn't to me!

Sometimes I hear you praying with others and it sounds as if you are speaking more to them than to me. You are so concerned about whether they approve your prayer that you forget who you are talking to. Many times your heart has been bursting with a real prayer, but you have held back and remained silent in case the others didn't approve. What a pity!

How I love it when people stop performing and become really honest with one another as well as with me. I wish there were more prayer meetings like that. Sometimes hardly an honest word is spoken in the whole meeting. People spar with one another; they fence, even in prayer. They correct each other's doctrine and criticise each other. How can I answer prayer like that? What am I to answer?

I know how critical and judgmental Christians can be; I am on the receiving end enough to know that! So I understand your reasons for wanting to remain silent. I don't want the critics running my church. I want those who are open to be led by my Spirit and to encourage you, and others like you, to walk boldly and confidently in my Spirit.

138

Humble and Confident

———o———

There have been times when I wanted to speak through you but you haven't dared to speak in case others disapproved. You have been afraid of being wrong or mishearing what I've said. I don't punish you on such occasions; but I am sad because I really want you to trust the Holy Spirit to speak through you. It doesn't matter whether others approve. Better to please me than men.

I know you are put off by those who are always speaking out and making contributions, especially those who seem to pray those beautiful, eloquent prayers. Well, I want you to know that the simple prayer of your heart is as beautiful to me as any other prayer.

I love the humble approach. Mind you, I don't want grovelling. I like you to come humbly but confidently. I am your Father. No Father wants a snivelling, grovelling child.

I appreciate that my children have many styles of praying. I don't mind that because I like variety. Some are very brash in their approach. It surprises people that I quite like that. Often there is real faith behind such prayer and I **always honour faith.** Such people receive very positive answers.

I like my children to be bold and confident, even though they are to be humble and gracious. If that brashness oversteps the mark and becomes pride then I have to take measures to humble that child. But whether the style is loud or quiet, what matters is that the prayer comes from the heart.

There is nothing false or superficial about me. Jesus hated hypocrisy and expressed my loathing of it. But I love honesty. I am glad, therefore, when my children are honest.

139

Full of Joy

——— o ———

My dear child, I want to tell you how much I rejoice in you. It grieves me that so many of my children do not really believe I enjoy them. They are constantly distracted by their inadequacies. They imagine I look at them with a frown instead of a smile.

Think of the joy a father and mother have when their child is born. **What great joy I had when you were born again!** I caused all heaven to rejoice. Heaven could only rejoice in you because I rejoiced.

I want my joy to be in you and your joy to be full. Many of your inhibitions have gone, haven't they? I love to break through all that stuff. It's great when you want to skip and dance and rejoice with me. This is my joy in you. Don't you realise that I was already rejoicing before it even occurred to you?

Joy is not an emotional response to situations. I am not an emotion; I am Spirit. **Joy is a fruit of my Spirit in your life.** I don't want to see that joy suffocated by problems and cares that concern you.

I never take my joy away from you. It is always within you and can always be expressed in your life.

140

My Surprises

—— o ——

I don't take delight in everything you do. At times you rightly expect to be disciplined. But on other occasions I surprise you. Instead of punishing you, I give to you and cause you to rejoice. You have thought, 'Why should that happen? What have I done to deserve this?' Nothing, my child. I like surprising you. I only reprimand you when necessary. I achieve much better results when I bless you; you are motivated to obey me when I encourage you. Not many people would like me if I was only interested in correcting them. Those who think I am never satisfied have a very false view of me. I am very different from that, as you well know!

People are filled with joy when they meet with me, when they are born again, filled with my Spirit, healed or when they receive an important answer to prayer. On such occasions they are so thankful. This is why I love to do these things in their lives. I love to see their joy and receive their thanks.

141

Rejoice Always

———— o ————

I know what you are wondering. If I am the God who desires such joy in my children, why do they experience so many things that are a denial of my joy?

When my Son came and lived among you, his joy raised him above others. But his life was not easy. He was constantly rejected and mistreated, ridiculed and persecuted. But he never lost his joy.

I understand the difficulties in your life. I know the tensions, problems, opposition and the ridicule you face because you believe in me. Didn't I say that in the world you would have trouble?

You have begun to discover that **if you praise and rejoice in me in the midst of the difficulties, my power is released in the situation**. Things may not change immediately but your perspective certainly changes, and you begin to realise that I am much bigger than the problem. Then you know I am able to meet the need.

My child, giving thanks in all circumstances is a real act of faith. I love to see my people walking by faith and trusting me.

You have come through many difficulties, moments of darkness and despair. You have been afraid and overcome by a sense of failure. You have felt judged and criticised.

Do you remember what I said to you in such times? 'Rejoice!' Sometimes you've argued with me, haven't you? 'I don't feel like rejoicing. I can't rejoice. It would be unreal if I did.' I tell you to rejoice always! And my Spirit will encourage you to do so.

Rejoice in my generosity. Rejoice in me, my child. I rejoice in you – and in giving to you. Why not rejoice in receiving from me?

142

I Am Holy

—— o ——

My dear child, I am holy. I sense your reaction immediately. I know how afraid you have been of my holiness. Yet I am holy by nature. My love is holy. My grace, mercy, righteousness, truth and faithfulness are all expressions of my holiness. You are afraid only because you don't understand the true nature of my holiness.

I know you are longing to be in heaven with me. You will be able to enjoy me without all the temptations and problems caused by the world, the flesh and the devil. Did you know heaven is the place of my holiness? Those who surround my throne acknowledge me as holy. There is no sin, fear, shame, guilt, sickness or pain. All the host of heaven rejoices and praises me. They have a wonderful time because they can enjoy my holiness unhindered.

You see, holiness is great! It brings tremendous happiness into the lives of my children. Unholiness mars their real enjoyment of me.

Are you beginning to get the idea? Holiness is not something to dread but to long for, just as you long for heaven. In fact these two things are one and the same. **If you long for heaven you long for holiness, and if you long for holiness you long for heaven.**

I am leading you towards the fulfilment of my promises. I will raise you at the last day and you will reign with me in glory. This is why I want you to be holy as I am holy. This is not merely a pleasant wish; it is essential. Only the holy can inhabit heaven. Without holiness no one will see me.

143

Heaven is Yours

———— o ————

Your fears originate because you think of yourself as unholy and you are afraid of judgment. Many passages in the Bible indicate that men suffer terrible affliction when I judge them in my holiness. Yes, it is true – there are harsh judgments awaiting the unholy.

If you belonged to the world and not to me, you would have every justification to be afraid of confronting me in my holiness. But as it is, there is no need to fear. I want to reveal myself to you in my holiness. This will not be a devastating experience for you, but a wonderful one. If you belonged to the kingdom of darkness you would need to shy away from holiness. You would not want the light of my truth to shine into the inner recesses of your being.

But I have saved you from the dominion of darkness and have already made you a child of my Kingdom. This Kingdom is within you. Do you hear what I am saying, child? **You already have the gift of heaven.** It is birthed within you.

As I work in you by the power of my Spirit, so I am causing the holy life of heaven to be expressed more fully in you. I myself, in my holiness, am being lived out in your life.

When my holiness comes up against the unholy, fleshly desires, you experience conflict. You make the mistake of thinking those desires disqualify you from my holiness. They don't. If they did, every one of my children would be disqualified from heaven. So I want to put that fear in the dustbin where it belongs.

144

You Are Holy

—— ∘ ——

Remember what I have done for you in my holiness. Jesus gave his holy life to cleanse you from all your unholiness. I have put my Spirit within you; he is holy. **You have the Holy One living within you, child. You are made holy in my sight. You are sanctified. I have cleansed you of your unholiness.**

I call you my dear child because you are dear to me. But I could also call you my holy child – a saint. Isn't that extraordinary? You are a saint. That means you are one who is sanctified, called by me and set apart for my purposes.

When you were born again I gave you the gift of eternal life because I wanted you for myself. **To be holy is to be set apart for me.** Obviously, if you are set apart for me, you are also set apart from sin and the devil's dominion, from fear and injustice. You are set apart *from* all that is evil and set apart *for* all that is good. Isn't that wonderful?

Why be afraid of my holiness when it means that you are saved and set apart for all that is good? Isn't the devil a liar? He wants you to imagine you still belong to him, instead of me. Those who belong to me inherit my holy life and will reign with me here in heaven. I am looking forward to having you here with me.

Listen, dear one, I didn't set you apart only to lose you somewhere along the way. I will certainly bring you to the fulfilment of what I have planned for you. That's encouraging, isn't it?

145

A Holy Life

———— o ————

I know your heart. There is that element of striving within you. You think you will only arrive in heaven if you do everything right. Well, it doesn't work like that. You will be in heaven because I have already done the right things for you. You can rejoice in that.

Don't misunderstand me. I am not suggesting that it doesn't matter what you do now. **Because you are holy I want you to live a holy life.**

Oh, there we go again. Fear! This fear is very deeply ingrained in you, isn't it? Every time I tell you that I expect holiness in your life you get very fearful. Let me ask you a question. Who lived the holy life, I mean a perfect holy life? That's right – Jesus. Was he miserable? No! The anointing of joy upon him raised him above his companions. Was he fearful, depressing or legalistic? Did he restrict people so much that they avoided his presence? No! Only the traditionalists wanted to avoid him because they were content with a formal kind of religion. Those who recognised their need were attracted by his holiness.

Now I am going to say something that will surprise you. I am going to work out my holiness in you so that you are really attractive as a person. As with Jesus, some religious ones are going to feel very awkward about your holiness; it will be a challenge to them.

I am going to make you more and more like Jesus, changing you from one degree of his glory to another. You are going to become more loving, joyful, faithful, peaceful, patient, kind, generous and gentle! You will be full of faith and able to exercise his power and authority in greater measure.

This is not a bad idea, is it? Why be fearful of such things? Don't you want to be like that? You think it's impossible? Well, just remember who is speaking to you! Nothing is impossible for me. I am able to work this out in you because I am who I am! Good news?

146

Co-operate With Me

———— o ————

Now, my dear child, as with so many things I do in your life, I do require your co-operation if you are going to live in holiness. I have given you a holy nature, but you have to let that life be worked out through your daily experience. Don't try to be holy by your own efforts. You cannot put on a performance of holiness for the benefit of others. No, **allow my holy life to shine through you.** Out of your innermost being rivers of living water will flow, the rivers of my holiness in you. Isn't that wonderful?

I love to see the fruit of my Spirit growing in you. I rejoice to see the gifts of my Spirit being used by you. All these activities of my Spirit are aspects of my holiness. The fruit is holy; the gifts are holy. And both are working in you! So there is more of my holiness shining through your life than perhaps you realise!

147

Resist the Liar

———— o ————

I know what concerns you – it's the unholy parts, isn't it? You think that a few unholy thoughts disqualify you from enjoying my holiness. My Spirit in you is much bigger, more impressive and powerful than a few puny thoughts!

It is time you were aware of the enemy's tactics. You see, because I have given you a holy life, there is nothing he can do to take that holiness away from you. He can't steal your new birth or your eternal inheritance. So he tries to prevent you from enjoying your life with me. He attempts to deceive you into thinking that you are not really accepted and couldn't possibly be holy.

He does this by planting unholy thoughts in your mind and encouraging fleshly attitudes. I've watched him do it. You have fallen for his tactics again and again, haven't you? Instead of resisting the enemy, you have thought yourself a terrible failure. Then he accuses you in an attempt to make you feel condemned. He suggests you are not holy. How could you be holy with such thoughts and attitudes?

Unfortunately, my child, you have agreed with him sometimes. But now you understand the source of these thoughts, you can stand against them. You don't have to put up with any of his lying tactics.

Oh, I know what you are thinking. It's not just the thoughts, but the desires that concern you. I know, I know; but the thoughts give birth to the desires. This is why the enemy feeds these thoughts to you again and again. When the thoughts become desire, you lose your resolve to stand against them. Then you are more likely to yield to temptation. Along comes the enemy again with his condemning thoughts: 'See how unholy you are. Look what you have done. A true child of God, sanctified and called to be a saint, wouldn't do anything like that.' Don't believe his lies.

Listen, my dear child. I have saints all over the world. I have millions of children, and they all sin. They all fail me and do unholy things. They are all aware of the same kind of conflicts that rage within you. I don't allow this to disqualify them from the inheritance I have chosen to give them. I have to teach each one of them personally not to believe the lying deceptions of the evil one, but to believe the revelation of my truth.

If anyone knows who is holy, it is me! So don't argue with me any more. **If I say you are holy, you are holy!** Because you are holy, you are called to be holy. If you believe you are unholy, you will certainly do unholy things. But if you believe you are holy because of all I have done for you, then you will live the Jesus life, won't you? Not perfectly. You have not yet reached the stage of perfection. There is a long, long way to go before you are at that stage!

148

You Have Made Progress

——— o ———

Let us consider this together for a moment. You are more loving than you used to be, aren't you? Before you were born again and part of my Kingdom, you didn't love in the way you do now. I wonder where that love came from!

You are certainly happier now than when you walked in this world's ways, even though sometimes you are disappointed with yourself when you fail me. You are more peaceful. You lose that peace when you worry, but it is restored when you trust me. **You have made progress, child.**

And lots of your prayers have been answered, haven't they? You see, there goes the enemy again. He points out all the ones that apparently haven't been answered. Remember those that have. You have faith and trust in my word now, don't you? This is more progress!

Consider your relationships. I know you still find these hard at times. Some people are really difficult to love, aren't they? But you are not as judgmental as you used to be, neither are you so critical. Some people you love now, you could not have loved before. That is progress.

All this is progress in the sanctifying work of my Spirit. These things have not happened by your own effort. They are my work in you. Aren't you encouraged, child?

149

Be Holy

———— o ————

Now, my child, I have something serious to say to you. Encouraging you to be holy is the most important thing I am doing in your life. So I do want you to turn away from those sins. You know the ones I mean. They are a constant contradiction to the life of Jesus in you, aren't they? You don't have to give in to such temptations, you know. Sometimes you feel the pressure will only be relieved if you indulge yourself.

The trouble is, if you indulge yourself once, you want to indulge yourself again and again. Then you get caught in a trap. That sin becomes part of you, and you lose the desire to be set free from it. So I have to speak a strong word to you to bring you to your senses. In my holy love, I discipline all my children for their good.

I am very tolerant. I wait until you realise you need to be set free from this pattern of behaviour and the attitudes which displease me.

You see, when you lose your appetite for sin, you really want to be set free from it. Then I can act. I have had a lot of experience in dealing with children like you. I deal with you at very close quarters because I live *in* you. I know you so well, child. I know how you think and react. **I don't live in you as a divine spy, but to enable you to enjoy my life.**

150

I Came

——— o ———

My dear child, I am a holy God. But in my Son I was not afraid to come among the unholy to touch their lives with my holiness. You see, I make the unholy clean, but the unholy can never tarnish me.

Jesus was not afraid that he would be corrupted or yield to temptation. He was tempted in every way that you are, and yet he never sinned. He could share every experience, except sin. He mixed with the prostitutes, outcasts and sinners, touching the corrupt with his holy love and power.

You see, in love he came as a servant and washed the disciples' feet. He didn't come with a blast of trumpets and with great acclamation that the King of heaven was now walking on earth. **He came and lived the life my children had to live, expressing holiness in the midst of a corrupt and perverse world.**

He gathered around him disciples who knew the same kind of dilemmas and conflicts that you experience. He had to be very patient with them while he trained and taught them, just as I have to be patient with you.

Some people think that he cannot really have enjoyed his humanity, but he loved it. Even though there was rejection, persecution, and people often met him with unbelief and ridicule, nevertheless, he really enjoyed being human. He had to leave his divine glory so that he could become life-size.

He didn't enjoy the process of crucifixion, but went joyfully to the cross because he knew what the outcome of his sacrifice would be. He reached out to people when they needed healing and help. He taught them from my heart. He enjoyed it. It was hard work, mind you. He got tired, just like everybody else; and sometimes the lack of faith in his disciples was very frustrating. But he fulfilled his task; and so I am able to welcome you into my Kingdom.

151

The Devil Defeated

———— o ————

I demonstrated how holiness can be lived out in a human being. That was fun. The devil thought he would catch Jesus out at some point. He tried hard enough in the wilderness! He thought he had what he wanted when he saw him hanging on the cross. I can hear his shriek of anguish when he suddenly realised he was defeated! All his demonic powers were overcome because **Jesus offered me a perfect sacrifice, uncontaminated by any evil.**

I even enjoyed sending Jesus to Hades to preach to the departed. It was good to take my holiness there. They needed it. These are things that many of my children never even stop to ponder.

152

Go in My Holiness

—— ० ——

Now, my child, just as I came among men in my holiness, so I am sending you among them in your holiness. I don't want you to tuck yourself away in some kind of spiritual prison. I want to see my children where the action is! **Purity is best demonstrated by generosity,** by giving freely what you have received freely. I want you to radiate my holy joy where it matters.

Don't be afraid of what the religious ones say. They opposed me and they will oppose you. Go where there is need, where people want help and are longing to be set free. Take my holiness into the gutters and ghettos. Take my love where people have lost hope and don't know which way to turn.

I draw you close to me to encourage and strengthen you. I want you to know tender moments when I express my affection for you. Then you will be aware of my love and faithfulness, no matter where I lead you.

Many think of holiness only in terms of behaviour patterns. They look at others through their spiritual magnifying glasses to see whether everything is morally correct. I wish they would turn their magnifying glasses on their own hearts!

Holiness includes righteousness but is much greater than moral behaviour. **It includes obedience to my word, going in my name to those who need me.** I bless those who reach out to others with my love. I encourage them and provide abundantly for them.

153

My Holy Judgment

———— o ————

My dear child, I am no longer among you as a human; now I reign in glory. The whole host of heaven proclaims my holiness. You often feel unworthy to come before my throne because you regard it not only as the seat of my majesty, but also of judgment. But the blood of my Son has cleansed you of your unworthiness. Now you can worship me because you are truly accepted.

I will judge nations in my holiness. Those who continue in rebellion and unrighteousness can expect to reap the reward they deserve. In my holiness I cannot condone sin. I cannot treat rebellion lightly. It is not my desire to condemn anyone. Two things will happen when people come before my judgment seat and are confronted by my holiness. My children will rejoice, for this will be the fulfilment of their longing to know me as I really am. Their hope to be transformed into my likeness will be realised when they see Jesus face to face.

Judgment will be fearful for those who have rejected holiness. My anger and punishment will be on those who fight against the truth and walk in their own ways with stubborn hearts. **If people don't desire holiness on earth, they don't belong in heaven.** They would only be out of place.

I long, therefore, to see stubborn hearts and minds changed by the power of my Spirit. My kindness and mercy is meant to lead to repentance. I never stop speaking words of faith where there is unbelief. I want my people to hear, to turn to me in repentance and receive the life I offer them.

How many really want holiness? How many want to please me? I wish there were more, don't you?

You don't need to live with a fearful sense of judgment hanging over you. You have passed from death to life. You are my child, my holy child, a child of my Kingdom, in whom I delight.

154

Holiness is Wholeness

———— o ————

My dear child, **holiness is wholeness**. This means I want you to be healthy in every way – spirit, soul and body. I want my holy life to touch every part of you.

My Holy Spirit has lived in you ever since you were born again. I want your mind to be consecrated to me and set upon things that are wholesome, for you to be free from negative thinking. I want you to enjoy my holiness, to feel my love for you instead of being bound by fear and feelings of unworthiness. I want your will to be submitted to my will. I want you to be careful how you use your body because it is a temple of my Holy Spirit, a sanctuary of my holy presence.

I want your body to enjoy me. I want your soul to enjoy love. **My holy love will bring you real joy, happiness and fulfilment.** But if you step outside my boundaries, this will bring tension, confusion and fear.

I am always with you and I will never allow you to be tempted beyond that which you are able to endure. You are always able to say 'No', my child. Being tempted gives you an opportunity for victory. Temptation strengthens you when you resist it.

If there are some occasions when you fail and yield to temptation, don't be too discouraged. All my children fail at times. When you yield to temptation, I don't throw you out of my Kingdom. I wait for you to turn back to me in repentance. Then I cleanse and restore you.

155

I Always Do What Is Right

——— o ———

Think of my righteousness as being the very best for
you. Sometimes my children think they know better
than me, and opt for the joy of the moment instead of
obedience to my word. They enjoy themselves for a
while, but afterwards realise I knew what was best.

I am very patient while this process is taking place. I
have to be, because sometimes it takes my children a
long time to work through all the things they want to do
before they are prepared to do what I want.

I always judge with righteousness. I don't assess
things, weighing up one thing against another to see
which is the lesser of two evils. I always see to the heart of
the matter. I don't simply judge the outward action but
the motive and intention that lies behind it.

**Because I am righteous, I have always done what is
right in your life.** I have never done anything unrighteous to you. The enemy has attacked you, and
others have dealt with you unrighteously at times. This
wasn't my work, so don't blame me! I put things right
and restore you.

156

True Righteousness

———— o ————

Many make up their own rules and regulations. This is a form of self-righteousness. They disobey my specific orders, but require obedience to their traditions. In the name of righteousness, some put people under false restrictions which I haven't placed upon them. They imagine that what *they* think is righteous must be righteous in my eyes.

You have had experience of this, haven't you, child? You have listened to respected men, more experienced than you, who have given the impression that my righteousness is harsh, restricting and virtually impossible to accomplish. You now see that some of these ideas are inconsistent with my heart. **I am much more tender, compassionate, loving and gracious than men!** You see, my dear child, I want right heart attitudes as well as right behaviour.

Love righteousness as I do. I love what is right. Love justice, truth and peace and reach out to others and be willing to get your hands dirty in the world's affairs. I want you to reach those who are depraved, unlovely and seemingly unlovable.

This to me is true righteousness; but the self-righteous will not go to such people. I am angry with those who have no care or compassion for the lost, poor, needy or desperate. Some religious people are like that. Some worldly people are the same. Their actions will determine their reward.

I have freed you in many ways. Now I want you to take my truth to others so that they can be liberated. Will you do that for me, child? Will you take my truth where there is deception, deceit, fear, unbelief and unrighteousness? Will you allow me to declare that truth through you so others are set free? Because you are so thankful for what I am doing in your life, you will do this for me, won't you? Thank you, child.

157

Liberty and Licence

———— o ————

My truth sets people free, not only from sin but from legalism. My Son became a curse to deliver people from the curse of the law. Why are people so legalistic? Because they are afraid of freedom. They fear that liberty will lead to licence. Both legalism and licence are sinful in my sight. I desire liberty for my children, the liberty that can only be expressed by living the truth.

To live in true liberty you need to depend on my grace. You have to love me and my ways more than yourself. When people box themselves up in legalistic attitudes they don't need to depend on my grace. They don't have to exercise faith in me.

It is much easier to live in prison, where everything is provided for you, than to live in the world. But I don't want my children living in prison. I have provided the truth to set them free.

Religious people judge those who fall into sexual sin and temptation. They imagine these to be the worst sins in my sight. How little they know and understand my heart.

You only have to examine my word to see how mightily I can use those who once fell into moral sin, but whose hearts belong to me. This does not mean I condone their sin; but I don't condemn them for it. I restore them when they turn back to me. I don't remove my call on their lives.

If I was to dismiss every one of my children for their moments of rashness and failure, who could I use? Men have so often concentrated on the failure and have missed my heart. I will always forgive when my children truly repent and turn from their sin.

My dear child, men won't like it when you speak like this because they don't like it when I speak in such ways. That is why so many rejected Jesus and the things he said. You see, men judge me as well as you. Those with harsh, hard and judgmental hearts try to make me like them. They constantly bring others under judgment and condemnation while I am trying to encourage them. They even imagine they are doing my will. They weary me. I love them but they weary me.

In the parable, the unmerciful servant received forgiveness and love, but then judged his fellow servant. He acted in unrighteousness and was judged by his own actions.

Those who apply judgmental passages of scripture to others always seem to excuse themselves. Did Jesus want to come in righteous indignation into the temple with a whip? How many times had he already been into the temple with words of compassion, forgiveness, life and truth? How many times did he bring healing and deliverance? His righteous act of judgment was a last resort.

The self-righteous ones, the traditionalists and religious legalists take no account of my heart. They think outward conformity satisfies me. I long for people to know more of my heart. I want to fill their hearts with my merciful forgiveness, my tender compassion and my gracious love. **Don't judge others, child – love them.**

158

Lord of Glory

———— ° ————

My dear child, I am the Lord of glory. I alone am worthy of honour and praise. I am bathed in inexpressible light, a radiance beyond anything you could envisage.

Jesus emptied himself of the glory that was his in heaven. He had to reveal my glory in what he said, and he did this so that you could comprehend it. He didn't come to glorify himself but to honour me through his obedience. He walked in holiness and righteousness, justice and truth.

He didn't seek his own self-esteem. He drew men to me and to my Kingdom. **Jesus was the human expression of my glory.** He deserves all the praise and honour you can give him. He is the Lamb in the midst of my throne, reigning in majesty and glory. Draw near to me; come before my throne with a sincere heart and in full assurance of faith. This is where you belong – in my glory.

159

My Glory in You

——— ◦ ———

I want your words and works to glorify me, child. You don't radiate my glory in the full way Jesus did, and I don't expect that. But through my Spirit working in you I am transforming you into my likeness from one degree of glory to another.

It is true, my child, that ever-increasing glory is being reflected in your life. This happens in a number of different ways. My presence within you radiates through your face, your body, your life-style. You reveal my glory in a dark and sinful world.

I want you to know that the cloud of my glory overshadows you. You never need to live under a cloud of oppression or darkness when you can live under the cloud of my glory. Wherever you go, that cloud goes with you. My divine glory is your inheritance.

You can do glorious things at any time and in any place, even when you feel you have nothing to give. The words you speak with boldness and confidence as revelation from my heart bring me glory. When you step out in faith, trusting my word, you bring me glory. When you confront sinners with their need to repent, reaching out to the lost with my love, you bring me glory. When you obey the leading of my Spirit and do what I ask, you give me glory. There are already many ways in which I am glorified through you, although there is always room for improvement.

You would like an experience of my glory, wouldn't you, child? Do you expect to see a cloud of glory, or to be enveloped in some kind of mystical experience? Such things happen, but **my glory is reflected in the way you reveal Jesus to others.**

In this way, you *add* to my glory. And that is even more important than receiving a revelation of my glory. Don't you think it is a great privilege, child, to be able to add to my glory every day? I think that's wonderful. This is why I have called and chosen you.

You will add to my glory in the future and in heaven. You will stand among the redeemed and proclaim my glory, honour and praise, I shall hear your voice and be pleased. You will experience my glory eternally!

160

The Reward Outweighs the Cost

———— o ————

I want you to live in the hope of glory. No matter what you experience now, glory awaits you. Jesus will come again as the Lord of glory. Beyond this life you will come into the full radiance of my glory that at present you only know partially. When you see me face to face, you will be transformed into my likeness. This will be the completion of what I have planned and my glory will be reflected perfectly in you.

I promise that you will share in my glory, provided you share in the sufferings of Jesus while you are on earth. **The cost of following me is nothing compared to the glory that is to be revealed in you.** I will give glory, honour and peace to those who obey me. The reward far outweighs the cost, child.

There are always those who seek glory without cost. They want reward but are not prepared for obedience. Every man will be rewarded for what he has done.

My deepest sorrow about sin is that it deprives people of the glory I desire for them. All have sinned and fallen short of this glory. I grieve over those who are deceived because they follow false gods and miss the glory that could be theirs if they put their faith in Jesus. But I rejoice in all who receive salvation from me. You are a child of my glory. I see you already seated in heavenly places in Jesus.

I was also glad in your death and the rich welcome I gave you into my eternal Kingdom. It may surprise you to hear me say this. You see, my child, in my eyes this has already happened. I know it lies in the future as far as you are concerned, but I can see the end from the beginning. And I know you will enjoy me eternally as much as I enjoy you.

161

Child of Glory

—— o ——

My dear child, your destiny is assured. I see you already reflecting my glory in the way I have planned. I see my purpose fulfilled, even while it is being worked out. I see you walking in my ways, resisting temptation. I see you affirming your faith in me and reaching out to others, seeking first my Kingdom and my righteousness. I see the rich reward that awaits you and I rejoice.

I regard you as a child of glory, not as a child of the earth. You are now working for things that last, not the things that will pass away.

Don't see yourself as purely human, but in terms of the destiny that awaits you. It is worth working for my Kingdom and putting me first, isn't it, beloved child?

162

You Glorify Me

———— o ————

I am thankful you don't mind paying the cost of being faithful. Listen carefully to me, child. Does it surprise you to know that I, your Lord and God, am thankful to you? You have always been the one to give me thanks. There have been few occasions when you have allowed me to thank you.

You glorify me by the way my love pours out of you to others, by the time you give to them, the affection you share with them and your concern in praying for them. I am glorified because you have wanted to be more effective in loving and ministering to others. You have glorified me with your praises.

I love to see you rejoicing in me, glad that you are alive in Jesus. I love to see your heart skipping and dancing – and your body, too!

You glorify me in the way you resist temptation, when you refuse the offers of the world, the flesh and the devil. I rejoice when you deny yourself, take up your cross and follow me. **Every act of self-denial in your life has added to my glory,** when you have obeyed me out of love. It is better to obey grudgingly than not at all; but you only add to my glory when you obey out of love.

My child, I know the sacrifices you have made, the cost you have faced. I know also the longing in your heart.

You love me so much, you long for more of me. Listen child, you add to my glory even by your longing. I will reward you.

163

Cycles of Growth

—— o ——

You have often condemned yourself for not living constantly in the full flow of revelation from me. I have watched you agonise over this. I have tried to comfort you but you have found it difficult to receive my words of truth.

Once you have tasted the best, nothing less is good enough, is it? But I give you this promise, child. You will know other times like this. Throughout your life there will be periods of exceptional blessing. Don't be disappointed that you are unable to live on the mountain top all the time.

My dear child, do you find this difficult to receive? You do realise that I use you at all times, not only when you experience exceptional blessing. The other times encourage you to seek me and to pray for revival. You would like to live in heaven on earth, wouldn't you?

Let me remind you what Jesus said. Every fruitful branch is pruned to make it more fruitful still. You have these glorious periods of fruitfulness, followed by times of pruning when I deal with selfish things such as pride, wrong motivation and disobedience. Then follow periods of growth, which lead to seasons of further fruitfulness and blessing. This is a continuous cycle.

The fact that I take you through seasons of pruning is evidence that I love you and that you are already fruitful. Yet I have heard your complaints at such times: 'Oh Lord, I am not as fruitful as I was'. Of course you are not, dear foolish child. How can you be so fruitful during the pruning season?

You have to bow to my wisdom, don't you? Remember, Jesus accomplished a great deal in three years. **Allow me to deal with you in the way I know best, and more of my glory will shine through your life; you will be more fruitful than in the past.** I have prepared good works for you to walk in.

164

My Glory in Jesus

——— o ———

My Spirit lived in Jesus and took him through all the stages of his manhood, through the times when he grew in wisdom and through the years of his ministry. He preached about my Kingdom, reached out to heal the sick and delivered those bound by evil spirits. He spoke my word, gave my promises and declared my truth.

My Spirit led him through times of rejection, false accusation and mockery, through every temptation, peril and danger. My Spirit led him through the agony in the Garden of Gethsemane, through the pain of crucifixion. There he yielded his Spirit to me and was victorious over all the principalities and powers of darkness.

I remember the morning I raised Jesus. I had seen the despair in the hearts of those who had followed him. Few of them retained their hope. I saw the darkness that had covered the world but I knew what I would do.

I remember the moment the stone was rolled away. Joy filled my heart as life flowed into the corpse that was my Son. I saw him lay aside the grave clothes, folding them neatly. He walked out into the garden. I saw the unbelief turn to joy in the hearts of my disciples when he appeared to them. I remember the day I raised my Son.

When Jesus returned to the glory of heaven, we sent the Holy Spirit upon all who believed in him. Jesus brings me glory by taking what is mine and declaring it to you. My child, the Spirit of Jesus is within you. This is the victorious, triumphant Spirit who lived in him and saw him through all those experiences.

That same Spirit who lives in you, will lead you victoriously through all the experiences of your life, through all opposition, rejection and pain. My Spirit will take you through death itself into the glory of resurrection. You shall have a new risen body in which to reveal my glory for all eternity.

Jesus has gone before you to prepare a place for you. You will reign with me in my everlasting Kingdom. How I rejoice in this! I am longing for you to come and take your appointed place. I am glad you have my Spirit to lead you in triumph. When Jesus appears, you will receive the crown of glory that will never fade.

Appendix of Bible References

1. I HAVE PERSONALITY
Gen 1:3; Ps 29:3–9; Ps 33:6–9; Jer 23:29; Isa 44:24; Jn 1:1–4,14; 8:30

2. IN MY IMAGE
Deut 32:6b; Gen 1:26–27

3. NO ACCIDENT
Matt 22:36–40; Ps 138:8; Rom 8:28

4. CREATED IN LOVE
Rom 8:15; Eph 1:4; Ps 139:13; Ps 33:13–14; Ps 121:8

5. MY PLAN FOR YOU
Eph 1:4–5,13–14; 2 Cor 3:18; Eph 2:8–9; Titus 3:5

6. MY WAY OF SALVATION
Rev 22:13; Gal 1:3–5; Col 1:13; Acts 4:12

7. I CARE FOR YOU
Jn 1:10–11; Isa 53

8. YOU ARE SAVED
Isa 43:11; 1 Jn 1:9; Eph 1:3

9. LET ME LOVE YOU
Matt 11:29; Eph 2:8; Jer 33:6b; 1 Jn 4:19; Ps 62:1; Isa 30:15

10. THE LOST CHILD

11. I LOVE YOU BECAUSE I LOVE YOU
Jer 31:3; Phil 1:6

12. I LOVE YOU MORE THAN YOU LOVE YOURSELF
1 Jn 3:1; 1 Jn 4:16; Isa 53:5; Isa 49:15

13. DON'T BE AFRAID OF LOVE
Lk 6:19; Heb 12:9–10; Heb 4:13

14. I AM GENTLE WITH YOU
Matt 11:29; Isa 50:5; Lk 22:27; Jn 13:1–17; Ps 46:10

15. I AM YOUR FATHER
Rom 8:14–15; Eph 1:7–8; Ps 130:7

16. YOU MAKE IT DIFFICULT FOR YOURSELF
TO RECEIVE LOVE
Rev 12:10–11; Isa 43:4; Ps 103:10

17. I LOVE THE PERSON YOU REALLY ARE
1 Sam 16:7b; Heb 4:13; Ps 38:9; Rom 5:8; Jn 6:63

18. YOU DON'T NEED TO PRETEND
Eph 4:25

19. YOUR APPEARANCE
1 Sam 16:17b; Jn 7:24; Lk 16:15; Ps 24:3–4; Rom 12:1

20. THE REAL YOU
Ps 45:11; Matt 6:6

21. OUR PRAYER MEETINGS
Phil 4:4–6; Matt 26:41

22. BE OPEN
Ps 62:8; Heb 4:12

23. GIVE AND YOU WILL RECEIVE
Matt 7:2; 2 Cor 9:6

24. NO FEAR IN LOVE
1 Jn 4:18

25. YOU ARE ACCEPTED
2 Cor 6:2; Jn 15:9; Jn 15:13

26. I WATCH OVER YOU
Ps 139:13–16; Rom 11:5

27. PEOPLE
Eph 4:3; Rom 16:1–18; Ps 105:14–15; Matt 6:14

28. EVERY DETAIL
Lk 12:7; Ps 20:7

29. I LEAD YOU STEP BY STEP
Phil 2:13

30. DON'T WORRY ABOUT THE FUTURE
Jer 29:11; Ps 119:105; Matt 6:34; Num 22:28; Jn 16:27

31. ALL OF ME
Col 2:9-10; Jn 14:15-17; Eph 1:18-19

32. ALL OF YOU
1 Cor 6:19-20; Rom 12:1-2; 1 Pet 1:18-19; 2 Cor 9:6-11

33. I AM MERCIFUL
Ps 103:8; Jn 15:2

34. TRUE LIBERTY
Gal 5:1; Matt 11:29; Lk 6:36; Eph 2:4

35. WHEN I FORGIVE, I FORGET
Ps 103; Isa 53:5

36. FORGIVE
Matt 6:12,14-15

37. THE FIGHT

38. LOVE IS PATIENT
1 Cor 13:4; 1 Thess 5:14; Eph 4:2

39. LOVE DOES NOT BOAST
1 Cor 13:4; 1 Cor 1:28-31

40. LOVE IS KIND
1 Cor 13:5

41. LOVE COVERS SINS INSTEAD OF EXPOSING THEM
1 Cor 13:5-7; Heb 8:12; Rom 4:7-8

42. MY SIN RECORD
1 Pet 1:15

43. YOUR SIN RECORD
Isa 1:18

44. LOVE NEVER FAILS
1 Cor 13:7; Ps 13:5; Ps 25:2; 1 Cor 13:12; 1 Cor 15:42–44; Ps 147:11

45. TRUSTING OTHERS
Jn 2:24

46. I HAVE CHOSEN YOU
1 Jn 3:1; Isa 43:1; 2 Cor 5:17; Isa 55:7b; Matt 28:20b

47. I DISCIPLINE IN LOVE
Ps 94:12; Heb 12:10; Matt 6:33; Jn 16:8; 1 Cor 11:32

48. I ENCOURAGE YOUR FAITH
Matt 28:20b; 1 Kings 19:11–13

49. YOU CAN DO WHAT I ASK
Ps 94:9; 2 Kings 18:7a; Phil 4:13; Mk 9:23b, 10:27

50. I NEVER DESPAIR OF YOU
Isa 43:4a

51. MY LOVE MAKES YOU CLEAN
1 Thess 5:23–24; Jn 15:3; James 1:7

52. I ENJOY YOU
SS 2:10; Zeph 3:17

53. ENJOY BEING YOU
Ps 139:7,23–24

54. RECEIVE AND GIVE
Jn 15:5

55. I AM GRACIOUS
Eph 1:3; Matt 7:8

56. CHILD OF MY GRACE
Eph 3:20; 1 Tim 6:17b; Rom 8:32; Ps 37:4

57. I AM GENEROUS
2 Cor 8:7; Lk 6:30,34–35,38

58.   THE OLD CAR

59.   THE WAY OF LOVE
Phil 2:5; Jn 13:15; Jn 15:10–12; 2 Jn 6; Isa 48:17–18

60.   LOVE IN MY NAME
1 Jn 3:16–18; Gal 15:6b

61.   A HEART OF LOVE
Gal 2:20; Rom 6:1–14; Eph 2:10; Jn 15:5; Matt 6:10

62.   GO IN LOVE
Jn 13:34

63.   I GO IN LOVE
Matt 10:1; Lk 14:27–33; Lk 9:2

64.   I GO IN YOU
Matt 5:11–12; Isa 42:6–7; Isa 6:8; 1 Cor 12:27–28; Prov 3:6

65.   THE RIGHT TIME

66.   SPREAD MY LOVE
2 Cor 2:14; Matt 9:36–38

67.   MY KINGDOM OF LOVE
Lk 12:32; Lk 17:21; 1 Cor 4:20; 1 Cor 13:1–13; Rom 14:17

68.   YOU ARE FILLED WITH MY POWER
Lk 4:38–39; Lk 5:13; Lk 8:27–37,51–56; Jn 2:1–11; Jn 6:5–13;
Matt 8:23–27; Matt 17:24–27; Acts 1:8

69.   MY POWER IN LOVE
1 Cor 4:20–21

70.   NOT BY MIGHT OR POWER
Gal 5:6; Jn 12:37; Lk 4:4–12

71.   I LOVE WORKING MIRACLES
Ps 77:14

72.   LET ME CARRY THE BURDEN
Lk 6:19; Matt 12:15; Ps 68:19; 1 Chron 14:10–11a,13–14,16;
1 Chron 15:13

73. LOVING DIFFICULT PEOPLE
Gal 6:12

74. BE REALLY FRUITFUL
Jn 15:8

75. GIVE YOURSELF TIME TO RECEIVE
Prov 4:23; Ps 68:9

76. I HEAL
Ex 15:26; Matt 12:10; Matt 8:2–3

77. CAUSES OF SICKNESS
Ps 107:20; Ps 106:13–15,28–29; Jn 14:1; Phil 4:7

78. I DON'T WANT YOU TO BE SICK
Gal 4:13–14

79. THE SICK WOMAN

80. JESUS HEALED
Matt 14:36; Matt 12:15; Isa 53:5

81. SICKNESS IS DISTRESSING
Prov 4:20–22; Matt 6:10

82. RECEIVE YOUR HEALING
Matt 19:26; Mk 9:21–24; Matt 6:14–15

83. I HATE SICKNESS
Isa 57:1–2; 1 Cor 15:55–57

84. I WAS THERE IN THE NIGHTMARE
Isa 43:2; Matt 27:46; Ps 40:1–3; Prov 12:17–21; Matt 5:43–44;
1 Thess 5:18; 1 Cor 6:7; Ps 43

85. THE BATTLE BELONGS TO ME
Jer 20:11; Rom 8:37; Isa 54:16–17; 2 Cor 10:5

86. I AM LIGHT
Jn 8:12; 1 Jn 1:5; Eph 5:8–11; Matt 5:14–16

87. POWERS OF DARKNESS
Eph 6:12; Jn 8:34; Rom 6:16; Jn 3:19–20

88. I DISPEL THE DARKNESS
2 Cor 11:14–15; Lk 9:42; Col 2:15; Matt 18:18; Isa 35:8–9

89. THE LIGHT OF THE WORLD
1 Jn 4:4; Jn 8:42–44; Col 1:13; Matt 5:16; Isa 41:10

90. LIVE IN FREEDOM
Gal 5:1; Jn 8:36; James 4:7

91. MY SOVEREIGN WILL
Isa 53:8; 1 Jn 5:4

92. THE ENEMY'S TACTICS
2 Cor 2:11; 2 Cor 12:7; Lk 22:31–32; Rom 8:34

93. VICTORY
Lk 9:1–2; Ps 91:11; Jn 12:31; Jn 16:11

94. I AM YOUR SHIELD
Ps 18:2; 1 Pet 5:8; 2 Tim 1:7

95. I HATE DARKNESS
Isa 8:19–20; Nahum 3:4; Eph 5:11–13

96. FIGHT THE GOOD FIGHT
Jn 8:44; 2 Cor 4:4; Jn 16:33; 1 Jn 3:7–8; Ps 44:4–8; Rom 8:37; 1 Jn 5:18–20

97. I AM THE GOD OF JUSTICE
Ps 72:4,12–14

98. IT IS FINISHED
Rom 3:10–12; Rom 6:23; Jn 3:17–18; Jn 19:30

99. MY RIGHTEOUS JUDGMENT
Rom 2:5–8

100. I LOVE EVERYONE
Jer 10:10–12; Isa 45:20–21

101. MY COVENANT PEOPLE
Jn 5:23,39–40; Jn 15:23; Rom 3:20–22; Rom 11:25–32; Matt 24:14

102. THE SON AND I ARE ONE
Jn 10:30; Jn 5:23; Jn 13:20b; Jn 14:6,9; Jn 15:23

103. JUDGING OTHERS
Rom 9:15–16; 1 Sam 16:7; Matt 21:31–32; Jn 8:42–47; Ps 9:4; Jn 8:15;
Matt 7:1–2

104. THE FORGIVEN

105. HELL
2 Pet 2:4–10; Rom 6:23; Matt 13:42; Matt 25:30

106. MEN FORM THEIR OWN JUDGMENT
1 Jn 2:16–17; Eph 1:3; Deut 11:26–28; Jn 3:36; Jn 12:47–48; 2 Cor 5:10;
Ps 79:6

107. THE NARROW WAY
Lk 11:49–51; Rev 6:9–11; Lk 9:23–26; Matt 7:13–14

108. NOT UNDER WRATH
Eph 2:1–10

109. I AM THE TRUTH
Jn 14:6; 1 Jn 1:5; Jn 1:14; Jn 8:32; Ps 26:2–3

110. THE TRUTH WORKS
1 Cor 2:4–5; Matt 24:35; Lk 8:15; Rom 12:2; Prov 2:1–5; Prov 4:20

111. DON'T JUDGE MY WORD
Jn 6:23; 2 Tim 3:16

112. CLING TO THE TRUTH
Jn 17:17; 1 Thess 5:16–18; Col 3:15; 2 Cor 5:17; Rom 8:1–2; 1 Cor 3:16;
Eph 1:6; Rom 8:37–39; Rom 2:11; 2 Pet 1:3; Heb 12:2; Prov 4:20–22

113. THE MAN WITH THE STOOP

114. FEED ON THE TRUTH
Col 3:16

115. THE WALK

116. I AM FAITHFUL
2 Tim 2:13; Matt 24:35; Jer 1:12

117. YOU WANT TO BE FAITHFUL
Jn 14:23 Matt 7:24–27; Ps 18:2,31; 1 Tim 6:17; Ps 103:2–3

118. DO YOU BELIEVE?
Ps 145:13; Jn 14:13–14; Isa 55:8–9; Lk 11:1–8; Lk 18:1–8; Ps 66:17–20;
Matt 21:22; Ps 37:4

119. TRUE FAITHFULNESS
Eph 5:17; Mk 11:24; Rom 4:18–21; Lk 8:15; Jn 8:19; Jn 14:7; Jn 17:9–19;
Jn 15:12–13

120. TRUST ME
James 1:22–25; Phil 1:6; Jude 24

121. I AM WISDOM
Prov 8:12–31; Isa 11:2; Ps 49:3; James 3:17; Rom 13:14; Matt 5:27–30;
Mk 9:43–47; 2 Cor 10:5; Eph 4:17–24; Heb 4:15

122. WORDS OF WISDOM
2 Tim 3:16; Jn 6:63,68; Col 3:16; Jn 14:25; James 1:5; James 3:17;
Dan 2:20–23; Prov 12:8; Prov 28:1; Prov 2:6

123. THIS IS WISDOM
Prov 2:6,9–10; Prov 3:13,17; Isa 32:17; Prov 9:10; Ps 111:10; Prov 28:26;
Prov 11:2; James 3:13; Lk 2:40; Lk 2:52; Ps 119:160

124. MY AUTHORITY
Col 1:16–17; Job 1:6–12; Job 2:1–6; Ps 47:7–9; Ps 2

125. MY CRITICS
Rom 2:1–3; Matt 7:21–23; James 4:1

126. MY AUTHORITY IN JESUS
Mk 1:22; Lk 4:36; Jn 8:28; Jn 5:19

127. MY AUTHORITY IN YOUR LIFE
Matt 7:21

128. SUBMIT JOYFULLY
Ps 119:47,56–60; Ps 100:2a; Phil 4:7; 1 Cor 1:5–7; Heb 13:20–21;
Matt 21:21–22

129. AUTHORITY IN MY CHURCH
Heb 13:17; 1 Tim 3:1–5,9–10

130. TRUE AUTHORITY IN LEADERS
Jn 12:43; Eph 5:21

131. I GIVE MY LIFE
Ps 27:14; Ps 37:7; Ps 46:10; Matt 20:1–15

132. RECEIVE THE HOLY SPIRIT
Lk 11:9–13; 1 Cor 1:4–7; Jn 7:38–39; Heb 7:25; Rom 8:31–32

133. THE GARDEN

134. PRAISE ME
Jn 10:10b; Gal 3:1–5

135. DON'T LIMIT ME
Heb 4:16; Matt 23:13

136. TRUE WORSHIP
Matt 18:20; Gal 5:13–15; 1 Thess 5:14; Jn 4:23–24

137. TRUE PRAYER
Jn 2:24; Acts 1:24

138. HUMBLE AND CONFIDENT
1 Pet 4:10–11a; Acts 5:29; Lk 18:9–14; Heb 10:19–25; Matt 6:5–8

139. FULL OF JOY
Lk 15:7; Ps 119:111; Ps 19:8; Zeph 3:17

140. MY SURPRISES
Ps 21:6; Ps 126:1–3

141. REJOICE ALWAYS
Heb 1:9; Jn 16:33; James 1:2–4; Acts 16:23–26; 1 Thess 5:16–18;
Phil 4:4–7; Jn 13:3–17

142. I AM HOLY
Isa 6:1–8; Rev 4; Deut 26:15; Jn 6:20; 1 Pet 1:15; Heb 12:14

143. HEAVEN IS YOURS
Jn 3:20–21; Lk 17:21

144. YOU ARE HOLY
Heb 9:14; 1 Cor 6:19; Heb 10:10; 1 Cor 1:2

145. A HOLY LIFE
1 Thess 4:3,7; Heb 1:9; Lk 1:37

146. CO-OPERATE WITH ME
2 Cor 7:1; Jn 7:38–39; Gal 5:22; 1 Cor 12:1–11

147. RESIST THE LIAR
2 Cor 2:11; James 4:7; Eph 4:27; James 1:14–15; Deut 14:2; 1 Pet 2:9

148. YOU HAVE MADE PROGRESS
James 1:18; Jude 24–25

149. BE HOLY
1 Cor 10:13

150. I CAME
Jn 1:5; Heb 4:15; Heb 2:18; Matt 18:12–13; Jn 13:1–7; Phil 2:6–11;
Heb 12:2–3

151. THE DEVIL DEFEATED
Lk 4:1–13; 1 Jn 3:8b; 1 Pet 3:18–22

152. GO IN MY HOLINESS
Matt 5:14–16

153. MY HOLY JUDGMENT
Heb 1:3b; Ps 9:7–8; Gal 6:7–8; Jn 3:17–18; Ps 1:5; Jer 2:35; 1 Pet 1:13–16

154. HOLINESS IS WHOLENESS
Eph 4:17–24; Phil 4:8; 1 Cor 3:16–17; I Cor 10:13; Titus 2:11–12

155. I ALWAYS DO WHAT IS RIGHT
Heb 12:11; Jn 7:24

156. TRUE RIGHTEOUSNESS
Phil 3:4–9; Lk 11:46,52; James 2:13b; Isa 61:1–3; Mk 7:5–13; Ps 9:8

157. LIBERTY AND LICENCE
Gal 3:13–14; Gal 5:1–6; 2 Sam 11:12–25; Ps 51; Rom 14:13;
Matt 18:21–35; Rom 2:3–4; Rom 3:20–22; Rom 14:4

158. LORD OF GLORY
Ps 24:10; Rev 4:11; Ez 1:26–28; Jn 8:54; Jn 7:18; Heb 10:22

159. MY GLORY IN YOU
2 Cor 3:18; Ps 34:5; Jn 17:24; Ex 40:34–35; 2 Chron 5:13–14;
2 Chron 7:1–3; 2 Thess 1:11–12; Jn 17:4; Rev 5:13

160. THE REWARD OUTWEIGHS THE COST
Rom 8:18; 1 Thess 4:16; 1 Pet 4:13–14; Rom 8:17; Matt 16:27; Rom 3:23

161. CHILD OF GLORY
Phil 3:20; Jn 6:27; 1 Cor 9:25; Matt 6:33

162. YOU GLORIFY ME
Jn 12:25–27

163. CYCLES OF GROWTH
Ps 73:25; Jn 15:2; Ps 77:6–13; Eph 2:10

164. MY GLORY IN JESUS
Mk 14:35–36; Jn 20:6–9; Jn 7:38–39; 1 Cor 15:42–44; Jn 14:2–3;
2 Cor 2:14; James 1:12; 1 Pet 5:4

THE TRUTH THAT
SETS YOU FREE

THE TRUTH THAT SETS YOU FREE

COLIN URQUHART

Hodder & Stoughton
LONDON SYDNEY AUCKLAND

To all those whose
desire is to live
in the Truth, and
to know how they
can encourage others
by speaking the
Truth to them in love

Acknowledgments

I want to thank the many, many people who have encouraged
me to write this book; those who have attended Direct
Counselling courses and conferences, and whose lives have
been changed radically as a result. A book can never be the
same as 'live' ministry, but I trust this will convey to you the
essence of the truth of Jesus Christ that will set you free; and
that you will see how you are able to communicate the truth to
others that they too may be liberated.

My thanks to my secretaries – Helena, who has borne the
brunt of the word processing, Barbara and Samantha – and
others who have helped.

My thanks also to my friends in the Middle East, especially
Dr Susheela John. Most of the book was written while there
for a time of ministry.

And of course I am deeply grateful to the Lord for His
enabling, and for a wonderful wife who is so understanding
whenever I am absorbed in writing.

To God be all the glory for whatever way He is able to use
this book to minister His Truth into the lives of His beloved
children.

Throughout this book I have used the pronoun 'he' as it is

important the teaching of the Truth is applied to each individual. Of course the Truth is equally applicable to every 'she'. The use of the masculine does not represent any sexist stance by the author!

The biblical quotations are from the New International Version, except where indicated. The use of bold and italic type in them is my own.

Contents

PART 3 OVERCOMING THE ENEMY

PART 4 DIRECT COUNSELLING

PART 1

THE TRUTH

1 Glorious Liberty

'It is for freedom Christ has set us free', Paul proclaims boldly. 'You were called to be free', he says. And yet many Christians do not live in personal freedom. They live more like victims than victors, victims of their past hurts or of their present problems. To suggest they are always led in triumph through Christ is met either with astonishment or unbelief.

They feel inadequate, useless, spiritual failures! Some even doubt God's love for them because they have sought to experience His love – but in vain! This failure reinforces their sense of inadequacy. They do not see how they could be used by God; and they expend considerable nervous energy trying to conceal their spiritual inadequacy from other Christians.

Perhaps counselling is the answer? After all, many others seem to need this and there are an increasing number of people ready to offer counsel.

In time even this often leads to disillusionment. It is good to have someone to talk to, someone who gives you time and takes a genuine interest in you. But there is the pain of going over past hurts, of having to relive things best forgotten. And there always seems to be another part of the puzzle to be discovered, as if you have to go deeper into yourself, or further into your past, to find the root cause of all this personal inadequacy and failure. And the benefits of such counselling seem so short-lived!

This can lead to a certain resignation: 'Perhaps I should learn to live with the problems. People will have to accept me as I am. At least it helps to talk, but will I ever really be free?' Such freedom as there is seems to disappear as new problems arise; the same old feelings of insecurity and inadequacy re-emerge. Will it ever get better? 'What is really wrong with me?'

Going deeper into yourself, or further back into your past, is diametrically the opposite to the teaching of the New Testament. No wonder such an approach to problems fails to bring true liberty. Neither does looking at yourself produce the faith that will enable you to face the difficulties which will inevitably arise in the future.

The purpose of this book is to show you how you can experience the freedom of which the scriptures speak: 'the glorious liberty of the sons of God'. In New Testament times Christians were so famous for the freedom they enjoyed, Paul suggests that others would want to send spies among them to see why they enjoyed such liberty.

People were genuinely set free by the power of the Gospel; so much so that they needed to be taught how to use, and not abuse, that freedom.

People only resort to unbiblical kinds of ministry, either because they do not know the Truth of what God has done for them in Jesus, or they do not understand these truths. And so they cannot believe what Jesus has accomplished for them. If their knowledge, understanding and faith are limited, they can only experience a limited freedom.

You never have to justify the Truth. If you have to justify the ministry you either exercise or receive, something seriously is wrong. Many involved in so-called 'inner healing' are trying to justify their approach from scripture, with zeal but no convincing arguments! The reason for this is simple. Methods will not rescue people from their bondages; but the Truth will. **Jesus affirms that it is the Truth itself that will set us free.**

Therefore we need to know and understand the Truth of what God has done for us through Him; for when we believe the Truth it impacts our lives in the way God intends. Then we can enjoy 'the glorious liberty' He desires for His children, the freedom He has made possible through faith in Jesus.

Does God want us to be healed? Undoubtedly! Does He want to free us from the hurts of the past and the emotional inadequacy of the present? Without question!

However, these objectives will not be achieved by looking into yourself, or back into your past. They can only be achieved by taking hold of the Truth and making that Truth your own. This book will encourage you in doing just that.

I have led a number of conferences under the title, 'Direct Counselling'. These have been directed at those involved in pastoral and counselling ministries. It would be no exaggeration to say that these conferences have brought about major changes in the lives of those attending. By the end of these conferences it was as if I was speaking to an entirely different group of people from those who arrived at the beginning.

I do not claim the credit for this, for I have only used the time available to share the Truth with them; and this has had the liberating effect on them that Jesus promised.

Many write subsequently to share how their ministries to others have been revolutionised. People who have received 'counselling' for years are set free at last!

To give one example: A minister came on one conference and the Truth impacted his life and ministry to such an extent he sent his wife on a subsequent conference. He later wrote to thank me for sending back his 'new' wife and commented how people were now being set free through her ministry with astonishing speed.

That is the effect of the Truth on people's lives, not the truth about themselves or their past, but the Truth of all that Jesus has done for them.

At another conference a lady who had just had two years of counselling therapy commented that the Truth had done for her in two days what counselling had been unable to do in two years – set her free! You only had to look at her to see the evidence of what she was saying. Gone was the frown, the worried expression, the drawn and pinched look; she now appeared radiant and peaceful.

Surely it should not be difficult for Christians to find such joy when Jesus has already done everything necessary to set them free, no matter how damaged they have been or how horrendous their past experiences!

In this book I am going to share with you the essence of the teaching given at these conferences. I pray that as you read this book you will be directed afresh to the TRUTH that will set you free; and that you will see how God can use you to speak that Truth into others' lives that they too might enjoy 'the glorious liberty' of God's children.

2 The Wonderful Counsellor

God sent His Son, the Word of God, into the world to bring us the Truth. He came as the Light to speak into the spiritual darkness of the world.

Jesus came to us as God's Word, God's Truth, God's Wisdom. He came as the Wonderful Counsellor, the Holy Son of God.

Yet whenever Jesus spoke, a clear division took place between those who believed what He said and those who rejected His words, those who obeyed Him and those who denied Him. Often it was the religious people who refused to believe; they were so entrenched in their traditions that they could not recognise the Truth when they heard it! They were so busy being religious, they failed to recognise Him as their Messiah and Saviour, and so were not able to receive the life He offered them.

Yet prostitutes believed in Him and turned to Him; they recognised Him as the Holy One. Even swindlers and con-men received salvation. Beggars came and sat at His feet, cried out to Him and were healed by Him. Outcasts, demoniacs, lepers were set free by Him.

You would think that if the Holy One was walking around, the unholy wouldn't dare go near Him. Yet His holiness wasn't expressed in religious piety that repelled the world. His holiness attracted sinners; they were drawn to Him not because He said the things they wanted to hear, but what they needed to hear: the Truth. **The prostitutes, outcasts, swindlers, beggars and sick flocked to Him because He was the only Counsellor who had ever given them hope.** To the religious ones they were the scum of the earth, today's equivalent of the drug-pushers, the child abusers, the alcoholics.

They stood for hours in the hot sun to listen to Him teach, for here was someone who could get them into heaven despite what they were! **The Wonderful Counsellor didn't judge or condemn them but gave them a future and a hope.** No matter how depraved their lifestyles, no matter how inadequate they felt, even if they had lost all sense of self-worth, **here was someone who said they mattered!** Because they believed Him many of them went ahead of the religious ones into the Kingdom of heaven. They received the life Jesus came to give.

Jesus did not preach sentimentality, neither was He looking for an emotional response to His Gospel. He said:

> Enter through the narrow gate. For wide is the gate and broad is the road that leads to destruction, and many enter through it (Matt. 7:13).

He wanted to set people free from everything which bound them and caused destruction; and He wanted to give them God's life in all its fullness.

Here was the man who spoke the truth; the Wonderful Counsellor. The crowds flocked to hear Him, to hear the Truth that would set them free. He said:

> If you hold to my teaching, you are really my disciples. **Then you will know the truth, and the truth will set you free** (John 8:31–2).

The Truth will set you free from your depravity, your bondage, your unbelief, your guilt, your fear, your sickness. Whatever your need, **the Truth will set you free!** This was the message Jesus came to bring! **God's Kingdom life, eternal life, the fullness of life for you – NOW!**

As you read the Bible the Wonderful Counsellor is speaking to you with all the authority of God Himself. **If you need counsel, you can turn to Him and listen to His words, the words of the Wonderful Counsellor.** And you can be sure that everything He says to you will be true, for **He is the Truth!** Jesus said:

> I am the way and the truth and the life (John 14:6).

Even His opponents recognised that He taught and acted with genuine authority. The religious ones could not match such authority.

ANOTHER COUNSELLOR

At the Last Supper His disciples were grief-stricken because the One in whom they had placed their hope was going to leave them. But He promised:

> I will ask the Father, and he will give you another Counsellor to be with you for ever – the Spirit of truth (John 14:16–17).

The promised Counsellor, the Holy Spirit, is the Spirit of truth. Jesus had come with the words of truth, now He promised to give His followers the *Spirit* of truth. Although He was returning to the Father He promised that this other Counsellor would never be taken from them.

Jesus made it clear that 'the world cannot accept him, because it neither sees him nor knows him. But you know him, for he lives with you and will be in you' (John 14:17).

The Wonderful Counsellor was *with* them, but the other Counsellor would be *in* them.

If you are born again the Wonderful Counsellor, Jesus, will be with you always; and the other Counsellor, the Holy Spirit, will be in you always. The Counsellor lives in you! The Word of Truth is with you and the Spirit of Truth is in you. What more could you need? The Word and the Spirit together have the answer to every situation or need that could arise in your life.

Both these divine Counsellors will always agree together. They are never at odds with one another.

> When the Counsellor comes, whom I will send to you from the Father, the Spirit of truth who goes out from the Father, he will testify about me (John 15:26).

The ministry of the Holy Spirit living in you is to testify to you about Jesus. Why? Because the answer to every need in your life is contained in what Jesus has done for you. It is not some new technique of ministry or prayer that will set you free; **you simply need the Spirit of Truth to testify to you about Jesus.**

> It is for your good that I am going away. Unless I go away, the Counsellor will not come to you; but if I go, I will send him to you . . . But when he, the Spirit of truth, comes, he will guide you into all truth (John 16:7,13).

Into what truth will the Holy Spirit guide us? The Truth of Jesus!

> He will not speak on his own; he will speak only what he hears, and he will tell you what is yet to come. He will bring glory to me by taking from what is mine and making it known to you (John 16:13–14).

The Holy Spirit will never act independently of Jesus or the Father. There is always unity and agreement in the Trinity!

THE COUNSELLOR AT WORK

A woman was caught in bed with her lover. There could be no doubt that she was guilty of adultery. According to the law she should be stoned to death. The religious ones brought her to Jesus thinking that this time they could catch Him out. He claimed He had not come to overthrow the law but to fulfil it. Yet He had been preaching mercy, forgiveness and love. How could He reconcile such teaching when this woman deserved death? Jesus told them:

If any one of you is without sin, let him be the first to throw a stone (John 8:7).

On hearing this the people began to drift away beginning with the eldest, until Jesus was left alone with the woman.

'Has no-one condemned you?'
'No-one sir', she said.
'Then neither do I condemn you,' Jesus declared. 'Go now and leave your life of sin' (vv. 10–11).

'Religious' people are very good at judging others. Yet Jesus, who had the right to judge, had come to save and heal, not judge. He was not being soft with the woman; He was being merciful, expressing God's desire to forgive, not condemn. But He also made clear she was to leave her life of sin.

Like that woman we stand 'naked' before Jesus because He can see our hearts. He could judge us; but in His grace and mercy He wants to forgive us and set us free.

To believe Jesus is to receive eternal life; to disbelieve Him leaves a person in the condemnation we all deserve (John 3:16–18). In Him God has provided not only the Way of Salvation, but also the Truth that will enable us to live in the freedom He desires for His children. **Through the Wonderful Counsellor God sets us free completely from what we have been, and**

through the Holy Spirit He enables us to be what He wants us to be.

These are the Counsellors you need and if you are filled with the Holy Spirit, these are the Counsellors God has given you. They will work together for your total well-being, if only you are prepared to co-operate with them.

This book will show you how to do just that!

3 The Healing Nature of the Gospel

The Gospel is the good news of what God has done for us in Jesus Christ. Everything He said and did revealed His Father's character. Jesus said: 'Anyone who has seen me has seen the Father' (John 14:9). Jesus loves because it is God's nature to love. He is merciful and gracious because He reveals God's mercy and grace.

God alone has the right to judge sin because He alone is righteous by nature. Instead of sending His Son to judge He sent Him to save, to offer men the way out of the condemnation they deserve.

Jesus demonstrated His love for the world; He showed that it is His will to liberate people from bondage and to heal them in spirit, soul and body.

It is a common fallacy to say: 'Jesus accepts me just as I am.' Everyone is totally unacceptable to God in his or her natural state. 'All have sinned and fall short of the glory of God.' All are therefore under condemnation and will remain so eternally, unless they place their faith personally in the saving work of Jesus Christ. The good news is that we can be made acceptable to God, that we can live in a relationship with Him of total acceptance and love.

This is only possible for those who believe personally what

Jesus has said and done for them. Such faith makes them one with Jesus and they are able to share in His standing before God. Because He lived a life of total obedience when on earth, Jesus remained in a relationship of total acceptance and perfect unity with His Father. Those who believe in Him share that acceptance. **His life becomes their life, His acceptance their acceptance, His inheritance their inheritance.**

REPENT AND BELIEVE

The key to such a relationship is made clear by Jesus at the very beginning of His ministry:

'The time has come,' he said. 'The kingdom of God is near. Repent and believe the good news!' (Mark 1:15).

These are the two important keys Jesus gives us to a life of complete freedom in Him: repentance and faith.

Repentance involves much more than being sorry about your sins. It involves a complete change of mind and attitude. The one who repents turns away from a life of sin and has a completely new perspective on his life. He accepts God's goals and plans for his future, and submits to His purposes.

To repent, then, is to turn away from what you have been. Faith enables you to embrace the Truth of all that Jesus has done for you, so that you can enjoy the life He came to give you, becoming the person He wants you to be.

Repentance and faith are essential at the beginning of the Christian's life, for without these no one can be born again, enter God's Kingdom and receive the gift of eternal life. However, both repentance and faith need to be a way of life for every believer. There is little point in someone turning to Christ if he then turns back to his own ways. He needs to remain at one with Jesus, believing the Truth of what He has said and done for him.

The Christian who lives by these principles will walk in continual freedom. He will refuse to turn back to a self-centred life or to his past. He will remain turned to Christ. He will live the new life Jesus came to give him. Like Paul, he will 'reach out for that which lies ahead'. He will 'take hold of that for which Christ Jesus took hold of me' (Phil. 3:12).

You can be such a believer!

WRONG CONCEPTS OF GOD

Wrong attitudes to difficult circumstances often reflect wrong concepts of who God is. Many believe that God wants to punish them rather than be gracious to them; that He wants them to be sick instead of knowing Him as their Healer; that they are objects of His wrath rather than His mercy. They think it is impossible for them to please Him. Clearly they do not understand the status they have before Him through what Jesus has done for them. Instead they see themselves as spiritual failures, they feel useless and more aware of their negative attitudes than of His positive love!

For example, some claim it is difficult to think of God as 'Father' because of their catastrophic relationships with their human fathers. It is obvious that even the best, most loving father can in no way be compared to God in His love and Fatherhood. But emotions can be so powerful that they swamp reason.

When we look at events through the pain and hurt of negative emotions we inevitably have a distorted view of the Truth. However, when we begin with the revelation of Truth given us through Jesus, and then allow the truths of His Word to impact different areas of our lives, we discover that God views us in far more positive ways than we view ourselves.

It is a tragic mistake to begin with 'my own ideas of God'. That is to create a god after your own understanding. Such a god could not save or heal you, meet your needs or give you a sense of total well-being. **It is mistaken to judge God through the mishmash of your ever-changing emotions and circum-**

stances. You need to begin with the biblical revelation of who He is and allow the Truth of what He has done for you to influence your thinking and emotions. Jesus wants you to be free to enjoy the life He died to give you now. And He wants you to be certain that nothing could ever separate *you* from His love; that you will reign eternally with Him in His glory!

THE TRUE GOD

To describe who God is would require a book in itself, volumes even. All we can hope to do now is to touch on some key aspects of His nature crucial to our faith. Other aspects of His character will become clear later.

> The Lord, the Lord, the compassionate and gracious God, slow to anger, abounding in love and faithfulness, maintaining love to thousands, and forgiving wickedness, rebellion and sin (Exod. 34:6–7).

Of the multitude of scripture verses we could choose, we will begin with these words spoken by the Lord to reveal Himself to Moses. They point us to five key aspects of His character that are often emphasised in the scriptures.

Compassionate
God is compassionate. This means that He is not merely sympathetic, but merciful. Jesus did not come to heap pity on us; we have more than enough of self-pity already! To be compassionate is to 'suffer along with', to share in another's predicament. By sending Jesus to share our humanity God showed His compassion.

The God of the Old Testament is the same as the God of the New. Jesus came from heaven to give us a clear revelation of the nature and character of God. He showed compassion because His Father is compassionate by nature. He had compassion on the sick and healed them. He had compassion on the multitude and fed the people. **His compassion led to action, to definite results.**

Ultimately His compassion would lead Him to the cross!

Gracious

Jesus's compassion was expressed in the way He graciously gave of Himself to people.

Grace is the 'free, unmerited favour of God'. In simple terms it is **God giving His everything to those who deserve nothing.**

We are saved by grace, brought into a living relationship with God, by His activity – not through anything we have done for ourselves, or through any merit of our own. We could never deserve anything from Him. **He gives because He has chosen to give to those who trust in Jesus.** Everything we receive from Him is a demonstration of His grace. 'From the fulness of his grace we have all received one blessing after another' (John 1:16).

Only through our complete identification with Jesus (which will be explained later) are we able to receive the life and liberty He wants to give us.

Slow to Anger

Because death is His just and holy judgment on sin, God could wipe men from the face of the earth if He so chose. In His mercy and grace He has chosen not to do so, but has provided a way of escape from the judgment we deserve.

Even when we were spiritually dead and under condemnation because of our sins, **He chose not to vent His wrath on us, not to judge us as we deserve, but to offer us the way of salvation. He is slow to anger!** Through Jesus He draws us to Himself that we might experience His mercy and grace and come to know His love.

Those who are one with Jesus need have no fear of eternal punishment.

Abounding in Love

To know God is to know eternal and perfect love. His love is spiritual, not emotional. It is not based on feelings or circumstances, but on who He is. **God is love and therefore He loves. He loves because it is His nature to love.**

Many who seek counsel complain that they do not 'feel' loved by God. This is not surprising for such a statement suggests a basic misunderstanding about God. He is Spirit, not an emotion. **Once you believe in His love you experience His love, especially in the ways He cares and provides for you.** Having accepted His love, you may on occasions 'feel' His love, although such feelings are incidental and not the basis of a loving relationship with God. **It would be impossible to live the Christian life if we only believed in God's love for us when we had emotional feelings of being loved by Him!**

God 'abounds' in love. He overflows with love. So it cannot be difficult to know or receive that love together with the benefits accompanying such a privilege. And we shall see how we are able to do this.

Jesus did not demonstrate God's love by putting His arm around people and saying: 'There, there, it's all right! God loves you!' In fact He said remarkably little about love; He simply demonstrated it in action. And that love led Him, not only to identify totally with you in your need, but to give His life for you on the cross to liberate you from that need.

Abounding in Faithfulness

Not only does God abound in love towards us; He abounds in faithfulness. He is not begrudgingly faithful because He has given promises He must keep. It is His nature to be faithful. To deny His Word would be to deny Himself.

The Father will never deny His Son. He accepts all who put their faith in Him, regardless of what they have been or have done in the past. He will not turn away any who come to Him. **He honours the faith of all those who claim the efficacy of His blood to forgive their sins and meet every need in their lives.**

The Lord is faithful to His Word, and promises. He watches over His Word to perform it. He is faithful to all those who put their trust in Him. God is not fickle and does not change with moods! **Jesus Christ is the same yesterday and today and for ever; He reflects God's unchanging nature, that He is always totally reliable and dependable.**

Righteous

Because He is righteous by nature, God is righteous in all that He does. He is the standard by which everything and everyone is judged. **We could not be righteous before Him if it were not for Jesus and what He has done for us. He puts us right with His Father so we can approach Him with confidence. Those who are made righteous through Jesus have nothing to fear from the righteous God.**

This is the amazing work Jesus has accomplished through the cross: He makes righteous before God those who have been unrighteous and were previously totally unacceptable to Him. This is possible only because Jesus has offered to the Father the sacrifice of a totally righteous life on behalf of sinners, even though He was subjected to every temptation we can experience, was continually rejected, persecuted, falsely accused and even hated by those who opposed Him. He demonstrated the life of love in the midst of continual difficulty and then in love offered His life to the Father on our behalf. It is almost impossible for us to comprehend such love. But this is God's nature.

The Lord is righteous in all his ways and loving towards all he has made (Ps. 145:17).

He is Holy

Righteousness is one aspect of holiness. It is impossible for us to describe God's holiness adequately. He is whole, perfect and complete in Himself. He is therefore above and beyond all He has made.

Yet Jesus accepted the limitations of a human life and lived in holiness, full of mercy, full of grace, full of love, of joy, power and authority. **It is that fullness of life He gives to those who put their trust in Him.**

In everything He showed Himself submissive to the will of His Father:

> For I have come down from heaven not to do my will but to do the will of him who sent me (John 6:38).

> I do nothing on my own but speak just what the Father has taught me (John 8:28).

And so Jesus shows that submission to the will of His Father is an indispensable part of living a life of holiness on earth.

His purpose is that we should be like Him.

> He chose us in him before the creation of the world to be holy and blameless in his sight (Eph. 1:4).

This is clearly not possible through any self-effort or personal achievement on our part. We cannot solve our own problems, let alone make ourselves holy! This is what God Himself will work within the believer, but only with his or her co-operation. To this end, God has made provision to deal with everything in our lives that is not like Him or is opposed to His purposes. **It is His intention to free you, therefore, from everything that is a hindrance to becoming more like Jesus. He is intent on changing you from one degree of glory to another.**

> For those God foreknew he also predestined to be conformed to the likeness of his Son . . . (Rom. 8:29).

> Therefore we do not lose heart. Though outwardly we are wasting away, yet inwardly we are being renewed day by day (2 Cor. 4:16).

It is good news that He who has begun a good work in you will bring it to completion! It is good news that God has made provision for you to become like He is!

MAN'S NATURE WITHOUT GOD

People are only ready to take hold of the good news if they first believe the bad news. This, stated simply, is to say that apart from Christ all are unacceptable to God and are living under condemnation. In other words they face judgment because of their sin.

> For all have sinned and fall short of the glory of God (Rom. 3:23).

Jesus Himself said: 'Whoever does not believe stands condemned already because he has not believed in the name of God's one and only Son' (John 3:18). What a contrast to those who do believe:

> I tell you the truth, whoever hears my word and believes him who sent me has eternal life and will not be condemned; he has crossed over from death to life (John 5:24).

God does not want to condemn; He wants to save and in Jesus has provided the only way of salvation. To receive this salvation involves passing from death to life.

Paul asserts that God 'wants all men to be saved and to come to a knowledge of the truth' (1 Tim. 2:4). Jesus makes it clear that this can only happen through faith in Him.

> I am the way and the truth and the life. No-one comes to the Father except through me (John 14:6).

Those who refuse to repent and believe are in grave danger:

But because of your stubbornness and your unrepentant heart, you are storing up wrath against yourself (Rom. 2:5).

How essential then, to repent and believe. **There can be no substitute for these two commands Jesus gives us.** They enable us to appropriate the life He offers, and then enable us to live in the fullness of that life.

There can be no substitute for His truth. Jesus warns His opponents:

But unless you *repent*, you too will all perish (Luke 13:5).

His opponents were very religious but they did not believe in Him. They sought to please God through self-righteousness instead of finding their true righteousness in Jesus. Again we see the contrast with those who accept Jesus:

Yet to all who received him, to those who *believed* in his name, he gave the right to become children of God (John 1:12).

Whoever *believes* in him shall not perish but have eternal life (John 3:16).

Whoever *believes* in him is not condemned (John 3:18).

Repent and believe. Repent and believe. Repent and believe. These are the keys to receiving all that God has to give us, including the freedom we are to enjoy as His children.

We dare not substitute anything for these two truths.

Counselling techniques can never replace obedience to the Truth Jesus proclaims. He has made clear that it is only by continuing to believe His words that we can be His disciples, know the Truth and enjoy the freedom He died to make possible for us. Jesus said this to those who believed in Him:

If you hold to my teaching, you are really my disciples. Then you will know the truth, and the truth will set you free (John 8:31–2).

THE ONLY WAY OF FREEDOM IS THE WAY OF TRUTH!

Every Christian needs to know the Truth, therefore, if he is to enjoy the freedom this alone brings. Those who desire to help others come into freedom need to do so in the way the Truth of God's Word indicates; not by taking people more deeply into themselves or into their past lives, but into the Truth. They need to know and understand the Truth that will set them free from sin and failure.

The Lord is near to all who call on him, to all who call on him *in truth* (Ps. 145:18).

Nothing can, or needs, to be added to what Jesus has already accomplished for us. **Faith in what He has said and done leads to complete freedom – from sin, past hurts, personal failure and inadequacy, bondages and sickness in all its forms.**

4 The Blood

> In him we have redemption through his blood, the forgiveness of sins, in accordance with the riches of God's grace that he lavished on us with all wisdom and understanding (Eph. 1:7).

God created in love, and desires to have a relationship of love with those He made. Love is always vulnerable. Beings that can love must also have the capacity to hate.

God wants His people to obey Him as the outworking of their love for Him. They are to acknowledge His Lordship and supreme authority in their lives by willingly submitting themselves to Him. They have freedom to disobey, be stubborn and even rebellious. **God had to give them His complete freedom, with absolutely no restraint placed upon the use of their wills, or it would not have been possible for them to love.**

We know to our cost that Adam, and in Adam all mankind, came to a point of choosing self rather than God. He yielded to the temptation of the devil, who himself had acted similarly in heaven. Created as one of the celestial beings, subservient to the Lord, he was thrown out of heaven, having rebelled against God's authority, desiring to make himself the object of worship and admiration from others. Jesus said:

I saw Satan fall like lightning from heaven (Luke 10:18).

This was God's judgment. There could be no rebellious beings in heaven. The devil's purpose ever since has been to tempt mankind to follow him in his rebellion. Instead of serving the Lord he wants us to rebel against Him; instead of submitting to God's authority, he wants us to rise up in rebellious independence.

All of us were infected by Adam's sin: his rebellion tainted all mankind. All are born with a sinful nature and therefore inevitably sin! Even an innocent-looking baby is born with a sinful disposition, and it is not very long before he reveals it!

We are all aware of the drive within us to please self, to be the central focus of interest in our own lives. That drive tears man away from God's purposes and leads him into the sins of selfishness and self-indulgence, placing self instead of God on the throne of his life. Inevitably this causes a rift between man and God, an alienation within their relationship.

God had to rectify this situation. Man needed a Saviour to deliver him from his rebellion and foolishness. Even before the creation of the world God knew He would need to provide us with such a Saviour. He knew man would abuse the freedom He had given him. In His love, God decided not to do away with sinful humanity, although that is what mankind deserved. The story of Noah and the flood clearly shows us that God could so easily have wiped out humanity and started again; but this was not His purpose. **He wanted to redeem, to purchase back for Himself those who had been lost to Him because of their sin – everyone.**

God could not ignore sin as if it didn't matter. Because God's just and holy judgment on sin is the death penalty, someone who was Himself sinless had to suffer that death penalty, someone who was subjected to all the temptations we experience and yet remained innocent. **An innocent life had to be given on behalf of the guilty.** So Jesus purchased men for

God with the shedding of His blood, offering His own sinless life on behalf of sinful mankind.

Jesus obeyed the Father. He did everything that Satan failed to do and that man couldn't do. He pleased the Father in every way and in every detail. There was no charge that could be justly brought against Him. He was without sin, pure in every way. On the cross He shed His innocent, perfect and guiltless blood on behalf of sinners.

There are three ways in which we need to understand the significance of the shedding of Jesus's blood:

1 THE BLOOD WAS SHED FOR GOD

This was the price God required in order that all our sin, and everything in our lives that had destroyed fellowship with Him, could be forgiven and cleansed. **The righteous requirements of God have been satisfied by the blood of His Son.**

Because all had sinned and fallen short of God's glory, no man could make such an offering. The only way such a sacrifice could be provided was by God becoming man Himself. **This is the evidence of His amazing love; that He saw the complete helplessness and hopelessness of man's situation, and so became man in Jesus.**

Jesus offered Himself to the Father on our behalf. It is only because He shed His blood that we can know God as our Father and receive His forgiveness for our sins.

No man can inflict crucifixion on himself. Jesus was not allowed to take a route of self-destruction. The manner of His death had to be inflicted on Him by those for whom He died. So He was unjustly accused, unjustly condemned, and unjustly nailed to a cross; and yet He prayed:

> Father, forgive them, for they do not know what they are doing (Luke 23:34).

When we consider the meaning of the cross we shall see that it is very significant that suicide was not permitted. Many Christians today try to put their old natures to death, instead of realising that they have been crucified with Christ.

In the blood, our heavenly Father sees the holy, perfect and innocent offering of total self-giving love. When He looks upon any individual man, woman or child, He sees a sinner; He sees the rebellion, all that is unholy, ungodly, and unrighteous. He knows about the independence, pride, lust, jealousy and greed. He sees it all.

But when someone believes in the blood of Jesus, He sees not the sinner but the innocence, the perfection, and the worthiness of the blood. No one comes into relationship with God the Father without that blood.

There is never a day in your life, never an hour, a minute, a second, a moment of time when you have any other means of access to God except by the blood. Many believers lose sight of this basic truth: **I could not even dare to speak to God today if it was not for the blood of Jesus.** The ground of my acceptance is always His blood.

If I ever try to come into God's presence on any basis other than the blood, I have fallen into error because I am coming not in His virtue but in some virtue of my own. I am coming on my own terms, on my own ground, on my own initiative rather than by the means of my acceptance by Him.

2 THE BLOOD IS SHED FOR US

When we approach God through the blood, He sees us through the virtue of the blood; innocent, made worthy, righteous, and holy. Christians talk in negative unbelief about themselves only because they do not understand what Jesus has done for them in the shedding of His blood. They concentrate on their unworthiness rather than on His grace and mercy through which they have been made worthy. They feel unacceptable and unable to enter the Holy of Holies **'with a sincere heart in full assurance of faith'** (Heb. 10:22).

There is absolutely nothing you can do, or need to do, to deserve God's acceptance, love or blessings. Jesus has already done everything for you! The fundamental problem for many Christians is that they do not truly believe God has totally forgiven and accepted them through Jesus's blood. There is no point in looking at themselves and their unacceptability. They can only fix their eyes on Jesus and marvel at this miracle of grace.

To live in the power of Jesus's blood is to live every day in His freedom. Paul said:

It is for freedom that Christ has set us free (Gal. 5:1).

You are set free from sin, guilt, fear, from bondage to Satan and even self when you put your faith in what He has done for you in the shedding of His blood! He wants to see you walking in that freedom, not in condemnation.

Because of your faith in Jesus's blood, the Father says: 'I forgive you.' This is the expression of His grace, mercy and love for you.

He also wants to reproduce in you that same forgiving grace, so that when others sin you forgive them. He is merciful to you, so you are to be merciful to others.

The shedding of Jesus's blood satisfies every need. Nothing is beyond the power of the blood; no sin, sickness, or need. Every negative is dealt with.

3 THE BLOOD ANSWERS EVERY ACCUSATION OF SATAN

The devil is described as *the accuser of the brethren*. Sin gives him ground for accusation. Why is there no condemnation for those who are in Christ Jesus? Because once forgiven, Satan's ground of accusation is removed from under his feet. **He has no valid accusation against those made righteous through Jesus's blood.** Even when a believer sins he is forgiven and cleansed from all unrighteousness once he has confessed his sin. He is restored to the place of innocence, righteousness and worthiness in God's sight, and Satan cannot rightly accuse him!

The devil will never be forgiven. As a believer you always stand on higher ground! **You do not have to listen to any of his lies or accusations. Instead, you can be thankful for your complete forgiveness. The Lord keeps no record of your wrongs.** There will be no mention of them on the Day of Judgment. You are forgiven!

You are so totally acceptable to God that He has come to live in you, and you live in Him. He sees you as now made holy with direct access into the Holy of Holies.

Because of the blood you need not fear God's wrath or punishment. **Jesus suffered the punishment you deserve and now you can live at peace with Him.**

Praise God for the precious, holy, life-giving blood of Jesus!

5 The Cross

I have been crucified with Christ and I no longer live, but Christ lives in me. The life I live in the body, I live by faith in the Son of God, who loved me and gave himself for me. I do not set aside the grace of God, for if righteousness could be gained through the law, Christ died for nothing! (Gal. 2:20–1).

God has not only made it possible for our sins to be forgiven; He has dealt with the root cause of our sin.

We are all aware of internal conflicts. It seems sometimes as if a great spiritual battle is being fought within us. The Holy Spirit is urging us to believe and obey God's Word. At the same time something within us is trying to drag us back into sin, tempting us to please self and walk in the flesh.

This conflict did not exist before your new birth. When it was your nature to sin, you did so without any reference to God's purpose for your life. The Righteous One was not living within you causing you to feel uncomfortable about your sin. Now, however, the Holy Spirit living within you warns you not to sin and convicts you when you do! He urges you to be restored to a right relationship with God.

When you first believed the Gospel, God put you into Christ and placed the Spirit of Christ in you.

And you also were included in Christ when you heard the word of truth, the gospel of your salvation. Having believed, you were marked in him with a seal, the promised Holy Spirit, who is a deposit guaranteeing our inheritance (Eph. 1:13–14).

Notice the sequence here:

1 **You heard the word of Truth, the Gospel of salvation.** You may have heard through reading the Bible, listening to a sermon or a friend testifying. One way or another you *heard.*
2 **You believed what you heard.** Faith was essential for the message to become effective in your life.
3 **He incorporated you into Christ as a work of His grace,** but not until you believed!
4 **God demonstrated that you had His 'seal of approval' by giving you the Holy Spirit.** So God now lives in you.
5 **Your eternal inheritance is guaranteed.** You do not need to fear the future or even death. Your eternal destiny is assured.

You are in the Righteous One and the Righteous One is in you. No wonder you feel uneasy, when you realise you have grieved Him. No wonder you experience conflict! This is the inevitable result of the Holy Spirit's presence within you. But if you condemn yourself because of this conflict, you are placing yourself under false condemnation.

DEAD

God has done everything to enable you to have victory in this conflict. When Jesus went to the cross He took not only the sins we committed; He took us, the sinners. 'I have been crucified with Christ!' says Paul.

The weak, jealous, self-centred, sinful 'I' was crucified with

Christ! **That person no longer exists.** This was true for Paul, it is true for you also. God did not incorporate into Christ the sinner you were, but the new creation you are now!

A Christian lives by faith in what God has already done for him. Jesus has not only died for you; **you have died with Him.**

> Don't you know that all of us who were baptised into Christ Jesus were baptised into his death? We were therefore buried with him through baptism . . . (Rom. 6:3).

Water baptism signifies that the person you once were is not only put to death but has been buried with Christ. The old life is dead, buried and finished with. You are now a new creation. A new person came into being when you were born again. You cannot be born again unless the person that you were has first died!

Faith is being sure of what we hope for and certain of what we do not see (Heb. 11:1). **God wants you to be sure and certain that you have died and that your life is now hidden with Christ in God!** He does not tell you that you have to put yourself to death; Jesus has put your old nature to death with Him on the cross!

Instead of believing the old life has gone, many turn to counselling and prayer techniques which take them back into the past which is dead! Understanding your past will not enable you to live a victorious new life. We dare not substitute any method of ministry for faith in what God has done.

You are to reckon yourself dead to the old life and alive in Christ. Going back into the old can never enable you to live the new life. The secret of living in victory is to know that you have been separated from your past, that you have died with Christ and are now living a new life in Him. There can be no substitute for faith. As Paul says: 'The life I now live in the body I live by *faith* in the Son of God who loved me and gave Himself for me'!

Your feelings, thoughts and experiences will sometimes

seem to deny the Truth, and later we shall see how to believe the Truth in the face of all those things which oppose faith.

A NEW LIFE

Jesus took you to the cross to make it possible for you to receive a new life. It is no longer your nature to sin; you have a new nature: **'Christ in you!'** He has given you His Spirit to enable you to live this new life.

You can walk in righteousness as you continue to trust in Jesus and what He has done for you. If you do not live the new life you will inevitably sink back into the old. It is potentially possible for every decision, every action, and every word to be done 'in Christ', as you learn to follow the leading of the Holy Spirit.

Yet the way many Christians see themselves, and the way they feel about themselves, seems to deny this totally. They fail so often that they wonder at times whether they could really have been placed in Christ. They remain self-centred, victims of their negative feelings because they do not believe the old has gone!

Jesus said you would be tempted, but God will ensure that you will never be tempted beyond your ability to endure or resist. **You have died, but sin hasn't!**

God has put into you the resources to say 'No' to sin; you can resist temptation and anything that grieves the Lord. It is never true for a Christian to say, 'I couldn't help it'. The sinner sins because it is his nature to sin. A believer can choose to sin but it is no longer his nature to sin. He has the choice to please God or himself. If he continues to make the wrong choices he can find sin irresistible; but that's only the result of a pattern he has allowed to develop. He has given himself to a particular sin so much that it has become a habit and is working death in him; whereas the Spirit wants to work life in him. **He is a new creation but lives as if in the grip of old patterns of behaviour.**

In the old life you were susceptible to any temptation. The

devil could manipulate and use you because there was no righteousness within you. You yielded easily to the temptations and desires of the flesh in order to please self. Now you have the choice of living in the old life or the new, of walking in the Spirit, pleasing God, or in the flesh, pleasing self.

Although crucified with Christ, this does not mean you will automatically walk in the Spirit. The only way to resolve this conflict between the flesh and the Spirit is by faith! It cannot be done through prayer alone; it can only be accomplished by faith, which begins by believing what God has done for us in Christ.

> If we have been united with him like this in his death, we will certainly also be united with him in his resurrection. **For we know** that our old self was crucified with him (Rom. 6:5–6).

We know this. We are sure and certain of it. **The old life was put to death with Him.** We no longer have to yield to the temptation of sin. We no longer have to walk in independence or selfishness. We know this! Those living in the past or who keep raking up the past, do not believe this Truth. **They cannot walk in the assurance of the new life if they don't believe that Jesus has already dealt the death blow to their old life.**

FREE FROM SIN

We know that we were crucified with Him so that the body of sin, which wants to do all the things that oppose God, is done away with.

> . . . Anyone who has died has been freed from sin (Rom. 6:7).

If you feel that you are losing the battle against the conflict within you, it is because you do not believe you have been freed from sin. Not only are your sins forgiven; you have been freed from sin!

The death he died, he died to sin once for all; but the life he lives, he lives to God. **In the same way, count yourselves dead to sin but alive to God in Christ Jesus** (Rom. 6:10–11).

Jesus only had to die once to accomplish salvation for all mankind. The crucifixion was an event in history that will never have to be repeated. **In the same way** you have died to sin once and for all! That too is an historical event; it happened when Jesus died. You died with Him. So you are not to keep trying to put yourself to death. HE HAS ALREADY DONE THAT. **You no longer live!** What a relief!

Sin ruled in that old life. Jesus is to rule in the new life. Sin hasn't died; but you have died to sin. That is as much an accomplished fact as the crucifixion.

Other people can still hurt and fail me, but I don't have to react with bitterness and anger because it is no longer 'I' who live but Christ who lives in me. He lives in me in love. He will enable me to forgive, to bless even those who hate me, to express His life through my life. The old life that was a contradiction to His life is now dead and buried. I can choose to sin, but I am no longer bound by my old sinful nature. **My new nature is Christ in me, the hope of glory!**

It is at once obvious that neither you nor I manifest the new life perfectly. Understanding my old life will not enable me to live the new. Going back into what is dead cannot possibly enable me to live the new life. As Paul says, the life I now live must be lived by faith in Jesus Christ! You are not to dig up or resurrect what is dead and buried with Christ.

The devil wants you to do just that. He wants you to believe that you are not truly crucified with Christ, that the old has not passed away, that you are still in bondage to sin. If you believe him you will keep looking back, thinking that somehow the answer to the freedom you desire lies in trying to unravel your past. This is the devil's snare. He will point to the fact that you sin so readily and have so many hurt feelings and bad memories that you could not possibly have died with Christ.

To believe the devil is to deny the Truth. And Jesus says that it is the Truth that will set you free. The enemy knows how to keep a person in bondage: tempt him to believe his feelings, his fears, his experiences, and so deny the Truth of what God has done for him.

You are called to 'live by faith in the Son of God' – not the devil's lies! So do not set aside what God has graciously done for you. **In His love Jesus took the old, hurt, disobedient, rebellious, rejected failure that you were and put you to death on the cross.** Now He has come to live in you to enable you to live the new life.

Hear it again: **'You died, and your life is now hidden with Christ in God'** (see Col. 3:3). Ask the Holy Spirit to give you revelation of this wonderful Truth. You have died. Don't do anything that would deny this great Truth. Your water baptism was the funeral service of your old life. It has gone, and good riddance!

6 In Christ

Occasionally I have heard people say that they long to have such an intimate relationship with God that they will be able to add to the revelation of scripture. Such is the pride of man! Who could possibly add to what God has already accomplished in Jesus? Those who say such things demonstrate that they do not understand what He has already done. It is complete. We only await His return for the total fulfilment of all He has promised, and only God Himself knows when that event will take place!

We do not have to seek for any revelation beyond that which God has given us in His Word. Any true prophetic word will guide us into a further understanding and application of the Truth of His Word in our lives, for the Holy Spirit is the Spirit of Truth who guides us into all the Truth of His Word. He takes the things of Jesus and declares them to us.

ST DEFEATED

We are products of our experience, circumstances and the influence of people around us. Many see themselves as victims of their past. They feel condemned to a life of failure and rejection, as their track record shows. Certain patterns of negativity have become so deeply ingrained in them that they can see no way of ever being different, even though they may profess faith in Jesus Christ.

This certainly should not be the case, and does not need to be so. Suppose someone who claims to be born again and to have received the Holy Spirit comes to you and says: 'I'm no good. I'm just a failure. I always get things wrong. I constantly fail God. I know He wouldn't want to heal me. He certainly couldn't use me to perform a miracle in anyone else's life.' At such a tirade of negativity you would know immediately that this is not humility but the product of unbelief. Your objective would not be to condemn or judge the person who is weak in faith, **but to encourage him to see the Truth about his life now that he is in Christ.**

It may be his initial response to the Truth is negative: 'Oh, I can't believe. I have been rejected so often that I fear God will reject me. I dare not ask Him for anything in case He refuses me. He must think I am awful. How can He possibly love me? And if He does, why has He allowed so much trouble in my life?'

This all-too-common scenario points again to alarming unbelief and even self-deception. Again it is not our business to judge but to help. We will not do that by trying to help the person to understand his past experiences of rejection, failure and futility. We need to lead him into the Truth that will change his own perception of himself, so that he no longer sees himself as a hopeless failure, but as one who can lead a liberated and triumphant life.

Such a thought may seem totally beyond him, but this is because he does not recognise the Truth about himself now that he is born again. Perhaps he is ignorant of the Truth, so cannot understand. It is not prayer that he needs initially but a good dose of the Truth. This diagram will help us to understand the nature of the problem and how it can be overcome. I want to emphasise that we are talking here about someone who is born again, who has yielded his or her life to Jesus

Christ and has received the gift of the Holy Spirit. He is therefore a 'saint', but feels that he is St Desperate or St Defeated. He is certainly not St Victorious!

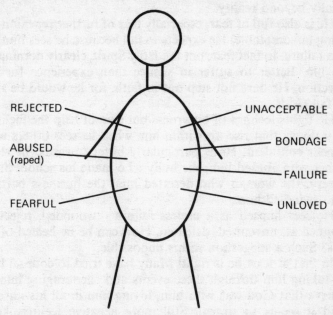

REJECTED

UNACCEPTABLE

ABUSED
(raped)

BONDAGE

FAILURE

FEARFUL

UNLOVED

How does he view himself? He tries to believe he is accepted, but *feels* rejected. He has a long case history of rejection which, let us say, began in early childhood when deserted by his father or mother. The ensuing divorce and rejection by a step-parent caused deep unhappiness. There was rejection at school from one particular teacher whom he could never please; rejection also from other children who bullied him. He was jilted when he had finally managed to commit himself to a relationship; and then, to crown everything, he felt totally rejected by his minister and church who seemed so wrapped up in their activities that they had no time for him. So saint he may be (according to God's Word), but he must be St Rejected!

No matter how many times well-meaning Christians now put their arms around him and tell him that he is loved, his feelings tell him that such a suggestion, though desirable, is totally beyond reality.

He is also full of fear, especially fear of further rejection, of being unacceptable. He expects to fail because he sees himself as a failure. In fact fear, not the Holy Spirit, clearly dominates his life. Better to suffer in silence than experience further rejection. He dare not step out in faith, for he would be sure to fail God!

He fights feelings of bitterness but cannot help the feelings of jealousy that rise up within him when he sees others who appear confident. He is particularly bitter towards the step-father who abused him, the bully who made his school life a misery, the woman who deserted him, the business partner who swindled him.

He sees himself as a useless failure – wounded, rejected, laughed at, unwanted, defeated. How can he be healed of all this? Such a suggestion seems impossible.

In that at least he is right! Many have tried to counsel him by taking him through these events and encouraging him to believe that God was with him, loving him in all his misery. And it seems so unreal. Still more negative feelings keep coming to the surface, more negative memories that need to be dealt with. He is taken farther and farther back in experience, but all to no avail. If he is honest he still *feels* the same. He has appreciated the time and attention given him, but he does not see himself as being any different. He is comforted to a measure by the fact that God knows all about his seemingly endless ordeal, but perplexed as to why He doesn't do anything about it. What a picture of negativity he is!

Of course, God does not need to do anything to liberate St Defeated or St Rejected or St Hopeless; He has already done it! God clearly states this. Let us point St Defeated towards the Truth.

When he was born again he became a new creation. His old life passed away and he was given a new life (2 Cor. 5:17). He died and his life is now hidden with Christ in God. His water baptism signified that he was dead and lay buried with Christ (Rom. 6:4). The person he was before his new birth no longer exists, therefore. So it seems nonsensical to take him back over a past that no longer exists, to encourage him to understand a person who is now dead and lies buried!

The scripture affirms that he is a son of God, that the Lord forgave him all his sins when he turned to Him in repentance. He is now righteous in God's sight; but all this seems totally unreal in the light of his feelings about himself. He reads that God has blessed him in Christ with every spiritual blessing in heaven (Eph. 1:3), that he has come to fullness of life because he is in Christ (Col. 2:10), that he has everything he needs for life and godliness, that God *always* leads him in triumph through Christ – and it all seems so unreal in the light of his feelings and his own concept of himself.

Of course, unwittingly, **he has been encouraged in this low self-image by all those who have helped him probe the secrets of his past failures and hurts. They have simply joined him in denying the person he now is in Christ.** They have aided him in denying the Truth instead of believing it.

So the truth, or his limited understanding of it, remains as head knowledge. He needs it in his heart, which still seems so full of negativity. He agrees wholeheartedly with those who assert that this journey from the head to the heart is the longest journey in the world!

How can these things be true, for one who is so full of negativity?

Without realising it he is living a lie, and those who have directed him back into the past have helped him in that lie. He does not understand the truth of who he is as a born-again believer.

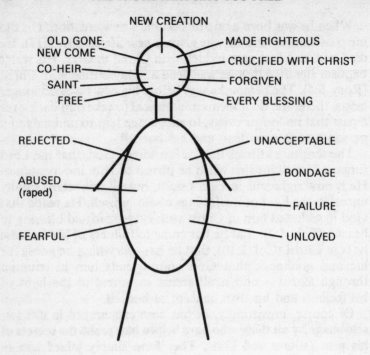

THE TRUTH

'For he has rescued us from the dominion of darkness and brought us into the kingdom of the Son he loves' (Col. 1:13) **The Kingdom of God is now within him.**

Jesus is in him, for 'the secret is this: Christ in you, the hope of glory' (Col. 1:27).

God Himself has come to take up residence within him in the person of the Holy Spirit. His body is, then, a temple of the Holy Spirit.

The truth is that he is not filled with rejection, failure, fear etc., but with God, the life of His Spirit and His Kingdom. All those things he has received only as head knowledge are certainly true and they are his route to true freedom. He is not to look back, but to the Truth. He is not to look at himself but at the Truth! He is to fix his eyes on Jesus, not take an occasional glance at Him (Heb. 12:2). He is to set his heart and mind on things above, not on earthly things – including himself.

Above all, he is to reckon himself dead and made alive in Christ.

First, however, he must realise that his feelings and many of his thoughts (prompted by the enemy) are lying to him. **He is not who he feels he is, but who God says he is. When he believes what God says, his feelings about himself will change because his perception about himself will be different.** The Truth will set him free from his negativity. While he persists in thinking of himself as a failure he will continue to live as a failure.

FACTS AND TRUTH

St Defeated is confused because he wrongly believes facts to be the truth. Let me explain by giving a simple example.

A born-again believer is told by his doctor that he has cancer and has only a short time to live. He is shown X-rays which show clearly the existence of the tumour. He feels the symptoms in his body. Clearly the facts indicate he has cancer. It would be foolish of him to deny these facts and claim the cancer didn't exist.

These are the facts, but not the Truth! The Truth is that by the stripes of Jesus he is healed. The facts state he has cancer; the Truth says he is healed. Which is he to believe?

The facts are natural; the Truth is supernatural. The supernatural is far more powerful than the natural! He has to choose, then, whether he is to put his faith in the facts or the Truth, in the natural or the supernatural.

The Truth is able to change the facts but the facts can never change the Truth. So a believer can trust in the natural prognosis or in the Truth.

Truth is a person: Jesus! He said: 'I am the Truth', and, 'the Truth will set you free'.

St Defeated's history is a series of facts of events he has

experienced. It would be foolish to suggest these things had never happened! But they are not the Truth about him now that he lives in Christ and Christ in him. He needs to concentrate on the spiritual, supernatural Truth that has changed the facts and made him a new creation. The more he concentrates on the facts, the more he will deny the Truth of what God has done for him in Christ.

He needs the help of those who will build him up in the Truth, not help him to deny it by concentrating on facts of the past which are not the Truth about him now. **How can he be expected to believe in who he is now, if people are helping him to deny his new identity by encouraging him to believe the rejected, hurt, weak and useless failure is still alive. He is not! That person is dead and buried, crucified with Christ. Realising this is at the heart of his victory.**

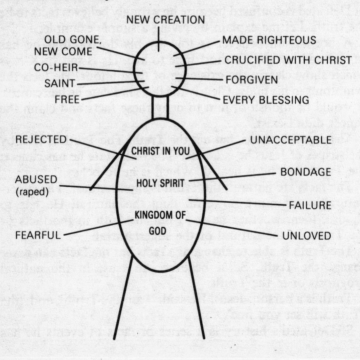

At the time of the crucifixion Paul was an enemy of Christ; later he came to understand that he had been crucified with Christ. Jesus did not have to die again when Paul became a believer. He accepted then what Jesus had done years before, when Paul was still an unbeliever.

When Jesus went to the cross He took every sinner with Him; 'one died for all, and therefore all died' (2 Cor. 5:14).

This is supernatural truth that can change the natural! When Jesus went to the cross He took you with Him.

Jesus Christ identified totally with you so that you could be identified totally with Him! His death became your death, so that His life might become your life.

HEALING?

Your old life does not need to be healed; it is dead! The dead cannot be healed! Neither do they need to be! The good news is that you are not the person that was born into the world, but the new person that was born when you put your faith in Jesus. At that point you appropriated what He did for you on the cross.

You do not have to try to kill the old life; it is already crucified with Christ.

> For you died, and your life is now hidden with Christ in God (Col. 3:3).

> Therefore, if anyone is in Christ, he is a new creation; the old has gone, the new has come! (2 Cor. 5:17)

The old life of sin has gone. When you came to Christ, giving your life to Him, you came in repentance recognising that you had sinned and needed God's forgiveness. **When you confessed your sins, He forgave you completely and eradicated the past with all its failure.**

> In him we have redemption through his blood, the forgiveness of sins, in accordance with the riches of God's grace (Eph. 1:7).

Not only did He forgive you, but He made you righteous in His sight. You were 'justified', made totally acceptable in God's sight, not because of what you had done but because of what He had done for you. **The old was totally unacceptable; the new totally accepted!**

> God made him who had no sin to be sin for us, so that in him we might become the righteousness of God (2 Cor. 5:21).

> How much more, then, will the blood of Christ . . . cleanse our consciences from acts that lead to death, so that we may serve the living God! (Heb. 9:14).

You have been made righteous in God's sight; you can serve Him in love and freedom! You only have to believe the Truth!

7 Spirit, Soul, Body

It is important to understand how spirit, soul and body operate in relation to one another. Your soul, often described as your personality, has three principal functions:

1 **Your mind or intellect,** giving you the ability to reason and understand.
2 **Your emotions or feelings** which are affected considerably by your thinking.
3 **Your will;** your ability to make choices or decisions. In the soul life this ability is influenced greatly by both your thinking and feelings.

Before your new birth you were spiritually dead. It was as if your human spirit was in a coma waiting to be brought to life by God's Spirit. This happened when you were born again.

God is Spirit and therefore He makes direct contact with us through our human spirits. It was not possible for you to have a spiritual relationship with Him until your new birth. At that moment His Spirit came to live in your spirit.

Jesus made it clear that a person must be born of the Spirit if he is to see God's Kingdom. He knew that it was possible to

serve God, love Him even, with the soul; but this did not make
a person spiritually alive.

Among many Christians there is considerable confusion
between the soul and the spirit; some even erroneously equate
the two. Paul says:

> May your whole spirit, soul and body be kept blameless at
> the coming of our Lord Jesus Christ. The one who calls you
> is faithful and he will do it (1 Thess. 5:23–4).

Clearly he sees a distinction between the soul and spirit and
asserts firmly that God Himself will ensure both are kept
blameless! In Hebrews we read:

> For the word of God is living and active. Sharper than any
> double-edged sword, it penetrates even to dividing soul and
> spirit, joints and marrow; it judges the thoughts and
> attitudes of the heart (Heb. 4:12).

In dividing for us the soul and spirit, the Word shows us what
is of self (the soul) and what is truly of God, working through
the Spirit.

The following diagrams help us to understand the relationship between spirit, soul and body. Before you were born
again, your soul and body acted independently of God. You
may have wanted to live a 'good' life; or you may have lived a
very immoral and ungodly life. In either case your soul and
body acted independently of God. You may not even have
believed in His existence. If you did, you still made decisions
without a heart submission to the Lord and therefore to His
purposes.

Your body houses both your spirit and soul but cannot take
any actions without direction from your soul. So, before your
new birth the following represents the way you functioned:

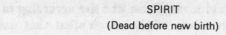

SPIRIT
(Dead before new birth)

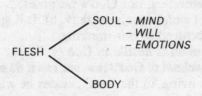

SOUL – *MIND*
– *WILL*
– *EMOTIONS*

FLESH

BODY

THE FLESH

When the soul and body act independently of God this is called in the New Testament, 'living in the flesh'. It must be remembered that **your flesh can do many seemingly good things, but independently of God.**

In the world you are surrounded by people who live 'in the flesh', with no submission to God and His purposes. Obviously many of them do 'good' things. They can be loving and care for others. They can be very religious, but without submission to the Lordship of Jesus Christ in their lives. Before your new birth you lived 'in the flesh' because it was then your nature to do so.

Now we must see what the scriptures say about this 'flesh' life, the soul and body acting independently of God.

1 Jesus said: **'The Spirit gives life; the flesh counts for nothing'** (John 6:63). Most people do not believe that this self-life, with all its 'good' and religious activity, counts for nothing in God's sight. Nevertheless this is the truth, for nothing that *we* do can make us acceptable to God. We cannot be saved either by our good deeds, or by our religious activities and observances. This was a bitter pill for the very religious Pharisees to swallow!

2   In Romans 8, Paul says: **'Those who live according to the sinful nature have their minds set on what that nature desires'** (v. 5). Those who want to please themselves maintain their independence. Their thinking revolves around themselves, not God's purposes.

3   **The mind of sinful man is death** (v. 6). It is spiritual death to be self-centred in our thinking.

4   **The sinful mind is hostile to God** (v. 7).

5   **It does not submit to God's law, nor can it do so** (v. 7). Even if a person living 'in the flesh' decides he wants to please God, he finds he is unable to do so.

6   **Those controlled by the sinful nature cannot please God** (v. 8). They may want to do away with the obviously bad or wicked things that self can perpetrate; but they still want self to dominate their lives. They want to be independent, to be in control!

7   Paul recognised that: **'I know that nothing good lives in me, that is, in my sinful nature'** (7:18). His estimate of the value of the flesh agrees with what Jesus said: 'Apart from me you can do nothing' (John 15:5).

8   Therefore Paul urges us to **'put no confidence in the flesh'** (Phil. 3:3). Put no confidence in this self-life, in soulishness. It is completely unreliable.

9   **Those who please God do not walk according to the flesh, but according to the Spirit.** Because you have been crucified with Christ, you no longer have to walk in the flesh. Because you have received the Holy Spirit, you can walk in the Spirit.

10 We now have to face an uncomfortable truth. Before you were born again it was natural or instinctive for you to walk in the flesh, for life to be centred around self. **Now that you are born again and Jesus lives in you, your life is to be centred on Him.** However, you can still choose to please self instead. Before you were in spiritual bondage and instinctively pleased self. Now you are freed from that bondage but can still choose to please

self instead of God. He will never take away your ability to choose. If He did so it would be impossible for you to love.

If you do not accept God's estimate of the flesh, you will continue to walk in it. Jesus did not try to reform your flesh life; He took it to the cross and put it to death, so that you can be liberated from it. As far as God is concerned the flesh is so corrupt and deceived that it cannot be reformed, only put to death.

THE ANSWER TO THE FLESH

Every believer has to accept this death of his self-life. So Paul asserts:

11 **Those who belong to Christ 'have crucified the sinful nature with its passions and desires'** (Gal. 5:24). Anyone who is born again belongs to Christ. The believer does not have to crucify himself. **He is already crucified!** Yes, even the passions and desires of the flesh have gone to the cross.

The believer has crucified the flesh, not by trying to put himself to death, but by recognising that when Christ died, he died also. Everything that belonged to that self-life, and is therefore in opposition to God's purposes, has been put to death by virtue of what Jesus Christ has done.

To fight your self-life only stirs it up – the very opposite of recognising that you have died with Christ. To delve into your life before you were born again is to suggest that you were not truly crucified with Christ, that His work for you was somehow incomplete, that there is something you have to do to add to what He has done for you.

12 It is not only a question of reckoning that self-life crucified with Christ, but also of putting on the life He gives you:

Clothe yourself with the Lord Jesus Christ, and do not think about how to gratify the desires of the sinful nature. (Rom. 13:14).

Paul deals with this more fully in Colossians:

Put to death, therefore, whatever belongs to your earthly nature (3:5).

He then lists several works of the flesh which are objects of God's wrath:

You used to walk in these ways, in the life you once lived. But now you must rid yourself of all such things as these: anger, rage, malice, slander and filthy language from your lips. Do not lie to each other, **since you have taken off your old self with its practices** and have put on the new self, which is being renewed in knowledge in the image of its Creator (vv. 7–10).

To say that your old life has been crucified with Christ is to acknowledge that 'you have taken off the old self with its practices'.

This need not be confusing if you realise that the Truth is like two sides of the coin:

The Objective Truth is that when Jesus went to the cross He took you with Him. Your old self-life was crucified with Him.

The Subjective Truth is that you have to believe this is what He did and then realise that **you can 'put to death therefore' whatever belongs to that self-life: not fight it, stir it up, look at it, talk about it, but deny it by reckoning it as dead.** It is essential to concentrate, not on fighting the old, but on putting on the new!

In the same way, **count yourselves dead to sin but alive to God in Christ Jesus.** Therefore do not let sin reign in your mortal body so that you obey its evil desires. Do not offer the parts of your body to sin, as instruments of wickedness, but rather offer yourselves to God, **as those who have been brought from death to life;** and offer the parts of your body to him as instruments of righteousness (Rom. 6:11–13).

It is clear that the only way for a Christian to live is by faith: 'The righteous will live by faith' (Rom. 1:17). In the Gospel a righteousness from God is revealed, 'a righteousness that is by faith from first to last'. **Faith believes that you were crucified with Christ.**

> The life I live in the body, I live by faith in the Son of God, who loved me and gave himself for me (Gal. 2:20).

I am no longer bound by my past. I no longer have to allow 'self' to dominate my life. Now I am free to follow Christ and to live a life pleasing to Him. I will do this, not by fighting what is dead, but by concentrating on the new life He has given me. **I do not have to try and improve that 'self' life; I am free to live the new.**

THE NEW LIFE

Let us extend the diagram to see how we can live this new life given to us in Christ.

The Holy Spirit now lives in your spirit; you are alive spiritually. Your body is the vehicle for doing God's will, but cannot act without direction from your soul. As you submit your soul to be governed by His Spirit, He will inform your mind of His will. **God has given you a mind not to argue with Him, but to be able to understand what He says to you and translate it into action.**

Your soul needs to be submitted to the Spirit, therefore. Then even your emotions will be brought under the authority of the Spirit. You will no longer be governed by feelings (which are unpredictable and unreliable) but by the Holy Spirit.

HOLY SPIRIT

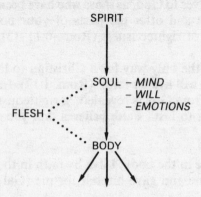

The key word here is 'submission'. While the soul and body remain submitted to your spirit (working in conjunction with the Holy Spirit) you are in God's order. But if you choose to please 'self' (to walk in the flesh) you elevate the soul above the spirit; you are then out of order:

GOD'S ORDER: SPIRIT   OUT OF ORDER: SOUL
                     SOUL   SPIRIT
                     BODY   BODY

When you are out of God's order your spirit is crushed, the Holy Spirit grieved, and self (the soul) is placed in the dominant position.

Remember, the soul is capable of doing many religious, good and seemingly worthy things, but if they are done independently of God they count for nothing. They serve only to elevate self.

It is clear that many Christians strive to please God by soulish activity. What they do is determined by what they want to do for God, instead of submitting themselves to Him and His direction for their lives.

JESUS'S TEACHING

Jesus Himself made it clear what is to be done with this soul life. (The Greek word can be translated either 'life' or 'soul'):

Whoever finds his life [soul] will lose it, and whoever loses his life [soul] for my sake will find it (Matt. 10:39).

This is a key truth. Many want to hold on to their soul life. They want to remain in control of their lives; **they are not prepared to 'lose' their soul life by reckoning themselves dead and by submitting themselves wholeheartedly to Jesus Christ.** The endless quest for inner healing is evidence of this. Such healing is soul healing. But Jesus said that this soul life is not to be healed, it is to be lost. It is not to be the focus of attention but denied:

If anyone would come after me, he must deny himself and take up his cross and follow me. For whoever wants to save his life will lose it, but whoever loses his life for me will find it (Matt. 16:24–5).

Notice these points from what Jesus says here:

1 **He is addressing 'anyone' who wants to follow Him,** to be a Christian.
2 **The Christian MUST deny himself,** not concentrate on himself or his healing!
3 **WHOEVER wants to save his life will lose it.** This is true for anyone.
4 **WHOEVER loses his life will find it.** Whoever submits himself to God will find what he is looking for.

So what are we looking for? Love? Joy? Peace? Of course! The qualities of patience, kindness, goodness, faithfulness, gentleness, self-control? Certainly!

Do we need God's power? Yes! Do we want to exercise His authority? We need to!

Well, none of these things is accomplished by looking at self or trying to heal self. They are all the work of God's own Spirit. **So when the soul life is submitted to the Spirit the life of God's Spirit floods through the soul, giving the believer precisely what he wants and needs.**

This is what people experience when first baptised in the Holy Spirit. Unfortunately all too often they return gradually to 'soulishness', trying to improve self instead of denying self.

SPIRIT:	Love, Joy, Peace
	Fruit of the Spirit
	Power
	Gifts
SOUL:	Fruits and gifts of the Spirit to be expressed through the soul and
BODY	

Jesus makes some very extreme statements about discipleship, showing us what is involved in denying self.

If anyone comes to me and does not hate his father and mother, his wife and children, his brothers and sisters – **yes, even his own life** – he cannot be my disciple. And anyone who does not carry his cross and follow me cannot be my disciple (Luke 14:26–7).

What does it mean for a disciple to hate his own life? He is to hate it whenever his soul or self-life takes the throne instead of being submitted to God. He is to hate the very idea of his soul hindering God's purposes instead of being a vehicle to express the Holy Spirit's life. He is to hate allowing others, even those who are precious to him, to be more important than Jesus. **The Lord is to be pre-eminent at all times.**

This does not mean that he will deny his responsibilities to his family. If he is out of God's order his loved ones will suffer because of the conflicts and tensions he experiences as a result. If he is truly submitted to God, His love, joy and peace will flow through him to the benefit of those around him. God's power and authority will be able to operate in his life in the way God intends. Jesus also said:

The man who loves his life will lose it, while the man who hates his life in this world will keep it for eternal life. Whoever serves me must follow me (John 12:25–6).

The death and resurrection principle is central to the teaching and ministry of Jesus:

I tell you the truth, unless a grain of wheat falls to the ground and dies, it remains only a single seed. But if it dies, it produces many seeds (John 12:24).

The way to be fruitful is to die to self, not try to heal self!

When first baptised in the Holy Spirit it is common for believers to experience the life of the Spirit flooding their souls. They are more aware of His love than ever before; they experience His joy in greater measure. They are at peace with God in a new way; they experience the peace that passes understanding. Changes in their attitudes and behaviour take place because of the fruit the Spirit is producing in them. They are more patient, kind, faithful, etc.

The soul always wants to assert itself again, to take back control. Before being filled with the Spirit, the believer needed to submit himself to God. That submission has to be maintained if the flow of God's Spirit through the soul is to be maintained.

To return concentration to the soul, to the self, is the worst thing that could happen. Immediately the Spirit is grieved, for He cannot influence the believer in the way He desires.

This was already a problem in New Testament times. Paul asks the Galatians:

> After beginning with the Spirit, are you now trying to attain your goal by human effort? (Gal. 3:3).

I have been saddened to see so many lose their spiritual vitality and joy because they have turned in upon themselves and have become introspective, instead of radiating to others the life that was so obviously within them. I have seen churches which have experienced a significant move of God's Spirit, lose the anointing when their members become obsessed with so-called 'inner healing'.

On the other hand it is wonderful to see people change as the Holy Spirit brings them revelation that they have died with Christ, that now they are a new creation. They do not have to improve themselves or heal themselves. They have already been set free completely from their past to live the new life. So great is the power of the Truth that people are changed when they believe it!

"THE TRUTH WILL SET YOU FREE" – JESUS

Paul tells the Galatians:

> It is for freedom that Christ has set us free. Stand firm, then, and do not let yourselves be burdened again by a yoke of slavery (5:1).

THE MIND OF CHRIST

Jesus has set you free. That is an accomplished fact brought about by what He did on the cross. You do not have to return to the slavery of the past, to religious law, to soulish ways, to fleshly lusts. You are free to follow Jesus Christ, your Lord and Saviour.

Therefore, I urge you, brothers, in view of God's mercy, to offer your bodies as living sacrifices, holy and pleasing to God – this is your spiritual act of worship. Do not conform any longer to the pattern of this world, **but be transformed by the renewing of your mind.** Then you will be able to test and approve what God's will is – his good, pleasing and perfect will (Rom. 12:1–2).

The more the soul expresses the life of the Spirit, the healthier it will be and the more able to fulfil God's purpose for your life. We all recognise our need to reflect more of Jesus. **This does not happen through self-improvement, but through having the mind of Christ.**

Jesus climbed a high mountain with Peter, James and John and there He was transfigured before them. His human body became a radiant, glorious body. The Greek word 'transfigure' is used only four times in the New Testament, twice to describe this event (Matt. 17:2 and Mark 9:2); and twice to describe what God is doing in us as His children.

And we, who with unveiled faces all reflect the Lord's glory, are being transformed into his likeness with ever-increasing glory, which comes from the Lord, who is the Spirit (2 Cor. 3:18).

The word translated 'transformed' here is the same Greek word for 'transfigure'. Whereas the process for Jesus could be an instantaneous one because He lived in perfection, for us it is a gradual one. We are being 'transfigured' with ever-increasing glory! How? By our minds being renewed by the Truth:

Do not conform any longer to the pattern of this world, but be transformed by the renewing of your mind (Rom. 12:2).

You are 'transfigured' by the renewing of your mind; by your thinking coming in line with God's thinking, with His Word.

You will never be transfigured by soul-searching or soul-
healing – only by faith in the Truth!

To have the mind of Christ does not mean that every thought
you have comes from Him. It means that you now have the
ability to think as Jesus thinks. The Holy Spirit encourages you
to see yourself and others as Jesus would; to have this attitude
of faith towards your circumstances.

It is only by checking your thinking with God's Word that
you can determine whether you are truly thinking with the
mind of Christ.

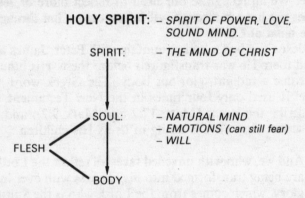

HOLY SPIRIT: – *SPIRIT OF POWER, LOVE,
SOUND MIND.*

SPIRIT: – *THE MIND OF CHRIST*

SOUL: – *NATURAL MIND*
– *EMOTIONS (can still fear)*
– *WILL*

FLESH

BODY

THE BODY

Your soul is in a pivotal position between the spirit and the
body. 'God is Spirit, and his worshippers must worship in
spirit and in truth' (John 4:24). You have direct communion
with God through your spirit. This is where revelation occurs.

Your body on the other hand is in touch with the world
around you, which offers constant temptation to the senses.
The body craves to be satisfied and would yield to these
temptations unless kept in line by your soul.

To submit your soul to the Spirit gives you life and peace.
To allow the soul to be controlled by bodily senses is spiritual

death. The Holy Spirit draws your soul towards the Truth; your body is intent on pleasing self.

If you want to please God, you will ensure your soul is kept under the influence of the Holy Spirit. You have to remember that at any time your soul can deny Him instead of honouring Him. It is for this reason that Jesus said that anyone who would be His disciple would have to deny himself *day by day*.

God gives you the Truth of His Word, not to find fault with you, but to set you free. The enemy constantly accuses and tries to make you feel condemned. But Jesus died to set you free.

The more you analyse yourself, your soul life, the less likely you are to live by faith. The more your soul looks to the Lord, the more you are delivered from self.

My soul finds rest in God alone (Ps. 62:1).

God's Spirit cannot act directly on the body; He has to work through your soul. He is drawing your soul to love and obey God; your body wants you to love the world. In this life you will always know this conflict.

So you have to decide whether the supernatural or the natural is going to reign in your life. **Neither God nor the devil can do anything in you without your consent.** You are given the sovereignty of your life. You can either yield that sovereignty to God, or maintain it for yourself, which is precisely what the devil suggests you should do. He wants you to concentrate on that soul life, not 'lose' it!

SUBMIT

You have to keep your soul humble before God in order to please Him. Jesus Himself is the example of this. In His humanity He denied Himself in order to obey the will of His Father:

Your attitude should be the same as that of Christ Jesus: Who, being in very nature God, did not consider equality with God something to be grasped, but made himself nothing, taking the very nature of a servant, being made in human likeness (Phil. 2:5–7).

Your attitude should be the same, says Paul. Jesus never acted independently of His Father. This was the very thing Satan tempted Him to do in the wilderness immediately before His ministry began. What a temptation it must have been to turn stones into bread when you haven't eaten for forty days, especially if you have the power to do so! But Jesus would not even consider doing anything at the devil's instigation; He acted only in obedience to His Father's wishes. **Jesus kept His soul life in constant submission to His Father.** That was why He could always exercise authority over the enemy and all his demonic powers.

Submit yourselves, then, to God. Resist the devil, and he will flee from you (Jas. 4:7).

Many try to resist the devil without first submitting themselves to God; and then they wonder why often they seem to be defeated rather than victorious. Instead of submitting they hold on to self. Their heart cry is: 'Love *me*. Accept *me*. Let *me* know that you appreciate *me*.' A far cry from losing self!

And often well-meaning Christians help them unwittingly in their sin. They try to encourage this self-life. The truth is that of myself I am a totally unacceptable failure, unable to do anything to please God. **But in Christ I am a new creation, made righteous and totally acceptable to God through Him.**

8 Living in Love

Jesus tells His disciples to 'remain in my love' (John 15:9). You can only remain where God has already placed you: 'in Christ'. To live in Him is to live in love.

To live in God's love is not to live in emotional sentimentality, but in the One whose love is eternal, steadfast, strong and utterly reliable. Jesus's command to remain in His love follows one of His most faith-encouraging statements:

As the Father has loved me, so have I loved you (John 15:9).

By definition, God cannot do anything imperfectly or half-heartedly. Everything Jesus does He does well! (Mark 7:37). To say that He loves is to say that He loves perfectly.

This means that God loves you, and every other born-again believer, perfectly. In other words there is no one else in the world that He loves more than you, for it is impossible to improve on the perfect!

It is not a question of whether you 'feel' this love, but that you believe in your heart that God loves you perfectly.

THE FATHER'S LOVE FOR JESUS

Jesus loves His disciples in the same way that the Father loved Him. The Father loved Him perfectly; we could not expect anything less. These are some of the ways in which the Father showed His love for Jesus:

1   **Jesus enjoyed unity with the Father.** 'The Father and I are one.'
2   **He could do nothing without the Father.** 'I can do nothing of myself.'
3   **Jesus knew He could depend on His Father to work.** He had not come to do His own will but His Father's will. He knew His prayers would be answered, that when He confronted opposition, sickness or even death, He would prevail.
4   **He knew the Father had entrusted all things to Him,** a sign of the love and trust between them.
5   **And yet the Father did not allow His love for Jesus to intrude on the purpose for which He sent Him to the world.** He allowed Him to be opposed, hated, rejected, mocked and crucified.
6   **Jesus entrusted Himself to the Father, even to the point of death, expecting that He would be raised.**
7   **Jesus was totally secure in knowing who He was, where He had come from and where He was going.**

Of course there are many other ways in which the Father and Son demonstrated the love and unity between them. Each of these points is to be reflected in our lives as His disciples, because of this truth: **in exactly the same way that the Father had loved Him, so Jesus has loved us**. This is demonstrated in the experience of those first disciples and in the lives of those who follow Him faithfully today.

JESUS'S LOVE FOR YOU

1   **Because of what He has done for you on the cross, you have been reconciled to God; you are one with Him.** You live in Jesus and He in you. You live in God and He in you

(1 John 4:15). You participate in the divine nature through His very great and precious promises (2 Pet. 1:4).

2 **Just as Jesus could do nothing without the Father, so apart from Jesus you can do nothing!** (John 15:5). Through faith in Him all things become possible for you (Mark 9:23). You can do all things through Him who strengthens you.

3 **As you believe the promises of Jesus, you will live depending on Him,** as Jesus lived in dependence on His Father. He will be with you always. He will give you whatever you ask in His name. In His love He died for you to make it possible for His Spirit to live in you, thus empowering you to do the things to which He calls you.

4 Just as the Father entrusted all things to Jesus, so He has entrusted to us as His Body the commission to make disciples of all nations. **As a member of His Body, He has given you His Kingdom, His Spirit, authority over all the power of the evil one, so that you can fulfil your part in His desire for His Kingdom to come, and His will to be done on earth as in heaven.**

5 **Like Jesus, you will be hated, rejected, persecuted, mocked for your faith.** Some will even suffer torture and martyrdom. This is the inevitable cost of bringing love to a sinful and hurting world. Such suffering for the Kingdom should never cause us to question God's love, for He is with us, no matter what we suffer for His name's sake. He brings us through triumphantly.

6 **You can let yourself die, by 'losing' your soul for Jesus's sake.** You will then find your true identity in Christ. You have been crucified with Christ. Instead of fighting for the survival of the flesh, you can rejoice that Jesus has dealt the death blow to the person you once were!

7 **Every born-again believer can be totally secure in Jesus's love. He knows he has been born of the Spirit, born 'from above'. He knows the Lord is with him always, and he is sure that when he dies he will enjoy his eternal destiny with Jesus**

in heaven. Nothing in all creation, either in heaven or earth, can separate him from God's love in Christ Jesus!

You have the assurance from Jesus: I shall lose none of all that he has given me, but raise them up at the last day (John 6:39). The believer does not need to fear death!

This is total security, but has nothing to do with emotion or 'feeling' loved.

THE INSECURE

As the love of the Spirit flows from your spirit through your soul, that love is bound on occasions to touch your emotions. But this is not 'soul-love', born of emotion; it is that which comes from the Spirit touching your emotions. And the nature of these two kinds of love is very different.

The same is true with joy and other aspects of the Holy Spirit's life within you. As this joy flows through your soul, you will sometimes 'feel' that joy and your body will want to express that joy. But this is not emotional joy. When Paul says: 'Rejoice in the Lord always', he is pointing out that at all times your focus needs to be on Jesus, no matter what our feelings or circumstances. This means that there will be many occasions when you will need to rejoice in Him as an act of the will, yet you could not feel less like rejoicing! You decide to turn away from your circumstances and feelings, focus on Jesus and rejoice in Him.

Soul-centred or self-centred Christians rarely rejoice and constantly doubt God's love for them. Many will claim they are unable to do otherwise. Once someone is born again and made one with Jesus, this certainly is not true! Nothing can separate a believer from God's love in Christ; but if he does not believe that he is loved, he will not see his need to rejoice. It is not healing he needs, but faith.

Soul-centred people concentrate on feelings. They are the ones who only believe they are loved if they *feel* loved. They believe the devil's lie that they are being hypocritical to rejoice in the Lord and praise Him when they do not feel like doing so!

In such people there is a craving to be loved, accepted, appreciated, wanted. They constantly seek encouragement and easily become dependent on ministry from others. It seems that their continual cry is: 'Love me, love me. Please tell me that you love me, that you really appreciate me.' Assurances of your love, or even of God's love mean very little. Such assurances have a short-term effect; it is not long before they want further assurances that they are loved.

This is no way for a Christian to live, with a basic insecurity, doubting they are loved, accepted and appreciated by the Lord and by others. However, the answer is not to minister to the insecurity by examining it, seeking to find the reason for it. **Their basic problem is one of unbelief, for it is only faith in God's love for them that can truly heal them of the insecurity. And faith NEVER comes from examining yourself, only through a revelation of the Truth, by hearing God's Word!**

It is the Truth, and only the Truth, that can set a person free from insecurity and self-doubt, giving him the assurance that God has loved him in Christ.

The truth will show him that God has declared His love for him in Jesus. It is only as he loses self, submitting his soul to God, that the love of the Spirit will flood his soul. It is only as he believes in the power of Jesus's blood that he will know he is accepted in the beloved, that he is already made totally righteous in God's sight. And if he is accepted by God he then can begin to find a new security in his inter-personal relationships.

He will know he is appreciated as he sees the fruit produced by the Holy Spirit's activity flowing through him. He will discover that God is able to use him; he is not a useless reject!

Once again it must be emphasised that the answer of the New Testament is not to concentrate on the soul by seeking to heal the soul. Insecure people are already too self-centred. **Concentrating on the self-life will only encourage them to be more so, and will give them the impression that the answer to their need is in themselves and not in Christ.**

Every need has been met in Jesus. Those who imagine they must be totally outside of God's love can only come into a true awareness of His love and acceptance through revelation of the Truth in their hearts. Then the Holy Spirit will saturate their souls with His *agape* love, so different from the soul-love based on emotion. As they obey Jesus and 'lose' their souls, they find the true love they need, a love that will never change with circumstances, a love that enfolds them eternally. A love that is expressed in positive action rather than emotion; and yet a love that satisfies emotional need when it is allowed to flood the soul.

The more anyone becomes abandoned to God's love, the more secure in that love he becomes, conscious that no matter what the feelings, problems, circumstances, opposition or suffering, nothing can separate him from God's love. His security comes from his faith in that love, quite apart from whether he feels His love or joy!

LOVING OBEDIENCE

The importance of knowing God's love, though, is not to give us security but to enable obedience to the Lord. It is through obedience that the believer will remain in His love:

> If you obey my commands, you will remain in my love, just as I have obeyed my Father's commands and remain in his love. I have told you this so that my joy may be in you and that your joy may be complete (John 15:10–11).

The soul-centred Christian becomes so wrapped up in his self-concern that he loses sight of his need of obedience. He *feels* unable to obey, to reach out to others in love.

It is not the self-centred soul life that God loves. He loves the new creation this believer has become, the one who is in Christ and in whom Christ lives. He loves this one that is totally accepted in His beloved Son.

There is a danger of encouraging people to believe that God loves what He does not love. He definitely does not love soulish self-centredness. The soul life of every believer is in the process of being sanctified with ever-increasing glory, as the believer submits himself to the Holy Spirit and the Word of God.

It is obedience to 'lose' your soul life; disobedience to concentrate on that life. **The only way to obey Jesus is to do what He says.** And He has made it clear that *anyone* who would be His disciple must deny self and take up his cross daily – irrespective of who he is, or what problems or needs he has! ANYONE means ANYONE.

It is not for us to turn round to Jesus and tell Him He was wrong. We would invite a similar rebuke to the one Peter received for disagreeing with what Jesus said: 'Get behind me, Satan!' . . . 'you do not have in mind the things of God, but the things of men' (Matt. 16:23).

You abide in Jesus's love by submitting yourself to God's will, walking in His truth, and living in the fullness of His joy.

When we seek any other way than His way, there are inevitable tensions between God and ourselves. The Holy Spirit within the believer, on the other hand, encourages a sense of peace, well-being and fulfilment whenever he does what God wants.

The world craves after self-fulfilment. Jesus's answer to this is to tell us to 'lose' self and then we will find true fulfilment. To concentrate on self is in direct opposition to 'losing' self!

God has put His love into the believer so that this love can flow out of him as a river of living water. He defeats his own ends if he sits around waiting to be loved instead of seeking to love others by giving to them. For we are to love others in the same way that Jesus loves us!

ANXIETY

Some consider this impossible because they feel so burdened by anxiety. Paul tells us:

Do not be anxious about anything, but in everything, by prayer and petition, with thanksgiving, present your requests to God. And the peace of God, which transcends all understanding, will guard your hearts and your minds in Christ Jesus (Phil. 4:6–7).

Paul does not suggest a person should examine the cause of his anxieties. Instead he tells him to turn to God:

1 **You are not to be anxious about anything.** This only endorses what Jesus said: 'Do not worry about your life' (Matt. 6:25). This is a command from God, and you are able to do whatever He commands you.
2 **In every situation you are to pray.**
3 **You are presenting your requests to God,** not man.
4 **You are to pray with thanksgiving** because the Father will answer the prayer of faith. There will be times when you need to persevere in prayer until you know you are genuinely thankful. Many are defeated because they do not pray through in this way. Instead of being thankful they resent their circumstances.
5 **When you pray with thanksgiving, God's peace will descend on you.**
6 **This peace is beyond understanding.**
7 **It will guard your heart (spirit) and mind (soul) in Christ Jesus.** You will be able to cope, no matter how desperate your circumstances may seem.

This is a far cry from those who seek to minister into people's anxieties by substituting something completely different from what we read in God's Word. It is by turning to God that a person will be lifted up:

Come near to God and he will come near to you . . . Humble yourselves before the Lord, and he will lift you up (Jas. 4:8,10).

God wants every believer to develop his own relationship with Himself, and this is done by personal faith in His Word and prayer. **The only way to learn how to pray is to pray!** Jesus said:

> Therefore do not worry about tomorrow, for tomorrow will worry about itself. Each day has enough trouble of its own (Matt. 6:34).

The Lord knows about the circumstances each of His children has to face. He will never allow any to be tempted beyond what he is able to endure (1 Cor. 10:13); **neither will He allow him to be overcome by events.**

In His sovereign overruling of your life, He ensures that you will have enough to cope with on each day. If you take tomorrow's burden on yourself as well as today's load, you will be overburdened. It is then that you will feel you cannot cope.

You feel overcome by events when you try to deal with today, tomorrow and the possible problems of the future all at once! This is not the way Jesus tells you to order your life.

Many disobey what He says, and then blame Him for the consequences. If we only obey Him we will find that in His love He cares for us, enables us, sustains us in every difficulty, will not allow us to fall and will lead us in victory!

9　Faith

The righteous will live by faith – not counselling! They put their faith in God daily. They trust in what He says and in what He has done for them, so that He will impact their lives in practical ways. They realise that faith is more than believing a series of doctrinal statements about God. It is putting their complete trust in the One of whom the Bible speaks.

When Jesus dealt with individuals who came to Him for help, He asked questions to see if they believed He would do what they asked. He often made it clear that their faith was the cause of their healing:

> 'Go! **It will be done just as you believed it would'**. And his servant was healed at that very hour (Matt. 8:13).

> She said to herself, 'If I only touch his cloak, I will be healed.' Jesus turned and saw her. 'Take heart, daughter,' he said, **'your faith has healed you.'** And the woman was healed from that moment (Matt. 9:21–2).

> Then he touched their eyes and said, **'According to your faith will it be done to you'** (Matt. 9:29).

> Then Jesus answered, **'Woman, you have great faith!** Your

request is granted.' And her daughter was healed from that very hour (Matt. 15:28).

When Jesus saw their faith, he said to the paralytic, 'Son, your sins are forgiven' (Mark 2:5).

Then he said to him, 'Rise and go; **your faith has made you well'** (Luke 17:19).

Jesus said to the woman, **'Your faith has saved you;** go in peace' (Luke 7:50).

I have heard people try to explain away this concentration on faith; they claim that Jesus didn't really mean that faith can heal! Then why did He say so? Jesus was certainly capable of saying what He meant! He chose to say, 'Your faith has healed you,' because that is precisely what He meant.

This demonstrates the great power that faith in Jesus brings into a believer's life. It is the voice of Truth who said: 'It will be done just as you believed it would,' and, 'According to your faith will it be done for you.'

It seems that only when people were so demonically bound did Jesus not look for a response of faith until after the healing. (Although even Legion, who had two thousand demons, came and fell at the feet of Jesus begging for help!)

No matter what the cause, faith in Him was enough to produce healing. Sometimes, as in the case of the paralytic who was let down through the roof, sin may have been either the cause of the sickness or a hindrance to receiving the healing. But sin could easily be dealt with by the forgiveness Jesus offered.

UNBELIEF

When Jesus first appeared to the Eleven in His risen body 'he rebuked them for their lack of faith and their stubborn refusal to believe those who had seen him after he had risen' (Mark 16:14).

Just as faith is very powerful in a positive sense, so is unbelief in a negative way. Jesus seemed to be disappointed, and even frustrated with His disciples when they failed to act in faith. For example, when He came down from the Mount of Transfiguration, He said to the nine disciples who had failed to heal the epileptic boy:

> O unbelieving and perverse generation . . . how long shall I stay with you? How long shall I put up with you? Bring the boy here to me (Matt. 17:17).

Not the most encouraging thing He ever said! But He wanted to shake them out of their unbelief. He emphasised to them afterwards that they had not been able to drive out the demon, 'because you have so little faith' (Matt. 17:20).

Jesus made it clear that **'Everything is possible for him who believes'** (Mark 9:23). Yet in Nazareth, 'He could not do any miracles there, except lay his hands on a few sick people and heal them. **And he was amazed at their lack of faith'** (Mark 6:5–6).

Faith is a choice. You have to decide whether to believe what God says in His Word, or those things which oppose faith. There are five main opponents to faith which we must mention briefly:

1 **REASON** – your natural, rational, reasoning power. Reason will limit God, because reason is natural, not supernatural. As you submit your mind to the influence of God's Spirit, He will guide you into the truth of God's Word, which is supernatural truth. This will not limit your thinking abilities but will expand your mind. **You will think with the mind of Christ. You will see the supernatural possibilities because you have all the resources of God's Spirit and Kingdom available to you.** For this reason you are urged to 'set your mind on things above' (Col. 3:2).

2 **EMOTIONS** – It is often much easier to believe feelings than God's Word. But feelings are unreliable and change

readily from moment to moment, often in relation to your thinking or the circumstances in which you are placed. The truth, on the other hand, never changes. 'Heaven and earth will pass away, but my words will never pass away' (Matt. 24:35). Truth is eternal. **Believing the Truth will change your feelings. Believing your feelings will often cause you to deny the Truth!**

Like reason, your emotions are given you by God; so they are important. The soul, including the emotional side of your life, is to be the servant of the Spirit. God wants you to express His love, joy and peace; not believe the negative self-centred emotions which contradict His purposes.

These negative emotions dominate some people's lives, which is evidence that they need the mind of Christ. It is only by believing you are who God says you are that you will have victory in the emotions.

3 **CIRCUMSTANCES** – These too are often negative. Jesus does not promise us an easy life. 'In the world you will have tribulation,' He says – and everyone believes that! However, He teaches us to approach our circumstances with faith, to speak to 'mountains' and command them to move. He gives believers authority to bind and loose, to prevent or permit on earth **whatever** is prevented or permitted in heaven (Matt. 18:18). They are not to accept them with a resignation that suggests God wants them to be stuck with these problems.

Circumstances are not to rule you; you are to learn how to exercise faith and so overcome your circumstances.

You have to choose whether to believe the facts or the Truth, which is able to change the facts. You have to make your choice in each situation!

4 **SATAN** – The enemy does not want you to act with faith, or to exercise the authority you have as a believer; so he appeals to your reason. 'Be reasonable', is typical of his suggestions. He also appeals to negative feelings, encouraging you to concentrate on yourself and your circumstances rather than on Jesus and God's Word.

His aim is to tempt you to concentrate on self, to encourage you to soulishness and so prevent you from walking in the Spirit.

The devil is the deceiver. He tries to deceive by suggesting you will be freed from your problems by concentrating on healing your self-life. He wants you to concentrate on self rather than 'lose' your soul as Jesus instructs you. **He wants you to believe you are in bondage to your past, instead of recognising that you have died and are now set free to live the new life.**

God does not condemn us even when we have been deceived. A person is only deceived when he firmly believes he is right, but isn't. It is deception to think that we will be set free by practices claimed to be 'consistent with the truth'. What is wrong or inadequate with the Truth itself? Jesus says that the truth will set us free, not something that is claimed to be akin to the truth! Often the things which are said to be 'consistent with the truth' are a subtle denial of the Truth. The enemy can appear as an angel of light!

The devil is also the accuser of the brethren. He attempts to make them feel condemned and so disbelieve what God has done for them in Christ. He wants to steal, kill and destroy. He will try to steal the Truth from you because he knows that he is overcome when you operate in faith in God's Word. He cannot undo what God has done for you; he can only try to encourage you to disbelieve it! Accusation is an effective way of doing this. 'You are a failure', 'You are no good', 'Call yourself a Christian?', 'Look at yourself!', 'How could God love you?'

Never listen to his lies. Listen to the Truth!

5 **TRADITION** – Many fail to realise how their church traditions often contradict the Truth. Jesus warned the disciples: 'Be on your guard against the yeast of the Pharisees and Sadducees' (Matt. 16:6).

A little yeast affects the whole batch of dough. The disciples came to realise that Jesus was warning them against the teaching of these religious groups. Jesus warned:

You have let go of the commands of God and are holding on to the traditions of men (Mark 7:8).

And He pointed out the devastating consequences of this:

Thus you nullify the word of God by your tradition that you have handed down. And you do many things like that (v. 13).

God calls every believer to live by faith in His Word, not traditions which nullify His Word!

Without faith it is impossible to please God (Heb. 11:6).

Everything that does not come from faith is sin (Rom. 14:23).

And that includes traditions!

BEING SURE

No wonder, with all these things opposing faith, that Paul speaks about fighting the good fight of faith. It will certainly be a fight, but a victorious one!

The nearest the New Testament comes to a definition of faith is in the well-known verse of Hebrews 11:1.

Now faith is being sure of what we hope for and certain of what we do not see.

Notice that faith is not trying to believe something that is impossible to believe. It is being *sure* and *certain*. **You are only in a position of faith concerning those things about which you are sure and certain.**

In all probability you are sitting in a chair as you read this. Before sitting down, you did not stand over the chair saying: 'I believe this chair will take my weight. I believe it. I really believe it. This chair will take my weight.' You were so sure and certain that it would support you that you sat down without giving the matter a thought. (No doubt someone, somewhere, will be sitting on a rickety chair that inspired doubt and challenged faith!)

If I were to say to you: 'Jesus is Lord! Do you believe that?' you would immediately say 'Yes', if you are a born-again Christian. You would not need to deliberate or think about your answer. You know He is Lord. You are sure and certain about this.

God wants you to be as sure and certain about everything He says in His Word, including all the things He has done for you and all He says about you.

He wants you to be sure and certain that you have died and your life is now hidden with Christ in God. He wants you to be sure and certain that you have been crucified with Christ, that you no longer live but Christ lives in you.

He wants you to be sure and certain that you have 'lost' your life, your soul, that you have submitted yourself to the authority of Jesus and the rule of His Spirit in your life.

He wants you to believe, to be sure and certain, that the old has gone and the new has come; that you are a new creation. He wants you to be sure and certain that He has blessed you in Christ with every spiritual blessing in heaven, that you have fullness of life in Him, that He will meet every need of yours according to His riches in glory in Christ Jesus.

Paul says: 'The only thing that counts is faith expressing itself through love' (Gal. 5:6).

You are not sure and certain of these things if you are trying to crucify yourself, fight yourself, heal yourself. In which case you need to ask the Holy Spirit to give you revelation of these truths so that they live in your spirit.

OLD OR NEW

The following shows two possible scenarios for a person's life. You belong to either one column or the other. **You cannot belong to both.** You have to decide whether you belong to the old or the new!

OLD	*NEW*
A sinner	A saint
Belong to Kingdom of darkness	Belong to Kingdom of God
Bound by sin	Set free from sin
Condemned	Forgiven
Unrighteous	Made righteous
Unredeemed	Redeemed
Unholy	Holy in Christ
Satan your father	God your Father
Child of darkness	Child of Light
Victim of your old nature	A new nature: Christ in you
Fallen	New creation
No eternal inheritance	Co-heir with Christ
Unworthy	Made worthy
Unacceptable	Accepted in Christ
No glory	Already glorified
No place in heaven	Seated in heavenly places
Without God's power	Filled with power through the Holy Spirit
Sick	Healed by His stripes
A failure	God's child
Ruled by law of sin and death	Ruled by Spirit of life
Spirit of fear	Spirit of power, love and sound mind

What a contrast! And remember you cannot belong to both sides. **If you belong to Jesus Christ everything in the right-hand**

column is true for you: everything. It may be tempting to think of yourself as being partly in both columns, but this is only because you don't share God's perspective on your life!

Many seek 'counsel' because they see themselves on the wrong side of the line. It is fatal to minister to them as if they are right in that assessment. They are only in the left-hand column if they are not yet born again.

We shall see later that some very broken people have to go through a process of conversion to be rescued from the old and brought into the Truth. But once they have reached the point of new birth they are made new and *everything* in the right-hand column is true about them whether they realise this or not!

Satan wants the Christian to disbelieve what God has done for him. He is powerless to undo God's work; so he tries to entice the Christian to believe he is still bound by the past, and therefore unable to live in the good of his new life in Christ. **Satan is a liar and the father of all lies.** Going back into the old can never liberate a person and make it possible to live the new life. That can only be lived by faith in Jesus. It is a lie to suggest I can only live the new if I dig and delve into the old. **The old has gone, crucified with Christ. It has already been dealt with. I have already been set free from my past by what He has done. Faith accepts what He has done for me.**

Nothing can be added to the finished work of the cross. Paul wrote the letter to the Galatians in white-hot anger. He had preached the good news of the cross to the Galatian church. But he was followed around by other preachers who suggested that faith in what Jesus had done was insufficient for salvation. To this needed to be added observance of the law, including circumcision for Gentile believers.

Paul was livid and suggested that the Galatians must be under some kind of curse to believe such a thing. What made Paul so angry?

The suggestion of these other preachers undermined the whole cause of the Gospel, suggesting that faith in Jesus and what He did on the cross, was insufficient for complete salvation. Such an impression is often given today. To the initial response of faith in Christ some seem to suggest must be added counselling, inner healing or healing of the memories! Paul would be equally livid if he were ministering today. He would not be able to understand how believers could be so deceived.

He asked the Galatians whether they had received the Holy Spirit and seen God working miracles among them through observing the law, or by believing what they had heard of the truth as he had proclaimed it. His questions could have only one answer: by believing what they heard!

The same is true today. The only way to freedom is by believing what we hear in God's Word about the finished and complete work of salvation accomplished on the cross. In that act everything was accomplished for your total well-being in spirit, soul and body.

Faith reckons Jesus's death as your death; His resurrection as your resurrection. The one who is accepted in Christ becomes as acceptable to God as Christ. He is made whole by what He has already done.

PART 2

COUNSELLING OTHERS
WITH THE TRUTH

10 Anointed by the Spirit

Any counsellor needs to be completely dependent on the Holy Spirit, the Counsellor God has given us. It is *His* truth we are to give, not our own advice! And He directs us to Jesus. So our real task is to show believers they are able to look directly to the Lord for leading and guidance, for help or healing. The Holy Spirit lives within them to reveal the Truth of Jesus to them and so enable them to walk in freedom in the power of God.

BORN AGAIN

When seeking to help others, it is first essential to ensure that they have been born again. This may seem obvious, but this is by no means the case. To be born again a person has to come to repentance and faith in Jesus Christ and all He has done on the cross.

Many today are not 'birthed' properly. They have been asked to make a sincere, but often superficial, response to the Gospel. It is common to hear people use such phrases as: 'He has made a commitment'; or 'She has asked Jesus into her heart'.

Both these phrases are non-scriptural and do not necessarily mean that the person has either repented, or put his or her faith in Jesus Christ crucified and risen.

Over the years many people with major problems have been referred to us by churches all over the nation and beyond. It has been amazing how it has been assumed by those ministering to them that they were born again, yet this sadly is often not the case. We have needed to lead them to repentance and faith and into a personal relationship with Jesus. So first they needed to hear the good news of what Jesus has done for them on the cross.

It is unwise to take it for granted that a person understands the cross, simply because he goes to church! Many do not know that they have been crucified with Christ.

The sad thing is that many of those referred to us have been subjected to prolonged ministry by those who have *assumed* they are born again, simply because they have made 'commitments' or attend church services. Frequently we find that they have never been confronted with the need to repent. On more than one occasion people have said to me: 'Why should I repent? I'm an Anglican!'

It goes without saying that church affiliation is no passport to heaven – **only the new birth, following repentance and faith.**

Bringing someone to repentance, faith in Jesus and new birth will itself resolve many issues in his or her life. In addition, the believer needs to be baptised in the Holy Spirit, for then the life of the Spirit will infuse his or her soul. This again will resolve many issues, for such an event leads to a great awareness of the Lord's presence in the believer's life.

Worship becomes more meaningful for he now knows the One to whom he prays. He experiences the life of Jesus flowing through him and out of him as never before. Love and joy fill his soul and he knows God's peace, in a new way. There is a great increase in the fruit of the Spirit in his life and he will soon find he can use the gifts of the Spirit, if encouraged to do so.

This, of course, does not herald the end of all his dilemmas. The life of the Spirit needs to continue to infuse his soul. **He needs not only to be baptised in the Holy Spirit, but to live submerged in the Spirit.** Paul tells the Ephesians to continue to be filled with the Holy Spirit. This needs to be a continual process that begins with a definite event performed by Jesus Himself!

BAPTISM IN THE HOLY SPIRIT

We have seen that at the point of new birth the Holy Spirit brings life to the human spirit of the new believer. We have seen also the need for every Christian to continue to submit his soul and body to the Lord so that the life of the Holy Spirit can flow through him and out of him as rivers of living water.

Jesus is the Baptiser in the Holy Spirit:

He will baptise you with the Holy Spirit and with fire (Matt. 3:11).

To baptise is to immerse, to infuse completely. When a person is baptised in water his body is immersed to indicate that his old life is dead and lays buried with Christ. He arises out of the water to live the new life in Christ.

When he is baptised in the Spirit his soul is 'immersed' in the Spirit. The life of the Holy Spirit floods through his soul, empowering him to live his new life in Christ. Jesus said:

You will receive power when the Holy Spirit comes on you; and you will be my witnesses . . . (Acts 1:8).

Water baptism signifies the person has been incorporated by faith into Christ. **Baptism in the Holy Spirit empowers him to live in Christ.**

Water baptism is into Christ. **Baptism in the Holy Spirit is given to the individual believer by Christ Himself** in fulfilment of His promise.

It goes without saying, therefore, that these two events should not be confused; both are intended by God for every believer! In some cases the two events may happen consecutively on the same day, as with Jesus. He submitted Himself to be baptised by John the Baptist; but the Holy Spirit came on Him when He came up out of the water – not while He was in it!

> As soon as Jesus was baptised, he went up out of the water. At that moment heaven was opened, and he saw the Spirit of God descending like a dove and lighting on him. And a voice from heaven said, 'This is my Son, whom I love; with him I am well pleased' (Matt. 3:16–17).

For others, the two events are separated by several years, not because this is God's intention, but usually because the believer has not been taught that a baptism in the Holy Spirit is available and necessary for him.

Often people are perplexed as to why they are not baptised in the Holy Spirit. Usually they think this is the case because they have not spoken in tongues. They are putting the cart before the horse. You do not speak in tongues in order to be filled with the Spirit, but because you have been filled! The baptism comes first, and this is a promise from God to be appropriated by faith, and then the tongue! Jesus says:

> Ask and it will be given to you . . . everyone who asks receives . . . how much more will your Father in heaven give the Holy Spirit to those who ask him! (Luke 11:9–13).

If the person has already received prayer to be baptised in the Holy Spirit on a number of occasions, I point out that it is not more prayer he needs, but faith that God has honoured His promise! **Once people believe they have received they will have no difficulty in speaking in tongues.**

Once again we see how people are prone to exalt experience above God's Word. When we believe the Word we enter into the necessary experience. (This is not to say that on occasions there may be some other reason for a person not receiving. In practice, though, I have found this to be rarely the case.)

It is common for the person's whole demeanour to change

when he suddenly realises that God has already given him the blessing. 'You mean, *I am* baptised in the Spirit?' they often ask. When assured of God's faithfulness many have prayed in tongues there and then, without receiving any further ministry!

Once again this shows the power over the individual of unbelief and faith. It is tragic when this has not been discerned by pastors or counsellors, who suggest there must be some moral reason why God has withheld the blessing. This only confirms the person's own worst fears and leads to intensive introspective soul-searching, which does nothing to encourage faith!

ANOINTED

But you have an anointing from the Holy One, and all of you know the truth (1 John 2:20).

This is true for every born-again believer. John then points out the implication of having such an anointing:

As for you, the anointing you received from him remains in you, and you do not need anyone to teach you. But as his anointing teaches you about all things and as that anointing is real, not counterfeit – just as it has taught you, remain in him (1 John 2:27).

Consider these points:

1 **The believer has 'an anointing'.** This does not mean that he should refrain from seeking further anointing, but it does indicate that he has already received an anointing.
2 **This anointing comes from God, the Holy One.** He anoints the believer with His own Spirit, the Holy Spirit.
3 **This anointing enables all who receive it to know the Truth.** The Spirit of truth will reveal Jesus, the Truth, and His words of truth to the believer.

4 **This anointing remains in you as a believer.** God does not take it away. He knows you need constant revelation of the Truth.

5 **Because of this anointing you don't need anyone to teach you.** You don't need to use anyone else as a substitute for the Holy Spirit. He will bring you the Word you need in every situation. He will be your Helper, your personal Counsellor.

Obviously John does not mean that you would never need to be taught the Gospel. 'Teacher' is one of the God-given ministries to the Church (1 Cor. 12:28). In this context John is saying:

> See that what you have heard from the beginning remains in you. If it does, you also will remain in the Son and in the Father (1 John 2:24).

The Holy Spirit reminds us of what we have been taught. We are to look to Him for His counsel. God has given you the anointing to do this.

6 **This anointing will teach you about all things.** You have the Teacher within you. He will point you, not back to your past nor inwards to yourself, but to the aspect of God's truth you need at any particular time.

It is no excuse to say that you do not hear the Lord's voice clearly. Jesus said that His sheep know His voice. He knows you. He knows what to say to you and how to say it. You hear His voice, but may on occasions push His words away because you don't like what He is saying!

7 **This anointing is real, not counterfeit.** The Holy Spirit will never lead you into deception, or intò anything which contradicts God's Word.

8 **This anointing teaches you to remain in Jesus,** to live in Him. He said:

> If you remain in me and my words remain in you, ask whatever you wish, and it will be given you (John 15:7).

What greater promise could you want? 'Whatever you wish!' This is true, not only for you but for any Christian who turns to you for help.

If he does not allow Jesus's words to live in him what are you to do? Certainly not substitute something else for His commands! The Holy Spirit will give you the right words to say to that person at that time. You speak in the name of Jesus; so you will say what He would say in that situation. You would do better to remain silent if you are not prepared to speak the Truth in love.

Peter at Caesarea Philippi had to face the uncomfortable fact that not everything he said was the truth. One minute he was speaking revelation from the Father in heaven; the next he was contradicting Jesus and being told he was Satan's mouthpiece!

The lesson to learn from this is never to contradict the Truth!

Why contradict what can set you and others free? To disagree with the Truth is to remain in bondage or even make the situation worse!

If anyone speaks, he should do it as one speaking the very words of God. If anyone serves, he should do it with the strength God provides, so that in all things God may be praised through Jesus Christ (1 Pet. 4:11).

When you speak a word from God into people's lives, things will happen to them. Life or healing can be imparted to them by the Lord. Paul says:

For in him you have been enriched in every way – in all your speaking and in all your knowledge. **Therefore you do not lack any spiritual gift** as you eagerly wait for our Lord Jesus Christ to be revealed (1 Cor. 1:5,7).

This is true for you as you counsel others; it is also true for those you counsel. Paul is speaking about every believer, 'all those everywhere who call on the name of our Lord Jesus Christ – their Lord and ours' (v. 2).

In Christ, every believer has been enriched in every way. He may not know or believe this. He almost certainly won't *feel* it. Nevertheless this is the Truth.

How could anything less be the Truth if he lives in God and God in him? He has been enriched in his speech, which means that he is able to agree with the Truth and speak it over his own life and circumstances. He has been enriched in all his knowledge, meaning, of course, knowledge of the Truth!

I need to repeat time and time again, that you will find what a person needs is not someone else to pray with him, but someone to direct him to the Truth. This was Paul's intention when penning his epistles to different churches. For the most part he is not bringing his readers fresh revelation, but reminding them of what they had already been taught. He regularly used such phrases as 'You know that . . .', 'We know that . . .'. He points them again and again to Jesus and to what He has done for them.

All the gifts of the Holy Spirit are available for you to use. And the Holy Spirit is within to help every Spirit-filled believer in his need. However, you want to help him hear the Lord for himself and to realise these spiritual gifts are his too. He has his own anointing from the Holy One and needs to flow in the anointing.

It is all too common for believers to experience a baptism in the Holy Spirit that transforms their Christian lives – but only for a few weeks. During that time they know considerable victory over their problems because they are so aware of Jesus and His love. But slowly they return to soulishness; they take their eyes off Him and back on to themselves and their circumstances. Then instead of overcoming their problems they feel overcome by them!

For a while their souls were submitted to God but slowly their self-life reasserted itself, and it seemed that the blessing of the Spirit diminished.

That is how it seems experientially; but God has not taken anything away from the believer. He simply is no longer living in the full good of what God has given him. So it is important to:

1 **ensure that the person is born again**
2 **ensure he has been baptised in the Holy Spirit**
3 **ensure that he is living submerged in the Spirit.** In other words, he is walking in the Spirit, seeking to live in obedience to Jesus.

It will prove to be a self-defeating process to try and counsel people while ignoring any of these three essential elements in any believer's response to the Gospel. Without his desire for all three, any help you can give him will be severely limited.

The Holy Spirit is the only one who can live fully the teaching of Jesus. **He does this in the lives of believers who are prepared to co-operate with Him.** Nobody can live the Christian life in his own strength or by his own efforts. He will either experience constant failure, or will construct a legalistic cage for himself.

God's perspective on a person's life is often totally different from his own perspective. The Christian sees a problem or series of problems that he wants God to deal with; **the Lord sees someone He loves, who needs to draw near to Him and to live in the Spirit.**

THE MINISTRY OF THE HOLY SPIRIT

The Holy Spirit living within the believer has a ministry to that person. **The one seeking to help needs to co-operate with this ministry, not replace it.** It is not his own spiritual expertise that will stand the person in good stead in the years ahead, but the believer's own relationship with His Spirit. The counsellor may be able to help in some way to establish the person more firmly in that relationship; but from the beginning his purpose is to direct the person to Jesus not to himself for ministry!

The Holy Spirit has a number of important functions to perform in the believer. The following is only a selection of these:

1 **He is the Spirit of truth, who will guide the believer to the Truth: God's Word** (John 16:13).

2 **He will remind the believer of all that Jesus has done for him or her** (John 14:26).

3 **'The Spirit helps us in our weakness'** (Rom. 8:26).

4 **The Holy Spirit is given to help us in prayer.** Scripture says: 'Pray in the Spirit on all occasions' (Eph. 6:18). This will involve the gift of tongues, available to all Spirit-filled believers.

5 **He who speaks in a tongue edifies himself,** builds himself up – the very thing needed by the one seeking help (1 Cor. 14:4)

6 **He who speaks in a tongue speaks to God** (1 Cor. 14:2). The Holy Spirit within will pray to the Father for the person in precisely the right way. He always knows what to pray; and you can be sure the Father listens to the voice of His own Spirit.

7 **The Holy Spirit intercedes for us** (Rom. 8:26).

8 **The Holy Spirit wants the controlling interest in the Christian's life.** He wants to lead and guide him, but will only work with his co-operation. He will never force the believer to respond.

9 **The Holy Spirit 'will not speak on his own; he will speak only what he hears'** (John 16:13). What the Spirit says is what the Father says to the believer.

10 **'He will bring glory to me by taking from what is mine and making it known to you'** (John 16:14). He will reveal Jesus to the believer.

11 **He will empower the believer to do whatever God asks of him.** So it is never true for a Christian to say: 'I can't' – if he trusts himself to the Holy Spirit working in and through him.

12 **The believer does not lack any spiritual gift** (1 Cor. 1:7). All are available to him. In 1 Corinthians 12, Paul is talking about the use of the gifts in a public context, 'for the common good'. In worship, not everybody is to exercise all of the gifts on every occasion! The Holy Spirit gives 'to each' a particular manifestation of the Spirit. So this does indicate that everyone present is expected to use the gifts!

The public use of gifts is to be exercised in an orderly fashion. But this does not mean that a believer can only ever expect to manifest one gift. All the gifts are available to him all of the time for his personal use, as and when he needs to make use of them, which is often!

There is little point in God providing these gifts to help the believer, if he or she either ignores them or never learns to use them!

13 **The believer should 'eagerly desire spiritual gifts'** (1 Cor. 14:1). In other words, to use what God has made available to him. Paul sees no competition between love and gifts. The Christian is not to live either a life of love or use the gifts. He expects both: **the gifts to be used in love.**

To desire gifts eagerly is not to say, 'Lord, I'll have this if you want to give it to me.' It is to long for the gift, plead for it to be manifested in the Christian's life.

It is obvious, therefore, that counsellors are to help believers to function more effectively in the power of the Spirit. In doing this they need to use all the Spirit's resources themselves. For He gives wisdom as to what to say and how to say it. Hours of fruitless conversation can be prevented by using the words of knowledge and wisdom the Holy Spirit gives.

The counsellor needs to avoid any pride in the use of the 'things' of the Spirit. He is not to show off his spiritual expertise, but to encourage the believer to hear God for himself!

11   The Authority of God's Word

AS MUCH AS YOU WANT

Jesus journeyed secretly to Tyre, but 'he could not keep his presence secret' (Mark 7:24).

A Gentile woman whose little daughter was possessed by an evil spirit, sought Him out in her desperation. She begged Jesus to drive out the demon. He told her:

> First let the children eat all they want, for it is not right to take the children's bread and toss it to their dogs (v. 27).

I used to have great problems with this verse, for it seems that Jesus is calling the woman a dog! What is even more remarkable is that instead of being offended, the woman agrees with Him.

> 'Yes, Lord', she replied, 'but even the dogs under the table eat the children's crumbs' (v. 28).

Jesus commended the woman for her great faith and told her that the demon had left her daughter.

Why should Jesus admire her faith? She knew she did not

have a place at His table; she was only a Gentile 'dog' with no right to make any claims upon Him. But she believed that just one crumb from that table would be sufficient for her daughter to be healed.

Look at Jesus's first words in response to the woman's request:

First, let the children eat all they want.

If a crumb could secure the healing of her daughter, what could the whole meal do for the children, who have the right to sit at the table and eat 'all they want'?

Every born-again believer is a child of God who has his or her place at the table. He can eat as much as he wants – but you cannot eat for him!

Every Christian has as much of Jesus in his life as he chooses. He spends as much time in prayer, with the Word, in worship, in fellowship, in ministry, in witnessing, as he chooses.

Encourage others to feast on the truth. One crumb healed the girl. What impact can the whole feast have on a person's life? **We can lead people to the table but we cannot force them to eat!**

Jesus issued an invitation to *all* who were wearied or burdened: 'Come to me,' He said 'and I will give you rest.' He didn't tell people to go to the pastor, the minister, priest or counsellor. He said: 'Come to me'. That is still His invitation.

There will be those who will need help in coming to Jesus, the spiritually immature, those who need to be taught the truth and receive revelation of all that God has done for them. However, it is important that they should genuinely desire to follow Jesus, to be disciples, to honour Him as Lord and King.

Unfortunately, many today want to use another as an intermediary between God and themselves. They are so insecure in their own faith and relationship with God, they use someone else as a substitute for Him. They approach a man or woman instead of coming directly to Jesus.

A woman visited her pastor and for an hour poured out a

long tale of woe concerning all her problems. A famous evangelist was visiting the church and walked into the pastor's study. The pastor thought he would avail himself of the famous man's wisdom and experience. 'This lady would like to tell you about her problems', he said. The evangelist looked straight at the lady and asked: 'Woman, have you talked to God about these things?' She confessed she had not. 'Well go and talk to Him,' retorted the evangelist, 'and stop wasting the pastor's time!'

Why do people seek help from others? Often because of the inadequacy of their own relationship with God. They are content to use the better relationship of the one to whom they go, rather than devote themselves to prayer and the Word and to meet with God themselves. They want to use someone else as a crutch rather than develop their own spiritual relationship with God.

Often they are spiritually lazy people. Even when told what to do by someone who counsels them, they don't do it and still return for further help.

This is not to say that we should never seek counsel or advice from other believers. Far from it. We all benefit at times from the encouragement others can give us and the wisdom they can speak into our lives, but never as a substitute for faith in God and in His Word. The Lord says:

Counsel and sound judgment are mine; I have understanding and power (Prov. 8:14).

When people come to you for help they often expect you to pray over them for a quick solution to their problem. They want the power of God to come upon them to resolve all the things that concern them. Often it is revelation of the Word they need before prayer, truth before power. **Your prayer may alleviate the problem for a short time; but unless they are walking in the truth they will very quickly fall back into bondage when the next difficulty arises.**

Some will think that in coming to you they will receive their answer through your faith. God expects believers to believe! It is fine for them to believe together, to agree in faith; but not to look to others as a substitute for faith in Jesus.

THE AUTHORITY OF THE WORD

It is important to establish that the one you are seeking to help acknowledges the authority of God's Word. Without that submission to the Word, there is not a proper submission to God Himself, for He cannot be separated from the Word He has spoken.

Neither will there be the faith that can come only from learning to trust God over and above negative thoughts, feelings and circumstances.

Those who love Jesus will not only respect His Word; they will obey it, which is another way of saying they will believe it and act upon it. And the Father and Son come to make their home with such a one!

Jesus replied, **'If anyone loves me, he will obey my teaching. My Father will love him, and we will come to him and make our home with him.** He who does not love me will not obey my teaching. These words you hear are not my own; they belong to the Father who sent me' (John 14:23–4).

One crumb from the table was enough to heal the woman's child. God's Word sets before us the whole feast. Jesus is the Word of God; He is the living Bread that has come down from heaven.

I am the bread of life. He who comes to me will never go hungry, and he who believes in me will never be thirsty (John 6:35).

Again the emphasis is on coming directly to Jesus; on believing personally in Him.

You come **with** the one you are seeking to help, not **for** him. You believe **with** him, not instead of him!

In Proverbs we read:

My son, pay attention to what I say; listen closely to my words. Do not let them out of your sight, keep them within your heart; for they are life to those who find them and health to a man's whole body. Above all else, guard your heart, for it is the wellspring of life. Put away perversity from your mouth, keep corrupt talk far from your lips. Let your eyes look straight ahead, fix your gaze directly before you. Make level paths for your feet and take only ways that are firm. Do not swerve to the right or the left; keep your foot from evil (Prov. 4:20–7).

We must note a number of key truths from this passage:

1 **A 'son' is being addressed** – someone in a personal relationship with God.
2 **This son is to pay close attention to the words God speaks to him.**
3 **He is not to let them out of his sight!**
4 **They are to be kept in his heart.** He has to receive them into his heart by believing them before he can keep them there.
5 **These words are life to him,** not simply good advice.
6 **They will bring health to his whole body.** God works from the inside outwards. Satan attacks from outside and tries to get into the believer's thinking. If the life of God's Word is in his heart, then health will radiate from the believer's spirit through his soul and will even give life to his mortal body.
7 **The 'son' is to guard his heart** so that nothing that contradicts God's Word is allowed to take root there.
8 **His heart is a 'wellspring' or fountain of life if filled with the truth of God's Word.** From that source life will well up within him.

9 **He is to put away perversity from his mouth.** He is not to say anything about himself, others or his circumstances which contradicts what God says. Any such contradiction is perversity. A Christian can say the right things in the prayer meeting, when being counselled or when on his guard. It is what he says at other times that reveals what is truly in his heart.

10 **He is to keep corrupt talk far from his lips.** If he believes the truth, he will speak the truth and live by the truth.

11 **'Your eyes are to look straight ahead',** the child of God is told – not back, not in at himself, but straight ahead.

12 **He is to fix his gaze directly before him.** This means he is not even to **glance** behind him!

13 **He is to make level paths for his feet.** He does this by walking in the truth. John said:

> Dear friend, I pray that you may enjoy good health and that all may go well with you, even as your soul is getting along well. It gave me great joy to have some brothers come and tell about your faithfulness to the truth and **how you continue to walk in the truth** (3 John 2–3).

Why was Gaius's soul getting on so well and why was he enjoying good health? Because he was faithful to the truth. He continued to walk in the truth.

14 **The believer is to take only ways that are firm,** rocklike. The only way to do this is not only to hear the Word, but put it into practice!

15 **He is not to swerve to the right or left.** He is not to turn from the truth of God's Word by listening to men's ideas or opinions. Neither is he to allow himself to be drawn into types of ministry which contradict God's Word.

16 **He is to keep his foot from evil!** If he continues in the Word, to abide in Jesus, he will walk in faith, in righteousness, living in the Spirit! This will keep him from evil!

> I say then: Walk in the Spirit, and you shall not fulfil
> the lust of the flesh (Gal. 5:16 NKJ).

You will notice by now that **we are not isolating healing from the living out of the whole Gospel.** Neither are we coming to the scriptures with some interpretation that will support preconceived ideas. We are seeking to see what the Bible teaches us about who a Christian truly is and how he is to live as a result.

SPEAK THE TRUTH

We want the Word itself to shape our thinking, inform our speech and be the basis for our actions. Those who only listen to God's Word but don't do it are deceived:

> **Do not merely listen to the word, and so deceive yourselves.**
> **Do what it says** . . . But the man who looks intently into the
> perfect law that gives freedom, and continues to do this, not
> forgetting what he has heard, but doing it – he will be
> blessed in what he does (Jas. 1:22,25).

James also emphasises the importance of what the Christian *says*. The tongue can bring either blessing or curse. It is like the rudder of a ship. Although only a small part of the body it directs the course of the person's life.

We would all like to think that God directs the course of our lives. He certainly wants to. In reality we can sin and be disobedient, rebellious, or simply unbelieving, in which case we steer off-course from the way God intends. Repentance will bring us back on course; but it is better not to go off-course in the first place!

If the heart is a fountain of life because it is filled with the truth, then the mouth will speak the Truth. **Many curse themselves by speaking negatively about themselves, instead of blessing themselves by speaking the Truth** – the words that are Spirit and life. How important, then, to agree with God's perspective on your life and to tackle negative issues in the way His Word indicates.

> Set a guard over my mouth, O Lord; keep watch over the door of my lips (Ps. 141:3).

You place your life under the words you speak. We all experience conflicting thoughts within and have to question whether they are of God, self or even the enemy! We have to choose which of these conflicting thoughts to believe. What we say is the proof of the choice we have made!

Refuse, therefore, to say anything about yourself or others that conflicts with God's revelation of truth.

David understood the importance of God's Word:

> **Preserve my life according to your word (Ps. 119:25). Strengthen me according to your word (v. 28).**

> **I run in the path of your commands, for you have set my heart free (v. 32).**

> **Your word is a lamp to my feet and a light for my path (v. 105).**

> **For your love is ever before me and I walk continually in your truth (Ps. 26:3).**

> **For the word of the Lord is right and true (Ps. 33:4).**

> **The law of the Lord is perfect, reviving the soul (Ps. 19:7).**

Dare we substitute anything else for the Truth? To love people is to love them with the Truth, even if this involves confrontation. At all times we are to speak the Truth in love. We are not to allow our love or the use of our time to be manipulated by those who do not want the Truth!

God has given us the Counsellor to guide us into all the Truth, not to help us avoid its claims upon us. Freedom comes through believing that truth, not denying it!

12 Counselling the Seriously Hurt

For some the process of conversion can only be accomplished over a period of time. It is truly a matter of rescuing them from the dominion of darkness, of lifting them out of a deep pit.

To explain what this involves I am going to take an extreme case. Perhaps you will never have to deal with such a situation, but if you see what is involved in this act of rescue, you can apply the necessary principles to other cases. For obvious reasons I have used a different name for the person concerned.

Sally was born into a satanist family and dedicated to Satan at birth. She was brought up to hate, not love; to curse, not to bless. She was abused as a child and placed in prostitution as a teenager to lure men into satanism. She was taught that her body belonged to the devil and had to be given to him. So she commonly experienced 'orgasm' with demonic powers.

Sally became pregnant and gave birth, only for the child to be taken from her immediately for ritual sacrifice. Although throughout her pregnancy she knew this would happen, it was a traumatic event for, having given birth, she found to her surprise that she wanted to keep her child.

She grew more and more desperate but could see no way of escape from her situation. She came to us through others who had been delivered from satanism. She knew nothing of the Gospel, except the distortion of it taught her by satanists.

Sally had great fear of the blood of Jesus that would be the very means of her deliverance. (Satanists are taught that if they take the cup at Holy Communion they will die immediately.)

The first thing was to accept Sally and give her the opportunity to get out of her situation by offering her a home while she was led out of darkness into light. She moved into one of our households with those who would be directly responsible for ministering to her. Another girl shared a room with her for reasons which will become clear.

During her time there Sally was abducted by satanists while out for a short walk near the place where she was staying. She was subjected to horrific sexual torture, but finally released because she had been 'de-programmed' as her abductors put it.

What they meant was that by that time she had been born again and so refused to renounce Jesus, despite the torture. She had learnt how to resist the enemy, instead of yielding to his demands.

After her return she was attended by a Christian doctor and loved back to full health by her household.

Now, many years later, completely set free from her past by Jesus, Sally is working with needy children and is a faithful witness for her Lord and Saviour. How was she brought out of such terrible bondage? By the Truth, brought to her by the love and power of the Holy Spirit working through believers.

It was not a question of taking Sally back into her past; who would want to revisit a past like that? But during the process of coming to Christ she needed to pour out to Him the black and evil things stored up within her. This could only happen over a period of time.

On each occasion those helping her encouraged her to bring all these vile things to Jesus and gave her assurance of His forgiveness. At first this was not easy for her to receive, but the speaking out of the evil within her brought a certain release. Slowly she was able to believe that Jesus not only forgave her, but accepted her and was ready to give her a new life, make her a new person. For this she began to long.

In the early stages the nights were often extremely difficult. Not only was she subjected to nightmares but also to visitations of the demonic powers to which she had given her body for sexual 'intercourse'. The young woman sharing her room would stand with her in prayer, teaching her to resist the enemy.

It was not long before Sally was able to commit her life to Jesus Christ. She had certainly been through deep and thorough repentance. She was then baptised in the Holy Spirit so that she could herself exercise authority over the enemy and all his forces.

She was now taught, not only the power of the blood and the cross, but her place and inheritance in Christ. Her grasp of the Truth was to be crucial during the time of her abduction.

As a believer she now needed to be fruitful for the Lord. Within a few months of coming to us, she was a radiant Spirit-filled believer, part of our ministry team and able to minister to others.

She travelled with me on occasions and sometimes gave a very powerful testimony at evangelistic meetings. **She would emphasise that her situation and deliverance were due to the power of the cross. Her understanding of who she was now in Christ had completely transformed her life and enabled her to know that God could use her.** The past no longer existed; the Truth had set her free!

In the early stages of her Christian walk the enemy would make renewed attacks on her encouraging her to look back. He tried to produce physical symptoms to suggest that she was not truly set free. Sally learnt to resist all these attacks.

Many were deeply affected by her testimony and turned to Christ. However, before one meeting when she was due to give her testimony again, the Lord made it clear to me that she should not do so. He had been pleased to use her in this way for a season, but knew the cost to her in having to review such a past. (Sally was always discreet about what she said publicly.)

When I told Sally what the Lord had said to me she replied: 'I'm so glad you said that. I never used to have any problems giving my testimony, but on the last couple of occasions I have found it difficult. I felt the Lord saying that He didn't want me to look back any more – not even in testimony.'

Sally did testify again, but not about her past – only about what God was doing in her in the present.

As the Holy Spirit took charge of Sally's life, He chased out all the areas of darkness. There was no need to do any digging or delving!

THE NECESSARY INGREDIENT

If it is possible for someone like Sally to be set free, become a vibrant believer and a fruitful child of God's Kingdom, loving and ministering to others, then this must also be possible for others whose history and problems seem insignificant by comparison.

Many believers have been brought up in Christian homes, belong to churches, and still are not free. They are forever looking back or within, living more in defeat than victory.

And yet others come out of backgrounds where there has been drug, alcoholic and sexual abuse, who have encounters with the Lord, believe what He did for them on the cross, are set free and never look back. They immediately become witnesses to others with similar backgrounds. Many are in full-time ministry within a few months of being saved, full of evangelistic zeal and fervour.

Why should there be such discrepancy? Not because God favours some more than others. **The truth of what He has done on the cross is the same for all. The inheritance every believer is given in Christ is the same. Each has the same Word in his or her Bible and the same Holy Spirit living within.**

So what is the difference? In a word, FAITH. Some have their backgrounds where they need to be: behind them! Others are always looking back, forever looking in and analysing themselves – and are even encouraged to do so by their 'counsellors'.

The truth is that each born-again believer, no matter what his past, is crucified with Christ; he has died. It is no longer he who lives but Christ who lives in him. The only way for him to live now is by faith in the Son of God who loves him and gave His life for him, that he might be set free completely.

It is for freedom that Christ has set us free. Stand firm, then, and do not let yourselves be burdened again by a yoke of slavery (Gal. 5:1).

Paul affirms that the Gospel, 'is the power of God for the salvation of *everyone* who believes' (Rom. 1:16). This is true for everyone – irrespective of how awful, traumatic or damaging their past life has been.

The Gospel is not the power of salvation for everyone who is counselled, but for everyone who believes! Hence the need to bring people, even seriously damaged people, into faith in the Truth. Without that faith, even those with minor problems will wallow around in introspective failure and defeat.

Those who counsel need, therefore, the dynamic of faith in their own lives. They also need to have a firm grasp of the Truth. They cannot convey to others what they do not have themselves! It is easier to try and apply some system of ministry than to walk in faith and obedience to God's Word. There has always been the temptation to prefer law, even 'counselling' law, to faith.

COMPLETE SALVATION

Because Jesus has met every need on the cross:

He is able to save completely those who come to God through him, because he always lives to intercede for them. Such a high priest meets our need (Heb. 7:25,26).

What Jesus has done on the cross is complete. He was able to cry out in triumph just before His death: 'It is accomplished' or 'It is finished'. Everything needed for our total salvation has been completed.

Jesus saves *completely* all those who come to God through Him. And He always intercedes for them! He stands before God on your behalf!

The amazing prophecy in Isaiah, chapter 53, gives a vivid description of the meaning of the cross. Not only did Jesus carry our sins, He also met every human need in that act. **He was identified with us, that we might be totally identified with Him.**

His appearance was so disfigured beyond that of any man. (Isa. 52:14).

Even the disfigured can identify with Jesus because He was identified with them.

He had no beauty or majesty to attract us to him, nothing in his appearance that we should desire him (Isa. 53:2).

Those who have no natural beauty, or who do not think of themselves as beautiful, were on that cross with Jesus.

He was despised and rejected by men (v. 3).

All who feel despised and rejected can know that their condition was shared and overcome by Jesus. He suffered rejection to deliver us from rejection and make *any* who put their trust in Him totally acceptable in God's sight.

He took up our infirmities (v. 4).

All sickness was overcome by Christ's victory at Calvary.

And carried our sorrows (v. 4).

He met every need of body and soul on the cross.

Yet we considered him stricken by God, smitten by him, and afflicted (v. 4).

All the afflicted find their Saviour in Jesus; in what He has already done. Those who think God has given them a rough deal in life can know that Jesus was given the roughest deal of all in order to set them free from every need.

He was pierced for our transgressions, he was crushed for our iniquities (v. 5).

He took all sin upon Himself; He was even crushed so that all who feel burdened, crushed even, by their sins, their failure and need, could be set free.

The punishment that brought us peace was upon him (v. 5).

Because He has punished Jesus for your sins, God will not punish you for them as well. God will not punish the same offence twice. The price has already been paid for you to have peace with God, no matter how grave your sins.

And by his wounds we are healed (v. 5).

The healing of every person's need in spirit, soul or body, took place on the cross. God does not have to do anything further to give us that healing. Faith in Him and what He *has done* releases God's healing power into our lives.

When you confess your sins, Jesus does not have to be crucified all over again so that you can be forgiven. He has done the work already. You are laying hold of the forgiveness made possible through His finished atoning work.

The same is true for your healing. Jesus does not have to do anything more than He has already done. Faith lays hold of

His finished healing work. The shedding of His blood makes it possible for us to be whole in spirit, soul and body.

You can see already how Sally needed every one of these truths about the crucifixion to become real in her experience. It was not a question of trying to heal her soul life, but of leading her to Jesus, to the cross, so that she could be delivered completely from the past. She had to be taught the Truth that she needed to lose her soul to Jesus in order to find it. And as she submitted her soul to God so the power of His Holy Spirit began to infuse her soul life to create the character of Jesus in her.

The former condition of the believer does not alter the fact that every Christian has to lose his soul. He has to be prepared to reckon himself dead or he will struggle to live the new life, and will experience more defeat than victory.

The Gospel works! The Truth really does set people free! Even a former satanist can become a beautiful, Spirit-filled child of God, radiating the love and person of Jesus – through faith in what He has already accomplished.

The Lord has laid on him the iniquity of us all (v. 6).

Yes, even the worst of those iniquities have been laid on Jesus. All the sins of unbelief, all the negativity that grips so many people. All was laid on Him!

He was oppressed and afflicted (v. 7).

Jesus was oppressed to the extent that He cried out: 'My God, my God, why have you forsaken me?' (Matt. 27:46). But through His victory on the cross He overcame all the oppressive powers of darkness, so that any who have been bound by Satan can be set free.

And having disarmed the powers and authorities, he made a public spectacle of them, triumphing over them by the cross (Col. 2:15).

To God the old life of every believer is as unacceptable as Sally's. It is not a matter of degree. The flesh is the flesh and cannot be improved, accepted by God or healed.

Once again we can see the truth of what Jesus taught us: 'Repent and believe the good news.' There is a simplicity in the Gospel which causes it to be powerful and effective to *anyone* who believes, of any race or culture, and of any intellectual ability.

It is often those who exalt their reason above the Word, their souls above the Spirit, that find it difficult to accept humbly the work of the cross in their lives. As Paul has pointed out:

> We preach Christ crucified: a stumbling-block to Jews and foolishness to Gentiles, but to those whom God has called, both Jews and Greeks, Christ the power of God and the wisdom of God (1 Cor. 1:23–4).

No wonder he went on to say:

> I resolved to know nothing while I was with you except Jesus Christ and him crucified (1 Cor. 2:2).

Jesus shared the lot of the broken-hearted and was Himself wounded so that:

> He heals the broken-hearted and binds up their wounds (Ps. 147:3).

Isaiah chapter 53 begins with a question:

> **Who has believed our message and to whom has the arm of the Lord been revealed?** (v. 1).

And there is the heart of the issue! 'Who has believed?' We do not need sophisticated ministry techniques; we only need to believe what He has done! **To all those who do believe, the arm of the Lord is revealed! They experience the power of God's Word, of His truth setting them free.**

For the message of the cross is foolishness to those who are perishing, **but to us who are being saved it is the power of God** (1 Cor. 1:18).

Through what happened to His 'physical body through death', Sally is made holy in God's sight, without blemish and free from accusation (Col. 1:22).

You who once were far away have been brought near through the blood of Christ (Eph. 2:13).

She came to realise that her every need had been met on the cross. No wonder Jesus cried: **'It is done!' 'It is accomplished!' 'It is finished!'**

13   Confronting with the Truth

If someone seeking help needs to be brought to genuine repentance, then the only effective way to help him is to bring him to repentance.

If he is not in a position of faith about the matters which overcome him, you need to teach him the truth, praying as you do so that the Holy Spirit will cause the Word to become revelation to His heart.

If he is being disobedient, is self-centred or self-obsessed, instead of denying himself, taking up his cross and following Jesus, then you will need to confront him with Jesus's claims on his life. The truth is often confrontational, as Jesus demonstrated in His ministry.

If the one who seeks help is living in resentment and bitterness because he has not forgiven those who have hurt or rejected him, then you need to show him his need to forgive.

OBEDIENCE

Can you hear what is being said? **In all these situations it is not healing that is needed, but obedience to God's Word.** Obedience will bring about significant changes in a person's circumstances because that obedience will be the product of significant changes of attitude.

It is not true to say of any born-again believer that he or she cannot obey God's Word. It is to enable precisely this that God Himself in the person of the Holy Spirit has come to live in him or her!

> Therefore everyone who hears these words of mine **and puts them into practice** is like a wise man who built his house on the rock. The rain came down, the streams rose, and the winds blew and beat against that house; yet it did not fall, because it had its foundation on the rock. But everyone who hears these words of mine and does not put them into practice is like a foolish man who built his house on sand. The rain came down, the streams rose, and the winds blew and beat against that house, and it fell with a great crash (Matt. 7:24–27).

The difference between the man who built on rock and the one who built on sand is that the former put the Word into practice while the latter did not! **Notice, both heard the Word; but while one did it, the other didn't!**

If you have someone before you who is not putting the Word into practice his life will remain on sand until he does so. It is your responsibility, therefore, not to comfort him with a few moments of prayer, but to face him with his need to live the Truth – not just listen to it! This is the route to freedom which is why Jesus said:

> If you hold to my teaching, you are really my disciples. Then you will know the truth, and the truth will set you free (John 8:31–32).

He also makes it clear that anyone who loves Him will obey His teaching (John 14:23). So disobedience to God's Word is a demonstration that a crisis of love towards Him exists on the part of this particular person. Anyone who loves, concentrates on the one he loves. Nothing hinders denying self and loving

Jesus more than a wrong love of self, a love of the flesh rather than the things of the Spirit.

Those who are guilty of this self-love will not usually thank you for making them aware of it, and may even deny this is true of them. In fact, they may claim to hate themselves, not love themselves, because they have such a low estimation of themselves.

To love self has nothing to do with how you view yourself but on how much time you spend thinking about yourself, being concerned about self, speaking about yourself, concentrating on yourself and all your problems!

A mother may have a delinquent child who causes her great concern. Yet, for all his faults, this child is her child and she loves him – no matter what he does to test that love, or to cause her to be exasperated with him.

In much the same way many Christians live in constant disappointment with themselves, but this does not make them any the less self-centred or self-concerned. They continue to love the self-life, even though they are fed-up and frustrated with themselves.

There is no point in ministering into a self-life that is to be denied, or to heal a life that is to be reckoned dead.

DEAD TO SIN

We must appreciate that some suffer unnecessary defeat, however, because they do not believe they have died to sin. Their sense of failure stems from the fact that it seems sin is very much alive in their lives. They expect to sin, so they do!

The flesh cannot be disciplined; it has to be denied alto-gether. **To indulge the self-life in just one area gives the whole of that self-life power over you.** Instead of recognising the need to reckon yourself dead to sin and alive to God in Christ Jesus (Rom. 6:11), one area of disobedience keeps that self-life very much alive and influential!

To battle against the flesh is self-defeating, as we have seen, and results in confusion. While protesting that he hates his flesh life, many a Christian does the very thing that maintains its influence over him; he talks about it! He only does this because he does not truly believe he is crucified with Christ or that the scripture is right when it tells him that he died to sin.

When we do not proceed according to God's Word He allows us to suffer defeat, until we are prepared to put into practice what He says. At that point the Word becomes rock beneath your feet.

Many are concerned about the works of the flesh, but not the flesh itself. They refuse to die! They know they belong to Christ Jesus but refuse to believe what this involves.

> Those who belong to Christ Jesus have crucified the sinful nature with its passions and desires (Gal. 5:24).

This verse does not say that the believer needs to crucify his flesh; it states that because he belongs to Jesus he *has* crucified his flesh together with these desires he knows to be contrary to God's will.

Many suffer defeat because on the one hand they want victory in a particular area, but refuse to deny themselves to obtain the victory. A person may hate himself for having lustful desires and yet still read pornographic magazines or watch X-rated films! A person with a problem of greed may talk about wanting to diet while tucking into another cream doughnut.

The flesh is in direct opposition to the Spirit. It is only by denying self and walking in the Spirit that a person becomes self-disciplined. This 'self' is not allowed to run his life.

Regeneration does not alter the flesh; it gives you a new life, makes you a new creation so that you no longer need to live according to the flesh, but are now empowered to live the new life. The flesh, with its desire to sin, is overcome by concentrating on the new life by fixing your attention on Jesus, not constantly looking at yourself.

The self wants to lead; so does the Holy Spirit. Who is to be given the pre-eminence?

THOSE WHO WANT TO BE HELPED

Remember, it is deception to hear what God says and not to do it. **You cannot minister to deception. You can only expose it so that the person can repent of it.**

> The man who says, 'I know him', but does not do what he commands is a liar, and the truth is not in him (1 John 2:4).

Sometimes you may wonder whether a particular person really wants to be a disciple and follow Christ, whether he has any intention of living by the Truth, or even if he wants to be healed. This may seem harsh, but it is better not to waste time on those who are unprepared to submit to Jesus. You cannot help them until they are prepared to acknowledge His authority in their lives. It is better to devote your time to those who genuinely are looking to Jesus to help them; those who are prepared not only to look at the medicine bottle but to take the spiritual medicine it contains, even if the Truth seems unpalatable at the time. One thing is certain: it will do them good!

The enemy is good at sending his emissaries, those who will take your time, sap your energy, but who have no real desire to serve Christ. These are usually the demanding ones!

In the early years of my ministry the Lord showed me how to distinguish between those He led to me for help, and those who were the enemy's deploys. The former would show deference to how busy I was; there would be a humility and graciousness about their attitude. The others would be demanding and manipulative. They were not concerned with Christ's way, but only in getting their own way!

> This is the verdict: Light has come into the world, but men loved darkness instead of light because their deeds were evil

. . . **But whoever lives by the truth comes into the light,** so that it may be seen plainly that what he has done has been done through God (John 3:19,21).

Why have former generations, which have experienced such remarkable revivals and general outpourings of God's Spirit, not needed soul-healing as it is practised today? Because the cross was preached and people were 'soundly converted'. They were not asked to raise a hand or come forward to make some token act of commitment. They were truly born again because the preaching confronted them with what was expected of them as believers: a holy and righteous lifestyle. They had to face the issue of sin at the very outset. **They were not led to a counsellor but to Christ,** and were taught that their whole trust and confidence must be in Him alone.

They 'prayed through' to a saving knowledge of Jesus, often with tears and sometimes over a prolonged period, not just a few minutes.

Many want a solution to a particular crisis, but without cost to themselves. They would prefer to continue to live self-indulgent, carnal, disobedient lives, using the excuse that they feel unable to believe or to pray. Instead of overcoming the flesh they are overcome by the flesh, and do not want to take the necessary steps to alter this situation.

Even some who have received the Holy Spirit are soulish; they are not prepared to deny themselves in order to follow Christ. They are so full of self-concern that they will talk about themselves at every opportunity. **They want attention, not self-denial. They want to survive, not die!**

Those who want to love and care for such people will not help them by pandering to their wishes. Jesus would never compromise His claims on people's lives. On one occasion 'many of his disciples turned back and no longer followed him' (John 6:66) because they found His teaching too demanding. On another occasion a rich young man went away sorrowful because Jesus told him that his wealth prevented him from following Him.

Jesus is not a spiritual pill to be taken for a headache; He is the Lord of glory who is drawing to Himself a people for His glory. **It is not His purpose for people to take hold of Him to bolster up or 'heal' the self-life which is to be denied, reckoned dead, crucified with Him and buried in the waters of baptism!**

SOULISH LIVES

Some years ago I asked the Lord why the move of the Holy Spirit that the churches were enjoying, usually called the charismatic movement, was having so little effect on the world. You would think that if God was enduing His people with power from on high, there would be a considerable impact on the nation, as there has been in times of genuine revival.

The Lord made clear to me that although He had made available all the resources of His Spirit to His children, most were still living soulish lives. They were trying to use His resources for their own soulish ends instead of for their intended purpose. So the evangelistic zeal of the early years of the charismatic movement, when great numbers of people came to a saving knowledge of Jesus Christ and were filled with the Holy Spirit, had been followed by years of inward-looking longing for soul-healing on the part of many.

Did the enemy hijack what began as a genuine move of God? You can come to your own conclusion. The Church is to fulfil the great commission to make *disciples* of all nations. Jesus's call to disciples is to deny self (not concentrate on self), take up their crosses and follow Him – out into the world, not into an endless series of healing seminars!

We experience healing as we respond to God's call with obedience and faith, not by becoming introspectively soulish. It is the devil's lie to say: 'I can't follow Jesus until all these wounds of the past are dealt with.' They have already been dealt with!

Jesus's call to the disciples to follow Him came at the beginning of His relationship with them. 'My sheep hear my voice and follow me', He said. This means He is walking ahead of you and you are following behind. If you turn around and go back into the past, you have turned your back on Jesus. That is walking away from Him, not following Him. Instead of reckoning the old dead, buried and finished with, you are proclaiming by your actions that you believe it is very much alive and has an influence over you greater than Jesus Himself!

When praying with someone who thought himself unusable by God because of his considerable personality problems, the Lord gave me a simple question: 'What do you do with a delicate, out-of-shape, china tea-pot? Answer: Make tea in it, of course!' God does not wait until we attain a state of perfection before He uses us. If that were the case He would have no one to use.

The secret of receiving from God is not to concentrate on self, but to look away from self. It is in giving that you will receive. Paul says:

I pray that you may be active in sharing your faith, so that you will have a full understanding of every good thing we have in Christ (Philem. 6).

It goes without saying that the Christian needs to know the Truth so that he has a faith to share. The more he speaks this out to others the more he is built up in that faith himself, and able to live in the good of the truth he is proclaiming.

PAST PROBLEMS

The more a person concentrates on his problems, speaking about them, the more he is stuck with them. He needs to speak of these things only once as he brings them to the cross of Jesus. He can then be sure that what he has spoken of is 'under the blood'.

It goes without saying too that there are things in our lives which should not be suppressed or buried; they need to be brought out into the open, into the light of Jesus so that they are then dealt with by the power of the cross.

There have been many occasions when I have had to listen lovingly and patiently while a person 'unburdens' himself. Then, together, we can bring these matters to Jesus – SO THAT THEY WILL NEVER BE SPOKEN OF AGAIN.

If, subsequently, the person tries to go over the same ground again, I will immediately stop him. 'Stop! That has already been brought to the cross. It is already dealt with.' 'I don't *feel* that it has gone', may be the reply. In which case I will point out: 'You will never *feel* that it is dealt with until you *believe* what Jesus has done for you. **The right feelings will follow faith, not precede faith!**'

With such people you have to be loving but firm. It does not help them if you allow them to manipulate you into spending time going over the same ground again and again. To do so is to give ground to the enemy and feeds the false idea that some deep work of deliverance is needed. This has led to great bondage for some who have been subjected to hours of so-called 'deliverance' which it seems is never completed; there always seems to be something more, something deeper, something farther back. The person is left wondering how he will ever get to the root cause of it all, how long it will take. He is helped momentarily, or so he thinks, because of the prayer and attention he has received; but he is no nearer believing the Truth: THAT HE IS DEAD AND HIS LIFE IS NOW HIDDEN WITH CHRIST IN GOD.

He is no nearer reckoning himself as dead. Quite the opposite. He has lost ground because he fears he will never be completely free to live the new life, as there are still nasties from the old life holding him back. We can see how readily deception has come into this whole process.

Can a born-again believer have problems that relate to his past? Most definitely. But the way to deal with these is not to go back into the past. He has a problem as to how to relate to his past. This simple diagram will help explain this:

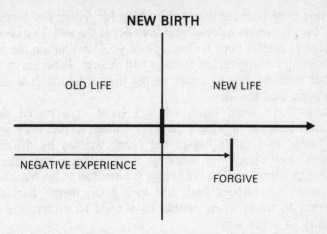

The cross separates him from his old life. He does not have to go back into the 'flesh' in order to live in the Spirit. Such a suggestion is spiritually ridiculous. **You would not suggest that a person has to relive sin in order to be forgiven. The fact that he confesses it to Jesus and brings it to the cross is sufficient for the miracle of forgiveness to take place.**

And once under the blood it is never to be mentioned again. It is dealt with once and for all. So with any other need from the past.

FORGIVE AND FORGET

Why should this person talk again and again about certain things from the past? Because he has not forgiven those who perpetrated those things. Therefore the bitterness, resentment and hurt remain.

It is no small thing to forgive those who have caused rejection, rape, abuse and other traumatic events. However this is Jesus's method of 'inner healing'; and the only one which truly works! As soon as the person is willing to forgive those that have caused the hurts, the 'healing' follows.

Some will claim they cannot forgive. This is a common

reaction only because they are looking for *feelings* of forgiveness. **Forgiveness is a decision; it is an act of the will. You choose to forgive, despite your feelings.** Once you have taken the step of deciding to forgive, the feelings will change. Inherent in this is your decision not to speak of the matter again! It is dealt with once and for all.

There have been times when I have experienced deep rejection because of what others have done to me. As I write this book, two other books are being written by different authors: one about our work at Roffey Place, the other a biography about me. I have been a frustration to both authors at times. 'What about such and such a situation?' they ask, referring to times when people have tried to undermine my ministry in some way.

'What about it?' is my reply.

'What have you to say about it?'

'Nothing!'

'Nothing? Why not?'

'Because I have forgiven the people concerned. Therefore I am not free to speak of those matters again. It is as if those things never happened!'

To their credit both authors have accepted this, although as writers no doubt regretting having to omit what to some would have been interesting reading!

Jesus says we have the authority to forgive or to retain sins. As He has shown us such great mercy, dare we refuse to be merciful to others? **How dare we hold on to hurts when Jesus will never hold against us the things He has forgiven!** They are forgotten; there will not be any mention of them again, even on the Day of Judgment. It is as if those sins had never happened.

And so it must be with the hurts we have received. **The one who refuses to forgive is a victim of his own lack of mercy.** The more a person appreciates how merciful God has been to him, the easier he will find it to be merciful to others. Those who are forgiven much, love much!

Of course every Christian needs to forgive immediately those who grieve, hurt, persecute or reject him, so that no root of bitterness grows up within him.

Anyone who is truly repentant has certainly tasted God's abundant mercy. An unrepentant Christian needs to repent before healing is ministered to him, and if necessary he needs to forgive any who have wronged him. Jesus said:

> For if you forgive men when they sin against you, your heavenly Father will also forgive you. But if you do not forgive men their sins, your Father will not forgive your sins (Matt. 6:14–15).

'I can't forgive' is often a cover-up for 'I am unwilling to forgive'. The resentful person's attitude is: 'Why should I forgive? It was not my fault! I was the one who was wronged. Why should they be let off, they deserve to be punished. They don't know the misery they have caused me – and they don't care! Why should I forgive?'

Where emotions are involved reason is easily distorted. The spiritual answer is clear: **'You need to forgive. You will remain a victim, not of the hurts so much as of your own unwillingness to forgive, until you do!'**

I have found it helps others greatly when I explain that forgiveness is a decision. You choose to forgive. You do not wait until you have the right feelings before you make the right decisions.

To forgive, a person does not have to be taken back over past events to relive them, any more than he has to relive past sins! **His problem is not in the past, but how he relates to the past.**

Anyone can sit down and consciously remember past hurts if he is foolish enough to do so, just as he can remember past sins. I can remember the events in my life that have caused me great distress, but because I have forgiven those concerned I can think of these events with no pain. What is the point of speaking of these things? I am better employed in speaking the truth in love to encourage others and build them up in Christ!

What of the deeply hurt personality who has suffered such great traumas that the events have been blotted out from conscious memory? It is best to leave such cases to those qualified to deal with them. However, anyone ministering in the power of the Holy Spirit is able to use the gifts of the Spirit. It should never be necessary to go digging and delving into a person's past. The Holy Spirit is able to give words of knowledge and wisdom which will penetrate to the heart of the matter and show how to deal with it speedily.

When praying with people the Holy Spirit has frequently made me aware of something in a person's past. When I have questioned him or her the response is often: 'Oh, I'd forgotten about that' – not because the matter had been forgiven, but buried. There and then the person can forgive and be set free from something that has been allowed to influence them subconsciously for years, without ever realising that this was the case!

Realise now that you do not need to allow anything from your past to hinder you in living the new life.

And when counselling others beware of those who constantly make excuses for themselves because they are unwilling to face the cost of following Jesus. They do not want to deny self, but talk about self. They don't want to obey the Word, only excuse their disobedience. They are unwilling to devote themselves to prayer and the Word, to seek God and meet with Him. So they meet with you instead! Their claim of 'I can't' is really 'I won't', or even 'I stubbornly refuse to'. Instead of drawing near to God in His love, they try to manipulate love from you!

You will not help them by allowing them to do so. Lovingly, gently, but firmly lead them into the Truth that will set them free!

14   Some Counselling Principles

We have seen that the first thing to do is to ensure the person before you is a born-again believer and has been baptised in the Holy Spirit. Once this is established how are we to proceed?

It must be made clear that the one counselling needs to be led of the Holy Spirit. So there can be no set formula. Every person and situation is unique. To try and apply some ministry technique will only result in bringing people into bondage, not freedom.

There can be no substitute for anointing. Never try to minister like some other person does; that also is bondage. You are unique and the Holy Spirit wants to operate in and through you to help others. It is not a question of reading a book or going to a series of seminars to learn how to do it, trying to apply someone else's system.

I am not going to give you a system. I would not dare to use one myself. This chapter will contain a series of useful hints, of 'do's and don't's', learnt from thirty years' experience of seeing the truth set people free.

You do not have my anointing, and I don't have yours. If you believe God is calling you to help others, then receive from Him the anointing to go with the call. Do not assume that you have the anointing automatically. The call and the anointing are distinctive.

It is the anointing that breaks the yoke of bondage (Isa. 10:27 NKJ). The proof of the anointing is the way the Spirit moves upon others as you minister the Truth to them.

If God has called you to a particular ministry, He is certainly prepared to anoint you for that ministry! So don't model yourself on someone else's anointing; get your own!

So here are some principles of how to counsel others with the Truth, principles I believe you will find useful:

1   **At least half (if not more) of your attention needs to be on what the Holy Spirit is saying, rather than on what the person is saying.** The Holy Spirit will take you directly to the heart of the problem, if you listen to what He is saying. And that may be very different from the perspective the person has about his need.

Often you have no way of knowing whether the person is telling you the truth. He may want to conceal something because he fears your reaction or rejection. Very few people will tell someone they don't know, the deepest secrets of their hearts; they are even less likely to tell someone they know well, as they have to live in relationship with that person afterwards.

2   **Treat the information you receive from the person as potentially unreliable.** It may be the truth; it may not be. The person may be acting out a role they have been playing for years. So it may sound very plausible. This is not to suggest that everyone you help is insincere or deliberately setting out to mislead you. It is simply to warn you not to accept everything that is said to you at face value!

3   **Realise that many will say what they think they ought to say.** Everybody likes to be accepted by others. It will be important to the person that you accept him. So this desire is likely to affect what he reveals, even subconsciously. He may not want to hide anything, but dare not verbalise the very thing that needs to be said.

4   **There is the kind of personality that sets out to shock you deliberately.** His testimony is even more unreliable. He is likely to say a series of outrageous things which at best are gross exaggerations, at worst downright lies!

5   **The person has come with a specific intention in mind. You need to determine as quickly as possible what that intention is.** He wants you to minister into that particular area, not other areas. Most want a quick, slick answer to their dilemma. They do not want to be confronted with the inadequacy of their prayer life (which may be why they come to you, not Him), their ignorance of or disobedience to His Word. Yet these things almost certainly have a direct bearing on the situation, and its solution.

6   **The information you receive from the Holy Spirit is far more reliable.** How do you know that the Holy Spirit is leading you? At one level you cannot be sure; there is always an element of trust. Not every thought you receive is from the Holy Spirit! Experience helps. But your ability to hear God clearly comes from your own relationship with Him. I normally spend at least half an hour a day (often longer) listening to what God says to me. It is difficult to turn on His voice like a tap simply because you are in a counselling situation. The Lord wants each of us to be sensitive to His voice at all times.

7   **Use the gifts of the Spirit, even while the other person is speaking.** Ask for a word of knowledge to bring you directly to the heart of the problem; or a word of wisdom to enable you to know how to deal with it. In some situations you will need to use the gift of discerning of spirits.

8   **Learn to listen carefully to, and take heed of, the 'inner witness of the Spirit'.** The Holy Spirit shows us when a person is being sincere or false; He will give you the question to ask or the appropriate word to speak, even though you may not understand its particular relevance.

9   **When the Spirit reveals something to you follow it through sensitively.** You are not there to judge, accuse or condemn.

Suppose a believer comes with a particular business problem. Everything is going wrong, he is facing potential bankruptcy. He has prayed about the matter but has received no direct guidance from the Lord. So he comes to you for help.

While he is speaking, the Holy Spirit speaks the single word 'adultery' to you. What are you to do in such a situation?

You could stop him in his tracks and accuse him of adultery, but you need to test what you have heard.

I would ask the man: 'Are your relationships pleasing to God?' He may say they are. In which case I will continue to listen to the Spirit. If this 'witness' about adultery continues, I will put the question more directly: 'Have you ever had an adulterous relationship?' He may say that he has never had such a relationship, or only in the past before he was a believer.

If the witness of the Spirit is that he is lying then I need to be stronger still, but without direct accusation. I might say: 'As you are speaking I believe God is telling me that you are having an affair with another woman, and this is why you cannot get through to God as you pray about your financial situation.' You are submitting what you believe to be the truth about his circumstances.

At this point the man is likely to realise that he is discovered and confess to the sin, but not necessarily so! If he confesses then you need to use the Lord's resources of love, grace and mercy to restore the brother, making it very clear that the relationship needs to end. It is very likely that he has been in considerable conflict because of the situation and has needed someone to help him face the issues.

10 **If you see clearly the answer to a person's dilemma, help the person to see this answer for himself.** That is more effective than your telling him the answers.

11 **Do not be afraid to confront the person of his need to repent if that is appropriate; and encourage him to be specific about the issues about which he repents.** Remember that unbelief concerning the problem facing him is often a sin that needs to be faced.

12 **Your purpose is to build and encourage faith where it is**

lacking. Faith comes from hearing God's Word. So it is more important for the Holy Spirit to give you a Word that will encourage faith, than for you to give loads of spiritual advice.

13 **Jesus healed 'with a word'. One sentence from God will do more than many sermons.** So don't preach! You can tell the person the solution and find him completely unmoved. So . . .

14 **You will be amazed at the way people change simply by hearing the Truth. The Truth imparts life to people when they believe it.**

15 **If faith for a specific issue is lacking ask the Holy Spirit to speak a word of revelation to the person, either directly or through you.**

16 **If the matter needs more extensive teaching of the Word so that the Truth can set him free, arrange for a suitable time to do this.**

17 **Get to prayer as soon as possible with the expectation that God will speak into the person's heart either directly or through a word He gives you.**

I have learnt that you can correctly analyse the situation and tell the person the solution, all to little or no effect. But when God gives you a particular word of truth in prayer, the person immediately experiences release. He needs the truth of the Word in the power of the Holy Spirit.

18 **You may need to speak with authority against some work of the enemy.** However, in the case of a believer, you need to encourage him in this. A fuller treatment of this is given in Chapter 20.

19 **It may be appropriate to lay hands on the person, not as a friendly gesture, but to impart some particular blessing from God.** The time to do this, then, is when you and the person for whom you are praying expect God to do something specific!

It is good to ask the person what he expects to receive from God. If faith is already present in his heart, encourage him to be specific about what he is asking and expecting to receive. If he has only vague hope, open the Word to him before praying. Faith comes from hearing the Word.

20   **Because you want to encourage the believer in his walk with God, avoid the temptation to do the work for him.** Ensure that he is involved as fully as possible. Do not pray his prayer for him; encourage him to pray aloud, no matter how simple or halting his prayer. And do not be over-concerned that he does not include everything you would have said. It is the prayer of the heart that God answers. Maybe not everything needed is going to happen on this one occasion. The Lord is much more patient than most counsellors!

21   **So do not go beyond what the Holy Spirit is leading you to do on this particular occasion, just because you want to see more happen.**

These are, I repeat, a few helpful hints. They are not the twenty-one laws of counselling!

There is a great temptation to take short cuts, especially if time is pressing. If teaching is needed then arrange a suitable time with the person. Meanwhile it would be helpful to encourage him to read some faith-building book or booklet that is particularly appropriate to his need, especially suitable sections of the Bible!

THE RIGHT PASTORAL SETTING

When fulfilling my itinerant ministry I will refer a person in need of teaching to a local pastor, saying that this person needs to know his place in Christ, or to understand the cross or whatever aspect of the truth is relevant.

Sometimes the person is attending a church where the Truth of God's Word is neither taught nor believed. All sheep need to be fed – with the Truth! It is no wonder so many struggle if they are trying to survive on a diet that is based on tradition, men's views of life, or teaching that is experience based rather than being revelation of God's Word.

The Resource Centre of Kingdom Faith distributes teaching materials, books and tapes to many who seek to survive in such situations. These are faith-building materials, which will greatly encourage the person in his personal discipleship and walk of faith, but cannot be a substitute for belonging to a congregation of vibrant faith.

It is unfortunate that many languish in places where they do not receive the teaching they need because of an emotional or soul bondage to a denomination. They fail to realise that their true loyalty is to Jesus Christ. God is glorified by the fruit we bear. So every believer needs to be in a place where he will be raised up and released in ministry to be fruitful, rather than be stifled by the unbelief of the leadership!

Of course there are many fine denominational congregations where the truth is taught and practised and where people are released to be fruitful. It is also true that there are fellowships where the truth is taught, but there is little evidence of anointing and freedom in the Holy Spirit.

All this is encouragement to pray and believe for genuine revival in the Church, which will certainly involve a return to vibrant faith in God's Word and evidence of the life-giving power of the Holy Spirit at work among His people.

All too often the itinerant minister is expected to do in a few minutes what can only be done properly over a period of time in a pastoral setting.

15 The God of Promise

When teaching those already believers, Jesus made it clear that He expected them to believe. When we look at Jesus's teaching on prayer, we once again see the centrality of faith in what He said. Believers were encouraged to believe together in their prayer, meaning that when they were at one in their faith they could be sure of the answer they would receive from the Lord:

> Again, I tell you that if two of you on earth agree about anything you ask for, it will be done for you by my Father in heaven. For where two or three come together in my name, there am I with them (Matt. 18:19–20).

To be gathered in the name of Jesus is to be gathered together in faith! Jesus said:

> If you believe, you will receive whatever you ask for in prayer (Matt. 21:22).

'Whatever' must include healing or anything else for which we pray with faith. At first this seems a dangerous promise for Jesus to make. Does this commit our heavenly Father to give us what He does not really want us to have? Not at all, as other prayer promises make clear. He does say that we can have whatever we wish, but on certain conditions:

> If you remain in me and my words remain in you, ask whatever you wish, and it will be given you (John 15:7).

To live in Jesus is to live in the good of the position He has given us by virtue of our new birth. If His words live in us, we will both believe and obey them. These two things belong together. **If you believe, you obey. And if you obey, it is because you believe!**

Many believe the scriptures to be the divinely inspired revelation of truth. Assenting to the fact that the Bible is the truth is not the same as putting your faith in that truth. **In practice the only parts of the scriptures that we truly believe are those that we obey.**

Jesus intends His words to live in those who live in Him. He knows well that when this is the case we will live in submission to Him; and because His words live in us, we will not ask for anything opposed to His purposes. We will not be able to pray with any real conviction or faith for anything that opposes His will, for the Holy Spirit will inspire faith only for those things which are in line with God's purpose. It is important to take note of this inner witness of the Holy Spirit.

The outcome of praying for 'whatever we wish' under these conditions is that the Father will be glorified:

> This is to my Father's glory, that you bear much fruit, showing yourselves to be my disciples (John 15:8).

There is no doubt that Jesus links this fruitfulness with answered prayer:

> You did not choose me, but I chose you and appointed you to go and bear fruit – fruit that will last. Then the Father

will give you whatever you ask in my name. This is my command: Love each other (John 15:16–17).

Live in Jesus, let His words live in you; then you will be fruitful and the Father will give you whatever you ask in Jesus's name. This is the clear sequence of thought in what He teaches, and of the way in which this teaching is worked out in our lives. This reinforces the central message of this book: **living in the Truth will set us free, not only from our past, but also to live the new life – to live and pray with faith.**

In John 14:12–14 there is another sequence of thought:

I tell you the truth, anyone who has faith in me will do what I have been doing. He will do even greater things than these, because I am going to the Father.

And:

I will do whatever you ask in my name, so that the Son may bring glory to the Father. You may ask me for anything in my name, and I will do it.

Let us note these following points:

1 What Jesus says is preceded by the phrase, 'I tell you the truth . . .' signifying that He is saying emphatically that what follows is the truth, even if His hearers find it difficult to believe.

2 He is talking about *anyone* who has faith in Jesus.

3 **Anyone who has faith in Jesus will do what He has been doing:** listening to the words of His Father, being submissive to Him, proclaiming the presence of the Kingdom, acting with the authority of the Kingdom and demonstrating the works of power that accompany the Kingdom! This, He says, of *anyone* who believes!

4 The believer will do even greater things, for he will be able

to pray for the Holy Spirit to come upon people; something Jesus could not do during His humanity as the Spirit was not yet given because He was not yet glorified (John 7:39).

5 Jesus will do whatever you ask in His name as you live in faith and obedience.

6 In this way the Son will bring glory to the Father. God is glorified in you by the faith that leads to answered prayer.

7 You can ask for anything in Jesus's name and He will do it, because you are living in His Word.

It is all too obvious from these scriptures that many Christians look to others to pray for them with the hope that this will produce the necessary miracle, but without living in faith and obedience themselves. We must not be tempted into pandering to them in this way. The commission the Church has received is to make 'disciples' of all nations; and disciples seek to live by faith and in obedience to the Lord.

A WAY OF LIFE

Faith is a way of life: 'The righteous will live by faith' (Rom. 1:17). To live by faith is to live in Jesus and allow His words to live in you.

We dare not substitute anything else for what God says in His Word. **It will not be surprising to see poor results if we do not pay due attention to this need for faith and obedience in those we are seeking to help.**

This does not mean that we have to attain some state of advanced perfection before God answers our prayers. Quite the contrary. New believers see the Lord answering their prayers in ways that usually amaze them. But then they usually find no great difficulty in living in faith and obedience to the revelation of Jesus they have just received.

The God to whom we pray is the God of grace, and all that He does in us is the work of His grace. Every answered prayer is evidence of His grace. It is not that our faith and obedience earn us the right to answered prayer. **These, however, are the best, the most favourable, conditions for the grace of God to work effectively in our lives.**

It is amazing that God seems to give us so many answers when there is little faith or obedience. But it is clear that we should not presume on His grace. Paul asks:

> Shall we go on sinning, so that grace may increase? By no means! (Rom. 6:1).

Because faith is a way of life, abiding in Jesus and His words abiding in you, it is difficult to switch on faith because a particular need has arisen. This is why so many Christians turn to others for help. **Because they are not living by faith, they do not have faith for the particular situation facing them.**

Prevention is better than cure. Those who live by faith take the shield of faith against the enemy's attacks and with the sword of the Spirit, the Word of God, attack the things which oppose them.

Some have said to me: 'I don't belong to a faith church.' I feel like asking them: 'Do you belong to an unbelief church then?'

> Everything that does not come from faith is sin (Rom. 14:23).

> The only thing that counts is faith expressing itself through love (Gal. 5:6).

How important it is, then, not only to live a life of faith and obedience yourself, but to be part of a congregation committed to such a lifestyle of 'faith expressing itself through love'. Not faith in tradition, but in God's Word. Not just a friendly, loving group of people, but those who demonstrate their love for Jesus by their obedience to Him. 'If you love me, you will obey what I command' (John 14:15).

In His love and grace, God does not wait until we attain an advanced stage of spirituality before we see His power at work in our lives, or before answering our prayers.

Each believer needs to be obedient to the revelation of truth the Lord has given him. In helping people, therefore, we want to encourage their faith by speaking God's Word to them. We can assure them that they are able to put His Word into operation through the power of the Holy Spirit.

There is a great difference between counselling the disciple who loves the Lord and diligently seeks Him because he wants to glorify Him, and the one who is casual about prayer, the Word and his or her discipleship.

Those living in faith and obedience do sometimes need someone to stand with them in faith. With others it soon becomes apparent that they would be happy to lean on your relationship with God, instead of developing their own! This is why it is important to direct people to the Lord, to His Word which builds faith encouraging them to *live* in the good of what He has said and done.

It is no hardship to encourage those whose hearts are genuinely given to Jesus, no matter how immature they may be in faith. Such people are eager to learn and ready to apply the teaching of God's Word to their lives. Their attitudes are in stark contrast with those who hear, know well what they are to do, but don't do it! And yet it is the disobedient who are then prone to turn in judgment on God, blaming Him for the catastrophes which befall them.

It is tragic that so many who desire to glorify the Lord are in churches where they receive little teaching of the Word or encouragement in faith. Coming into a meeting elsewhere when faith is operating and God's Spirit is moving, they are quick to respond and often receive healing or the answer to some other need, only to return to their churches where nobody wants to know about the great things that have just occurred. They are too threatening for those bound by religion but not moving by faith – as was the case in Jesus's day!

GOD'S PROMISES FULFILLED

If we are learning to live by faith, we are learning to live by promise. Peter says that:

> Through these he has given us his very great and precious promises, so that through them you may participate in the divine nature (2 Pet. 1:4).

To live in Jesus, to live in God, to walk in the Spirit is, then, to live by these very great and precious promises. They are so great that frequently they seem beyond us; but this is only because God is so much greater than we are. Paul describes Him as the one:

> Who is able to do immeasurably more than all we ask or imagine, *according to his power that is at work within us* (Eph. 3:20).

This is the new life! Sharing in the divine nature, abiding in Jesus! His mighty power at work within us enabling us to live as children of His Kingdom.

Beware of divorcing the promises God gives from any conditions that He attaches to them. For no matter how many promises God has made, they are 'Yes' and 'Amen' in Christ (2 Cor. 1:20).

> Since we have these promises, dear friends, let us purify ourselves from everything that contaminates body and spirit, perfecting holiness out of reverence for God (2 Cor. 7:1).

We want to walk in the holiness of God, to seek first His Kingdom and righteousness, and so inherit Jesus's promise that everything else will be added to us. Be wise about praying with those who are laying claim to some promise, but without paying attention to the conditions that go with the promise.

The time to pray and agree together is when they are concerned to see the conditions, as well as the promises fulfilled in their lives.

HOLD FAST TO THE PROMISES

'The testing of our faith proves that it is genuine', says Peter (1 Pet. 1:7).

None of us likes to be tested, nor do we like to be kept waiting when we want something. Jesus teaches us to persevere in prayer, to be determined to receive the answer needed. It is easy to grow impatient, or to begin soul-searching to see if there is any fault that is preventing us from receiving the answer; or to begin concentrating on the problem instead of the truth.

> Consider it pure joy, my brothers, whenever you face trials of many kinds, because you know that the testing of your faith develops perseverance. Perseverance must finish its work so that you may be mature and complete, not lacking anything (Jas. 1:2–4).

Abraham 'did not waver through unbelief regarding the promise of God' (Rom. 4:20). **He was 'fully persuaded that God had power to do what he had promised'** (v. 21). So when someone has received a promise from God he has to hold fast to that Word believing God is faithful in fulfilling His Word.

The faith that perseveres, despite contrary circumstances, is the faith that is proved genuine and praises God. The one who stands the test 'will receive the crown of life that God has promised to those who love him' (Jas. 1:12).

So the one with genuine faith will not try to use you as a prop or substitute for his own relationship with the Lord; although he will appreciate your love and support during his time of testing.

It is important not to get in God's way when He is taking a believer through a testing time, a trial of faith!

You are helping him to keep his trust in God, so that He will supply his need. Where he has learnt to hold fast to God's Word and to pray through to victory, he will enter into a new dimension of faith that will stand him in good stead when facing future difficulties.

If a promise is not being fulfilled immediately, God must have good reasons for withholding the blessing. He is perfect in His timing. It may be that He will show you that the believer needs to sort out some particular area in his life. Maybe it is obvious to you, but not to him, that he is not truly in faith; he does not believe he has received the answer. You can encourage obedience or faith as the occasion demands.

This is your aim: to encourage dependence on Jesus and His promises, not dependence on you or any other human counsellor.

16   Fear

Unbelief in God's promises leaves the Christian in bondage to fear.

Fear is a soulish reaction either to certain thoughts or words (often inspired by the enemy), or to circumstances. Negative thoughts cause feelings of fear which can easily overwhelm a person. It is common for Christians to seek ministry for their 'fears', even to believe they need to be delivered from a spirit of fear. This is not usually the true nature of the problem. The believer does not have a spirit of fear:

> God has not given us a spirit of fear, but of power and of love and of a sound mind (2 Tim. 1:7 NKJ).

Why does he live in fear then? Because he allows his soul to dominate his spirit, instead of living in submission to God. So the life of his spirit is not able to influence his soul in the way God intends. Within his spirit there is power, love and a sound mind; but these qualities will not be real in his soul unless the Spirit has the pre-eminence in his life.

God's answer to fear is not to have the cause of your fear analysed. He simply says: 'Fear not' – no less than 366 times in scripture! He gives us good reasons for not being afraid: He promises to be with us always. If Jesus is with me, and His Spirit within me, I will only fear if I allow my soul to dominate my spirit.

I used to be an extremely fearful person, and my natural reaction in certain situations is still to be afraid. That is the response of my soul to the circumstances in which I find myself. If I dwell on those fears I will be paralysed into inactivity. So I have learnt to allow the Spirit to fill my soul with the Truth. This means I speak the Truth of God's Word to myself. I deliberately fill my mind with the Truth, so that my emotions can be influenced by that Truth, for then the fear will begin to evaporate. I cannot fear and trust at the same time.

I will often have to make a definite decision to move forward, despite any residual feelings of fear; for faith in God involves taking positive action. It is not a question of waiting until all the feelings of fear have gone before I step out in obedience to face the situation. Often we have to choose to obey God despite feelings of fear.

It is common for people to be afraid when they are confronted with the purposes of God. It seems He chooses people who will feel inadequate to His call on their lives so that they will put all their trust in Him.

The Lord makes it clear that this fear is a soulish response to what He asks of them. He makes it clear that it is not who they are that matters. He is not asking them to obey Him in their own strength. What matters is who He is and that He is the one who will be present with them to provide for them and protect them as they step out in obedience to Him.

The Lord said to Abram:

Do not be afraid, Abram. I am your shield, your very great reward (Gen. 15:1).

When Moses feared to return to Egypt to confront Pharaoh and lead God's people out of captivity, He said 'I will be with you' (Exod. 3:12). He could go in the name of 'I am who I am'. The Lord gave him assurance after assurance, and of course Moses fulfilled his task.

When the angel of the Lord appeared to Gideon as he was threshing wheat in a winepress for fear of the Midianites, he was assured, 'The Lord is with you, mighty warrior' (Judg. 6:12). When Gideon showed his reluctance to accept his commission, the Lord said to him:

Peace! Do not be afraid. You are not going to die (Judg. 6:23).

Jeremiah was reluctant to accept his calling to be a prophet to the nations; the Lord was very firm with him:

But the Lord said to me, 'Do not say, "I am only a child." You must go to everyone I send you to and say whatever I command you. **Do not be afraid of them, for I am with you and will rescue you,**' declares the Lord (Jer. 1:7–8).

And when God called Ezekiel to prophesy to His disobedient people, He said: '**Do not be afraid of what they say or terrified by them,** though they are a rebellious house' (Ezek. 2:6).

It seems that the Lord views fear as being the product of having faith in yourself. The answer, then, is simple: **Put your faith in Him, in who He is and His presence with you.**

This would not be a popular answer to fear in some counselling circles today! Nevertheless it is the Truth!

The person who is readily overcome with fear is allowing his soul life, rather than his spirit, to predominate. He believes the negative thoughts and feelings rather than allowing the power, love and sound mind of his spirit to infuse his soul with those qualities.

The Lord knows that we will all experience testing times, but He has given us wonderful promises concerning the way He will carry us through those times:

Fear not, for I have redeemed you; I have summoned you by name, you are mine. When you pass through the waters, I **will be with you;** and when you pass through the rivers they will not sweep over you. When you walk through the fire, you will not be burned; the flames will not set you ablaze. **For I am the Lord, your God, the Holy One of Israel, your Saviour** (Isa. 43:1–3).

You belong to the Lord; He has called and chosen you to be His very own. Therefore He promises to care for you in every way and to provide for every need:

And my God will meet all your needs according to his glorious riches in Christ Jesus (Phil. 4:19).

No matter how difficult the circumstance, no one and nothing can take His presence or His Spirit away from you, or separate you from His love, the perfect love that casts out all fear.

For I am convinced that neither death nor life, neither angels nor demons, neither the present nor the future nor any powers, neither height nor depth, **nor anything else in all creation, will be able to separate us from the love of God that is in Christ Jesus our Lord** (Rom. 8:38–9).

In all these things, Paul says, **we are 'more than conquerors through him who loved us'** (v. 37).

In the light of these truths, it makes little sense to concentrate on your fears or try to analyse their cause. Once your heart and mind are fixed on the truth, you will once again walk by faith and not fear.

The Lord said to Joshua:

I will be with you; I will never leave you nor forsake you (Jos. 1:5).

These were the words of strength and comfort he needed at that moment, faced with the great task of leading God's people to take possession of the Promised Land. Miracles would be needed to see their enemies vanquished. So the Lord impressed on him the need to live in the Truth, and gave him encouraging promises:

Be strong and courageous, because you will lead these people to inherit the land I swore to their forefathers to give them. **Be strong and very courageous. Be careful to obey** all the law my servant Moses gave you; do not turn from it to the right or to the left, **that you may be successful wherever you go.** Do not let this Book of the Law depart from your mouth; meditate on it day and night, **so that you may be careful to do everything written in it. Then you will be prosperous and successful.** Have I not commanded you? **Be strong and courageous. Do not be terrified; do not be discouraged, for the Lord your God will be with you wherever you go** (Jos. 1:6–9).

Living in faith and obedience to God's Word were crucial to the prosperity and success He promised Joshua.

And so with us. **The Lord wants you and every one of His children to prosper and be successful. This will only be accomplished as they choose to walk in the truth** (3 John 3–4). So the Lord warns Joshua not to be discouraged by his circumstances; He knew His servant would face difficulty as well as triumphant times.

The Lord wants your soul to prosper. So walk in the Truth and do not allow your circumstances to dominate your thinking.

The Lord's continual command to 'Fear not' is not a facile answer that avoids the real need. He knows it is the only answer that will meet the need.

Whenever you become 'soul-centred' you will be prone to fear, striving, failure and disappointment. Whenever you look at yourself or imagine that it is you on your own that has to face the difficult situation, you will inevitably have feelings of fear. This does not signify that God has taken His Spirit away from you, or that you need soul-healing. It simply indicates that you need to submit your soul life to the Spirit once again so that His life can infuse your soul with power and love. Then you will once again be able to rejoice in the Lord.

Though the mountains be shaken and the hills be removed, **yet my unfailing love for you will not be shaken nor my covenant of peace be removed,** says the Lord, who has compassion on you (Isa. 54:10).

17   Physical Healing

On the cross Jesus did all that was necessary for physical as well as spiritual and emotional healing. Some deny this aspect of the cross because not everyone for whom they pray is healed. It is dangerous to construct doctrine from experience, rather than from the evidence of God's Word! **When we believe what He says, then we experience what He promises!**

The forgiveness made possible through the cross has to be appropriated by faith, just as physical healing does. Some ask God to forgive them again and again because they lack that faith. Some ask for healing again and again for the same reason.

In Matthew, chapter 8, the writer gives us an account of the healing that attended Jesus's ministry, healing of physical sickness and deliverance from demonic powers.

He drove out the spirits with a word and healed all the sick (v. 16).

Matthew then explained why these things were happening:

This was to fulfil what was spoken through the prophet Isaiah: **'He took up our infirmities and carried our diseases'** (v. 17).

There is no question that the writer equated both deliverance and the healing of all sickness with the work of the cross. But why should he quote the prophecy concerning the cross at this early stage of Jesus's ministry, before the crucifixion had taken place?

While on earth Jesus ministered to that particular generation, and then only in one place at a time. **The cross made the total work of salvation available to everyone of every generation everywhere!** It was a 'cosmic' event with eternal consequences.

Usually those who fail to teach the healing power of the cross see little healing in their ministries. When we do not see God doing particular things, it is very tempting to attempt to justify our lack of faith! Jesus said:

> **If you believe,** you will receive **whatever** you ask for in prayer (Matt. 21:22).

'Whatever' must include healing!

GOD'S WILL TO HEAL

The saving work of Jesus is the healing work of Jesus. It is God's very nature to heal:

> I am the Lord, who heals you (Exod. 15:26).

It should not be necessary to have to explain God's willingness to heal, but there is so much confusion concerning this topic it is important to communicate what God's truth reveals to us.

There is no question as to whether Jesus wants to heal. The first who came to Him was a leper who said: 'Lord, if you are willing, you can make me clean' (Matt. 8:2). **Jesus simply removed the 'if' and said: I am willing. Be clean!** (v. 3). Immediately he was cured of his leprosy.

People talk about the 'sovereign will of God' as an excuse when people are not healed. Surely God has declared His sovereign will in Jesus? He has shown that every need is met in Him crucified. The Lord will never deny faith in what Jesus has already accomplished.

We must remember that God does not always have His way in our lives. Do you ever sin? Yes, you do! Does God ever want you to sin? Is it ever His will for you to sin? Of course not!

God wills all men to be saved and has provided the sacrifice for us that makes this possible. But are all men saved? No, only those who put their faith in the saving work of Jesus Christ.

God does not sit on His throne as a fickle Father deciding whether to forgive this one or not, or heal that one or not. He has provided the means for us to be forgiven, saved, healed, set free. **When by faith we take hold of the Truth of what He has done, we see the fulfilment of what He has promised.**

Part of the present-day confusion comes from the fact that often people try to minister God's healing at the wrong time. Even Jesus could not perform many miracles at Nazareth because of the unbelief of the people!

When they came seeking healing, He would ask questions of them to see whether they believed they would receive what they asked. **Faith, remember, is being sure and certain!**

Often people receive the laying-on of hands without any enquiry as to what they believe will happen as a result. Neither is opportunity given for any repentance that may be necessary so that nothing will hinder the receiving of what God wants to give! Is the sick person in a right attitude of forgiveness towards others? If not, God will not forgive that person. And if he is not forgiven, he is unlikely to be healed!

Those who administer healing in a pastoral context can deal with all these points *before* prayer; and they will obtain better results if they do! The laying-on of hands does not have to be a spontaneous thing at a public service. At such times some receive healing, but many don't! It is discouraging both to the sick person and to the rest of the congregation, to see the same people coming forward again and again, without anything apparently happening to them.

ANOINTING

Often anointing is administered in a way that is not true to the teaching of scripture. Notice what James says:

> Is any one of you sick? He should call the elders of the church to pray over him and anoint him with oil in the name of the Lord. And the prayer offered in faith will make the sick person well; the Lord will raise him up. If he has sinned, he will be forgiven. Therefore confess your sins to each other and pray for each other so that you may be healed. The prayer of a righteous man is powerful and effective (Jas. 5:14–16).

1 **The sick person should call for the elders to go to him.** It was not for the elders to take the initiative. The sick person needs to exercise faith!
2 **The elders should pray over him.** They are to pray with faith.
3 **They anoint him with oil.** Both the sick person and the elders can see this as the point at which they believe healing is given and received.
4 **It is the prayer of faith that effects the healing.**
5 **There should be open confession of sin by those present, with the assurance of forgiveness, 'so that you may be healed'.**
6 **The prayer of the righteous person** (made righteous through Jesus) **is powerful and effective.**

Again we would see much better results if we ministered anointing in the way God directs.

All this goes to show that wherever possible, due preparation can take place before prayer or anointing. Of course this is not appropriate in cases of extremity, with very young children (although the parents should prepare their hearts), the mentally handicapped or for minor irritants where spontaneous prayer is obviously called for!

PREPARATION

When ministering physical healing in a pastoral situation I have found that a few days of preparation for the sick person has been of immense value. I will share what I have found effective, but not as a blueprint for everyone to copy.

1 Most healing needs have been present for some time; so a few more days will not make any significant difference.

2 God is concerned about the whole person, not just the sickness. So this is an opportunity for God to meet afresh with the believer, spiritually as well as physically.

3 The person needs to consider if there is any sin which needs to be confessed, any area of disobedience or any relationship where forgiveness is called for.

4 Is the person in a position of faith? If not, time needs to be given to reveal the scriptures to show that it is God's purpose to heal. It should not be taken for granted that the person believes this. Everyone knows God *can* heal; the issue is whether the person believes God *will* heal him or her **when we pray.**

5 I give the person three or four scriptures of promise appropriate to his need and suggest he sits quietly three times a day and allows God to speak them to his heart. (I suggest he uses the method of prayer explained in my book, *Listen and Live*.) Faith comes from hearing the Word, so I suggest he reads the healing miracles in the Gospels. He is coming to Jesus, not me, for healing; so I suggest he asks the Holy Spirit to make these words revelation to his heart.

6 I then arrange a time when we will meet to pray. I actually fix a time for the healing! 'Now let's fix the time for your

healing.' This gives a focal point. **He needs to come, not expecting prayer, but to receive his healing.**

7 When he comes for this appointment I ensure *he* prays. He has the opportunity to open his heart to the Lord, to ask for forgiveness, to confess any lingering doubts and to state what he believes God is going to do about his need.

8 I then pray in whatever way the Holy Spirit leads, giving assurance of forgiveness first if necessary, praying for the anointing of the Holy Spirit to be upon us before I minister the healing.

9 I will pray 'in the Spirit and with the mind also', if necessary taking authority over the enemy.

This is not a form of ministry to be used legalistically. You can see the benefit of building people's expectation. There are always those who say that this is dangerous in case people are disappointed! **If we do not expect healing to happen when we minister, then what is the purpose of praying?**

I cannot say that I have always seen the total healing take place when ministering in this way; **but something always happens.** The person meets with God, the healing process is begun, perhaps faith is enlarged. Often, of course, the healing does happen there and then. In any case, we thank the Lord for what He has done, for we are told that we are to pray at all times with thanksgiving.

It is advisable to prepare the ground as well as possible. Did Jesus prepare people like this? Most of the healings recorded were in an 'itinerant' context rather than a pastoral one, when obviously such preparation is not possible. However, Jesus did ask penetrating questions, the answers to which showed that the person was able to receive the healing.

Most of my ministry is now itinerant and I must confess to a certain frustration at not being able to prepare people to receive, although at a public meeting I will always lead in a time of repentance and stress the importance of faith before ministering healing.

I do not take people through the above process of preparation if the Holy Spirit gives witness to pray immediately.

MINISTER WITH AUTHORITY

Jesus commanded His Church to heal the sick. We have His authority to do this in His name. Although faith is the central element in healing, especially on the part of the one who is sick, it is also necessary for those ministering to exercise authority in this area of ministry.

We have already seen that we are only able to exercise authority inasmuch as we are submitted to the Lord's authority. Because Jesus was completely submitted to His Father, He could exercise perfect authority over sickness and the demonic powers which plagued people's lives. He gives that authority to believers:

> I have given you authority to trample on snakes and scorpions and to overcome all the power of the enemy; nothing will harm you. However, do not rejoice that the spirits submit to you, but rejoice that your names are written in heaven (Luke 10:19–20).

The reason that believers have such authority is because their names 'are written in heaven'. **They belong to God's Kingdom which is far superior in power to the dominion of darkness.** The Holy Spirit living in the Christian is far greater than the power of darkness operating in the world.

We shall talk about deliverance later. Here we need to see this as part of the total ministry of healing to which God calls His Church.

God's Spirit is now upon the believing Church to enable God's children to continue Jesus's war against sickness. He said of Himself:

> The Spirit of the Lord is on me, because he has anointed me to preach good news to the poor. He has sent me to

proclaim freedom for the prisoners and recovery of sight for the blind, to release the oppressed, to proclaim the year of the Lord's favour (Luke 4:18–19).

He told the messengers sent by John the Baptist to report what they had seen:

The blind receive sight, the lame walk, those who have leprosy are cured, the deaf hear, the dead are raised, and the good news is preached to the poor (Luke 7:22).

We can rightly say that God wants all people to be saved; but He knows that not all will be saved. We can say that God wants all to be healed; but He knows that not all will be healed. We can even go as far as to say that ideally God would not want anyone to sin or be sick; and He tells us to pray:

Your kingdom come, your will be done on earth as it is in heaven (Matt. 6:10).

We do not expect to find either sin or sickness in heaven. So Jesus waged war on both while on earth. We are to do likewise.

It is clear that Jesus healed all who came to Him, but He did not take the initiative of going to people to heal all the sick in Israel. Healing the man by the pool of Bethesda (John 5:1–9) was the exception rather than the rule.

Our aim must surely be to exercise the faith and authority to heal all who come to Jesus with faith. It is significant that Jesus asked such questions as:

'Do you want to get well?' (John 5:6).

'Do you believe that I am able to do this?' (Matt. 9:28).

Just because someone came to Him, Jesus did not take it for granted that he either wanted healing or had the faith to be healed!

He also made it clear:

I tell you the truth, the Son can do nothing by himself; he can do only what he sees his Father doing, because whatever the Father does the Son also does (John 5:19).

If this was true for Jesus, it must also be true for us.

By myself I can do nothing . . . for I seek not to please myself but him who sent me (John 5:30).

I would love to see every sick person healed at every meeting at which I spoke! But like Jesus, I have to be completely dependent on God's leading; and so do you!

I have found that speaking words of command following words of knowledge to be a most powerful way of ministering healing in a public context. The one ministering is dependent on the Lord to make him aware of the particular needs to be met. When he commands the sickness to depart, speaking with authority, the healing happens there and then.

On such occasions people have frequently said that as soon as the word of authority was spoken, the power of God came upon them and they were healed. There have also been occasions when people have said to me that they were healed as soon as I mentioned their particular sickness; and yet I did not speak any such word. When the Spirit moves in this way some obviously hear directly from God and are immediately healed.

There is an interesting scripture which says that:

The power of the Lord was present for him to heal the sick (Luke 5:17).

Even in His ministry there must have been particular moves of God when many people received their healing.

We have seen that we should not isolate healing from the

whole Gospel. The exercise of authority is greater than commanding sickness to leave, but does include this. Jesus rebuked fever and it left immediately (Luke 4:39).

In His teaching on prayer, Jesus makes it clear that every believer is to speak with faith to the mountains of need.

> I tell you the truth, if anyone says to this mountain, 'Go, throw yourself into the sea,' **and does not doubt in his heart but believes** that what he says will happen, it will be done for him. Therefore I tell you, whatever you ask for in prayer, **believe that you have received it, and it will be yours** (Mark 11:23–4).

It is important to note that **the believer is to speak to the need himself, as an outworking of his faith; he is not supposed to be dependent on someone else to address the mountain for him!** When he speaks to the need he is to believe in his heart and not doubt that what he has said will come to pass.

Jesus makes it clear that to pray with faith means that we believe we have already received the answer to our prayer. This is different from the statements Christians often interpret as faith: 'I really believe God is going to do it.' That is hope, not faith.

Hope says it will happen.
Faith believes it has happened, even when there is no immediate evidence to substantiate that.

Authority is an outworking both of the believer's submission to God and of his faith in His promises. Jesus says that it is not the amount of faith that matters but the quality of it:

> If you have faith as small as a mustard seed, you can say to this mulberry tree, 'Be uprooted and planted in the sea,' and it will obey you (Luke 17:6).

Such faith is expressed by speaking to the need with authority with the expectation that there will be the desired result; faith inspired by Jesus who is the 'Author and Perfecter of our faith'!

DEALING WITH UNBELIEF

What can be done when counselling someone who does not have such faith in his or her heart?

1 **There is nothing you can do to change a person's heart.** This is the work of God alone.
2 **Pray that the person will receive revelation from God.**
3 **Encourage him to be honest with God about his unbelief or doubts.** He hates hypocrisy but loves honesty. He will forgive the unbelief.
4 **Encourage him to ask God to speak a word of faith to his heart.** This may happen at that precise moment or later, but the expectation is that God will speak such a word to him.
5 **When he has received such a word and has come to a position of faith, that is the time to minister healing to him.**
6 **The Lord may prompt you to pray for him before he has such a word; in which case you need to listen carefully as to how to pray on that occasion.** It may not be the right time to pray for the healing itself.
7 **When ministering remember that you are handling someone who is precious to the Lord. Whatever you do or say is to be in His name and is to be done, not only with authority, but with all the love and grace at your command.**

All ministry must be exercised in love if it is truly in the name of Jesus.

At all costs avoid wild, accusing, or condemning statements. These are said only out of your own frustration if you do not see things happening in the way you wanted or expected. It is easy, but does not help the situation at all, to blame the person with whom you are praying by saying he doesn't have enough faith, or there is some sin in his life that is preventing him from receiving the healing. This may be true, but **it is your responsibility to hear from God and bring a word of faith, correction or encouragement.** God never accuses us or makes us feel condemned; and you are speaking in His name!

So before ministering pray that the love of Jesus as well as His truth and power, will flow through you. You are speaking and acting in His name.

PART 3

OVERCOMING THE ENEMY

18 Opposing the Enemy

When dealing with those who were not believers, Jesus delivered them from the demonic powers which bound them, and then told them to follow Him. There is no evidence of His praying in the same way with those who were already believers. **Every believer has the responsibility to resist the enemy in his own life.** He is to submit to God and resist the devil who will then flee from him.

It is important, therefore, that every believer knows the authority he has over the enemy and how to exercise that authority. He needs to understand the enemy that opposes him, his tactics, and the various ways in which he tries to undermine his faith.

Believers have the authority to prevent and permit whatever is prevented and permitted in heaven. Jesus said:

I tell you the truth, whatever you bind on earth will be bound in heaven, and whatever you loose on earth will be loosed in heaven (Matt. 18:18).

To bind is to prevent; to loose is to permit. The Greek is difficult to translate simply. Jesus is saying that whatever is prevented in heaven, we have the authority to prevent on earth. Whatever heaven permits we can permit.

'Whatever' does not apply exclusively to demonic activity as we have seen, but must certainly include this. It is clear from Paul's teaching that we have spiritual opposition in heavenly places and this can affect what happens to us on earth.

> For our struggle is not against flesh and blood, but against the rulers, against the authorities, against the powers of this dark world and against the spiritual forces of evil in the heavenly realms (Eph. 6:12).

In this struggle, Paul tells believers to 'put on the full armour of God'. He uses the illustration of the pieces of armour to illustrate the essential elements in the Christian's defence against the enemy's attacks, and his ability to overcome him. These are:

1 TRUTH
2 RIGHTEOUSNESS
3 THE GOSPEL OF PEACE
4 FAITH
5 SALVATION
6 THE SPIRIT AND THE WORD
7 PRAYER

The Christian does not need to fall into such bondage that he needs someone else to take authority over the enemy on his behalf. He has the power to overcome the enemy himself! Each 'soldier' is to wear the armour, use the shield of faith and attack with the sword of the Spirit!

1 TRUTH: The Truth sets the believer free. **If he walks in the Truth he will walk in freedom and will not fall into bondage.**
2 RIGHTEOUSNESS: **If he lives in the good of the righteousness he has in Christ, he will not fall into serious sin.** When he does sin, he can confess his sins and will be forgiven and cleansed from all unrighteousness.

3   THE GOSPEL OF PEACE: Because of his faith in the cross of Jesus Christ, the believer has peace with God. Nothing can destroy his relationship of peace if he resists the enemy's attacks. The good news is that **he is at one with God, living in Christ and the Kingdom of God is within him.** He therefore has authority over the enemy, who has been thrown out of that Kingdom.

4   FAITH: **His faith in the Lord and His Word enables the believer to resist everything the enemy throws at him. He knows the Truth and can therefore resist his lies.** He knows his place and inheritance in Christ, so he can resist the enemy's attempts to make him doubt his worthiness, acceptance and love through Jesus. **He has the faith not only to survive but to overcome.**

5   SALVATION: **He knows that he is saved** and that this gives him a privileged position in relation to God, and power over the evil one. No one can snatch him away from Jesus.

6   THE SPIRIT AND THE WORD: The believer is filled with the Holy Spirit. **The One in him is greater than he that is in the world.** That Spirit of Truth guides him into all the Truth. So he can use the Word of God to refute the enemy, as Jesus did in the wilderness.

7   PRAYER: He is to pray in the Spirit on all occasions. **Not only will the Holy Spirit guide him as to what to pray, He will also fill his prayer with power.**

So God has made all these resources available to enable the believer to overcome the evil one. To walk in the Spirit is to walk in the Truth, to walk in the light, to live in Christ and allow His Word to live in him; then he will have nothing to fear, for he will be walking on the Highway of Holiness:

> No lion will be there, nor will any ferocious beast get up on it; they will not be found there. But only the redeemed will walk there (Isa. 35:9).

'The unclean will not journey on it; it will be for those who walk in that Way' (v. 8). This is the place where only the Lord's children can walk.

The lion represents Satan who 'prowls around like a roaring lion looking for someone to devour' (1 Pet. 5:8). And the wild beasts are the demons which serve Satan. Those who walk on the Highway of Holiness are out of their reach. They may snarl and make angry-sounding noises; but they cannot actually touch them.

Sin and disobedience makes the believer vulnerable to the enemy's attacks, which is a good incentive to walk in righteousness; but we do not always do what is sensible and right. We are told to ask for wisdom if we need it. Disobedience may seem relatively unimportant to the guilty one, but it is proof of a lack of wisdom. Those who disobey do not stop to think of the ways in which they are yielding themselves to the enemy's influence, making themselves vulnerable to him.

Persistent disobedience can certainly lead a person into bondage, even if he is a born-again Christian. Most of those bondages are broken by sincere heart repentance. **The power of the cross breaks the power of the sin that has temporarily bound the believer.** He only became bound through his own fault, through persistent disobedience or unbelief. Repentance restores him to the place of unity and peace with God.

THE NEED FOR WISDOM

But the wisdom that comes from heaven is first of all pure; then peace-loving, considerate, submissive, full of mercy and good fruit, impartial and sincere (Jas. 3:17).

Notice the qualities of this wisdom:

1 **It is pure.** To live in wisdom is to walk in purity, not sin. The wise choices are the right choices!
2 **God's wisdom is 'peace-loving'.** The wise believer will not

make decisions that disrupt his peace with God. He will choose righteousness, for sin causes him to lose this sense of peace.

3 **The wise believer is considerate to others.** He knows that faith has to be revealed in love, that the measure he gives will be the measure he receives back, that he will reap what he sows.

4 **He is full of mercy towards others,** because God has forgiven him for so much. He desires to have a forgiving heart.

5 **Because in wisdom he chooses to walk in the Spirit he bears much fruit for the Father's glory.**

6 **The wise man holds to the Truth, for then he will be impartial, judging everything by God's Word.** 'From now on we regard no-one from a worldly point of view' (2 Cor. 5:16).

7 **He has a sincere heart,** is a person of integrity and can be trusted.

Many of those who seek counsel have departed from the way of wisdom; hence the tensions and anxieties they experience. **It is not for us to judge them, but to bring them back to wisdom.** As we have seen this will inevitably involve the need of repentance, which restores a person to a relationship of peace and unity with God.

However, his lack of wisdom over a prolonged period of time may have led to real bondage in his life. It may seem to him that he cannot break free, that he needs deliverance.

BONDAGE

It is important for us to keep things in true perspective. Some want to blame demons for everything that goes wrong, so much so that they absolve themselves from blame. They refuse to face their responsibility for their sins or their need to repent.

There can be no doubt that the enemy opposes every

believer and uses demonic powers to accuse and deceive them. Many are oppressed because they have believed a series of lies which have come from the father of lies. Instead of exercising their authority to resist the devil, they have yielded areas of their lives to his influence.

Neither the devil himself, nor any of his demonic powers, have any rightful claims to a believer's life. The only ground they can occupy is that yielded to them by the believer – through sin, disobedience or by being deceived.

Nobody likes to face the fact that he has been deceived. We have all been deceived at times. We have all thought ourselves to be right when in fact we were wrong. That is the nature of deception!

God is infinitely patient with us. He does not judge or condemn us for being wrong or being deceived. **His Spirit gently but firmly leads us back to the Truth.** This may take time when we are full of self-righteousness, determined to defend a position we have taken because we do not want to admit we have been wrong. Because of pride we want to conceal from others that we have not only been deceived but have been used to deceive others. We have tried to influence them with our views which cannot be substantiated from the Truth!

Instead of holding on to pride, believers need to humble themselves before the Truth.

Although the Holy Spirit convicts the believer of sin, he is able to ignore this conviction if he so chooses. He can carry on with life, can still praise God and be aware of His love, yet resist the promptings of the Holy Spirit.

He may decide to persist in the sin. If he does so, it will take a greater and greater hold on him. At times he may feel uneasy about this because of the Holy Spirit's witness within him. But his love of the sin outweighs his desire to obey God; and so he persists in this area of disobedience. He thinks he can handle the situation; after all, God still loves him!

In time he will realise that this sin not only has a grip on him, but is affecting the whole of his spiritual life, his relationship with God and with others. He may pray about the matter, but for so long he has been deceiving himself, justifying the matter in his own eyes and even before God, that he cannot pray with much conviction or faith. The sin persists. He may seek someone's help, but without necessarily admitting to the real need. Or he may blunder on, putting on a good Christian front for others, while at the same time knowing he has slipped to a wretched state within himself.

His prayer life deteriorates, he loses his appetite for God's Word, which convicts him so clearly that he is loath to read it. He becomes tense and is prone to snap at those around him, especially those who love him. He grows withdrawn and morose.

He may come to the conclusion that if someone prayed with him he could receive a swift act of deliverance that would set everything right. A quick prayer of deliverance will do little good unless there is first genuine repentance. **He needs to submit himself afresh to God; then he can resist the devil himself with authority.**

The one who comes for prayer, but without true heart participation, may find temporary relief; but it is not long before the problem returns. This is because he has not faced the real problem: the condition of his heart.

He will need to repent of:

a   the original area of sin and disobedience,

b   persisting in this sin, ignoring the convicting work of the Holy Spirit,

c   allowing the enemy to deceive him in this area of his life,

d   instead of resisting the enemy, giving him ground on which to stand to accuse him,

e   the way this sin has affected his relationships and attitudes to others.

His real sin has been to disobey the Lord. Like David he needs to admit: **'Against you, you only, have I sinned'** (Ps. 51:4). And so David's prayer is also pertinent for him: **'Create in me a clean heart, O God, and renew a steadfast spirit within me'** (Ps. 51:10).

Genuine repentance comes from the heart and must involve a definite turning away from the sin as well as a fresh submission of his heart to God. Then he will be able to resist the enemy once again. Nobody else can resist the devil for him, but others can stand *with him* against the enemy.

He may travel around seeking ministry from anyone he considers more able to exercise authority over the enemy. He will try the 'experts' in deliverance. But unless he is prepared for a change of heart, any help he receives will be short-lived in its effect, no matter who prays for him. The return of the bondage is likely to give him the impression that he is in a hopeless condition; that the enemy has a grip on him that cannot be shaken off.

His persistent disobedience has given demonic powers the opportunity to influence him and even exercise some hold over him. Those demons will have to respond to the prayer of authority from others who minister to this Christian. Hence the temporary relief. But without a change of heart the believer is likely to return to the sin and disobedience and so give ground back to the enemy.

Genuine repentance on his part, coupled with fresh submission to God and a determination to resist the enemy, is the only way for the problem to be dealt with effectively. He will not be able to sustain victory in any other way.

DEMONS

Christians should not be surprised that they are resisted by demonic forces. Whether they like it or not they are involved in spiritual warfare. **To refuse to fight is to give the field to the enemy.** Every believer needs to know, not only how to withstand these enemy forces, but how to overcome them.

Often Christians do not recognise when there is enemy

activity. They need to exercise the gift of the Spirit known as the discerning of spirits, and to pay attention to the inner witness of the Holy Spirit. He causes them to feel wrong about certain people and situations the enemy is using, even though it may not be apparent what exactly is wrong.

Satan uses demonic forces to oppose believers, even those who are seeking to walk in faith and obedience. He will try to deceive, to lie and accuse, in an attempt to draw the believer off course. The one whose heart is set on righteousness is not easily swayed or deceived; but the enemy will use every device he has to try and disrupt the believer's walk with God.

Lack of discernment by Christians when under demonic attack plays into the enemy's hands. Some even assert that demons are not real; that Jesus only talked of them because He was using the thought forms of the day!

That is a blasphemous suggestion for it accuses Jesus of deliberately deceiving people, which is the devil's work, not His. He brought people the Truth, often correcting their misconceived ideas. He would not have cast out demons from people if they did not exist! Neither would He have taught about them if He knew them to be a figment of people's imagination. He tells us some interesting facts about demons:

> When an evil spirit comes out of a man, it goes through arid places seeking rest and does not find it. Then it says, 'I will return to the house I left'. When it arrives, it finds the house swept clean and put in order. Then it goes and takes seven other spirits more wicked than itself, and they go in and live there. And the final condition of that man is worse than the first (Luke 11:24–6).

1 Evil spirits or demons have personality. They are not vague powers or forces.
2 Demons can exist either within people or externally.
3 They seek places of rest. They want to take up residence within people if they can.

4   They can speak.
5   Demons can co-operate with one another.
6   They are able to plan and make decisions, so they have a
    certain amount of autonomy.
7   A 'clean house' is an invitation for greater demonic attack.
8   Some demons are more wicked than others.
9   They will take up residence wherever they are allowed to.

There is no doubt from either scripture or experience that the
enemy attacks the soul of every believer. He even attacked
Jesus at the level of the soul (and body when He was crucified),
but could not have any influence over His Spirit. Because He
lived in constant obedience and submission to His Father, He
could exercise total authority over Satan himself, thus denying
him any victory.

A disciple who walks in the Spirit, and so in the Truth of
God's Word, will be able to exercise authority over every
attack the enemy hurls against him.

**Satan cannot steal your inheritance from you, but he will try
to prevent you from living in the good of that inheritance.** He can
do nothing to change the Truth; so he will try to deceive you so
that you do not live by the Truth. Then you will not be able to
enjoy the freedom God intends for you.

**Satan cannot take away the gift of eternal life you have received
from God. Neither can he remove you from God's Kingdom.** But
he tries to steal the revelation of the Kingdom power and
authority the believer has, because then he will not exercise
his authority over the demonic forces deployed against him.

When the seventy-two returned to Jesus, delighted that even
the demons submitted to them, He pointed out that this
should not be their cause of joy. They needed to rejoice,
not in the fact that they could overcome those powers, but
why they were able to do so; their names were written in
heaven. **They belonged to the Kingdom of light which is
infinitely more powerful than the dominion of darkness!** Whenever light shines, darkness disappears.

They belonged to the Truth which is the answer to the lying, deceiving tactics of the evil one.

Because your name is written in heaven you have authority over every demonic force that opposes you. And you can exercise authority over the demons that attack others. Nothing will harm you, Jesus assures you. So you never need to fear those over whom you have power and authority.

This shows how irresponsible it is for Christians to allow themselves to get into bondage, either through sin or because they do not oppose those who come against them. To every believer is given the shield of faith in one hand, faith that enables him to resist everything the enemy throws against him. In the other hand he has the Sword of the Spirit, the Word of God.

Man does not live on bread alone, but on every word that comes from the mouth of God (Matt. 4:4).

With the Word of Truth he is able to overcome the lying, deceiving spirits which falsely accuse him. He needs to know the Truth that sets him free, and to live in the Truth which will enable him to maintain that freedom.

19 Deception

1 SELF-DECEPTION

Sometimes Christians want to be deceived. When a believer wants to hold on to some sinful area of his life and does not want to repent, the sin takes a firmer grip on him thus giving the enemy opportunity to place him in bondage.

We have also seen that the scriptures clearly teach us that **we are self-deceived when we hear what God says in His Word but fail to put it into practice:**

> Do not merely listen to the word, and so deceive yourselves. Do what it says. Anyone who listens to the word but does not do what it says is like a man who looks at his face in a mirror and, after looking at himself, goes away and immediately forgets what he looks like. But the man who looks intently into the perfect law that gives freedom, and continues to do this, not forgetting what he has heard, but doing it – he will be blessed in what he does (Jas. 1:22–5).

These are the alternatives facing each Christian: to deceive himself through disobedience to God's Word, or to be blessed by his obedience.

It is clear that self-deception was already a problem in the early Church of New Testament times and took a number of different forms:

a **A person is self-deceived if he claims to be sinless:**

If we claim to be without sin, we deceive ourselves and the truth is not in us (1 John 1:8).

b **A person is also self-deceived if he has exalted ideas about himself:**

If anyone thinks he is something when he is nothing, he deceives himself (Gal. 6:3).

c **He is deceived if he thinks he can fool God:**

Do not be deceived: God cannot be mocked. A man reaps what he sows (Gal. 6:7).

He will either sow to please his flesh, which is spiritual death; or he will sow to please the Spirit, which is eternal life. When Christians are perplexed as to why they should suffer certain problems, they need to consider what they have been sowing. A critical person reaps criticism. A judgmental person will be judged. Jesus makes it clear that he will be judged with the same judgment with which he judges others.

On the other hand, if he gives love he will reap love. If he is generous he will reap generosity and will not be in any need.

d **A Christian is deceived whenever he raises his reason and understanding above the revelation of God's Word:**

Do not deceive yourselves. If any one of you thinks he is wise by the standards of this age, he should become a 'fool' so that he may become wise (1 Cor. 3:18).

All these expressions of self-deception are examples of the Christian elevating his soul or self-life above the Spirit. This always spells trouble.

e **A man is also self-deceived if he appears to be a spiritual person, but speaks negatively, is critical and judgmental of others:**

> If anyone considers himself religious and yet does not keep a tight rein on his tongue, he deceives himself and his religion is worthless (Jas 1:26).

That seems a harsh evaluation of his religion. But Jesus said: 'For out of the overflow of the heart the mouth speaks' (Matt. 12:34). Jesus recognises that an unbridled tongue is a manifestation of a wrong heart.

f **It is self-deception to imagine that formal religion is able to save people.**

The difficulty with self-deception is that the guilty one usually fails to see his own sin. That is the nature of self-deception; it causes him to be spiritually blind. Try telling a critical person that he is critical and see the reaction you receive!

The Pharisees were the epitome of self-deception, performing their external religious duties while neglecting the most important elements of the law. Deceived because they imagined their words were pleasing to God, while their hearts were far from Him. Appearing righteous, yet full of corruption within.

Jesus warned against legalistic, formal religion. Paul also warned that the unrighteous would not inherit God's Kingdom:

> Do you not know that the wicked will not inherit the kingdom of God? Do not be deceived: Neither the sexually immoral nor idolaters nor adulterers nor male prostitutes nor homosexual offenders nor thieves nor the greedy nor

drunkards nor slanderers nor swindlers will inherit the kingdom of God (1 Cor. 6:9–10).

No universal salvation here! It is not a question of 'everyone will be all right in the end'.

g **Imagining that everyone will go to heaven is another form of self-deception.**

Jesus answered, 'I am the way and the truth and the life. No-one comes to the Father except through me' (John 14:6).

h **A Christian deceives himself if he imagines he cannot be influenced by others, by flirting with sin or temptation.**
Paul warns believers about the company they keep:

Do not be misled: 'Bad company corrupts good character' (1 Cor. 15:33).

He has the responsibility to witness to all and sundry, but that is not the same as allowing himself to be yoked with those who will try to suck him into the standards of the world, who will appeal to his flesh life and tempt him to compromise his walk with God.

2 DECEPTION

Satan is out to deceive believers. Here are some of the warnings we are given in scripture:
a **False Christs.** Paul says:

For if someone comes to you and preaches a Jesus other than the Jesus we preached, or if you receive a different spirit from the one you received, or a different gospel from the one you accepted, you put up with it easily enough (2 Cor. 11:4).

There are many other Jesuses being preached today, even within churches. Some preach a Jesus who is powerless to intervene in natural circumstances, or to answer prayer supernaturally. Some preach a Jesus who is not the same today as He was yesterday. They claim that He does not heal today or perform the signs and wonders experienced in the life of the apostolic Church. They preach a partial Gospel, a partial cross, a partial Jesus even!

The Jesus in whom we are to believe is the Jesus of scripture, the One who 'is the same yesterday and today and for ever' (Heb. 13:8).

b **False prophets.** Jesus warns believers:

> False Christs and false prophets will appear and perform great signs and miracles to deceive even the elect – if that were possible (Matt. 24:24).

All prophecy is to be tested, no matter who speaks or what miracles he performs.

c **False teachers.** The enemy seeks to deceive through those who teach a distortion of the truth.

> Even from your own number men will arise and distort the truth in order to draw away disciples after them (Acts 20:30).

d **False claims.** Jesus warns:

> Watch out that no one deceives you. For many will come in my name, claiming, 'I am the Christ', and will deceive many (Matt. 24:4–5).

e **False teaching.** Not only will false teachers arise, but the enemy will attack Christians directly. Paul tells Timothy:

> The Spirit clearly says that in later times some will abandon

the faith and follow deceiving spirits and things taught by demons (1 Tim. 4:1).

These things that are taught will appear reasonable, and even spiritual, but are deceptive works of the enemy, such as new age teaching, spiritism and the occult. The Holy Spirit gives true discernment as to what is of God. If even the elect can be deceived, it is obvious that not all are prepared to listen to the inner witness of God's Spirit.

We are to believe the whole counsel of God, not be selective in choosing only what we want to believe and rejecting the rest. A lack of submission to the authority of God's Word opens the door to the devil's deceptions.

If you do not believe what God says you believe something else instead. You have substituted something else for the truth!

How important it is, then, not to give the enemy a foothold, ground on which he can stand to accuse, deceive or condemn. How important to walk in the Spirit, in the Truth and to test every spirit to see that it is of God (1 John 4:1).

Many obviously do not do this. It is amazing how often prophecies are apparently received by a congregation without being weighed or tested in the way scripture instructs us.

HOW CHRISTIANS CAN BE DECEIVED

Believers need to have a good grasp of the Truth of God's Word, or else they are an easy target for the enemy's deceiving tactics. Peter warns:

Your enemy the devil prowls around like a roaring lion looking for someone to devour (1 Pet. 5:8).

So he instructs:

Resist him, standing firm in the faith (v. 9).

Self-deceit encourages the enemy in his deceit. Jeremiah warns that: 'The heart is deceitful above all things and beyond cure' (Jer. 17:9).

For this reason at new birth God gives believers a new heart and puts a new spirit within them. But that heart can get dirty with use. Paul encourages us to:

Purify ourselves from everything that contaminates body and spirit, perfecting holiness out of reverence for God (2 Cor. 7:1).

An unclean heart can easily be deceived. The serpent set out to deceive Eve in the Garden of Eden, and at that time her heart was right towards God. How much easier for his work to be accomplished if the heart is not right.

The way he set about deceiving the woman was by challenging the Word God had given to Adam. 'Did God really say . . .?' This is still his attitude; to challenge the believer's faith in God's Word, to cause him to doubt the authority of that Word, to set up his own ideas and reason against the Word. **Those he persuades to disbelieve will disobey the Word!**

Jesus says that those who are double-minded need to purify their hearts. Either you submit your mind to the thinking of scripture or you will inevitably be double-minded.

You also aid the enemy in his deceptive work if you push scriptural truth beyond what is revealed. The enemy often wants to push people too far so that they become unbalanced.

For example, the New Testament teaches clearly that we have authority to cast out demons. But it is clear by now that this is not always the answer to a person's problems. The one who sees a demon behind every problem, and deliverance as the answer to every need, will put many people into bondage instead of setting them free!

It is deceptive to engage in ministry which takes a person back into the flesh in order that he might be free to walk in the Spirit.

Again this is a contradiction to the truth of the Gospel, the good news of what Jesus Christ has done for us.

Believers are not to be like,

> infants tossed back and forth by the waves, and blown here and there by every wind of teaching and by the cunning and craftiness of men in their deceitful scheming. Instead, speaking the truth in love, we will in all things grow up into him who is the Head, that is, Christ (Eph. 4:14–15).

It is alarming to see how easily many Christians are misled by the latest fad of ministry, or how readily they will adopt one emphasis of scripture to the almost total exclusion of other emphases.

We are to speak the truth to one another in love, building up each other in God's Word. The more we do that the less likelihood there is of being deceived.

THE COUNTERFEIT

Satan's deceptions are embodied in false religions and cults which abound today. Some acknowledge Jesus, but not as God's Son. Others are completely ignorant of Him. Others still are directly and deliberately opposed to Him.

When a person turns to Christ it is important that he renounces completely his previous involvement in any of these activities. Jesus made it clear:

> He who is not with me is against me, and he who does not gather with me, scatters (Luke 11:23).

You cannot worship God and demons (1 Cor. 10:21). All counterfeit religions are demonic, worshipping false gods as if they were the truth.

Those who have been part of deceptive religions or cults need to be sure that their thinking has not been influenced by the

errors they previously believed. Once again we see how important it is for every believer to have a firm grasp of God's Word, which will bring correction to his thinking.

There is no place for superstition, fetishes or charms in a Christian's life. All such things must be destroyed along with any dependence there has been on them.

When ministering to people who have had occult connections or involvement with such organisations as Freemasonry, it is important that they themselves renounce these things. You cannot do this for them. If they renounce them, you can join in prayer that they will experience no residual influence on their lives from such things.

Likewise they need to renounce their involvement with eastern techniques of meditation, prayer or yoga. Also they need to stand against the negative spiritual effect of receiving treatment through certain alternative medical techniques which have occult roots. Some of these appear to do good physically, while placing the person in spiritual bondage.

Some have also been involved in 'therapy' which has been soul-centred and has therefore contributed to their longing and desire for soul-healing, instead of 'losing' their souls.

If an area of bondage persists despite prayer, a renunciation of former activities may well be needed, but must be coupled with an appropriation of the truth.

At first some may be reluctant to acknowledge the demonic origin of a religion or cult in which they have been involved. As we have seen, no one likes to admit he has been deceived. However, **walking in the Truth has to involve a renunciation of everything that opposes the Truth, whether in the past or present.**

Satan can appear as an angel of light. Sometimes there is a longing to hold on to 'culture'. There seems nothing wrong with this in itself; except that many cultures are intimately linked with the religions of those cultures. This is what leads to syncretism, the blending of different beliefs.

It was for this that God's people in Old Testament times

found themselves in persistent sin. They were frequently warned by the Lord not to intermarry with those of other religions, nor to have anything to do with their idols or religious practices. Their worship of the God and Father of Jesus Christ was to be pure and undefiled. When they failed to obey the Lord in this respect, trouble always resulted.

God is a jealous God (Exod. 20:5). He has chosen a people for Himself. Our faith cannot be in Him and in anyone or anything else at the same time. He expects a wholehearted obedience.

So-called 'inter-faith' services are another deception. It is claimed that this is a 'loving' thing to do and shows that as Christians we accept other people, quite apart from what they believe. But those of other religions are praying to what is false, and therefore demonically inspired. The truth and the false cannot be put together in that way.

The only way to love those who are deceived is to seek ways to share with them the Truth of Jesus Christ, not give them the impression that we respect their false gods and will join them when they pray to them.

Such attitudes are often called intolerant. It is right to be intolerant of what is false and deceptive. If we truly love people we want to see them delivered from their deception so that they embrace the truth. **It is better to be charged with intolerance than to be disobedient to the Lord.** To stand against deception is the way to love those who are deceived!

For some it is costly to renounce their former religion. It can lead to being isolated from families and even their nation; and perhaps losing their jobs as well. But to those who find life in Jesus Christ, the changes in their lives are so significant that the advantages far outweigh the cost, no matter how great.

There can be no compromising of the Truth, for whatever reason, in a Christian's life. Just as the Truth sets him free, so compromising that Truth will put him into bondage for this weakens his faith in Jesus.

PRAYER AND FAITH DECLARATION

Renounce areas of self-deception, asking the Holy Spirit to reveal things to which you have been blind. Encourage others to do likewise. When praying with them it is important that they renounce these things themselves rather than leave you to do this for them. When leading them in prayer, be sure that they vocalise their repentance, not as a form of words, but from the heart.

After teaching the Truth, I will lead in a time of silent prayer so that those present can speak from their own hearts to God. Then I will ask them to repeat a statement of faith after me, phrase by phrase. I will give an outline of these prayers in the following chapters. These should not be used as a set form or formula; I include them to show the kind of ground that is covered. Each situation is unique and you need to follow the leading of the Holy Spirit on each occasion.

In the name of Jesus and by the power of His blood, I renounce all self-deception. I ask the Holy Spirit to convict me of sin that I may not be blind to things in my life that oppose the Truth.

I choose to humble myself before God that I will not have exalted ideas about myself. I submit my mind to be instructed by the Spirit of Truth. With my mouth I intend to speak the Truth, not negatively about myself or others. I intend to live the Word of God, not only hear it.

Heavenly Father, I ask for the help of your Holy Spirit to enable me to walk in the Truth, not in self-deception.

I believe Satan no longer has any foothold in my life and cannot accuse me for my past failures. I am free, for Jesus has set me free!

In the name of Jesus and by the power of His blood I renounce every way in which I have allowed the enemy to deceive me.

I stand against any false ideas of God, the Lord Jesus Christ or the Holy Spirit.

I stand against any way in which I have been influenced by false prophecy, or by allowing others to speak untrue or deceptive words into my life.

I stand against the influence of all false teaching I have received. I forgive those who have taught me things opposed to the Truth; I pray for them, that their eyes and hearts may be opened to the Truth.

I choose to submit myself afresh to the Truth of God's Word, to be led and guided by the Spirit of Truth.

In the name of Jesus I take authority over every lying or deceiving spirit that has sought to have any influence on my life. I tell all such spirits that they have no hold whatsoever over me, or what I believe or think. I am free because Jesus Christ has set me free. To Him belongs all the glory.

In the name of Jesus and by the power of His blood, I renounce every counterfeit activity of the enemy; all influence there has been in my life through involvement with the occult, with false religions or cults. I renounce (Freemasonry, yoga or whatever may be appropriate) and I praise God that I am now free from the influence of all these activities. I renounce all superstition.

Heavenly Father, I thank you that your Holy Spirit of Truth will keep me walking in the Truth of your Word and I yield myself afresh to you; thanking you for your love and grace in bringing me out of darkness into your glorious light.

20 Dealing with Rebellion and Pride

Rebellion is deliberate – and often persistent – disobedience to the Word of the Lord and always leads to spiritual bondage.

Only genuine repentance will end the rebellion. But times of rebellion give the enemy advantages he is swift to accept.

> For rebellion is like the sin of divination, and arrogance like the evil of idolatry (1 Sam. 15:23).

No born-again Christian would willingly involve himself in witchcraft; such a thought would be unthinkable. And yet rebellion is regarded as being just as serious by the Lord.

Neither would most Christians evaluate stubborn independence as idolatry. You even hear some say, 'I value my independence'!

Satan, as Lucifer, rebelled when in heaven. He deceived Eve and then Adam rebelled, and the whole of mankind was infected with his sin. For acting independently of God's Word, both were thrown out of the garden.

Both rebellion and independence play straight into the enemy's hands. It is for these Satan was thrown out of heaven, and Adam and Eve from the garden.

Because of His mercy the Lord does not throw us out of His

Kingdom when we sin deliberately against Him. However sin yields ground to Satan, and that ground has to be retaken.

In some ways the Christian life is like climbing a mountain with the Lord. Each step takes us nearer the summit. Rebellion and independence cause us to slip down the mountain; and we continue to slip until we repent and rebellion ceases. We then start to climb again but have to retake the ground that has been lost. Although God forgives our sins, this does not mean that we are immediately restored to the same place we enjoyed before the rebellion.

The Lord certainly wants us back, and even higher up the mountain. Once again we have to devote ourselves to prayer and the Word of God and walk in obedience to regain the ground lost.

It is dangerous to look back when you are climbing; you need to be watchful as to where to place your next step. It is wonderful that God 'keeps us from falling' and will present us blameless before the throne of grace. However, Christians always regret the time wasted and the ground lost when they have departed from God's best purposes by choosing some independent way of their own.

Rebellion is not always obvious to those guilty of it. Some feel justified in having independent attitudes, and strongly self-willed people are usually reluctant to describe their attitudes as rebellious.

Stubborn refusal to accept what God says and act upon His Word is nothing less than rebellion, no matter what reasons or excuses are used by the guilty one to excuse his behaviour.

God places us under human authorities, and it is clear that He expects us to respect His authority as expressed through these human agencies. Any human expression of authority is bound to be imperfect at the very best! It is hardly surprising that so many find it more difficult to submit to others than they do directly to the Lord.

God does not call us to be one-man churches! He makes believers members of His body and teaches them to submit to one another as well as to the Head, Christ. Such submission involves a recognition of our interdependence, that we belong one to another.

LEADERS

However, although He expects submission to the human leadership in the Church, this does not give that leadership license to 'lord it over' people 'like the Gentiles' (Matt. 20:25). Yet there are frequent abuses of this leadership, both within denominational structures and in some new churches.

Biblical leadership is by example. A true spiritual leader is submitted to the leadership of the Holy Spirit in his own life (soul submitted to Spirit) so that he can lead others – not dominate them. His commission from God is to make responsible disciples, those who willingly submit themselves to the Lord, not servile people who do not think for themselves and who are prevented from making the important decisions which are an essential part of their personal response to the Lord.

This means that every Christian should place himself under true spiritual authority; not man-made authoritarianism which is the fleshly substitute for the real thing. Under proper teaching and leadership the individual believer's ministry will develop and prosper.

The believer is also to submit to the civil government, parents, husbands, employers, as well as to church leaders. This is not the place to go into a lengthy discussion on each of these areas of submission. **Any true submission comes from a right heart attitude towards others; while rebellion and independence indicate a wrong, self-centred attitude.**

We are urged to pray for those who lead us:

Remember your leaders, who spoke the word of God to you. Consider the outcome of their way of life and imitate their faith. Jesus Christ is the same yesterday and today and for ever (Heb. 13:7–8).

It is interesting to see that the statement about Jesus always being the same is made immediately after being urged to pray for our spiritual leaders. Notice what is said about these leaders:

1 **They speak the Word of God.** They lead and guide people in the way of truth.
2 **Their lives are an obvious demonstration of that truth.**
3 **You see at work in them a faith that is to be imitated.** They are fine examples of faith.
4 **They radiate faith in the Jesus who is the same today as yesterday!** You see something of the real Jesus in them, in the things they say and do, and in the fruit of their ministries.

Follow those who preach and live the truth and beware of the warning: 'Do not be carried away by all kinds of strange teachings' (Heb. 13:9).

It is not rebellion to leave a church where you are being neither led nor fed; it is common sense. In fact it could be construed as rebellion against God's Word to stay there, for you cannot grow spiritually unless you are being fed on a diet of truth; and you are not being properly led unless those in charge are going where the Holy Spirit is directing! God calls you to be fruitful, for in this He will be glorified. He will not be glorified by your remaining loyal to tradition but unfruitful at the same time.

True submission is not servility. Humility is not being humiliated.

PRIDE

Behind both rebellion and independence lies pride. Paul tells us to put *no* confidence in the flesh (Phil. 3:3). And Jesus says:

Apart from me you can do nothing (John 15:5).

Both James and Peter quote Proverbs 3:34:

> God opposes the proud but gives grace to the humble (Jas. 4:6; 1 Pet. 5:5).

We have seen the need throughout this book to keep the soul submitted to the Spirit; otherwise it will rise up in self-right-eousness. This may be expressed in pride, selfishness or unbelief – or a combination of all three because clearly they work together against the best interests of the disciple.

'Humble yourselves before the Lord,' says James (4:10). It is necessary to keep the self-life humbled before God. Every believer has to do this for himself; no one else can do it for him. Only through Jesus is it possible to have a personal relationship with God. Yet this inevitably produces respon-sibilities for the disciple. It is for him to walk with the Lord. And if he allows pride to assert itself, he will find himself in opposition to God, not walking with Him!

If God opposes the proud, then pride obviously gives the devil opportunity. He can work with readiness on the one who centres on self, instead of denying self.

Peter echoes James in his letter:

> Humble yourselves, therefore, under God's mighty hand, that he may lift you up in due time. Cast all your anxiety on him because he cares for you (1 Pet. 5:6–7).

To hold on to anxiety is to say that you intend to bear the burden and work things out for yourself when, in reality, Jesus took your burdens on Himself and His desire is for you to live by faith in Him. It is a form of pride to depend on self instead of God!

Peter continues by warning his readers: 'Be self-controlled and alert' (v.8). That self-life must be kept under control because the devil is prowling around waiting to take advan-tage; and we must be alert to his intentions.

Pride goes before destruction, a haughty spirit before a fall (Prov. 16:18).

We are told to 'give no opportunity to the devil' (1 Tim. 5:14). Pride does precisely that and makes the person vulnerable to his attacks. You cannot walk on the highway of holiness in pride!

This pride takes one of two forms. **There is the aggressive, self-assertive haughtiness where one person wants to exalt himself above others.** This is readily recognised as pride and is resented by others.

However, **there is a negative introverted pride that is usually not recognised for what it is, but is equally destructive to the Christian's well-being and also has a negative effect on those around him.** This is the kind of self-assertiveness that says: 'I am no good. I am a failure. I am not sure that anyone really loves me, or accepts me. I don't expect too much of God. I want to take a back seat. I don't want to push myself forward.'

And yet that is the very thing such people are doing; they are pushing their self-life forward. And a very negative self-life at that! Their words convey what goes on in their hearts. 'I' and 'me' pepper the statements they make. Their protestations about their humility leave you unconvinced.

As we have already seen, such attitudes are negative unbelief and show an absence of real faith in what Jesus has accomplished for them. **Their attitude is as full of pride and self-centredness as the one who is self-assertive.** Behind both aspects of pride there is the obvious fact that 'self' is still to the fore and very much in control. It is simply that the two kinds of people have a different kind of self-life, both equally destructive to their well-being.

True brokenness is needed in both cases, a dying to self in order that they may be brought to faith and liberty in God's Word.

While the assertive personality elicits no sympathy from others, the danger is that the negative ones trade on it! This

only adds to their problems because it confirms them in their self-centredness.

In either case the enemy has ground on which to stand and someone through whom he can readily work. Through the self-assertive one he will walk all over other people, crushing and bruising them. Through the introverted one, he spreads self-centred, negative unbelief to anyone who will listen.

The answer in either case is obvious: repentance and a true faith in the finished work of Jesus Christ. The question is how to bring them to that point. **You cannot make another person repent, neither can you work humility in his heart. This has to be the work of the Holy Spirit.** You can only seek to be His instrument in bringing that word which will be as the hammer that breaks the rock of their hard hearts, or the double-edged sword that cuts to the division of soul and spirit, that 'judges the thoughts and attitudes of the heart'.

The introverted one has a heart that is hardened against the Truth, as does the extrovert one! **Both prefer 'self' to the truth.** And both need that word from God that will penetrate their shells of self-protectiveness.

What is most serious is that there is a clash of wills between God and the individual. In both cases, **they do not want to let go of self.** They may hate themselves for what they are, and yet still cling to self. They fear losing their identity, and so cannot find their true identity in Christ.

Before either has the breakthrough needed, there will have to be a renunciation of self, a releasing of themselves to God. They will need to learn what it truly means to live for others and not themselves. Even their service of others has centred around self, wanting to prove their abilities on the one hand, or desiring recognition and praise to build up self-esteem on the other.

Either can be manipulative and so seek to exercise control over others. This is an opening for a real work of the enemy, as **a spirit of control is one of the most subtle and invidious of his activities among Christians.**

The proud extroverts exercise control by lording it over others; they use people for their own personal ends and to further their own ministries. They often treat people with disdain, are highly critical and take no notice of the scriptural instruction to count others better than yourself (Phil. 2:3). Such an idea seems to them ridiculous as they are so much wiser (in their own eyes), more capable, and everything would be done more quickly and with better results if only others listened to them and did as they were told!

It is the strong streak of independence, often coupled with considerable natural abilities, that makes it difficult for such people to be willing to deny self, to be broken before the Lord and therefore before others. Once this process has taken place, however, they can be mighty in God's purposes.

Saul of Tarsus was full of self-righteous zeal, convinced that he was serving God by persecuting the Church. No doubt he had listened to many testimonies from believers he had arrested, proclaiming Jesus to be the Christ; but he vigorously held on to his own religious views.

Yet once broken before the Lord he became Paul, the mighty apostle. Three days of blindness to show him how blind he had been, and several years in obscurity to prepare him for the ministry God had purposed for him! He could not have become the man of God he became without this breaking process, learning what it meant to lose self, rather than serve God with the mistaken zeal and self-righteous pride of the self or soul life.

It is equally difficult and costly, but in a different way, for those with a low self-image to lose self. **A spirit of control works through them, because the enemy can so easily control them. They are manipulative because they are readily manipulated by him.**

They are eager to get their own way, and will go to great lengths to obtain what they want. They manipulate others by using their time to talk endlessly about themselves and their problems. They accuse others of lacking love for them if they do not give them what they want. They often seem so considerate and loving, yet always seem to end up getting what they want – their own way! They can be very pleasant but you find yourself manipulated into doing what they want.

Such people are often very capable, but feel the need to have their abilities recognised by others. They appear easily hurt when they do not receive the thanks and acclaim they desire.

They are certainly self-deceived for they do not recognise their pride. They think of themselves as quite the opposite. Some of them see themselves as humble, others hate themselves for being so introverted and giving in to so many fears. They manipulate because they are convinced that others would not notice them or love them unless they manipulated their love. This is the pattern of life and relationships they have experienced over a lifetime; so the pattern is not always easy to break.

Once again, such believers need to encounter the truth, rather than simply have an experience of God's power. For it is only the revelation of the truth that will make them aware of their need; only the Holy Spirit can bring them the necessary conviction! **They need to see how they have allowed the enemy to manipulate and control them, and then stand against him.** You can pray and agree with them once they are prepared to acknowledge their need and renounce the way they have been manipulated and have sought to control others.

In humbling himself before God, the proud extrovert has to come to a heart knowledge that his flesh counts for nothing, that all he does apart from Jesus, that is not initiated and empowered by the Holy Spirit, is worth nothing. As he has spent a lifetime exalting his self-life he is going to experience much refining as he discovers what it means to 'deny himself, take up his cross and follow' Jesus. Only then can he understand his true position in Christ.

Often, while the process takes place, it seems to him that everything is falling apart. Whatever he puts his hand to goes wrong; in the past he was so capable while things were in his hands! But he will only discover the real power of the Holy Spirit in his life as he learns to depend on the Lord.

To tell the proud introvert that he needs to repent might meet with a response of astonishment, for he has such a low opinion of self he could not see what else there is to repent about. To him it seems he is always repenting.

Because of their insecurities the introverts feel they have to do everything possible to keep hold of what little self-respect they have, instead of letting go and discovering their true identity in Christ. They are afraid of a total loss of identity.

Many people go through a period when they appear to fluctuate between living in revelation of the new, and sinking back into the old ways of thinking and behaving. They want to believe the truth, but feel weighed down and pulled back by the old.

We need to stand in faith with them, standing firm against the devices of the enemy who wants them to stay bound by their old ways of thinking so that they cannot enjoy their inheritance in Christ or be fruitful for God. He would prefer them to stay bound, not to be released into freedom, and to continue to spread negativity and unbelief all around them. He must not be allowed to have his way.

CONFRONTATION

To help either the proud extrovert or the proud introvert, confrontation will be necessary. And these are not easy people to confront, which is why they have persisted in their manipulative behaviour for so long.

The one seeking to help either will need to be bold but in differing ways, for the extrovert and introvert cannot be treated in the same way because their personalities are so different. However, without strong confrontation they are unlikely to face their need.

Jesus was very confrontational in His style of ministry and we can learn much from Him in this. The reason for this is simple: **the Truth is confrontational by its very nature.** Light and darkness are utterly opposed to one another, as is the flesh to the Spirit. They are completely at odds. So if people are living in the flesh (and often imagining they are being spiritual) their deception has to be exposed. You are unlikely to receive many thanks for doing this. Such people will only be thankful when they come to a revelation of the truth that sets them free from the control that has operated through them.

The proud extrovert is likely to dismiss what you say; the introvert will suggest you cannot understand him!

It is important not to be deflected from your purpose, no matter what reaction you receive. You want to see these people set free, not persist in their bondage. And you must be prepared to love them, no matter what the cost to yourself. The extrovert will try to crush you and make you feel stupid; the introvert will accuse and try to make you feel insensitive and unloving. Remember both groups have had plenty of practice!

However the Truth is able to set anyone free. The cross is the power of God's salvation or healing to anyone who believes!

It is difficult to persist when those you try to help do everything possible to make you think you are wrong in your estimate of the situation and your approach to it. In love, persist and show them that you will not be shaken by their tactics. If they threaten not to have any more to do with you, do not pander to them. That is precisely what they want. They may threaten not to have any more to do with you, but if you have spoken a word of truth to them pray that the Holy Spirit will 'water' the seed you have sown. In nearly every case they will return and with a different attitude, more open to the Truth and therefore to the help you can give them.

And don't be too discouraged when people seem to be making good progress and then regress, at least temporarily. This is common. You are responsible for speaking the truth in love, but you cannot hold yourself responsible for the way in which others respond to that truth.

PRAYER AND FAITH DECLARATION

In the name of Jesus and by the power of His blood I renounce all rebellion and pride, and every way in which I have allowed the enemy to influence my life through my rebellious and proud attitudes. I renounce all my independent and self-sufficient attitudes, every way in which I have opposed the teaching of God's Word and have failed to put my trust and confidence in Him.

I renounce the spirit of control, every way in which I have allowed my life to be controlled or manipulated by others. And I stand against any such spirit of control being able to operate through my life to influence others.

I forgive those leaders who have sought to control me, and I pray that they will become men of true spiritual authority.

I renounce my aggressive, self-assertive pride, all self-centredness, every way in which I have tried to elicit sympathy and pity from others. I renounce all self-centredness and rejoice that the old has gone and the new has come, that I have died and my life is now hidden with Christ in God.

Heavenly Father, I thank you that you have forgiven me for every way in which I have spoken negatively of myself, denying my inheritance in Christ. Again I submit myself to the Truth that I may live in freedom from self, and all the influence of the false accuser. I praise you that you always lead me in triumph in Christ. Hallelujah!

21   Unforgiveness

We have already seen how important it is to forgive those who
have caused past hurts, to be in a right attitude towards all
who have affected our lives negatively. However, we also have
need of ongoing forgiveness. Jesus said:

> For if you forgive men when they sin against you, your
> heavenly Father will also forgive you. But if you do not
> forgive men their sins, your Father will not forgive your sins
> (Matt. 6:14–15).

Refusal to forgive others puts you outside God's forgiveness,
and that is serious! To be in a state of unforgiveness before
God is to be in rebellion against Him, and this will inevitably
hinder the flow of His provision and power in the believer's
life. It is clear from the parable Jesus teaches that **the
unmerciful servant's refusal to forgive the debt of his fellow
servant resulted in his return to the bondage, out of which his
master had taken him:**

> Then the master called the servant in. 'You wicked servant',
> he said, 'I cancelled all that debt of yours because you
> begged me to. Shouldn't you have had mercy on your

fellow-servant just as I had on you?' In anger his master turned him over to the jailers . . . until he should pay back all he owed. 'This is how my heavenly Father will treat each of you unless you forgive your brother from your heart' (Matt. 18:32–5).

These are strong words and demonstrate how essential it is to be merciful. 'Blessed are the merciful, for they will be shown mercy' (Matt. 5:7).

God wants us to be merciful so that our immediate response when others fail, hurt or offend us is to forgive them. Satan of course will do anything possible to stir up feelings of bitterness, anger and resentment. He knows God's Word. He knows that failure to forgive will make you vulnerable to his devices; so it is understandable that he will use every argument he can to persuade you not to forgive:

'Why should you forgive? The other was in the wrong.'
'You cannot forgive until he comes and asks for forgiveness.'
'It is for him to come to you to be reconciled; it is not for you to go to him.'
'It is too easy to forgive such a great hurt. He should be made to suffer first.'
'He deserves to be punished for what he did to you.'

Such are the statements of the father of lies! They appeal to the flesh, but utterly oppose the truth Jesus teaches us. No ground should be yielded to the enemy here.

Bitterness and resentment give him a foothold in a person's thinking and enable him to encourage feelings of self-righteousness, condemnation and self-pity (which is like a spiritual cancer that eats away within a person's soul).

Many who know there is no condemnation for them because they are in Christ Jesus, frequently have to fight feelings of condemnation. One of the chief reasons for this is that they condemn others, and so reap what they sow.

Do not judge, or you too will be judged. For in the same way as you judge others, you will be judged, and with the measure you use, it will be measured to you (Matt. 7:1–2).

Jesus then teaches the parable about looking at the speck of sawdust in your brother's eye, while you have a plank in your own! Your problem is greater because you have a wrong heart attitude towards the one who has offended you. If it seems right to point out the sin to your brother (Matt. 18:15), this needs to be done in love, not judgment. The aim is to be reconciled with him, not to judge or condemn him.

If his sin is deliberate because he has a wrong heart attitude then God alone can deal with him. This is no reason to condone a wrong heart attitude on your own part! Two wrongs don't make a right!

Forgiveness is a decision, not a feeling.

We live in a world where most live for themselves and Jesus warned that in it we would experience tribulation. There will be those who think nothing of defrauding and cheating you, lying, deceiving, falsely accusing, ridiculing you for your faith, taking advantage of you, and so on. The enemy working through human agents!

It is more hurtful when other Christians treat you like this; you would not expect them to be used by the enemy in such ways. Sometimes you are left wondering who you can trust!

Your own sinful attitudes or lack of wisdom may be a significant part of the total picture. So it is necessary to acknowledge before God the ways in which, even inadvertently, you have contributed to the problem. And then **you have to forgive, no matter how deep the hurts or how prolonged and persistent the sin against you.**

Then Peter came to Jesus and asked, 'Lord, how many times shall I forgive my brother when he sins against me? Up to seven times?' Jesus answered, 'I tell you, not seven times, but seventy-seven times' (Matt. 18:21–2).

This is the Gospel! **It is good news to know that the Lord has completely forgiven you! It is equally good news to know that you are to forgive!** Failure to do so will result in further pain for you and disruption of your peace, which will affect your walk with God; and He wants to spare you that!

> If your brother sins, rebuke him, and if he repents, forgive him. If he sins against you seven times in a day, and seven times comes back to you and says, 'I repent,' forgive him (Luke 17:3–4).

It would seem that someone such as this is lacking in genuine repentance if he keeps returning to the same sin; and yet Jesus says you are to forgive him. There is no alternative. After all this is how we often treat the Lord. We say we are sorry and ask Him to forgive a particular sin. We are determined not to repeat the sin, and yet find that it is not long before we are back before Him confessing the same thing again.

Was the confession of sin sincere in the first place? Oh yes. **But the sin persisted because the heart had not experienced change. The Lord will give you the change of heart once that is what you genuinely want.**

As we have seen, there is nothing you can do effectively to change another person's heart. You can ensure that your heart is right, full of mercy, love and grace.

Jesus teaches us the 'golden rule': 'Do to others what you would have them do to you' (Matt. 7:12). It is fatal to retaliate when others wrong you:

> Do not repay anyone evil for evil. Be careful to do what is right in the eyes of everybody. If it is possible, as far as it depends on you, live at peace with everyone. Do not take revenge, my friends, but leave room for God's wrath, for it is written: 'It is mine to avenge; I will repay,' says the Lord. On the contrary: 'If your enemy is hungry, feed him; if he is thirsty, give him something to drink. In doing this, you will

heap burning coals on his head.' Do not be overcome by evil, but overcome evil with good (Rom. 12:17–21).

Judgment is the Lord's prerogative, not yours! The love Jesus expects among His disciples is expressed in forgiving so completely that you pray for your enemy, feed him, give him something to drink!

Stand against the enemy's attempts to dredge up hurts. Sometimes certain events set off a chain-reaction within you, and old feelings of bitterness begin to rise up within you. In such circumstances it is good to say (aloud if you are in a suitable place) that all that pertains to those events is completely forgiven and is 'under the blood' of Jesus. He does not dredge up your sins, so don't allow the enemy to do so.

It is important to claim back from the enemy any ground that has been lost through unforgiveness. **When you forgive immediately, you have not lost any ground; in fact you have gained it.** Your immediate soul-reaction may be one of dismay to the events that have taken place; if you are living submitted to the Spirit, He will give you the grace to forgive immediately. Your faith has proved genuine in the crisis, and you have gained ground. We have already seen that we only have to retake ground we lose to the enemy. So it is best not to lose it!

The flesh does not like to forgive and will try to justify your reaction of outrage at the offence against you. If this fleshly reaction is not checked immediately it will gain a tighter grasp on you. You will get to the point where you know it is wrong, but feel powerless to react in any other way.

A jealous person does not want to be jealous, feels resentful towards the one causing the jealousy (as he sees the situation), but feels unable to rid himself of the jealousy. This is an emotional bondage which may involve needing to forgive others; but the jealous person has to acknowledge that the real problem is within himself. **'Nothing outside a man can defile a man', says Jesus. He is defiled by what is in his own heart.** So it would be wrong for him to accuse others for being the cause of his jealousy, even if someone has done something to trigger off this reaction within him.

When falsely accused, be like Jesus at His trial; say nothing! Do not seek to justify yourself before God or man. Forgive and be thankful that God is so merciful to you! Seek 'to live at peace with everyone'. Live a life of forgiveness.

Sometimes a person seeking counsel will claim: 'I can't forgive.' This is not true. What the person really means is, 'I don't feel it is right to forgive, and therefore I won't.'

The person will remain in bondage to the offender until he does forgive. He also places himself in bondage to the enemy. Encourage him to face his need to forgive, and to tell the Lord that he specifically forgives X for doing 'such and such' to him. He needs to be specific, to vocalise who he is forgiving and for what. Just as he is thankful that his own sins are under the blood, never to be held against him, so he is to regard the offences he forgives in a similar light.

The test of forgiveness is to be able to treat the offender with love, as if the offence had never taken place. This is the outworking of God's grace. He has given us:

> the ministry of reconciliation: that God was reconciling the world to himself in Christ, not counting men's sins against them (2 Cor. 5:18–19).

It is a vital part of reconciliation that you do not count others' sins against them, no matter how difficult that might seem at first!

PRAYER AND FAITH DECLARATION

Heavenly Father I thank you for your mercy and grace, that you have forgiven all my sins and cleansed me from all unrighteousness. I praise you for the victory of the blood and cross of Jesus, and that I can now live the new life in the power of your Spirit.

In the name of Jesus and by the power of His blood I choose to forgive all who have ever sinned against me, those who have rejected me or hurt me in any way, those who have opposed me or spoken ill of me. And I pray that every one of them will know the forgiveness of Jesus Christ and His acceptance.

In particular I choose to forgive N . . . for . . . I thank you, Heavenly Father, that you have forgiven me for all the negative attitudes I have had towards these events and those who caused them. I thank you that I am now set free from all harmful and negative influences these events have had on my life. And I thank you, Father, that the enemy cannot have any advantage over me now because of these things. I am free from all the hurt and from the influence of those who have caused it. My past is behind me. Now I can walk into the future with confidence, with a believing, forgiving heart, rejoicing in your love and mercy.

22　Strongholds and Curses

The enemy's purpose is to try to place Christians in bondage. He has no right to do this, and cannot succeed without the believer's co-operation, however inadvertently that is given.

The enemy is the tempter. You can only be tempted in an area where your flesh enjoys the enticements offered you. So what might tempt one Christian will not necessarily tempt another.

Bondage occurs when a believer yields persistently to a particular temptation so that a pattern of sin is established in his life. It is easy to recognise these bondages in others; so we need to avoid judging them and seek to restore those who fall into serious sin (Gal. 6:1). You can be thankful that by God's grace you have not fallen into that sin; but at the same time be sure that the enemy is not being allowed to have victory in your life in some other way!

Most Christians have to face the problem of habitual sin at some time. They will try to keep these sins secret. Yet their very presence leads to internal conflict which will seriously hinder the person's witness. This is often the problem in Christians who show great potential and yet never seem to realise that potential. Others cannot see what God sees. He knows what hinders the fulfilment of His purpose.

Struggling with an area of persistent sin causes many a believer to think of himself as a failure. He sees himself as weak, and feels a hypocrite for appearing to be different externally from what he knows himself to be internally.

There can be two main causes for habitual sin. **The believer continues to be tempted in a particular way because he does not truly want to be set free in that area.** He enjoys that particular sin; it appeals to his flesh and satisfies his soul in the wrong way.

His enjoyment of the sin produces further conflict. He may try to justify the sin as part of God's will for him. The heart can be very deceptive!

Alternatively, he knows clearly that the sin he enjoys is sin, and he hates himself for liking it. This produces further conflict within him. Part of him wants to be set free from this; another part doesn't. If only he didn't enjoy this sin it would be so much easier!

He confesses the sin to God, yet knows in his heart of hearts that he will commit the same offence again and will need to come back to the Lord for further forgiveness. While this process is going on it seems he is treading water spiritually. He can put much effort into his activities without making any noticeable progress. It seems there is little anointing or fruit in his Christian life.

All this serves the enemy's purposes, for he does not want the believer to make progress!

The other cause for this persistent sin is that for some reason the enemy may have had the opportunity to place this believer in bondage. It could be that this sin has become such a habit, the Christian feels powerless to oppose it.

Sin invites demonic attack. Take obvious examples such as lust or greed. The believer knows his lust is wrong but enjoys his lustful fantasies, reads the wrong magazines and watches the wrong videos or movies. He wants to walk with the Lord, but this is his area of weakness. Self-effort has proved futile; he keeps returning to the very things that feed the lust.

The enemy is good at putting the wrong materials before

him. He feeds lustful thoughts which affect the way he views the opposite sex (or the same sex in the case of those in homosexual bondage). He feels overcome. He asks for ministry, believing that he needs to be delivered from a demon of lust that has him in its grip.

This may well be the case, but it is a problem of his own making. It is possible for you to rebuke the demon and he will have to retreat, which will give the believer temporary relief; but unless the heart of the matter is dealt with, the problem or bondage will inevitably return.

A CHANGE OF HEART

There has to be a change of heart. For that to take place, the Christian must want the change of heart that only God can give him. He will need to desire genuinely the purity of heart and mind God wants him to have.

Without such a change of heart, the desire for the sin will remain; and he will struggle constantly, fearing further failure. With a change of heart the problem disappears. However, knowing his former weakness, he will be wise not to place himself in a position of temptation again. He is like a former alcoholic who learns to refuse alcoholic beverage. One drink could begin a slippery slide downwards again.

The example given of lust is true of any sin: greed, criticism, judgment, jealousy, etc.

The one who is persistently critical feels justified in his critical attitudes towards others and often does not recognise his sin. His persistent sin places him in bondage to critical spirits who are able to work through him to hinder and destroy others. Such a believer may be oblivious to the way the enemy is manipulating and using him.

When people cannot break free from such bondage, they often need to confess their sin to another and have someone stand with them against the enemy. It is not easy to stand alone against the very spirits you have attracted by your behaviour! However, a change of heart alters the ground on which they stand and their ability to withstand the enemy's devices.

Overcoming the enemy is a question of authority. A Christian will only be able to speak with authority to unclean spirits, of whatever kind, if he does not want the sin with which they try to entice him. Peter urges us to 'abstain from sinful desires, which war against your soul' (1 Pet. 2:11). The nature of the flesh never changes. Your flesh will always be enticed by sin, which is why it is so important to walk in the Spirit.

While the soul is submitted to the Spirit, the good things of the Holy Spirit flood through the soul. When filled with love for Jesus, there is little room for love of self; when the Spirit is flowing freely in your life, it is much easier to walk in the Spirit, and so give no room for the flesh:

> I say then: Walk in the Spirit, and you shall not fulfil the lust of the flesh. For the flesh lusts against the Spirit, and the Spirit against the flesh; and these are contrary to one another, so that you do not do the things that you wish (Gal. 5:16–17 NKJ).

> But put on the Lord Jesus Christ, and make no provision for the flesh, to fulfil its lusts (Rom. 13:14 NKJ).

Prevention is better than cure! Jesus Christ has set us free. So Paul advises:

> Stand firm, then, and do not let yourselves be burdened again by a yoke of slavery (Gal. 5:1).

You are yoked to Jesus and are no longer a slave to sin. It is never true for a Christian to say: 'I couldn't help it', when referring to his failure to resist temptation. **God will not allow us to be tempted beyond our ability to endure and always provides the escape route!** (1 Cor. 10:13).

Jesus has set you free to enable you to serve others in love and thus express your love for Him, not indulge the flesh (Gal. 5:13). Sin is by nature deceptive. It is the devil's lie that it will bring happiness and fulfilment. He suggests that to yield the heart to God so that the root of sin is dealt with would lead only to a sense of loss.

The opposite is the truth; for it is only submission to the Lord that will bring the release and freedom the believer wants. **A change of heart brings a change of desire.** You do not miss what you do not want! The mind set on what the Spirit desires is life and peace.

PERSONAL REVIVAL

Many Christians subject themselves to unnecessary torture and defeat over long periods of time through their failure to face the real issues, come before God and begin crying out to Him for the change of heart needed.

You can help by standing with a believer against his bondages, but remember this will be futile without his co-operation. It is for him to seek the change of heart he needs.

It is very helpful to be part of a body of believers who have the same aim; they want to live in personal revival, to glorify Jesus, to walk in the Spirit in ways that please the Lord. For by seeking God together many of these heart issues are addressed, because of the depth of the repentance taking place corporately.

In times of revival God challenges His children to face the need of practical holiness in their lives. They have to face honestly those areas of their lives which are a denial of being Christlike. As God works this sanctity in them, the holiness of God's people challenges the unholiness that exists in churches and in the world around. The holy people of God become leaven in the lump, light for the world and salt for the earth.

Then the nations will know that I am the Lord, declares the Sovereign Lord, **when I show myself holy through you before their eyes** (Ezek. 36:23).

Revival is the fruit that results from the way God dealt personally with the hearts of His children.

STRONGHOLDS

God has given believers every spiritual weapon they need to overcome the enemy.

> The weapons we fight with are not the weapons of the world. On the contrary, **they have divine power to demolish strongholds.** We demolish arguments and every pretension that sets itself up against the knowledge of God, and we take captive every thought to make it obedient to Christ (2 Cor. 10:4–5).

God transforms us into His likeness by the renewing of our minds. It is important that the enemy is not allowed to retain a 'stronghold' in a believer's thought life, an area of thinking inconsistent with the Truth of His Word. You could describe a stronghold as a wrong pattern of thought that has a considerable influence on the person, perhaps of criticism, anger, jealousy or lust.

Such 'strongholds' are often the aftermath of years of wrong thinking before being converted to Christ. At new birth the Christian's attitudes towards several areas of his life would have changed immediately; but he did not become instantaneously perfect! God's refining purposes continue within him. And part of that purpose is to rid his mind of any enemy strongholds.

Sometimes these are of a religious nature. Holding on to traditions, religious prejudice or denominational thinking is evidence of enemy strongholds. These result in resistance to change and unbelief. People will prefer their own thoughts to the Truth!

If the heart is full of truth, the person's thinking will be right. A stronghold in the mind resists the Truth, so must be pulled down, using the spiritual weapons God has provided.

Again the believer has to stand against these strongholds himself after facing the fact that they are present and are wrong. Unless his thinking is right, neither his speech nor actions will be as God intends. We have the authority 'to demolish arguments and every pretension that sets itself up against the knowledge of God'.

We have seen how important it is that the believer's heart is right with God, that he feeds on the Truth, 'eating' the Bread of Life, the Living Word that comes down from heaven. This will correct any of his wrong ideas or opinions.

And he will need to learn to reject immediately any thought that is a contradiction to God's Word. If he receives one negative, the enemy will follow that with another, and then another. Before long he will have been allowed to establish another stronghold of negative thinking which will have to be dealt with.

CURSES

It is, however, possible for Christians to experience an oppressive heaviness for which they can find no rational account. Things can go wrong, and apparently for no reason. They may realise that this is enemy opposition but do not know how to deal with it.

The Lord has put before us the way of blessing or the way of curse:

> This day I call heaven and earth as witnesses against you that I have set before you life and death, blessings and curses. Now choose life, so that you and your children may live and that you may love the Lord your God, listen to his voice, and hold fast to him. For the Lord is your life, and he will give you many years in the land he swore to give to your fathers, Abraham, Isaac and Jacob (Deut. 30:19–20).

Again the Lord emphasises how important it is to walk in the Truth, to obey His Word and so inherit the promises He gives us.

In reality many Christians curse themselves, obviously without intending to do so. **They do this by speaking of themselves in ways which deny what God says about them, when they choose to disobey, when they are guilty of unbelief instead of walking by faith.**

Some, however, have been converted from families that have been under curses for generations. This is no cause for fear. Curses are easy to break because of the victory Jesus has won on the cross. The Holy Spirit is more powerful than any other spirit, and Jesus has already disarmed the principalities and powers that are against us (Col. 2:15). We have the authority to break the power of any curse that stands against us.

When the believer breaks the power of a curse over his family, other members of the wider family are also set free, even if they are not themselves believers.

A believer is able to exercise faith to overcome hereditary disease. His inheritance now comes from above, not from former generations. It is not the Lord's purpose for him to live in fear of sickness, or in fear of communicating sickness to his children. With new life in Christ the curse can be cut off and cancelled.

The curse of the fallen nature is carried on from one generation to another. Christian parents can begin to pray for their children while still in the womb, and from birth they can enfold them in the love of Jesus and teach them the Truth. Their children can come to a saving knowledge of Jesus at an early age. The curse of Adam is then replaced by the blessing of Christ's living presence within!

Demonic strongholds have persisted in some families through the sin of former generations. For example, there may be a history of suicides in several past generations. The power of Jesus's blood is able to save the believer from such demonic activity. The believer can renounce the sin of their ancestors that caused the problem initially, and break the power of the curses that have resulted.

Other members of the family may 'pray' for them by invoking occult powers through involvement with spiritism, a cult or false religion. The believer need not fear; he has God's armour and protection.

However he would be wise to move on to the attack by binding the evil powers that are being invoked, and by praying for those family members involved. This is sometimes of great importance in a case of serious sickness. A spiritual battle can take place if the believer is calling on God, while others are calling demonic powers to influence the same situation.

Satan has no claim over one who has been purchased for God with the blood of Jesus. God's purpose for every believer is blessing not curse, that:

> From the fulness of his grace we have all received one blessing after another (John 1:16).

This is what God wants us *all* to receive so that we *all* overflow with blessing towards others.

Jesus bore even oppression for us so that we might be liberated from it. 'He was oppressed and afflicted' (Isa. 53:7). He became 'a curse' so that we might be delivered from the curse of legalistic religion, and be able to live in the power of His Spirit and the Truth of His Word – in freedom! (Gal. 3:13).

PRAYER AND FAITH DECLARATION

In the name of Jesus and through the victory of the cross I stand against any habitual sin in my life and the bondage that has resulted from this.

Heavenly Father, I repent of this sin (N . . .). I choose to turn away from it so that my life may no longer be under its

influence, and that I shall no longer grieve you in this way. Please forgive me for any way in which this sin has given the devil opportunity in my life, and for the ways in which my sins have influenced others negatively.

I choose to submit my heart afresh to you that you might work change in my life.

Thank you, Father, that I am yoked together with Jesus. I want to be more like Him. Change me into His likeness from one degree of glory to another.

In the name of Jesus and by the power of His blood I come against every enemy stronghold in my thinking. I have the mind of Christ, and choose to submit my thinking to the Truth of God's Word.

In particular I come against the stronghold of (Name them . . .). I now use the spiritual weapons that are mighty to the pulling down of strongholds and everything in my life which sets itself up against the knowledge of Christ. I believe those strongholds are now pulled down. I choose to submit my mind to the truth of God's Word. I will not allow any fresh strongholds of unbelief or negativity to be established in my thinking with your grace and help.

In the name of Jesus and by the power of His blood I now exercise the authority given me by Jesus Christ, and I break the power of any and every curse brought against me, or any member of the family to which I belong. The power of that curse is now broken, and I and the members of my family are delivered completely from any influence this has had on our lives.

I choose to bless all who have sought to curse me.

I praise you, Heavenly Father, that I do not need to live in any fear of the devil or future curse. You are my shield and I praise you for the victory you give me over every device of the evil one through Jesus.

PART 4

DIRECT COUNSELLING

23 Speaking into Others' Lives

Direct Counselling is just that. It is direct. It is concerned with the truth that sets people free, and aims at the heart of a person's problems.

Direct Counselling has to be centred on the revelation of God's Truth and can only be exercised in the power of the Holy Spirit, the Spirit of Truth.

THE FRUIT OF THE SPIRIT

You will need to experience the fruit of the Holy Spirit abundantly when you counsel. **These are the qualities of the Counsellor, and they need to be evident in anyone who counsels in the name of Jesus.**

Love is the first-fruit of the Holy Spirit. Without love for those you counsel your ministry to them will prove unfruitful. **Even if you speak the truth, others will find it difficult to receive what you say unless you speak the Truth in love.**

Joy You will need to maintain your joy throughout, no matter how despondent the one you are seeking to help. Even when you weep with those who weep you are drawing them to faith in God for their situation, to a place where they will **'rejoice in the Lord always'** and **'give thanks in all circumstances'**.

Peace   It is essential that you remain peaceful, no matter how agitated others become. This is a demonstration of faith in the face of difficulty. You will find no difficulty in doing this if you keep listening to the Spirit and remain in an attitude of forgiveness, no matter what you hear! **Discern, but don't judge!**

Patience   Often you will need an infinite supply of this fruit of the Spirit, especially when people are slow to respond to what God says to them. **Apart from faith in God's Word, being patient is the quality most necessary for counsellors.**

Kindness   **You will need to be a human agent of God's mercy again and again,** directing people to the truth that by His grace they are perfectly loved and made totally acceptable in His sight.

Goodness   You minister to people for their good. **So you are prepared to be confrontational if necessary,** even though you risk rejection as a result. And you want to be an example to others of the life of which you speak; that you are living in the good of what God has done for you in Christ.

Faithfulness   No matter who you are counselling, or what their problems, **you are to remain faithful to the Truth of God's Word.** It is faith in that Truth that will set them free; so you dare not depart from the Truth into reason, sentiment or emotion.

Gentleness   Even when you have to say strong things to people you will need to do so with a gentle spirit. **Jesus was very confrontational, but described Himself as 'gentle and humble in heart'.** So don't brow-beat people with the truth. Lead them into the realisation that all Jesus has done, He has done for them!

Self-control   Avoid showing facial response to what is said to you; **appear as impassive as possible.** Do not give away what you are thinking. The person may be looking to you for signs of approval, acceptance, judgment, even repulsion or rejection. **You are drawing him to Christ and His love and acceptance;** so you do not want him distracted by your reactions.

We have seen the need to depend on the spiritual gifts God has given us, especially the word of knowledge which enables us to understand the true nature of the problem, and the word of wisdom which enables us to speak the right word into the situation.

It is much better to trust the witness of the Holy Spirit who will never lie to you, than to the views of the person you are seeking to help.

In the case of a believer, the Holy Spirit within him will witness to the truth of what you say in the name of Jesus. He may smother the inner witness of the Spirit, preferring to believe his own reason or feelings. I have known it to take several months before some have been prepared to receive what God has said to them; wasted months because they were not prepared to face the Truth. But God will not change His Word for anyone. He waits patiently until he is prepared to receive and respond to His Word.

Often the perception God gives you of a person's problem is very different from the believer's own perception of his need. He will need a change of attitude before he is prepared to receive the Lord's Word into his life.

It is better to trust the way you believe the Spirit is leading you to pray and risk being wrong, than to ignore the prompting of the Spirit. If you have submitted yourself to be led by the Spirit you will seldom be mistaken, even though sometimes you will not understand why you feel moved to pray in a particular way!

On one occasion I felt moved to pray for a man to be healed of a kidney disease. He was asking for prayer for something totally different! Some time later I met him again. He told me that at the time he thought I was mistaken in the way I prayed for him, although he said nothing out of politeness. About two years later he had to have a hospital check-up for something entirely unrelated. During the course of the extensive examination he received, it was discovered that he had been living a normal life on less than half a kidney. 'You should be dead', the doctor told him, 'not walking around like this!'

You will certainly need to use the gift of faith, often in relation to the gifts of healings. It is worth noting that both words are in the plural. Gifts of healings are given to the Church. I would never allow anyone who claimed to have a gift of healing to pray for me. Those who minister in the occult make such claims. Those who minister in the Spirit recognise that they have the authority to heal, and God gives them the anointing to administer His healing grace to others, that they may receive gifts of healings. If the minister possessed these gifts himself he could clear the local hospital!

Not even Jesus made such a claim. He made it clear He could do nothing of Himself, but only what He saw His Father doing. He would never act independently of His Father. On occasions the power of God was present to heal the sick; so presumably even in His ministry there were occasions when the Spirit moved powerfully in this particular way.

There is little point in praying with people, laying hands on them or anointing them unless we and they expect things to happen. God will work miracles through anyone who believes (John 14:12), but the anointing of the Holy Spirit is essential. It is that anointing that makes us fruitful and successful in ministry. Those ministering submit themselves to the Spirit, then God's power can flow through their soul life and out of their bodies as rivers of living water.

We can go through the motions of ministry without anointing and not much will happen as a result. **We need anointing to speak the Truth so that people will hear God and respond,** and we need anointing to fulfil the commission to heal the sick in the name of Jesus.

When you do not see the results you need, don't blame the people to whom you are ministering; seek from Him the anointing that will break the yoke.

You will need to exercise the gift of the discerning of spirits. **It is important to discern to what degree you are coping with a situation that has arisen from someone walking in the flesh, and how much is due to enemy activity.**

When you prophesy over people, encourage them to test what is said. If you give them a major directive prophecy, show them that God will speak to them further Himself and will also confirm what is said through other witnesses.

When you pray in tongues over people, be open to receive the interpretation. Then you will be able to understand the way in which the Holy Spirit is leading you to pray. Often, you will flow easily from one to the other, tongues, interpretation, then tongues again, more interpretation, tongues, interpretation; and so on. In this way the Spirit guides the direction of your prayers and your understanding of the situation is greatly increased.

You will find that the Holy Spirit will go for the heart of the matter, not the superficial symptoms. So a person may come with a superficial request, only to find that God gives you a word that cuts to the division of soul and spirit, and tests the desires and intentions of his heart!

THE CRUNCH ISSUE

When seeking to bring someone to faith in Jesus Christ you can spend a great deal of time answering questions, parrying criticisms of the Church and the failures of some believers. The person will be no nearer the Kingdom of God as a result. There may be some vital questions to be answered; but you have to confront the person with the real issue as quickly as possible. 'Do you **want** to know Jesus?' It may be that you have to state the truth starkly. 'Your life is in a mess and only Jesus can alter that'; or to challenge boldly: 'You need to ask for God's forgiveness and surrender your life to Jesus. Are you prepared to do that?'

You may well receive a negative response. Do not always believe what you hear! It is likely that the person before you is in conflict, fearful about what will happen if he does surrender to Jesus.

On occasions I have found it right to call people's bluff: 'I don't believe that. I think you do want Jesus in your life but you are afraid of the repercussions.' On nearly every such occasion the person has admitted this is true and minutes later has come to Christ.

Jesus did not allow the woman at the well in Samaria (John 4:19) to slip off the hook by trying to initiate a discussion about the proper way to worship. He used a word of knowledge to reach her heart and her need; and her life was transformed. As a result the whole village came to hear Jesus.

This principle is true, not only in evangelism but in all counselling. **Listen to the witness of the Spirit and go for the heart.** Time and again people will try to avoid facing the real issue. **It is for you to keep the flow of conversation to the point.** You have achieved nothing if you have allowed the other person to dictate the course of the conversation by asking you questions that have been ideal openings for you to air your considerable spiritual knowledge! They have appealed to your soulish pride and have been successful!

SETTING PEOPLE FREE

Those who engage in lengthy counselling techniques often do so for their own soulish reasons. They want to be needed, to have a ministry that others will appreciate and even depend on. These are fleshly desires and are likely to lead into bondage both the one counselling and the one being counselled. When challenged about this their reactions show they do not want to 'lose their souls'; they think they have found a spiritual identity in the 'counselling ministry'. This is dangerous deception.

There are limitations to any counselling. Its purpose is to help and encourage the believer in his or her walk with God. **Counselling is not to replace that walk, or to try and find a slick alternative to discipleship.**

Imagine a person shackled to an iron ball and chain, which he is trying to drag along as he walks. How would you help him? Would you suggest that he turns round and counts the links on the chain? Or that he goes and examines the ball to discern its contents? Or that he discusses what the ball consists of, or how it could be lifted? Obviously not!

You would simply unshackle him at the ankle and let him go free! That is precisely the effect that Direct Counselling has. The truth unshackles a person and sets him free.

THE AIMS OF DIRECT COUNSELLING

1   **Your aim is to teach the truth to someone who does not know or understand what God has done for him in Christ, or to bring the Word of the Lord that will penetrate to the heart in the situation of need.**

2   **You aim is to help the person hear what God is saying to him in that situation; but he has to believe what God says and act on His Word. You are not helping him to find alternatives to faith and obedience.**

3   **You stand with a believer against any way in which he has allowed the enemy to put him into bondage;** but you do not do the deliverance for him without the necessary repentance and co-operation on his part. He has to exercise authority over the enemy, or the deliverance will only be short-lived.

4   **You do not take the person into the past, but into the Truth of God's Word, into what He has done for him in Christ.** It is this Truth that will set him free as he hears it, believes it and acts upon it.

5   **If necessary you help him to see that he needs to forgive** and not drag the weight of the past into his walk with Jesus.

6   **You are not to be used as a substitute for faith in God.** Prayer with you is not an alternative to walking in the truth as a disciple of Jesus.

7   **Allow the Word to do the work!** You will be amazed at the liberating power of the Gospel!

8   **Your sensitivity to the Spirit will help the person to see clearly the issues he cannot see for himself** because of the confusion that has resulted from trying to find his own solutions to his problems.

THE BENEFITS

It is rewarding to see that the time devoted to a person in this way, not only brings the liberty promised in scripture, but **you see him being built up in faith so that he will be able to withstand future trials,** and that he grows in his knowledge in such a way that he becomes an ambassador of the Truth to others.

I pray that you may be active in sharing your faith, so that you will have a full understanding of every good thing we have in Christ (Philem. v. 6).

It is rewarding to see a person being fruitful for the Kingdom of God, instead of feeling he is held back by the weight he has been dragging along because of his wrong self-image. It is encouraging to see a person rise up in faith and authority to overcome the enemy. It causes your heart to rejoice to see someone who was problem-centred become purpose-orientated, on fire with love for God and desiring above all else to do His will, instead of seeing himself as a problem, a failure, a nuisance.

What a difference between the new, assured of his place in Christ and of the Father's love for him, and the old, bound by fear and introspection!

This is not to say that he will have no further difficulties and challenges to face; but **he is now equipped to face whatever the future might bring because of his faith in God and His Word.**

But thanks be to God, who always leads us in triumphal procession in Christ and through us spreads everywhere the fragrance of the knowledge of him (2 Cor. 2:14).

Also he has now discovered to whom to turn in future times of crisis. **He has direct access to God through Jesus Christ.** With a sincere heart and full assurance of faith he can come into the Holy of Holies. He is learning how to pray things through with

God, to hear Him for himself, **to be Counsellor-led, not counsellor-dependent!**

Of course you have only helped him to establish a process that will need to continue for the rest of his life. But you have done what is asked of you by the Lord: to make disciples. You have not made his decisions for him, nor sought to lord it over him. You have taught him what it is to be a responsible disciple. And it will not be long before he disciples others, for now he has a grasp of the Truth that he knows will set others free.

The believer's spirit is sanctified and now the process of sanctifying his soul is taking place. Jesus prayed for His disciples: 'Sanctify them by the truth; your word is truth' (John 17:17).

Any believer is in good hands because the Lord Himself will sanctify him through and through, spirit, soul and body (1 Thess. 5:23). His purpose as a Christian is to live the life of the Kingdom God has placed within him. The measure he gives will be the measure he receives. **In the past he sowed into the Truth sparingly and reaped sparingly; now he can sow generously and reap generously** (2 Cor. 9:6).

He has learnt that he will not receive from God on his own terms, but on those the Lord lays down in His Word. **It is for him as a believer to believe, as a disciple to submit himself to God, as a child of the Kingdom to give cheerfully.** And he knows that:

> **God is able to make all grace abound to you, so that in all things at all times, having all that you need, you will abound in every good work** (2 Cor. 9:8).

He can believe the promise:

> **You will be made rich in every way so that you can be generous on every occasion** (2 Cor. 9:11).

Instead of the former self-pitying, poverty mentality, he can believe in the rich inheritance he has in Christ.

And all this is the work of God's grace! He will be eternally grateful for the love and mercy shown him by Jesus. **He will not easily set aside the grace of God,** for he will not want to return to the bondage to self he was in before he saw the need to 'lose' himself. He will not want to return to law once he has tasted the rewards of faith.

He has been liberated from Satan's grasp by his own grasp of the Truth and can exercise his God-given authority over the enemy.

So if the Son sets you free, you will be free indeed (John 8:36).

The Son has indeed set him free, and if he is wise he will heed the warnings of scripture not to return to a life of bondage:

I run in the path of your commands, for you have set my heart free (Ps. 119:32).

And so now he can truly be led in triumph. He is free because the Lord has set him free. He is learning to walk in the Spirit and experience freedom in every area of his life, which he yields to the sovereignty of the Holy Spirit.

No longer does he need to fear the spirits that are at work in the world, for:

You, dear children, are from God and have overcome them, because the one who is in you is greater than the one who is in the world (1 John 4:4).

He has the faith to overcome the world:

For everyone born of God overcomes the world. This is the victory that has overcome the world, even our faith. Who is it that overcomes the world? Only he who believes that Jesus is the Son of God (1 John 5:4–5).

And he knows an eternal inheritance awaits him:

> To him who overcomes, I will give the right to sit with me on my throne, just as I overcame and sat down with my Father on his throne (Rev. 3:21).

Like Paul there is a cry of joy and victory in his heart. **He has victory over the past and the confusion he has experienced for so long.** Now he does not need to fear the future, not even death:

> The sting of death is sin, and the power of sin is the law. But thanks be to God! He gives us the victory through our Lord Jesus Christ (1 Cor. 15:56–7).

Now he can set his heart on obeying the apostle's exhortation:

> Therefore, my dear brothers, **stand firm. Let nothing move you.** Always give yourselves fully to the work of the Lord, because you know that your labour in the Lord is not in vain (v. 58).

He is not only on the defensive; he now wants to influence others with the Truth that they too might be set free. He is no longer the enemy's punch bag, but is able to overcome him:

> **You give me your shield of victory, and your right hand sustains me; you stoop down to make me great . . . You armed me with strength for battle; you made my adversaries bow at my feet. You made my enemies turn their backs in flight, and I destroyed my foes** (Ps. 18:35, 39–40).

Of course he will need to guard against pride and a return to self-sufficiency. His soul will rise up above the Spirit if allowed the opportunity!

Be on your guard; stand firm in the faith; be men of courage; be strong (1 Cor. 16:13).

He finds his strength in the truth of Jesus Christ and will do well to remember that apart from Him he can do nothing!

You may lose sight of the one you have helped. You may continue in a relationship of mutual encouragement. In either case you can give him the advice Paul gave Timothy:

But as for you, continue in what you have learned and have become convinced of, because you know those from whom you learned it (2 Tim. 3:14).

Each of us has to learn to:

Throw off everything that hinders and the sin that so easily entangles, and let us run with perseverance the race marked out for us (Heb. 12:1).

We are constantly reaching out for what lies ahead of us, taking hold of everything for which Christ Jesus has taken hold of us. And we can be confident that:

He will keep you strong to the end, so that you will be blameless on the day of our Lord Jesus Christ (1 Cor. 1:8).

And when difficulties arise instead of being miserable or despondent, we can afford to be confident:

Being confident of this, that he who began a good work in you will carry it on to completion until the day of Christ Jesus (Phil. 1:6).

And we won't let the devil or anyone else tell us otherwise!

Further Study

For further reading:

Victory over the Darkness   Neil Anderson
(Monarch Publications)

The Bondage Breaker   Neil Anderson
(Monarch Publications)

In Christ Jesus   Colin Urquhart
(Hodder & Stoughton)

Personal Victory   Colin Urquhart
(Hodder & Stoughton)

Listen and Live   Colin Urquhart
(Hodder & Stoughton)

Anything You Ask   Colin Urquhart
(Hodder & Stoughton)

Receive Your Healing   Colin Urquhart
(Hodder & Stoughton)

Thriving on the Truth   Dan Chesney
(New Wine)

Toxic Love   Malcolm Smith
(Pillar Books)

Forgiveness   Malcolm Smith
(Pillar Books)

All the above are available from:
Kingdom Faith Ministries
Roffey Place, Old Crawley Road
Faygate, Horsham, West Sussex,
RH12 4SA

The following audio cassette series are also available:
BREAKTHROUGH:
by Colin Urquhart
A series of four cassettes about overcoming the enemy

BREAKING BONDAGES:
by Dan Chesney
Breaking repetitive behaviours
Dealing with thoughts and emotions
Winning over crises and anger
Living what we are

DIRECT COUNSELLING:
by Colin Urquhart
Twelve cassettes from a Conference covering the areas of
teaching given in this book; how to counsel with the Truth